THE NEW SEPARATION OF POWERS

The New Separation of Powers

A Theory for the Modern State

EOIN CAROLAN

OXFORD
UNIVERSITY PRESS

OXFORD
UNIVERSITY PRESS

Great Clarendon Street, Oxford OX2 6DP

Oxford University Press is a department of the University of Oxford.
It furthers the University's objective of excellence in research, scholarship,
and education by publishing worldwide in

Oxford New York

Auckland Cape Town Dar es Salaam Hong Kong Karachi
Kuala Lumpur Madrid Melbourne Mexico City Nairobi
New Delhi Shanghai Taipei Toronto
With offices in
Argentina Austria Brazil Chile Czech Republic France Greece
Guatemala Hungary Italy Japan South Korea Poland Portugal
Singapore Switzerland Thailand Turkey Ukraine Vietnam

Oxford is a registered trade mark of Oxford University Press
in the UK and in certain other countries

Published in the United States
by Oxford University Press Inc., New York

Reprinted 2011

ISBN 978-0-19-956867-3

Printed in the United Kingdom by
Lightning Source UK Ltd., Milton Keynes

For Ailbhe

Preface

This book is an expanded and updated version of a doctoral thesis on 'A Theory of Institutional Separation for the Administrative State'. As the title of that thesis indicated, the arguments and analyses which follow are primarily concerned with the administrative state and with the challenges which it presents for traditional theories of the separation of powers. Of itself, the separation of powers doctrine is a complex subject in relation to which much learned scholarship has been produced. This is true also of the concept of the administrative state. Given the wide-ranging and multi-faceted nature of these two topics, it would be impossible to deal comprehensively with all of the questions which their interrelationship raises, especially in so short a work as this. It is necessary, therefore, to emphasize at the outset the limited nature of the author's ambitions.

This book deals with universal themes but it does not at all purport to provide universal answers. On the contrary, it is concerned with a relatively narrow range of issues. This reflects the limited focus of the original doctoral thesis. Identifying the particular issues addressed in the thesis might provide useful clarification of what the book is about—or, more particularly, of what it is not about. This short introduction is intended, therefore, to explain a number of preliminary points which may be relevant to the interpretation of the material contained in the remainder of this book.

One important limitation to note is that the book is predominantly concerned with the situation in Irish and English law only. Although repeated references are made to other jurisdictions throughout the book—most notably the United States of America—the analysis is based on, and directed towards, the law and governance systems which exist in the Republic of Ireland and in England. This may be attributed to the fact that the doctoral thesis was originally conceived as a thesis about Irish law, which would contain comparative analysis based on the approach adopted to these issues in England and Wales. The initial impetus for the choice of this area as a suitable topic for the thesis was the striking similarity between the way in which Irish and English law dealt with administrative bodies. In particular, the Irish and English courts refer to very similar doctrines of rationality, reasonableness, and procedural fairness in reviewing the exercise of discretionary powers by administrative actors.

What was interesting about this situation, however, was the fact that these analogous approaches had been developed in the context of two very different constitutional systems. On the one hand, Ireland has a quasi-American system based on the separation of powers, the rule of law, and a written constitutional text which, inter alia, protects fundamental rights and expressly confers judicial review powers on the courts. The United Kingdom, on the other hand, has—or at least had—a system of government based on traditional notions of parliamentary supremacy. In form and in appearance, these two jurisdictions ought to have adopted very different approaches to the separation of powers and the administrative state. It could have been expected, for example, that the review of the conduct of administrative actors by reference to notions of substantive value or fundamental rights would have been more likely to occur under Irish than under English law. Yet the doctrine of procedural fairness has not only been accepted in England but, if anything, is applied with a greater degree of vigour by the English courts.

This was especially noteworthy in 2003 when work on the thesis commenced. At that point, the Human Rights Act 1998 had only recently come into force in England. Yet, despite the English courts' previous lack of a clear human rights competence and orthodox subordination to Parliament, they had been able to develop a regime which seemed, in practice, to accept the possibility of administrative discretion but also to regulate it in a way which provided some degree of protection for the rights and interests of individuals. The Irish courts, operating in a constitutional separation of powers system, had also accepted the legitimacy of administrative discretion and, rather than automatically striking it down as an unacceptable transfer of authority outside the centralized tripartite structure, sought instead to review it on procedural fairness grounds. That these two ostensibly different constitutional systems had arrived at effectively the same result raised the possibility that the actions of the courts were influenced, perhaps even subconsciously, by considerations which were independent of or distinct from traditional constitutional principles. The initial focus of the thesis was to consider what could possibly account for the similar approaches of Irish and English law to this issue. The objective was not to develop a model of institutional separation which could automatically be applied to administrative bodies in any contemporary system. On strict constitutional principles in both jurisdictions, the courts ought to have dealt with administrative decision-making in a very different manner. That they have developed closely analogous systems of review which depart from these principles suggested an incremental and ad hoc effort on the part of the judiciary to develop an alternative understanding of the proper place of administrative bodies in government. The courts' practical tolerance of administrative power seemed to indicate that they have accepted the emergence of an administrative state as a necessary feature of modern government. One of the key questions, therefore, would be how such a development might be legitimated.

Despite their differing constitutional systems, Ireland and England notably share very similar political structures. Both systems operate the Westminster model of cabinet government in which the leader of the largest party in the legislature tends also to act as the head of the executive branch of government. Both jurisdictions have bicameral legislatures in which the majority of power and influence is vested in the lower house. Both also have a distinct head of state who is formally independent of government and parliament but who exercises no significant political power. Overall, therefore, the vast majority of political power in both jurisdictions rests with the individual or party that controls the executive branch. Given the tendency in most jurisdictions to associate administrative bodies with the executive branch, this was significant for the issues of administrative legitimacy being considered in the thesis. In a system of executive dominance, could it be legitimate to entrust all responsibility and accountability for administrative decisions to a branch of government which already exercised very significant powers? Could this explain the courts' efforts to impose substantive limitations upon the way in which administrative bodies exercise their powers?

In Ireland, the Constitution's recognition of the tripartite separation of powers presented particular problems for this effort to explain, account for, and potentially legitimize the phenomenon of discretionary administrative decision-making. The tendency for judicial review of administrative bodies to be limited by reference to separation of powers principles highlighted the potential dangers of a system in which the formal rhetoric of constitutional tradition does not reflect either the realities of political power, or the steady development by the courts of an alternative approach to administrative action. The separation of powers was taken by some to suggest that administrative power was legitimate because of the involvement of both the legislature and the executive in the process by which power was exercised. By involving separate organs, the risk of unchecked abuses of power could be avoided. This legitimacy depended, of course, on a separation of influence which was more apparent than real. The potential effect of the traditional separation of powers was therefore to discourage the involvement of a truly independent branch of government in supervising the exercise of power by another organ, in favour of a formal check which lacked any real substance. As the thesis developed, this concern was reinforced by developments in the United States of America where President Bush's reliance on a strong conception of the unitary executive theory gave rise to similar concerns about the risks of the separation of powers theory being deployed in a way which, in fact, would limit the possibility for real inter-institutional checks and balances. The notion that President Bush's position as head of the executive entitled him to directly intervene in the exercise of any power that could be broadly classified as 'executive' meant, for example, that the President ordered the Environmental Protection Agency to set air quality standards which differed from those favoured by the Agency itself, in spite of the fact that the EPA's power to set such standards was conferred upon it by Congress and was obliged to be based on the best available science.[1] For different reasons, the actions of President Bush and the decision of the Irish Supreme Court in *TD v Minister for Education* illustrated the problems which could potentially arise in relation to the application of traditional separation of powers logic to a

[1] J Eilperin, 'Ozone Rules Weakened At Bush's Behest' *The Washington Post* (14 March, 2008).

governmental system characterized by executive dominance and administrative discretion. The concern, therefore, was that the traditional understanding of the separation of powers could serve as an obstacle to the acknowledgement, or the development, of a more appropriate account of institutional power in the administrative state. It was for this reason that the thesis sought to connect the two issues in order to identify how the separation of powers theory might be modified, or amended, to better account for contemporary practices with regard to administrative power.

Concerns about administrative power or executive dominance have a broad universal appeal. This is underlined by the extent to which the discussion contained in the thesis drew upon examples and insights from other jurisdictions. While such individual examples may have a certain degree of explanatory power, it is important to bear in mind that the issues which arise in any given system of government are necessarily shaped by the particular constitutional, political, and institutional context in which they arise. It is very difficult, as a result, to directly apply the logic of one system to the situation which exists in another. Even similar concerns can manifest themselves in different ways, or be directed towards different issues. For example, the issue of discretionary administrative decision-making is an important element of administrative law in Ireland, England, and in the United States. Yet, such discretionary decision-making can take very different forms within each system. Most notably, for example, a considerable portion of the American jurisprudence is concerned with regulatory rule-making. Making rules is a very significant element of administrative governance in the USA. Both Congress and the courts accept it and seek to regulate it on the basis of certain key process requirements. Yet traditionally regulatory rule-making, in the manner in which is exists in the United States, has not been part of the Irish or English systems of government. To the extent that the same process of framing regulatory rules or policies occurs, it operates in a very different manner and through a very different process. This means, of course, that concerns which might be expressed in a similar fashion across these systems are actually directed to different administrative practices—which obviously can affect the way in which they manifest themselves in practice. Thus, although the principles set out in this book could potentially apply to any institutional system in which administrative entities exercise power, it is important to emphasize that they were developed only with the Irish and English government systems in mind. That is not to say that they might not have relevance to other jurisdictions, or, indeed, could not be reproduced or replicated elsewhere. The key caveat is that they do not take account of the specific nuances which exist in other government systems.

This is particularly important with regard to the book's treatment of the US material. Frequent reference is made to US decisions and academic commentaries. This is largely because of the sophisticated nature of the American jurisprudence on this issue. This sophistication, however, also reflects the native complexity of the American system, which is necessarily shaped by the specific domestic considerations raised by US constitutional law, by America's political and federal system, and by the distinct character of American administrative law. For an author from another jurisdiction, this presents particular challenges. Most notably, it is necessary to bear in mind the limited extent to which an outsider can grasp the particular nuances of American administrative law without extensive and prolonged exposure to it. Thus, although the book consistently draws on American experiences and considers issues of relevance to the USA itself, it should not be regarded at any point as attempting to indicate how the American jurisprudence could, let alone should, be developed.

This reference to the problems posed by the distinct and individual characteristics of particular political or constitutional systems raises another point upon which preliminary clarification is required—namely, what is meant by the 'administration' or 'administrative bodies' within the book. Again, the administrative element of government is organized in different ways within different systems. Different states—even different political parties within a single state—will generally have different views of how decision-making power ought to be variously distributed between central government, local government, directly employed public servants, semi-state organizations, public–private bodies, regulatory agencies, third-party actors, and so on. There is an extensive and impressive literature on how this array of organizations ought to be identified or classified. From the point of view of this book, however, the central concern is not with the most effective or appropriate method of delivering government, but rather with the more normative question of how the vesting of discretionary power in those bodies which fall outside the traditional tripartite model can be legitimized and organized. Strictly speaking, the question whether a particular body is administrative or not falls outside the scope of that enquiry. This is particularly the case in light of the fact that the book rejects such functional classifications as arbitrary and lacking particular utility. What one system treats as administrative may be classified by another as private but that will not alter the extent of the actual decision-making power which it exercises. Similarly, the extent of ministerial power or influence over an institution will not be affected by the fact that one official is formally regarded as the direct servant of a minister whereas another is formally independent but obliged to advise and assist the minister as required. The aim of the thesis was to devise a system capable of ensuring a distribution of power which was based, not on formal classifications of institutions, but rather on real power and influence. The model outlined also assumes that all institutions may have a potential input into the governance process. This makes such issues of formal classification less important. That is not to say that the question of what organizations form the core of the administrative state is not important. On the contrary, it is a matter deserving of extensive analysis in its own right which could not be satisfactorily addressed in a book of this length. It is also an analysis which would necessarily be specific to a particular jurisdiction. For these reasons, this book does not address these issues but prefers a more open and universally applicable conception of the administration as decentralized governance. The administrative state is intended to refer here to government with a small g—that array of institutions, organizations, and actors which operate at some distance from the core central institutions. Quite where the boundary between the two exists will vary from jurisdiction to jurisdiction. In essence, however, this approach is based on the assumption that the tripartite separation of powers was concerned primarily with the key central institutions of government: Parliament, the Executive/Government, and the Courts. The purpose of this book is to examine the implications of the vesting of power in institutions which do not fit within this narrow traditional theory. Thus, any organization which exercises power in any way independently of these central institutions—even including, where appropriate, elements of the civil service—can potentially come within the notion of the administration envisaged in this book.

Finally, the other preliminary caveat to bear in mind is that the book retains much of the topical and temporal focus of the thesis in its original form. Chapters 6 and 7 are the newest additions to the book, and seek to provide a preliminary discussion of some of the more practical implications of the thesis. Although the other chapters have been updated where possible, the structure and logic of the arguments is very much based on the author's analysis of the emerging law up to early 2006. If the thesis was being written afresh now, other themes or insights might have emerged from a consideration of the more recent decisions of the courts since 2006, or other examples might have been used to illustrate the arguments being made. It is to be hoped, however, that developments have not significantly detracted from whatever utility the original arguments may have had.

Bluehaven
Dalkey
March, 2009

Acknowledgements

I have been immensely fortunate to have had the support of a wide range of friends and colleagues while working on this project. Very many people have contributed to this work in many different ways. Space precludes me from mentioning them all here but I would like to record my gratitude to everyone who helped me along the way. I am especially indebted, however, to a number of people, whose efforts deserve, at the very least, my specific and grateful acknowledgement.

I would like to thank the supervisors of my original thesis, Dr Gerard Hogan and Professor Hilary Delany, for their valuable advice, guidance, and direction; and to Professor John Bell of Cambridge University and Dr Colm O'Cinneide of UCL for agreeing to examine it, and for providing a host of helpful comments which contributed greatly to the development of this book. Professor Gerry Whyte of Trinity College, Dublin also gave very generously of his time and expertise during the *viva* process.

I would also like to thank the various members of University College Dublin, Trinity College Dublin, the University of Cambridge, and Harvard Law School who assisted me with my research during my time at each institution. Special thanks are due to Professor Colin Scott, Professor Daryl Levinson and Professor Mark Tushnet for taking the time to consider and discuss the ideas contained in the book. Their input and insight were invaluable in shaping its development and in avoiding at least some of the errors which might otherwise have been included. Those errors that remain are, obviously, my own.

A number of bodies generously provided funding to support various stages of the research. I am especially grateful for the award of a Post-Doctoral Fellowship by the Irish Research Council for Humanities and Social Sciences which allowed me the freedom to spend more time updating and expanding the thesis than might otherwise have been possible. The assistance they provide to research in Irish universities has made a real difference to the opportunities available to researchers in the area in Ireland. I would also like to thank Harvard Law School for hosting me as a Visiting Researcher for several months, as well as the Trinity Trust and Francis E Moran Trust for providing funding to support my stay there.

University College Dublin in general, and the School of Law in particular, have gone to great lengths to facilitate this research, for which I am immensely grateful. In particular, the financial assistance of the University Seed Funding Scheme and the School of Law's Research Awards considerably smoothed the process of bringing the project to a conclusion.

Alex Flach and Chris Champion at Oxford University Press have been a constant source of useful advice and direction, while Paris O'Donnell's assistance was invaluable and very much appreciated. I am also grateful to

Oxford University Press's anonymous reviewers for taking the time to read the original thesis, and for offering such constructive advice on how the book ought to be developed.

Finally, I would like to thank my family once again for all of the tremendous encouragement they have given me over the years. In particular, I am indebted to my parents for the inspiration and education they have provided over many, many years. The biggest debt of gratitude of all, however, is owed to my wife Ailbhe. Her insights have vastly improved this book, just as her love and support enhances each day. For this, as well as for so much else, I am forever grateful to her.

Summary Contents

Detailed Contents

Table of Cases

DECISIONS OF THE IRISH COURTS:

DECISIONS OF THE ENGLISH COURTS:

DECISIONS OF OTHER JURISDICTIONS:

United States:

Australia:

Canada:

South Africa:

New Zealand:

Israel:

1

The Role of Institutional Theory in a Constitutional System

A. Introduction

A 'central concept of modern constitutionalism',[1] the theory of the separation of powers enjoys a position of almost unparalleled global repute as a foundational tenet of liberal democracy. A doctrine of long-standing historical and political significance, it exerts considerable influence over the attitudes, opinions, and public pronouncements of academics, officials, and individual citizens alike. In recent times the theory has even attracted favourable comment from a number of prominent English academics—a notable development in a jurisdiction whose Diceyan heritage had inculcated an orthodox disparagement of the doctrine as a 'rickety chariot' of alien invention and dubious design.[2] Reforms of the United Kingdom's constitutional order in recent years have been welcomed by jurists such as Masterman[3] and Malleson as an overdue attempt to introduce elements of the separation theory into the British constitutional order.[4] Woodhouse has even raised the possibility of 'parliamentary sovereignty being replaced as the defining principle of the constitution by a more robust version of the separation of powers'.[5] In a similar vein, the Irish Supreme Court has proclaimed the doctrine to be 'of itself, a high constitutional value' through the ideological prism of which all other constitutional provisions ought to be perceived.[6]

The doctrine's recurring prominence as a basic staple of constitutional and political discourse suggests that the theory is one which attracts widespread support. The model's virtually universal acceptance should not obscure the fact

[1] E Barendt, 'Separation of Powers and Constitutional Government' [1995] PL 599, at 599.
[2] W Robson, *Justice and Administrative Law* (2nd ed., Stevens, 1947), at 14.
[3] R Masterman, 'A Supreme Court for the United Kingdom: One Step Forward, Two Steps Back' [2004] PL 48.
[4] K Malleson, 'Modernising the Constitution: Completing the Unfinished Business' (2004) 24 LS 119, at 123.
[5] D Woodhouse, 'The Constitutional and Political Implications of a United Kingdom Supreme Court' (2004) 24 LS 134, at 153.
[6] *TD v Minister for Education*, [2001] 4 IR 259, at 362 *per* Hardiman J.

that various aspects of it have been subjected to adverse academic comment. That the doctrine prevails and even proliferates in the face of such critical scrutiny could be taken to suggest that these attacks are inaccurate, ill conceived, or quite simply incorrect. This book will attempt to argue, however, that the theory's constitutional constancy is the result not of its innate ideological veracity but rather of its continued identification with a series of distinct institutional values which, in themselves, deserve support. It is these values, it is submitted, which underpin the continuing influence of the doctrine. This work will therefore aim to develop a revised institutional theory of separation which draws on these values whilst also managing to avoid the problems which the persistent invocation of the traditional theory involves.

An evaluation of the relative merits of rival institutional theories clearly demands the elucidation of some form of analytical criteria. The success or otherwise of a given theory of institutional arrangement can only be adequately assessed in the context of a full and proper understanding of the part which institutional theories play in the constitutional order. The remainder of this chapter will therefore be devoted to developing just such an understanding. If a clearer conception of the normative purposes underpinning the adoption of an institutional theory can be established, it should assist in the elaboration of appropriate evaluative criteria against which the separation of powers—or, indeed, any other theory—can be systematically assessed.

Institutional theory invariably constitutes only a single, albeit significant, element of the overall constitutional structure of a state. An analysis of the role and function of an institutional theory, therefore, ought obviously to commence with an examination of the place and purpose of constitutionalism in general.

B. Constitutionalism and the State

(1) The Social Significance of a Constitution

A constitution, in contemporary terms, tends to connote a written document which enshrines certain substantive and institutional principles. These values are generally enforceable by a judicial branch dedicated to upholding this ostensibly foundational text.[7] Constitutions, on this view, are generally regarded as a form of received and settled fact, a fixed declaration of those political precepts which are socially cherished as essential ideals. The written constitution is treated as a legal instrument of virtually sacred value, a higher-order statement of rules which serves as the foundation of social and political order in that state. The US Constitution, the Supreme Court has declared, constitutes that

[7] This was the logic used to justify the existence of the power of judicial review in the seminal American case of *Marbury v Madison*, 1 Cranch 137; 5 US 137; 2 L Ed 2d 60 (1803).

country's 'social fabric',[8] 'the only true foundation of every power in ... government'.[9] Similarly, the Irish Supreme Court has expressed the opinion that, in 1937, '[a] new constitutional basis for the State was laid',[10] thereby equating the enactment of a revised constitutional text with a recasting of the Irish state and its structures. As Budd J had previously proclaimed, '[t]he Constitution brought into existence a new State, subject to its own unique and basic law'.[11]

Martin Loughlin, however, has strongly criticized this tendency to treat the written constitution as antecedent social fact, decrying such 'constitutional legalism' for its failure 'to acknowledge the provisional character of constitutional arrangements'.[12] In contrast to the common conception of the document as fixed positivist fact, Loughlin proffers instead a dynamic vision of constitutional theory as a flexible framework which both structures and reflects the shifting character of everyday political practices. Constitutionalism does not denote an absolutist belief in the top-down authority of a particular text. Rather, its roots lie in a reciprocal relationship between political reality and constitutional practice.

This refusal to regard the constitution as the rigid and immutable foundation of social order is traceable, for Loughlin, to Schmitt's theory of the political.[13] Characterizing conflict as an essential and enduring feature of human existence, Schmitt's work, at its very simplest, can be taken to deny the very possibility of a permanent social settlement. This position echoes the views advanced by James Madison in Federalist Paper No. 10. Madison felt that '[a]s long as the reason of man continues fallible, and he is at liberty to exercise it, different opinions will be formed'.[14] Machiavelli's belief in the possibility that a perfect republic could emerge from a state's efforts to deal with internal discord can similarly be understood as an implicit acceptance of disharmony as an inevitable element of an effective theory of government. The reality is that there will always be an enemy to be countered. Politics arises from conflict, and requires it for its continuance. One man's unchallengeable truth will always be another's misguided dogma. There is, therefore, no universal good upon which all states and societies can be constructed. There is, instead, only the provisional personal conception of the good which must be defended against alternative understandings.

[8] *Brent v President of the US*, 35 US 596, 627 (1836).

[9] *Newton v Stebbins*, 51 US 586, 607 (1851), *per* Daniel J dissenting.

[10] *Maguire v Ardagh*, [2002] 1 IR 385, at 570, *per* Denham J.

[11] *Riordan v An Tanaiste*, [1995] 3 IR 62, at 81.

[12] M Loughlin, 'Constitutional Law: The Third Order of the Political' in N Bamforth and T Leyland (eds.), *Public Law in a Multi-Layered Constitution* (Hart, 2003) 27, at 48.

[13] C Schmitt, *The Concept of the Political* (1932), (G Schwab (tr.), University of Chicago Press, 1996). For further discussion of Schmitt's theories, see, for example, D Dyzenhaus, *Law as Politics: Carl Schmitt's Critique of Liberalism* (Duke University Press, 1998); C Mouffe, ed., *The Challenge of Carl Schmitt* (Verso, 1999); and WE Scheuerman, *Carl Schmitt: The End of Law* (Rowman & Littlefield, 1999). The interpretation of his work presented here is that provided by Loughlin as part of his wider analysis of constitutionalism.

[14] J Madison, *Federalist Paper No. 10* (1788) in I Kramnick, ed., *The Federalist Papers* (Penguin, 1987), at 123.

(2) The State, Politics, and Internal Social Divisions

The state provides a means by which human conflict can be successfully internalized. If it is assumed that conflict is inevitable, state structure may be regarded as a mechanism for the management of this perpetual conflict, creating a unifying entity with which the individual can himself identify, and which, just as significantly, allows him to identify others and their collective entities as an enemy:

> With the recognition of a 'we' that can be set against the 'they' of the rest of mankind, the friend–enemy distinction [which inheres in human relationships] is capable of being externalised.[15]

It is important to bear in mind that the state, if it is to be effective, does not need to seek to eliminate internal conflict entirely. Schmitt, in fact, regarded such a classically utopian vision of social harmony as an undesirable outcome. '[G]roup life without conflict—society without politics—constitutes a denial of the human condition which, if ever realised, would amount to a moral loss.'[16] This suggests that the state must provide for the effective management of domestic conflict on an ongoing basis. Disputes will inevitably arise but must be dealt with in such a way that the internal unity of the state is not destroyed. Intra-state conflict must be acknowledged and accepted as an ever-present element of the entity's existence. It should therefore be factored into the construction and design of the state structures. As Loughlin explains:

> Since the state [must be]... able to institutionalise domestic political antagonism at a lower level of intensity than that of friend *versus* enemy, one of its most basic achievements is that of being able to keep conflict and disagreement within a framework of order. For these conditions to be realised, however, the tensions that exist within the state must be actively managed.[17]

Loughlin, like Machiavelli,[18] sees the practice of politics—that is the active regulation of internal divisions—as one way in which the state undertakes this task. 'The conduct of politics ... is not built on the celebration of conflict: it is generated by the need to ensure its effective management.'[19] Efficacy is the touchstone of political action. The constitution, on this understanding of the state, thus appears not as a testament to the state's normative foundations but as a tool for the successful management of internal conflict. Accordingly, it is not the basis for the existence or creation of the state. Rather it is simply another way in which the state—the unified 'we' which has emerged—can actively and efficaciously address the potential danger of internal divisions. The constitution is a

[15] M Loughlin, note 12 above, at 34. [16] Ibid, at 35. [17] Ibid, at 34.

[18] N Machiavelli, *The Prince* (1513), (2nd ed., R Adams, ed., Norton, 1992). Loughlin prefers Machiavelli's conception of the practice of politics to that of Schmitt. Schmitt, he feels, sees conflict as a principle to be embraced whereas Machiavelli views it as an inevitability to be managed by the successful statesman.

[19] M Loughlin, note 12 above, at 39.

by-product of the practice of politics[20]—a purposive device whose true value lies in its instrumental efficacy rather than its ontological legitimacy. That is not to say, of course, that the moral or normative legitimacy of the constitutional order is irrelevant. As this book will argue, for the state to be legitimate and to continue to exist as a cohesive social entity, it is important that it acts, and is regarded as acting, in a way which is 'good'. The smaller point being made here is that this pursuit of the good has an important instrumental dimension. 'Writings about constitutions', on this view, 'are always undertaken in the service of political theory'.[21]

C. A Political Tool?—The Constitution as Unifying Force

(1) Substantive Constitutional Values

Constitutionalism's political utility therefore derives from the extent to which it supports the existence of a unitary sense of social consciousness. Preuss has noted how 'the common feeling of a group's oneness is the determining state-building social energy'.[22] The constitution, its existence and accepted authority predicated on the presence of a common identity, reinforces public belief in the reality of a homogeneous social unit, and thereby supports the state's efforts to successfully manage any internal conflicts. The establishment of a constitution proclaims the unitary nature of the state, and demands the obedience of the citizenry on that basis. By accepting its authority, the citizens also implicitly acknowledge their individual identification with the unitary vision advanced therein. This recognition of the authority of the constitution and of the state enhances the centripetal force of this centralized social identity, thereby also reducing the centrifugal pressures created by any internal political conflict.

It is clear therefore that public acceptance of the authority of the constitution is a key stage in the development of a stable governing structure capable of effective internal conflict management. The citizens must feel as if they owe allegiance to the constitutional order if the state is to profit from its adoption of a constitution. A positivist declaration of a shared normative conception of society is one obvious way in which the existence of the essential common identity can be both acknowledged and encouraged. If the stated conception is one which receives widespread public acclaim, not only is the homogeneity of the unit reinforced but, in addition, the mandate of the state to speak and act for the social unit—and thus also to exercise authority over it—is greatly enhanced. The enactment of a purportedly authoritative enumeration of a society's most

[20] What Loughlin refers to as the third order of the political.

[21] N Barber, 'Prelude to the Separation of Powers' (2001) 60 CLJ 59, at 63.

[22] UK Preuss, 'Political Order and Democracy: Carl Schmitt and his Influence' in C Mouffe, ed., note 13 above, at 157, cited with approval in M Loughlin, note 12 above, at 39.

fundamental beliefs implicitly confirms the existence of a normatively unified social entity. At the same time, its enforcement encourages the continuing public espousal of the designated social values into the future. If a constitution is widely believed to promote, support, and, in its operations, exemplify some objective concept of communitarian good, it is considerably less likely to lose the allegiance of its public at a given point in the future. This analysis is supported by de Toqueville's conclusion that:

> [f]or society to exist, and, even more, for society to prosper, it is essential that all of the minds of the citizens should always be rallied by and held together by some leading ideas.[23]

It is in this context that a theory of assertedly objective appeal has value. Schmitt's work may be taken to deny such doctrines the possibility of universal acclaim. It does not, however, disavow their utility. Schmitt suggests that opponents will invariably emerge to contest any particular position. From the point of view of state stability, the key requirement is that this opposition function at a manageable level of sub-constitutional conflict. Disputes at this level will be settled in accordance with constitutional rules which are uncontested by the parties. They do not need to be accepted by all but constitutional principles do require broad popular approval. Those concepts which have been derived from objectivity or reason are more likely to command that widespread public support which is so essential. As this work will subsequently propose an institutional theory of ostensibly universal value, this is a significant point.

The tendency in contemporary liberal democracies to textually entrench certain substantive normative values provides an instructive example of the operation in practice of the constitution-as-unifying-force. As Bamforth has noted, liberal democracies are inclined to evince an intuitive opposition to the coercive use of power by the organs of the state, demanding instead that any exercise of public power be legitimated by way of its compliance with the society's unifying normative vision.[24] Power can only be used for legitimate purposes, and in normatively legitimate ways. The insistence that legitimacy is essential, however, implicitly accepts the managerial authority of the state, while also reassuring the citizenry that such power will only be used for purposes that are normatively 'good'. Thus, not only is the authority of the state over the social unit affirmed, but the public's acceptance of such authority as a social good to which they owe allegiance is encouraged. The initial emergence of the unified state might not be predicated on its pursuit of an objective or external notion of the good, but the internal adoption of such an idea serves to enhance the individual's identification with, and belief in the value of, the common identity

[23] A de Toqueville, *Democracy in America* (G Lawrence (tr.), Harper, 1969), at 434.

[24] See N Bamforth, 'The Public Law–Private Law Distinction: A Comparative and Philosophical Approach' in P Leyland and T Woods, eds., *Administrative Law Facing the Future: Old Constraints and New Horizons* (Blackstone Press, 1997) 136, at 138.

upon which the state is, in actual fact, founded. The institution and enforcement of a central normative vision can therefore have the effect of cementing the cultural bonds of the state structure. Thus, for our liberal democracies to flourish, the public should have some degree of confidence in the constitutional order, their faith secured by that order's demonstrable commitment to a socially-accepted understanding of the communitarian good.

(2) The Institutional Arrangement

The institutional elements of a constitution can also support such a public belief in the integrity and veracity of the state's governing authority. The enactment of a lofty commitment to substantive normative goods is, by itself, insufficient to secure continued public confidence in, and allegiance to, the constitutional order. Individuals will not value a public statement of principles unless they have faith that the principles will be properly reflected in the daily actions of the state. Thus, 'the cultivation of a sense of even-handedness constitutes a vital aspect of the project of state-building'.[25] The prospect of unbiased institutional action proffered therein supports the effort to secure the continued acceptance by the public of the state's authority. Individuals are much more amenable to placing their faith in the values of the substantive aspects of the text if they are offered assurances that these values will function with equal and consistent force in every situation. This constancy is the very essence of their constitutional status. The constitution's authority as a formal declaration of basic social values rests on its related promise to ensure that the substantive values proclaimed therein will be recognized and respected as the community's universally binding normative constants. Its principles cannot be unevenly applied, ignored, or abandoned when convenience so dictates. As ostensibly authoritative norms, they must appear to be beyond question, above political debate or influence.

> The evolution of institutions of government that aspire to operate at one remove from direct manipulation by power-wielders removes certain decisions and disputes from partisan political processes and . . . serves to bolster faith in the system. The cultivation of a belief in the law-governed nature of the state is, in short, a means of generating political power and an especially powerful aspect of state-building.[26]

The state must therefore provide some form of institutional structure which confers on the constitutional text a reputation for such consistent and authoritative operation.

The substantive and institutional elements of a written constitution therefore play a significant part in the state's critical task of establishing and maintaining a shared sense of community. The substantive aspects of the text provide a unifying normative vision to which all can pledge allegiance, thereby confirming

[25] M Loughlin, note 12 above, at 40. [26] Ibid, at 41.

the existence of a communitarian cultural identity. The institutions of the state, meanwhile, offer a guarantee that this statement of societal values will operate in a suitably authoritative and even-handed way, enforcing the central tenets of the text with the unbiased consistency which befits their constitutional status. The constitution's utility as a political tool thus arises from the way in which it helps to counteract the socially destructive effects of domestic conflict by reinforcing a common social view.

(3) The Problem of Inevitable Conflict

This instrumental understanding of the constitution derives, in large part, from a recognition of the strong likelihood of political conflict. If, however, we have accepted such conflict as almost inevitable, it seems problematic to then rest the constitution's utility on its acclaimed (and thus also authoritative) status as a fixed declaration of shared social values. If internal conflict is to be an inevitable occurrence in the state, a settled conception of social values is clearly an impossibility. Conflict will inexorably arise over the normative values of the relevant society, thereby calling into question the extent to which an unchanging constitutional text reflects the views of the state's citizenry. If the substantive elements of the document fail to reflect such changes, the authority of the constitution will necessarily be weakened. In this case, its essential ability to retain the allegiance of the population at large would also be undermined.

It is obvious, therefore, that a fixed declaration of substantive social values will be unable, over time, to maintain its centralizing authority over the people of the state. The substantive normative elements of the text are, by themselves, insufficient to ensure that the constitution successfully fulfils its political function over an extended period of time. The institutional architecture of the state must be designed in such a way that it is capable of confronting the problems posed by internal normative conflicts. An institutional theory, it would seem, must constitute more than the mere organizational instantiation of a society's substantive normative views. Any comprehensive assessment of an institutional system's efficacy should therefore take all of these elements into account.

D. The Constitution and Changing Social Tastes

(1) Unifying by Example

A comprehensive analysis of an institutional theory must therefore reflect the extent to which it successfully performs this normative–systemic function. As Shapiro explains:

> [n]ormative–systemic arguments first point to the existence of norms of right conduct. They then urge that to vindicate these norms we should try to increase the incidence of

> right actions and decrease the incidence of wrong ones. A major mechanism for doing so is to reinforce attitudes important in the genesis of right actions and to attenuate other ones. This can be done in part by pursuing and observing certain social practices and appropriately endorsing them. … The arguments, in short, recommend programs for learning … through the construction of community institutions.[27]

On this view, the institutional architecture of a constitutional system is conceived as an orienting framework with a socially pedagogic role. The substantive elements of the constitution, it was argued above, attempt to authoritatively enumerate the 'norms of right conduct' in which the community believes. It then falls to the institutional aspects of the constitutional structure to encourage continued public faith in, and adherence to, this unifying normative vision. The initial adoption of the constitution as a public declaration of the good establishes a normative presumption in favour of the future actions of the institutions which apply its principles. The effective enforcement of the authoritative precepts of the constitutional order, if correctly carried out, can validate, reinforce, and, crucially, *instruct* the public in the application of this established normative vision. Mashaw maintains that 'our positive beliefs about what is, powerfully constrain and shape our normative beliefs about what is good and desirable'.[28] If it is to assist in the active management of internal conflict, an institutional theory should draw on the potential for the 'is' (the presumed fact that the constitution represents a vision of the good) to influence the public perception of the 'ought' (what is an appropriate vision of the good) in such a way that the cementing effects of the substantive elements of the constitution continue to endure. '[R]epeated exposure to representations or ideas'[29] can have profoundly taste-shaping consequences, thereby providing a means of regulating the problems raised by internal normative conflict.

There are echoes of this analysis in Hart's well known discussion of the reflexive way in which individual citizens respond to the orienting effects of legal rules. Hart correctly identified how the enactment of a legal rule or obligation 'mak[es] certain types of behaviour a standard' for society as a whole,[30] thereby furnishing individuals with a determinate yardstick against which, they are aware, their own behaviour is likely to be publicly assessed.

> [W]here rules exist, deviations from them are not merely grounds for a prediction that hostile reactions will follow or that a court will apply sanctions to those who break them, but are also a reason or justification for such reaction and for applying such sanctions.[31]

These rules, therefore, act as a guide for citizens in the everyday conduct of their lives, colouring their perception of what is in their society, and what ought to be.

[27] MH Shapiro, 'The Technology of Perfection: Performance Enhancement and the Control of Attributes' (1991) 65 *Southern California Law Review* 11, at 52.

[28] JL Mashaw, *Greed, Chaos & Governance* (Yale University Press, 1997), at 2.

[29] Ibid, at 3.

[30] HLA Hart, *The Concept of Law* (Clarendon Press, 1961), at 83.

[31] Ibid, at 82.

The values and standards proclaimed therein help to shape individual citizens' own opinions as to what constitutes socially acceptable action. Thus does Hart's concept of an internal understanding of an individual social unit develop—a point of view which, unlike its external analogue, fully captures the extent to which the laws (or constitution) of a state influence the intuitive actions of its population. The external observer is compared unfavourably to:

> one who, having observed the workings of a traffic signal in a busy street for some time, limits himself to saying that when the light turns red there is a high probability that the traffic will stop. He treats the lights merely as a natural sign that people will behave in certain ways. . . . In so doing, he will miss out on the whole dimension of the social life of those whom he is watching, since for them the red light is not merely a sign that others will stop: they look upon it as a signal for them to stop, and so a reason for stopping in conformity to rules which make stopping when the light is red a standard of behaviour . . .[32]

Through the conditioning effects of these express standards of public conduct, legal or (at a more abstract level of reasoning) constitutional rules have such unifying and taste-shaping effects.

(2) Unifying by Reaction and Response

Of itself, however, the general social recognition of a constitutional structure as a morally authoritative system deserving public obedience is not enough to forever forestall the possibility that internal dissent could produce seriously disintegrating effects. Hart's analysis suggests that it is generally sufficient for a rule to be recognized as a legal (or in this context constitutional) provision for it to be observed by the public, independently of the probability that it will actually be enforced. However, it can be argued that this general attitude of acquiescence is itself contingent upon the existence of a majoritarian belief that the system, as a whole, is efficacious.[33] Such efficacy, in the context of the issue currently under examination, rests upon the public's acceptance of the constitution's substantive values as normatively good. The institutional employment of these values can encourage this acceptance, it has been claimed, through a subtle process of habituation by enforcement. However, it is equally obvious that in the event of a sufficiently serious dislocation between constitutional principle and public belief, the unifying effects of the constitutional order would be negated. In light of this chapter's characterization of conflict as an inevitable ingredient in human affairs, this is a scenario which institutional taste-shaping, of itself, might not be

[32] Ibid, at 87–88.

[33] This argument derives from Hart's observation that the internal perspective is that of 'those who normally are the majority of society'. Ibid, at 90. The relationship between a system's efficacy and Hart's presumption of majority support is examined further in 'Revolt of Revolution—A Harten Analysis' (2002) 5 *Trinity College Law Review* 292.

able to prevent. Thus it is not enough for the state's institutional structures to reinforce a set vision by simple repetition. The state must also provide for some mechanism by which it can adjust to, and accordingly reflect, the shifting nature of public opinion.

If the constitutional structure of a state is to fulfil its designated function as an instrument of social cohesion, it must also be able, therefore, to react to the outcome of internal normative disputes, and to thereby evolve in such a way that it retains the allegiance of the public. This public allegiance, as already discussed, is a prerequisite for the maintenance of the constitution's status as an authoritative statement of public values, upon which the force of its unifying effects is contingent. The constitution's institutional structures should be taste-responsive as well as taste-shaping.

How might this be achieved? The state, it would seem, must provide institutionally for the possibility of future amendments to its initially authoritative statement of norms. The values which the constitution affirms must retain sufficient flexibility that they may be dynamically developed to reflect the prevailing social view. Public debate about the normative content of the constitutional order must be tolerated, indeed encouraged, by its institutions. As an apparent inevitability, it should obviously be incorporated in their initial design. If a state's institutions do not embrace debate, it is difficult to imagine how they might ever be equipped to respond to it.

(a) Institutional Design and Normative Debate—The Place of Public Justification

The importance, from the state's perspective, of engaging with this process of value evolution is reflected in the significance which several prominent theorists attach to the institutional value of public justification. Vile, reviewing the historical development of institutional theory, remarked that:

> the clash of interests in the real world is so sharp that the nature of the governmental structures through which decisions are arrived at is critically important for the content of these decisions. There has therefore been, since earliest times, a continuous concern with the articulation of the institutions of the political system and with the extent to which they have promoted those values that are considered central to the 'polity'.[34]

Thus, the consistent *public* enforcement of a particular set of values encourages their adoption as a template for the citizenry's interaction with both state institutions and each other. Rawls noted how:

> [t]he publicity of the rules of an institution insures that those engaged in it know what limitations on conduct to expect of one another and what kinds of actions are permissible. There is a common basis for determining mutual expectations.[35]

[34] MJC Vile, *Constitutionalism and the Separation of Powers* (Clarendon Press, 1967), at 1.

[35] J Rawls, *A Theory of Justice* (revd ed., Oxford University Press, 1999), at 49.

Internal debate is therefore not only tolerated but actively managed. An institutional structure which seeks to expose its processes to the public allows for debate but structures and orients it in such a way that the importance of the central constitutional text is ultimately confirmed.

Openly allowing for the possibility of public interaction encourages individual citizens to put their alternative perspectives to the institutions of the state. Dissent—Schmitt's ubiquitous engine of political action—is not excluded or ignored (and thus allowed to develop) but is brought within the institutional structures of the state.

A forum is provided for the presentation of conflicting normative views. This allows the state to establish its ownership of the debate at issue, imposing certain institutional strictures to which the participants in the process must conform. State control allows it to shape the ensuing public debate, effectively imposing a type of institutional etiquette in accordance with which all claims must be articulated. This requires any assertions of value to draw on the language, content, and form dictated by the existing constitutional text. The constitution's ostensibly authoritative status proclaims the existence of a social consensus, the continued value of which is implicitly affirmed by the attempts of individual citizens to invoke it. After all, a dissenter who seeks to rely on the existing constitution to support his normative stance will find it difficult to subsequently impugn the communitarian authority of the text.

An institutional theory which provides a forum for the articulation of varying domestic views plays a valuable part in preserving the unifying force of the constitutional order. For Rawls, this transparent process is additionally useful in light of the institutional opportunity which arises therein to reiterate by example the merit of the constitution's normative vision. The publicly-reasoned application of its principles, on this view, cannot but demonstrate to individual doubters the inherent veracity of the initial constitutional arrangement. The state's institutions should assist the political project of successfully managing internal normative dissent by demonstrably persuading the public that the constitution's central substantive values continue to operate in a way which is worthy of their social support.

> To justify our political judgments to others is to convince them by public reason, that is, by ways of reasoning and inference appropriate to fundamental political questions, and by appealing to beliefs, grounds and political values it is reasonable for others also to acknowledge.[36]

Rawls' understanding of institutional public justification, however, clearly connotes the existence of an objective external conception of social good. 'Public justification,' he suggests, 'proceeds from some consensus: from premises all parties in disagreement, assumed to be free and equal and fully capable of

[36] Ibid, at 27.

reason, may reasonably be expected to share and freely endorse.'[37] Disputes, therefore, result not from the possibility of divergent normative views but rather from the inability of certain individuals to identify the true principles of social justice by themselves. The reasoned public application of these principles therefore encourages these recalcitrant citizens to recognize the value of the objective (Rawlsian) concept of justice.

(b) Public Reason and Evolving Social Values

However, it has repeatedly been argued in the course of this chapter that the nature of mankind generally precludes the isolation of such a universally accepted objective good. Thus, Allan's more nuanced interpretation of public reason is preferable for the purposes at hand. In his consideration of this question, Allan accepts that individual citizens, when engaging in political or normative arguments, tend not to confine themselves to an agreed or objective premise from which all legitimate discussion must proceed. A society's view of its shared values will not remain forever constant. This means that the relevant institutional actors cannot be content simply to enforce a fixed normative view if they are to provide effective ongoing support for the authority of the state. It is not enough to trust that the exposure of the public to the way in which the constitution is practically applied will invariably convince them of its value. State institutions must not only allow the constitution to be justified and explained to the public, but must also ensure that the public regards the proffered justification as a reasonable one.

> A purported legal principle that had no counterpart in ordinary moral discourse could provide no justification for anything: its recognition would show that an insular preoccupation with the niceties of a technical legal craft had been substituted, unacceptably, for a proper concern for the requirements of ... the public good.[38]

Thus, Allan's concept of public reason requires *both* publicity and rationality. The public must observe the ostensible authoritative text in practice but must also accept and embrace it as a reasonable reflection of their social views. A difficult balancing act is therefore required. After all, if the institutions are obliged to respond to shifting public tastes, can they also produce the necessarily unifying taste-shaping effects examined above? Would not the claims of a constitution to social or normative authority inevitably be undermined if it was to regularly amend its supposedly central tenets?

In this context, Allan emphasizes that it is essential to provide some form of institutional adjudication. The existence of such a public forum, as the previous section has shown, has the advantage of encouraging normative dissidents to implicitly draw on the existing text when framing and presenting their

[37] J Rawls, *Justice as Fairness: A Restatement* (Belknap, 2001), at 27.

[38] TRS Allan, *Constitutional Justice* (Oxford University Press, 2001), at 292.

alternative views. However, the inclusion of an element of authoritative adjudication also allows for conclusive and yet dynamic resolution of such disputes. Institutional adjudication is not simply designed to allow those citizens lacking faith in the substantive constitutional structure to be shown the error of their ways. To see public adjudication in this way is to demonstrate an ill conceived and unquestioning acceptance of the constitution at issue as a tangible manifestation of the (chimeric) universal and objective good. On the contrary, a developed notion of the process of public adjudication should acknowledge the way in which it allows the state to position any emerging social views within the parameters of the existing understanding of the constitution. This reinforces its authority. Not only are the divergent social claims expressed in the rhetoric of the constitutional order, but also the institutions of the state will publicly ensure that the provenance of any determinative resolution is traced back to the constitutional text.

This analysis is very clearly illustrated by Dworkin's concept of interpretative integrity.[39] The notion of 'integrity' draws attention to the way in which the system attempts to seamlessly evolve to embrace any shifting social mores. Changes are publicly justified by reference to principles and values the authority of which has been confirmed by consistent public repetition over time. The taste-shaping effects of institutional activity condition the public to accept these principles as constitutive of the community's good. However, this general social acceptance also allows the system to respond to changing social tastes. The state's institutions publicly invoke these tenets to justify any changes they judge to be necessary, thereby investing these 'new' social understandings with the authoritative reputation cultivated by the public use and repetition of the 'old'. 'Constitutional adjudication ... resolve[s] our political disputes successfully ... as it instructs us in our shared political principles'.[40] This is a taste-shaping and taste-responsive technique which, Selznick notes, the law has long employed:

> By inviting argument and making the law forever fluid and debatable, the common law tradition [like constitutional adjudication] ensures that the law that is merges with the law that ought to be. ... Common law reason cannot escape social and political tradition: 'Custom must stand the test of reflection; reflection must yield to the verdict of experience'.[41]

Thus a picture of unity is presented to the public which binds new community values into the constitution's reputation as the authoritative exposition of normative social goods—even if that reputation originally rested on an alternative

[39] See, for example, R Dworkin, *Taking Rights Seriously* (Duckworth, 1977); and *Law's Empire* (Fontana, 1986).

[40] JL Mashaw, *Due Process in the Administrative State* (Yale University Press, 1985), at 43.

[41] P Selznick, *The Moral Commonwealth: Social Theory and the Promise of Community* (1992), at 450, cited with approval by Allan, above note 38, at 291. The passage is based in part on Blackstone's work in *Commentaries on the Laws of England.*

understanding of the state. Furthermore, the reputation of the state's institutions for even-handed and consistent treatment of the constitutional text reinforces public faith in the outcome of any such debate. It was noted in an earlier section how an aura of operational consistency can affirm the authoritative status of the constitutional text by confirming the public's view of its values as central social norms with a universally powerful force. In this context, this purported consistency serves to support the public assertion that the decision taken does not distort the normative unity of the constitutional order. Adjudication is thus a value-affirming exercise through the public use of which the institutions of the state are able to evaluate, synthesize, and ultimately legitimate the evolution of public views.

E. Conclusion

The most common contemporary evaluative approach to issues of institutional architecture and design is one which examines whether the implementation of a particular structural model generates results which reflect the normative values underpinning its initial adoption. This focus on goal achievement treats institutional efficiency as the touchstone of theoretical success. In constitutional terms, it is generally equated with the production of outcomes which accord with the system's stated normative values. As Barber explained, '[a] constitution is efficient in so far as it promotes the purposes for which it was established. It is inefficient in as far as it fails to fulfil these aspirations.'[42]

To turn to the specific example of the separation of powers, academics are inclined to argue about the extent to which its employment by the organs of the state yields liberty-optimal outcomes. It is beyond question that this is a valid means of inquiry. It would clearly be impossible to justify the continued usage of a doctrine which ultimately, in the situations it creates, fails to vindicate the normative value which justified its original utilization by the state.

However, the preceding section has shown that a focus on principles and values cannot exhaust the scope of an academic inquiry into the operation of a constitution. Constitutional theory is not simply a question of protecting basic principles or manufacturing norm-appropriate outcomes. To assess a model instrumentally on the basis of the extent to which its outputs reflect the foundational values upon which its employment is contingent is to adopt an unduly circumscribed understanding of the institutional structure's constitutional utility. Such a narrow view of institutional instrumentality necessarily ignores the two key lessons of the earlier aspects of this chapter: that the public's belief in the normative values upon which the institutions were initially erected is unlikely to remain constant over time; and that the way in which the institutions publicly

[42] N Barber, above note 21, at 65.

engage with and treat these values is arguably as significant (from the perspective of ensuring the constitution adequately fulfils its unifying function) as the normative integrity of the outcomes thereby produced. A proper conception of constitutional design must, it is clear, treat it as more than a mechanical exercise in producing norm-maximizing effects.

Such an approach may also be open to charges of indeterminacy and incompleteness. Not only does a focus on goals and values ignore the importance of institutional means, it also overlooks the fact that the pursuit of a particular goal or objective may be consistent with a multitude of governmental actions. In many cases, the simple identification of a constitutional value or objective will not provide any particular indication as to how that objective or value ought to be achieved. From the point of view of the constitution's purpose of providing determinate guidance on the appropriate exercise of governmental power, an institutional concentration on objectives alone is liable to encounter the problem that 'a given goal can be seen as consistent with liability or no liability, regulation or no regulation, constitutional right or no constitutional right'.[43] The reality is that '[g]oal choice may be necessary to the determination of law and public policy, but it is far from sufficient'.[44]

A comprehensive analysis of an individual theory of institutional arrangement should therefore assess the extent of its contribution to the maintenance and development of the social, cultural, and normative consensus which forms the centrepiece of the structure of that state. The theory should be examined not only for its compliance with the substantive values underlying its use, but also for the way in which it performs its critical taste-shaping and taste-responsive role. If it fails to fulfil this latter function properly, the likelihood is that the substantive values which the constitution espouses will remain fixed over time, ultimately leading to a loss of public belief in, and therefore allegiance to, the text. This would undermine its authority as a declaration of a shared social view, thereby damaging the state's ability to successfully manage its inevitable internal divisions.

This work must not, therefore, consider only the question whether the separation of powers theory, in its everyday incarnation, consistently produces libertarian outcomes. It should also explore whether the way in which the theory is institutionally employed publicly reinforces the constitution's legitimacy (and thus unifying force) as an authoritative statement of common social beliefs. The institutional devices (such as public adjudication) and process values (consistency, publicity, rationality) which support this task must form part of any full assessment of the constitutional utility of the separation of powers theory. Accordingly, the next section of this book will examine the separation of powers

[43] N Komesar, *Imperfect Alternatives: Choosing institutions in law, economics and public policy* (University of Chicago Press, 1994), at 5.

[44] Ibid.

doctrine in the light of this dual conception of its constitutional utility. The next chapter will therefore attempt to examine:

1) whether contemporary institutional instantiations of the theory tend to systematically produce norm-appropriate outcomes which reflect the substantive values underlying its usage;
2) whether the way in which the institutions engage with the separation of powers theory both reflects and reinforces the public's equation of the authority of the state with the pursuit, enforcement, and achievement of socially-accepted normative goods.

2

The Tripartite Separation of Powers Theory

A. A Universal Separation of Powers Doctrine?

(1) The Problems of a 'Pure' Theory

A preliminary problem for any purported analysis of the separation of powers is the absence of an agreed understanding of the theory. It is one of the peculiarities of the concept that, despite its status as an ubiquitous tenet of constitutional thought, it remains an analytical subject of considerable imprecision. As a doctrine, it defies universal definition. The most obvious instantiation of the theory—a pure Montesquian model of three distinct organs independently exercising power—has not been wholly reproduced in the institutional architecture of any modern state. There must accordingly be serious doubts about its contemporary relevance. This so-called 'pure' theory of the separation of powers is, in fact, generally regarded as a practically impossible, or even undesirable, mode of government, a reputation chiefly acquired after its inauspicious cameo appearance in the formative years of the American constitutional experience.

The seventeenth and eighteenth centuries marked the undoubted political and theoretical highpoint of the 'pure' conception of the separation of powers. At a time of rising resentment at the repressive orthodoxy of absolute monarchies and unrepresentative rule, Montesquieu's idealized depiction of the English organs of public life as a paradigm of fair and balanced government served as the template for those seeking to reform or replace existing state systems. It was to this blueprint that the American revolutionaries turned. Intoxicated by the potent taste of their new-found freedom, conscious of the historical significance of the opportunity to fashion their own social and political structures free from the constraints of traditional dogma, those charged with the creation of the American state predictably acted with an absolute conviction. In their words and deeds, they exhibited an ideological purity untainted by extended experience of the practical realities of government rule. Statements of principle and declarations of intent—whether rhetorical, political, or constitutional—were delivered in stridently aspirational terms, as befitted the character of men committed to the establishment of a determinedly radical state. Acting in the first flushes of their revolutionary ardour, their dedication to a faithful recreation of Montesquieu's abstract scheme was total.[1] Thus Virginia's constitution declared that:

> the legislative, executive and judicial powers of government ought to be forever separate and distinct from each other.[2]

This absolutist view was also evident in the constitution of Maryland, which similarly insisted 'that the Legislative, Executive and Judicial powers of Government ought to be forever separate and distinct from each other', adding that 'no person exercising the functions of one of said Departments shall assume or discharge the duties of any other'.[3]

Practical difficulties inevitably arise, however, when a theoretical abstraction is reborn in tangible form. The American constitutionalists, acting as midwife at the birth of this hybrid offspring of ideology and politics, could only expect to encounter such labour pains. As Barber has commented:

> A political philosopher can produce a utopian vision of the ideal world, uncluttered by the limitations inherent in all human endeavour. A utopian constitutional theory, on the other hand, [is] a waste of time.[4]

From a practical perspective, the hermetic division of governmental functions envisaged by these texts was impossible to achieve. The extensive powers exercised by the organs of the state could never be satisfactorily reduced to a simplistic three-way allocation of tasks. Further, the very notion of subjecting public bodies to a concept of independence so austere as to prohibit any substantial institutional interaction bore little relation to the realities of an efficient administration. Some degree of cooperation and coordination between branches is essential if the state is to function in a cohesive manner. 'It is naïve . . . to think of separation of powers rules as capable of creating sealed chambers, each of which must contain all there is of the executive, legislative and judicial powers. Overlap is inevitable.'[5]

The chastening experiences of the founders of the early American states demonstrated quite clearly the veracity of this view. It is an eloquent, if implicit, recognition of the practical difficulties which the earliest attempts at

[1] Although the theories of John Locke obviously also had a significant influence on the actions of these constitutional creators, it should be noted that 'Americans looked for specifics to Montesquieu, not to Locke': DAJ Richards, *Foundations of American Constitutionalism* (Oxford University Press, 1989), at 120. Locke's justification of revolutionary action against tyrannical rule was arguably his greatest influence on events in America. See AC McLaughlin, *Constitutional History of the United States* (Appleton-Century, 1935), at 96–98.

[2] Constitution of Virginia, adopted on 29 June, 1776. A copy of the constitution is available at <http://avalon.law.yale.edu/subject_menus/18th.asp> accessed 8 May, 2009.

[3] Maryland Declaration of Rights, Article VI, adopted on 11 November, 1776. The text of the declaration is available at <http://avalon.law.yale.edu/18th_century/ma02.asp> accessed 8 May, 2009.

[4] N Barber, 'Prelude to the Separation of Powers' (2001) 60 CLJ 59, at 62–63.

[5] P Bator, 'Constitution as Architecture: Legislative and Administrative Courts under Article III' (1990) 65 *Indiana Law Journal* 233, at 265.

institutional choreography encountered, that only a very short time after Maryland and Virginia saw fit to assert their commitment to Montesquieu's ideal in such absolute terms, the constitutional texts of neighbouring states opted instead to present their own division of functions in a more measured fashion. The fiery zeal of the revolutionary had been replaced by the practical realism of the politician. Madison saw the constitution of New Hampshire as a product of this gradual process, noting how its position as the last state to enact a constitution allowed it to be 'fully aware of the impossibility and inexpediency of avoiding any mixture of these departments'.[6] In his view, this constitution avoided the errors of the earlier documents, which bore 'strong marks of the haste, and still stronger of the inexperience under which they were framed',[7] displaying a more pragmatic degree of ideological circumspection. Its commitment to the separation of powers was expressed in considerably more qualified terms:

> [T]he legislative, executive and judiciary powers ought to be kept as separate from, and independent of each other as the nature of free government will admit; or as is consistent with that chain of connection that binds the whole fabric of the constitution in one indissoluble bond of unity.[8]

The American experience thus demonstrated the inefficacy of the purest conception of the separation of powers as a workable model of government. Today, the pure theory is accordingly treated with considerable scepticism. The South African Constitutional Court, for example, accepted in *S v Dodo* that 'there is in our constitution no absolute separation of powers'.[9] Worldwide experiences, the South Africans feel, have instead demonstrated that 'there is no universal model of separation of powers', and that 'in democratic systems of government in which checks and balances [exist] ... there is no separation that is absolute'.[10] To this end, the Canadian courts, like Kenny J in the Irish context,[11] have noted that their constitutional text 'does not insist on a strict separation of powers'.[12]

[6] J Madison, *The Federalist* (2nd ed., University of Chicago, 1990), Book 47, at 155.

[7] Ibid, at 156.

[8] New Hampshire. Georgia (1777), New York (1777), and Vermont (1786) are amongst the states which favoured a more qualified approach to their constitutional adoption of the separation of powers theory. The texts of these documents, and other from the same era, are available at <http://avalon.law.yale.edu/subject_menus/statech.asp#my> accessed 8 May 2009.

[9] *S v Dodo*, 2001 (5) BCLR 423; 2001 (3) SA 382, at para 22.

[10] *Re Certification of the Constitution of South Africa* (the First Certification case), 1996 (4) SA 744, at [106–8].

[11] Kenny J accepted in *Abbey Films v AG* that 'the framers of the Constitution did not adopt a rigid separation between the legislative, executive and judicial powers', a 'realistic' appraisal of the position which, Morgan notes, has not always been adhered to by the courts. *See Abbey Films v AG*, [1981] IR 158, at 171, and DG Morgan, *The Separation of Powers in the Irish Constitution* (Round Hall, 1997), at 26–32.

[12] *Re Reference re Secession of Quebec*, [1998] 2 SCR 217, at para 15.

These decisions reinforce Gwyn Morgan's remark that the 'Platonic ideal' of the *trias politica* 'has not been followed in any working constitution in the world'.[13] It would seem that a model of such pristine academic integrity is impossible to effect in practice. As the South African courts have confessed, '[n]o constitutional scheme can reflect a complete separation of powers; the scheme is always one of partial separation'.[14]

In its place, a variety of these partial theories of the separation of powers have emerged. Schemes of separation have been put forward from a host of theoretical and practical perspectives.

> [S]cholars [have] . . . staked claims for a de-evolutionary *versus* an evolutionary approach; a neoclassical *versus* a pragmatic approach; an originalist *versus* a non-originalist interpretation, or judicial literalism *versus* judicial interpretation.[15]

The existence of such myriad interpretations of the theory makes any overarching analysis of its efficacy very difficult.

(2) The Ubiquity of the Institutional Trinity

These differing doctrines do, however, tend to be united in their invocation of, and reliance upon, Montesquieu's original tripartite vision of the state. Although none of them seek to embrace and adopt it in its entirety, the three-way classification of state power as legislative, executive, or judicial recurs as a central feature of almost all understandings of the separation of powers. Differences arise not over the validity of this initial threefold categorization of the governing functions of the state, but rather over the particular inter-institutional allocation of power. Although the pure model of separation has been generally discounted as a viable institutional theory, its central threefold vision retains its influence as a guiding principle of power distribution. The model of a legislative–executive–judicial division of functions continues to appear as an essential element of most constitutional discourse. Disputes arise, not over its inherent validity, but over the mechanics of its actual operation. Contemporary theorists tend to implicitly accept the veracity of this threefold division of power, striving not to replace but to recalibrate it for the modern world. It is through its reliance upon the tripartite model of institutional power that a conception of the state becomes recognizable as a model based on *the* separation of powers theory. Thus, the tripartite model seems also a suitable starting point for any analysis of the separation of powers' efficacy as an institutional theory.

[13] Morgan, note 11 above, at 24. [14] 1996 (4) SA 744, note 10 above, at para. 109.
[15] R Brown, 'Separated Powers and Ordered Liberty' (1990) 139 *University of Pennsylvania Law Review* 1513, at 1522–1523.

B. The Separation of Powers as an Effective Institutional Theory

(1) Indeterminacy as an Institutional Problem

As an institutional doctrine, the theory of the separation of powers has a clearly defined role in helping to structure and direct the distribution and division of institutional power. Proffering a particular vision of institutional order, it ought to act as a guide to those who wish to establish an efficacious system of governance. After all, if an institutional theory is to convincingly support its claims of normative value, it must first perform its primary duty of organizing and arranging the allocation of institutional power in that state.

As a theory, the tripartite understanding of the separation of powers has always been notable for its communicative simplicity. The idea of three separate organs with independent powers is easy to explain and to appreciate. The imprecision of this idea did not hinder the global diffusion of the doctrine. Such an 'open texture, which enabled people to see in it what they liked, and take from it what they wanted, was no disadvantage to its reception or employment'.[16] This same simplicity, however, makes it problematic to apply. An institutional theory, it has been argued above, should actively assist in shaping the structure of a state if it is to retain any practical utility. It should therefore provide sufficiently specific criteria to decisively determine initial, and indeed ongoing, disputes over inter-institutional competences. The tripartite model, however, is so abstract that it is almost always unclear what it actually enjoins in an individual instance. As this section will seek to show, it would seem that the doctrine is, in fact, so indeterminate that it is ultimately devoid of any practical efficacy.

(2) Indeterminacy in Action

Easy to express, the Montesquian model, as an interpretative principle, is extraordinarily problematic to apply. Montesquieu himself made no attempt to establish a workable scheme of institutional separation and others since then have struggled with the doctrine's definitional indeterminacy. The key difficulty is the imprecision inherent in the theory's central terms. For example, the two dominant versions of the theory in the extensive US literature on this issue both depend, for their everyday usage, on essentially indefinable notions.

(a) The Formal Doctrine

The formalist conception of the separation of powers attempts simply to preserve the distributional integrity of the tripartite model. From a normative point

[16] C Munro, *Studies in Constitutional Law* (2nd ed., Butterworths, 1999), at 302.

of view, formalists trust entirely to the model's inherent veracity. When faced with a question of disputed competences, the formalist court or commentator is concerned chiefly to identify and classify the task at hand. Once characterized as a legislative, executive, or judicial function, the task is allocated to the appropriate institution. The initial classification effectively exhausts the formalist enquiry. This step necessarily involves, however, the adoption and employment of essentially arbitrary definitional criteria. How, for example, should an executive function be defined? And how can a court distinguish between a legislative and judicial task? The courts in Ireland and the USA have conspicuously failed to provide a convincing and determinative account of the critical characteristics of the respective institutional functions.

Irish judges, for their part, have intermittently attempted to develop an authoritative definition of the judicial function. The indeterminacy of this concept has meant, however, that they have been forced to rely on a capriciously chosen checklist of apparently important features. Kenny J in *McDonald v Bord na gCon (No. 2)* opined that the 'characteristic features' of the administration of justice were:

1) a dispute or controversy as to the existence of legal rights or a violation of the law;
2) the determination or ascertaining of the rights of parties, or the imposition of liabilities, or the infliction of a penalty;
3) the final determination (subject to appeal) of legal rights or liabilities, or the imposition of penalties;
4) the enforcement of those rights or liabilities, or the imposition of a penalty by the court, or by the executive power of the state which is called in by the court to enforce its judgment; and
5) the making of an order by the court which, as a matter of history, is an order characteristic of courts in this country.[17]

Like the efforts of earlier Irish courts in *Lynham*[18] and *Shanahan,*[19] however, this definition provides only a descriptive summary of the everyday workload of the contemporary court. An *ex post facto* overview of the average judicial caseload, it does not offer a suitably prescriptive analysis of the core concepts of the judicial function. The logic of Kenny J's position is hopelessly circular, relying

[17] [1965] IR 217, at 231.

[18] *Lynham v Butler (No. 2),* [1933] IR 74. In this case, Kennedy CJ, interpreting A 64 of the 1922 Free State Constitution, attempted to define the judicial power in a lengthy section which, he admitted, was offered 'by way of description rather than of precise formula'. Like the *McDonald* criteria, it functioned more as a description of what the court did than as an analysis of what it ought to do.

[19] *State (Shanahan) v AG,* [1964] IR 239. Here Davitt P, denying any attempt on his part to fully define the judicial power, nonetheless set out another lengthy description of what he saw as its essential features.

on the current nature of the court's activities to define its function into the future. The *McDonald* criteria reflect the judge's estimation only of what the courts do, rather than what they ought to do. In this, it owes more to historical happenstance than conceptual coherence.

The alternative, however, is for a court to content itself to 'say in a given instance whether or not the procedure is an exercise of [judicial] power, rather than to identify a comprehensive check-list for that purpose',[20] categorizing instances of institutional power on a case-by-case basis. This 'easier, if intellectually less satisfying' approach has been adopted by the US and Irish courts in several cases.[21] It is similarly affected, however, by the connected problems of indeterminacy and arbitrariness.

The Irish courts have oscillated between bold (but necessarily incomplete) attempts to identify the essence of institutional functions and a more realistic recognition that 'this question is likely . . . to be resolved on a pragmatic case-by-case basis rather [than] by reference to a pre-defined set of principles'.[22] Because the functions are so difficult to define, the court is forced to identify, distinguish, and allocate institutional powers on the basis of unconvincing, inauthoritative, and ever-shifting criteria. Thus in recent years the Irish courts have experimented with auxiliary options—namely the historical,[23] contextual,[24] and incidental[25] approaches. These methods differ considerably, however. The conceptual approach, for example, resembles the *McDonald* checklist in that it seeks to reduce an abstract and elusive concept to a precise and comprehensive definition. The contextual and incidental options, on the other hand, involve a more intuitive examination of the measure at issue, the existing institutional context, and the centrality of the power in question to the conduct of the body in question. Theoretical esoterics are eschewed in favour of a pragmatic and definitionally indeterminate approach. That the courts see fit to intermittently rely on such varying interpretative techniques—with Kearns J actually considering all three in the course of a single decision in *O'Donoghue v Ireland* without comment or complaint[26]—illustrates the problematic dearth of clarity or certainty in this area of the law.

From an American perspective, *INS v Chadha* provides an excellent example of the problems involved with this sort of case-by-case approach.[27] Faced with a legislative veto of the decision of an immigration judge to suspend Chadha's deportation, the majority, noting the impact of the decision on the applicant's

[20] *Per* McCarthy J in *Keady v Garda Commissioner*, [1992] 2 IR 197, at 204.
[21] Ibid, at 204.
[22] G Hogan and G Whyte, *Kelly: The Irish Constitution* (4th ed., Butterworths, 2003), at 627.
[23] Keady, note 20 above. [24] *O'Donoghue v Ireland*, [2002] 2 IR 168.
[25] *Murphy v GM*, unreported, High Court (O'Higgins J), 4 June 1999. For a further discussion of these three approaches, see Morgan, note 11 above, at Chapter 4, and in 'Judicial-o-centric separation of powers on the wane?' (2004) XXXIX *Irish Jurist* 142, at 154–158.
[26] [2000] 2 IR 168. [27] 462 US 919 (1983).

rights and liabilities, defined the power as a legislative one. Powell J, on the other hand, classified it as a judicial function—powerfully demonstrating the intensely subjective nature of the judges' individual analyses.

Similar problems apply to any attempt to identify the essence of the executive function. It is difficult to identify any clear conception of exactly what constitutes the executive. Thus the English courts have:

> continued to use the language of Queen and Crown to signify an executive which has been transformed almost out of all recognition since the seventeenth and eighteenth centuries.[28]

This reflects the fact that:

> this notion [of an executive branch] principally seems to exist to capture all that is excluded from the other two categories.[29]

Apparently incapable of definition in its own terms, the concept of the executive thus encounters the same difficulties as were outlined above in respect of the judicial function. Once again, courts and commentators are forced to identify executive organs on an effectively ad hoc basis.

The inconsistency inherent in this sort of palm-tree justice is directly attributable to the indeterminacy of the concepts which are central to the use of this formalist theory. The formal view of the separation of powers 'depends upon a belief that the legislative, executive and judicial powers are inherently distinguishable as well as separable from one another', a proposition which judicial experience has shown to be a 'highly questionable premise'.[30] The reality, as Stevens J recognized, is that:

> the exercise of legislative, executive and judicial powers cannot be categorically distributed among three mutually exclusive branches of government [because] governmental power cannot always be readily characterised with only one of those three labels. On the contrary . . . a particular function, like a chameleon, will often take on the aspect of the office to which it is assigned.[31]

(b) The Functionalist Approach

The functionalist conception of the separation of powers acknowledges the impossibility of the formalist school's neatly compartmentalized vision, opting to concentrate instead on the preservation of the normatively crucial inter-institutional balance. Aspiring, as it does, to ensure that no single body assumes a disruptive position of excess power, this concern for inter-institutional checking deliberately echoes the foundational objectives of the doctrine. Once again, however, the simplicity of the tripartite model is practically problematic.

[28] T Daintith and A Page, *The Executive in the Constitution* (Oxford University Press, 1999), at 26.

[29] Barber, note 4 above, at 71.

[30] Brown, note 15 above, at 1525.

[31] *Bowsher v Synar*, 478 US 714 (1986), at 749.

How is this notion of balance to be assessed, let alone secured? How can the respective institutional strengths of the three organs of the state be compared? One need only look at the way in which the legislature,[32] the executive,[33] and the judiciary[34] have, at various times, been characterized as the single greatest threat to civil governance to see that this is an impracticable task. Just as the formalist theory necessarily (and misguidedly) assumes the ability to accurately define and distinguish the three functions of the state, so the functionalist approach similarly rests on the system's chimerical capacity to define, adopt, and consistently employ the essentially indefinable notion of institutional balance.

Like its formalist rival, the functionalist approach tends to produce an ad hoc and uneven judicial treatment of separation of powers issues. Judges in the USA have been unable to successfully elaborate universal criteria for these cases. The central concepts of the tripartite model—the characteristic functions of each institution and the balance to be maintained between them—have proved impossible to define. Judges have accordingly been cast in a reactive rather than a prescriptive role, adjusting their view of the relevant criteria to reflect the issues raised in an individual case.

The consequence of the absence of comprehensive curial guidelines in the US courts has been that:

> the Court has appeared to decide each case as if it were the first of its kind, with each individual justice apparently weighing the costs and benefits according to some idiosyncratic scale of value . . . which may vary from case to case.[35]

This brief overview of the formalist and functionalist versions of the separation of powers theory demonstrates that they are both crippled by the central indeterminacy of the tripartite model. The nature of the branches, and the distinction between them, cannot, it is clear, be determined 'with mathematical precision'.[36] Definitional uncertainty, as Marshall and Jennings have acknowledged, is typical of all aspects of the theory.[37] The doctrine provides guidance and direction only to the extent to which it is supplemented by the court's own intuitive choice of independent evaluative criteria. The use of the tripartite

[32] Madison, like many of his contemporaries, regarded the legislature as the greatest institutional threat to constitutional government.

[33] See, for example, GH Hewart, *The New Despotism* (Benn, 1929), in which the former Lord Chief Justice railed against the dangers of increasing executive power.

[34] Academic commentary in the USA in the years after the Warren Court considered in some detail the argument that the court's power of judicial review makes it the most prominent threat to democratic government. This differs from Hamilton's traditional view of it as the least dangerous branch of government. See, for example, A Bickel, *The Least Dangerous Branch: The Supreme Court at the Bar of Politics* (2nd ed., Yale University Press, 1986), and R Bork, *The Tempting of America: The Political Seduction of the Law* (Free Press, 1990). Cf. A Hamilton, *The Federalist Papers* (Kramnick, I, ed., Penguin, 1987), Book 78.

[35] Brown, note 15 above, at 1518.

[36] *Springer v Government of the Philippines*, 277 US 189 (1928), at 211, *per* Holmes J.

[37] See G Marshall, *Constitutional Theory* (Clarendon, 1971) and I Jennings, *The Law and the Constitution* (5th ed., University of London Press, 1959).

model necessarily involves a choice between the Scylla of subjective inconsistency and the Charybdis of arbitrary determinacy. The formalists and functionalists face essentially the same problem of trying to construct an operational theory of power allocation from an institutional model, the details of which are hopelessly unclear. The tripartite theory provides a vision of constitutional governance but no guidance as to how to achieve it in practice. As Brown comments, the formalists and functionalists differ 'in the end [on] no more than a question of where the proper point lies in the flexibility/determinacy matrix'.[38]

(3) Indeterminacy of Objectives

The simple Montesquian model is therefore insufficiently specific to serve effectively as a directive principle of institutional organization. It is, of itself, too vague and imprecise to authoritatively regulate the institutional structures of the state. For the doctrine to function effectively, some external criterion or value is required capable of supplying the certainty lacking in its basic design. One solution would obviously be to interpret the theory in the light of the objective which it aims to achieve. Here again, however, issues of indeterminacy arise. The separation of powers has historically been justified by reference to several discrete normative values. Morgan, for example, identifies four policies which have been advanced, at various times, as the foundational objectives of the doctrine.[39] Gwyn, for his part, posits five.[40] These differing policies are not necessarily mutually exclusive. They do, however, variously suggest that the separation of powers doctrine aims, inter alia, to:

- prevent tyranny by ensuring that power is not vested in any single individual or organ;
- secure a balance between institutions such that they are capable of supervising each other's actions through a system of checks and balances;
- ensure law is made in the public interest by establishing a balance of power between institutions, or representative groups;
- enhance efficiency by giving responsibility for individual tasks to the most appropriate institutional actors;
- prevent partiality and self-interest by separating the personnel involved in decision-making;

[38] Brown, note 15 above, at 1530.

[39] These are (i) balance of power, (ii) efficiency, (iii) preventing conflict of interests, and (iv) ensuring law is public, objective, and precise. See Morgan, note 11 above, Chapter 2.

[40] '(1) To create greater government efficiency; (2) to assure that statutory law is made in the common interest; (3) to assure that the law is impartially administered and that all administrators are under the law; (4) to allow the people's representatives to call executive officials to account for the abuse of their power; and (5) to establish a balance of governmental powers': WB Gwyn, *The Meaning of the Separation of Powers: An Analysis of the Doctrine from its Origin to the Adoption of the United States Constitution* (Tulane Studies, 1965), discussed in Morgan, note 11 above, Chapter 2.

- ensure objectivity and generality in the creation of laws by separating the tasks of law creation and law enforcement; and
- allow elected and representative officials to supervise the actions of executive officials and call them to account if necessary.

There is, it is obvious, considerable overlap between several of these objectives. For example, it would be possible to devise an institutional balance which was capable of increasing the possibility that laws be enacted in the public interest while, at the same time, safeguarding the state from the ills of unilateral rule. Equally, however, these values are not neatly co-extensive. Securing the public-spiritedness of official acts requires a much more elaborate structure than one focused primarily on the prevention of tyranny. A citizen, intolerant of what he sees as intrusive government, may support the idea of avoiding a solitary concentration of public power but might object to the establishment of a more complex and instrumentally-calibrated institutional structure. An individual's view of what the separation of powers prescribes is dependent, in the first place, on his or her perception of its specific aspirational objectives. Does it dictate a simple separation of personnel, or does the doctrine demand the establishment of a particular institutional balance? Does it require that legislation be enacted in the public interest, or is the theory satisfied once legislation is expressed in sufficiently general terms? Does it, in fact, impose no limitations on the content or language of legislation, insisting only that laws be created by the designated legislative organ of that state? The separation of powers theory is clearly capable of encompassing a host of varying views of the state. It does not, in itself, indicate a particular hierarchy of values, nor provide any guidance as to the setting of appropriate priorities for objectives in cases of choice, or indeed conflict, between them.

This poses problems for those who seek to rely on the doctrine, or, indeed, to assess it. Barber emphasized that '[t]esting the efficiency of an institution requires the clear identification of its goals and a careful practical examination of its outcomes'.[41] With its ambiguous values and objectives, the separation of powers theory is too vague to support consistent usage and analysis. Its indeterminacy, once again, 'enable[s] people to see in it what they lik[e], and take from it what they wan[t]',[42] creating an impression of popular support for a single theory which in fact conceals beneath its surface considerable scope for serious disagreement on important constitutional questions.

(4) The Theory in the Courts

This view of the theory as all things to all people is most starkly demonstrated by the doctrine's frequent appearance on opposing sides of the same argument. This has been evident even as far back as the American case law of the early

[41] Barber, note 4 above, at 66. [42] Munro, note 16 above, at 302.

nineteenth century. The political, constitutional, and jurisprudential processes leading to the adoption of the legitimacy of judicial review by the US Supreme Court in *Marbury v Madison* are well known and need no more than the briefest description here.[43] Marshall CJ's rejection of the 'honied Mansfieldism of Blackstone's' equation of popular sovereignty with legislative supremacy was founded on the federal Constitution's clear classification of the people as ultimately supreme.[44] The Constitution was not only the source of the powers of government agencies but also of the limitations imposed on these organs of the state. The 'original and supreme will' of the American people, as expressed in their enactment of the Constitution, 'organizes the government and assigns to different departments their respective powers. The powers of the legislature are limited and defined.' The presence of such constitutional limits necessarily implies the existence of a body capable of adjudicating on alleged transgressions of these boundaries. As an issue of legal interpretation, the separation of powers principle clearly dictates that such questions ought to be entrusted to the judiciary. Of this, Marshall CJ had no doubt:

> It is emphatically the province and duty of the judicial department to say what the law is. Those who apply the rule to particular cases, must of necessity expound and interpret that rule. If two laws conflict with each other, the courts must decide on the operation of each. So if a law be in opposition to the Constitution ... the court must determine which of these conflicting rules governs the case. This is of the very essence of judicial duty.[45]

However, there were those who saw the theory instead as insisting on the exclusion of the judiciary from what, for them, was patently an issue of legislative action. Gibson J, for example, delivering a dissenting opinion in the 1825 Pennsylvanian case of *Eakin v Raub*,[46] questioned the validity of the supervisory jurisdiction of the courts. Adjudicating on the normative disabilities of an elected assembly—what Kelsen later portrayed as the exercise of a negative legislative power[47]—was not, according to Gibson J, a responsibility which ought to vest in the judicial branch. The significant point, however, is that his objection rested on his own view of the separation of powers as a principle which demanded that the organs of state not interfere in what were the prima facie areas of activity of their theoretically co-equal counterparts. As a dissenting judgment in a state court, Gibson J's decision was not, in itself, constitutionally significant. However, when compared with the views expressed in *Marbury*, it demonstrates quite clearly how the separation of powers theory can be plausibly

[43] 1 Cranch 137; 5 US 137; 2 L Ed 2d 60 (1803).

[44] E Corwin, 'The Higher Law Background of American Constitutional Law' (1928–29) 42 *Harvard Law Review* 149, 365, cited in Marshall, note 37 above, 104.

[45] 1 Cranch 137 (1803), at 177–178.

[46] 12 Sergeant and Rawle (Penn) 330 (1825).

[47] H Kelsen, 'La Garantie Jurisdictionelle de la Constitution' (1928) 44 *Revue du Droit Public* 197.

invoked in support of very different notions of judicial review. As Marshall remarked:

> In reality, arguments from the separation of powers, though frequently mentioned, are ultimately of little force on either side of the controversy. As a consideration in favour of review, the doctrine is too vague and (since better arguments exist) superfluous. As an argument against review, it is in its commonest forms unconvincing.[48]

The doctrine's chameleon-like capacity to serve both sides of an argument was again evident in *Myers v US*,[49] and in *Youngstown Sheet and Tube Co. v Sawyer*.[50] In both these cases, the majority and minority of the US Supreme Court both invoked the separation of powers theory in support of their very differing conclusions. In the latter case, for example, the majority invalidated a Presidential attempt to seize and operate steel mills in the midst of the Korean War. They based this decision on their strong conviction that the separation of powers ought to operate as a guarantee of liberty. To allow such a unilateral executive seizure of individual property rights, even during wartime, would constitute an unacceptable infringement of this value.

The minority, on the other hand, advanced an efficiency-based understanding of the separation of powers doctrine in support of their position that the executive ought to be able to carry out such acts without being obliged to have disruptive recourse to the other branches of government. The theory, in their view, created an executive power so that such managerial judgments could be made unilaterally in times of crisis.

Recent judicial allusions to the theory in Britain have also been notable for their vastly varying views of what the idea of a separation of powers involves. In Lord Steyn's eyes, the theory envisages an independent, institutionally separate court, charged with the intensive scrutiny of the other branches of government.[51] To Lord Hoffman, it requires judicial caution and restraint, constraining the ability of the court to investigate matters allocated by the theory to the other organs of the state.[52]

This uncertainty and confusion as to the institutional dictates of the doctrine has also characterized the recent attitude of the Irish Supreme Court to the theory. The court unanimously agreed in *TD v Minister for Education*[53] that the tripartite theory is a constitutional principle of considerable influence in the

[48] Marshall, note 37 above, at 108. [49] 272 US 52 (1926).

[50] 343 US 579 (1952).

[51] Lord Steyn, 'The Case for a Supreme Court' (2002) 118 LQR 382, at 383.

[52] Lord Hoffman, 'The COMBAR Lecture 2001: Separation of Powers' (2002) 7 *Judicial Review* 137. Cf. M Chamberlain, 'Democracy and Deference in Resource Allocation Cases' (2003) 8 *Judicial Review* 12. Lord Hoffman's view echoes the more traditional judicial view of separation of powers, evident in authorities such as *Dupont Steels v Sirs* [1980] 1 WLR 142.

[53] [2001] 4 IR 259.

Irish legal order. What was striking, however, was the extent of the differences between the members of the Court on the nature of the theory itself. Marshall had remarked in his work on the inability of advocates of the idea of a three-way institutional separation to conclusively determine whether a scheme of checks and balances constituted a central tenet of the theory, or rather a justifiable departure from its strictest demands. The Supreme Court seemed to share this confusion. Denham J, in her dissenting opinion, envisaged the existence of a system of scrutiny as a 'breach [of] a rigid concept of the separation of powers'.[54] Keane CJ, however, seemed to regard such inter-institutional restraint as a requirement of the theory itself, citing Hardiman J's words in the earlier *Sinnott* case[55] in support of his own conclusion that the principle 'exists to prevent the accumulation of excessive power ... and to allow each [organ] to check and balance the other'.[56] Hardiman J, for his part, evinced a more pragmatic attitude to such checks, appearing to view them as a practical necessity of the administration of power. He insisted that their instantiation in the Irish order did not denote that the constitution's brand of separation of powers was 'in any general sense a porous one'.[57] Murray J (as he then was) expressly acknowledged the existence of these varying views of the theory, admitting that it could be, and indeed has been, construed either as a 'distribution of powers' between branches, 'or [as] a balancing of power among these [organs]'.[58] That such contrasting conceptions can coexist beneath the same constitutional banner provides clear evidence that Marshall's accusations of unavoidable conceptual confusion were well founded.

The theory, in its various guises, is clearly capable of supporting diametrically opposite understandings of the state. It is uncertain, in any given situation, whether the doctrine in fact enjoins the separation or the blending of the state's institutions. Plausible arguments can be constructed in support of either point of view. Its utility as an institutional theory is seriously compromised by this. In reality, it seems no more than a political catchphrase of limited polemical utility, devoid of any sort of central ethos or ideological essence. It serves only as a rhetorical rallying point, a convenient label for an *a priori* conclusion reached on the basis of any number of external considerations. By itself, the separation of powers supplies scant guidance to the institutional actors of the state, offering equal backing for an array of diverse and divergent views. As Marshall so famously remarked, the theory is:

> infected with so much imprecision and inconsistency that it may be counted as little more than a jumbled portmanteau of arguments for policies which ought to be supported or rejected on other grounds.[59]

[54] Ibid, at 306. [55] *Sinnott v Minister for Education*, [2001] 2 IR 545.
[56] Ibid, at 286. [57] Ibid, at 367. [58] Ibid, at 329.
[59] Marshall, note 37 above, at 124.

(5) The Historical Origins of the Uncertainty

This problem is not simply a product of an inadequate contemporary understanding of the doctrine. Magill argues persuasively that this fatal indeterminacy is, in fact, an inescapable element of the theory of the separation of powers. Examining the historical emergence of the idea, she notes how it developed as an amalgamation of the older doctrine of mixed (and later balanced) government with the concept of the separation of government functions. Both ideas aimed to structure state power in such a way that the evil of tyrannical rule would be avoided—an objective which, it was outlined above, the separation of powers is generally accepted to share. These two theories, however, sought to achieve this end in clearly divergent ways.

United in their emphasis on the importance of ensuring an institutional 'balance', these theories actually defined that notion in very different ways. Separating the functions of government demanded a distinct division and separation of institutional competences between independent state organs. The mixed/balanced theories, on the contrary, required the cooperative participation of the state's distinct social classes, through their institutional representatives, in its governance.[60] It is scarcely surprising, therefore, that the modern 'marriage of the two [pre-constitutional] ideas is a troubled one'.[61] The contemporary lack of such clearly defined social classes leaves the institutions of the state as the locus for both separation and balancing. The institutions are supposed to be separate to avoid tyranny, but are also required to cooperate to achieve an appropriate institutional equilibrium. 'The system of separation of powers is equated with balance among the government departments,' thus, 'collaps[ing] both strategies into one objective.'[62]

The two theories are treated as complementary elements of a unified ideal, with the result that this ostensibly cohesive doctrine is, in actual fact, unclear as to whether it instinctively demands a system of separation or one of checks and balances. These twin pillars of the theory are actually uncomfortable ideological bedfellows, straining to conceal their differences behind a show of joint support for a tripartite model of institutional arrangement. Their shared attachment to the number three is insufficient, however, to obscure the fact that they incline in contradictory directions, seeking constitutional salvation by the very different paths of institutional separation or blending, with all the contradictory requirements such opposite approaches entail.

[60] See Chapter 5, below, for a more extensive discussion of the mixed theory of government.

[61] E Magill, 'The Real Separation in Separation of Powers Law' (2000) 86 *Virginia Law Review* 1127, at 1166.

[62] Ibid, at 1167. Magill goes on to note that this unified approach could only succeed if a causal connection could be established between the fact of functional separation and the existence of an institutional balance. This, however, cannot be satisfactorily established in the absence of measurable criteria of balance, forcing the separation of powers theory to rest its validity on a 'fanciful premise'. See ibid, at 1170–1174.

C. Value Shaping and the Separation of Powers

(1) The Problem of Hidden Normative Judgements

Indeterminacy, it has been demonstrated, affects all aspects of the tripartite separation of powers theory, necessarily casting doubt on the specifics of its details, ideals, and instrumental objectives. The doctrine, of itself, does not actually demand the adoption or indeed rejection of a particular scheme of institutional arrangement. It is but a convenient label for articulating various concerns about the regulation of the structure of the state, lending rhetorical colour to an argument advanced on essentially independent grounds. This indeterminacy of detail makes the model, taken seriously, an institutional theory of minimal merit. Necessarily unable to provide concrete criteria for the resolution of questions of disputed or uncertain institutional competence, the doctrine is incapable of fulfilling the primary role of any institutional theory—that of directing the arrangement and interaction of the organs of the state. That it has become a doctrine of such widespread and recurring constitutional import in spite of this problem is concerning in itself. However, its indeterminacy of objectives further undermines the theory's utility in a manner which is arguably more serious, adversely affecting its ability to discharge the constitutionally crucial task of norm reinforcement, identified in Chapter 1.

It was suggested in that chapter that an institutional theory, through its reliance on notions of public reason and justification, plays an important part in supporting and shaping the shared normative values of a state. The way in which the institutions openly invoke and employ common communitarian principles affirms the foundational status of these values, whilst simultaneously encouraging citizens to continue to rely on them in any future interaction with the state. It is essential that this process of institutional exposition sufficiently inform the public about the nature and characteristics of these constitutionally central values. The separation of powers, however, has been shown to lack such specifics. By itself, it is but a 'desiccated concept that waits for the introduction of a stronger normative thesis before it generates a full conception of the doctrine that can provide any institutional considerations'.[63] Any theory of separated institutional power depends for its details on the political vision upon which it is premised.

Yet, in many jurisdictions, these normative assumptions remain untested by political or judicial debate. This calls into question the extent to which the doctrine, as an institutional theory, is performing its value-shaping or value-reinforcing role. Instead of articulating a complete theory of the system's directive principles of institutional separation, discussions instead tend to

[63] Barber, note 4 above, at 65–66.

concentrate on individual aspects of the institutional arrangements at issue—the delegation of legislative power in Ireland, for example, or the position of the Lord Chancellor or the House of Lords in the UK. The intuitive simplicity of the tripartite model has the unfortunate effect that it can come to be used as an underdeveloped article of constitutional faith, a concept 'admired without being analysed, and imported to [a legal system] with little or no debate'.[64]

Commentators have remarked on how the American courts, for example, tend to treat the theory as an end in itself,[65] a 'self-executing safeguard' to be interpreted and upheld without any examination of the deeper normative origins of the judge's individual understanding of what the doctrine demands.[66] In this, American judges are not alone. This inclination to rely on the theory as if it reflected a single unitary vision of the state inhibits the public's ability to understand it properly. It has been demonstrated that the theory is little more than a broad rhetorical church, within which rival sects claim sanctuary. The theory is determinate (and thus usable) only when viewed from a particular political or theoretical perspective. Its portrayal in the courts as 'an ostensible theory of the constitution' conceals such subjective value judgements behind a putatively apolitical facade.[67] 'Separation of powers theory claims to be an exercise in constitutional theory, and in so claiming distinguishes itself from exercises in pure political theory' at the same time that it depends upon the adoption of controvertible political concepts for its institutional efficacy.[68] The political foundations of a court's interpretation of the doctrine are rarely made explicit in its judgment, however. The result of this is that the public is unable to understand or engage with the normative substance of the institutional decision. Public justification centres solely on a tripartite model which, when it is subjected to more intensive scrutiny, is cripplingly uncertain.

The contemporary approach to the separation of powers accordingly serves to shape, support, and encourage continued public allegiance to a tripartite model about which there are profoundly differing views. The model is treated as a value or end in itself at the same time that it gives sustenance to contrasting conceptions of the state and its structures. It is commonly used as an *ex post facto* label for a conclusion reached on other, crucially unspoken, grounds. It therefore fails to exert the vital unifying influence which an institutional theory ought to exercise, rallying the public behind a rhetorical standard which ostensibly unites all but actually persuades none.

The recent case law of the Irish courts provides the perfect illustration of this point. The presence of divergent judicial interpretations of the theory has been alluded to above. The majority of the court in the *TD* decision, it should be remembered, rested their conclusions chiefly on the doctrine of the separation of

[64] Morgan, note 11 above, at 297.
[65] See, in particular, Brown, note 15 above.
[66] *Buckley v Valeo*, 424 US 1 (1976), at 122.
[67] Barber, note 4 above, at 62
[68] Ibid, at 62.

powers. They did not advert to the political origins of their position, however. Favouring, as they did, a dogmatically strict understanding of the separation of powers, it is clear from closer examination of the judgments that these judges were decisively influenced by a majoritarian conception of democracy. At no stage, however, did they engage with the substance of that theory, nor attempt to justify it by the institutionally valuable process of public reason.

It is important to understand the factual circumstances in which the case arose, as these are unlikely to be familiar to any non-Irish readers. Article 42.4 of the Irish Constitution recognizes the existence of a right to free primary education. The relevant text provides that:

> [t]he State shall provide for free primary education and shall endeavour to supplement and give reasonable aid to private and corporate educational initiative, and, when the public good requires it, provide other educational facilities or institutions with due regard, however, for the rights of parents, especially in the matter of religious and moral formation.

The *TD* litigation was one of a number of similar challenges which arose out of the consistent failure of the state authorities to provide high-support secure units for the treatment and accommodation of disadvantaged children with specific behavioural needs. It was claimed that this failure contravened the children's right to education, which had previously been broadly defined by the Irish courts to include not only 'scholastic' instruction but also the general 'teaching and training of a child to make best possible use of his inherent and potential capacities, physical, mental and moral'.[69] In the High Court, the state authorities had previously indicated that they were in the process of implementing a plan to address these needs. For various reasons, however, these plans were not implemented, leading Kelly J to issue a mandatory injunction directing the state to implement the proposed policy plan immediately. The state appealed this order to the Supreme Court.

The majority of that Court did not question the entitlement of the applicant to the protection of Article 42.4. Rather, Keane CJ expressed the 'gravest doubts' about the judiciary's entitlement to enforce this type of socio-economic right, seeing in Kelly J's actions the 'far-reaching assumption by the courts of what is, prima facie at least, the exclusive role of the executive and legislature'.[70] This prima facie view reflected a clearly held *a priori* position. As the Chief Justice commented, 'a Rubicon has been crossed'[71]—but one which sprang, not from an express constitutional mandate, but rather from a political philosophy he personally regarded to be in the constitutional ascendancy.

The majority judgment of Hardiman J concurred in this opinion of the primacy of a 'strict separation of powers', going so far as to require the individual's

[69] *Ryan v AG*, [1965] IR 294, at 350.

[70] *TD*, [2001] 4 IR 259, at 285.

[71] Ibid, at 288.

express constitutional rights to be interpreted as subject to its values. Thus the long-standing assertion by an earlier Supreme Court that the judiciary's power was 'as ample as the defence of the Constitution requires'[72] was, in Hardiman J's view, to be restricted by reference to an understanding of the separation of powers which he saw as 'fundamental to all ... provisions' of the constitutional text.[73] This was not, in his opinion, to neglect the express references to the right to free primary education in the document. Hardiman J's perception of the separation principle's primacy necessarily required, however, that such claims could only be entertained in 'an absolutely extreme situation ... as an absolutely final resort in circumstances of great crisis, and for the protection of the constitutional order itself'.[74] Given the vindication of very significant, expressly guaranteed, and necessarily transient constitutional rights did not satisfy such stringent criteria,[75] it is difficult to imagine what would. The *TD* majority therefore chose to read express constitutional precepts in light of an implicit, perhaps only organizational, principle, which they elevated to the status of a 'high constitutional value'.[76] This was, of course, a permissible (if arguably novel) interpretation of the text. The difficulty lies in the fact that it was a decision evidently derived from unarticulated and unacknowledged assumptions of political theory. Hardiman J's judgment was inspired by the sort of basic majoritarian understanding of the democratic state about which Craig has been especially scathing:

> The assertion [of a counter-majoritarian difficulty with rights-based judicial review] is uttered as if this were a self-evident and straightforward proposition. It is, of course, nothing of the sort. It is based on an implicit conception of democracy, in which the essence of that concept is captured by the notion of majoritarianism. This certainly does not capture the totality of almost any sophisticated exposition of democracy, whether it be modern or classical in nature.[77]

That the court's conclusions proceeded from political theory rather than constitutional thought was made clear in the dissenting judgment of Denham J. She discussed at some length what was required by the concept of democracy. Citing the decision of Barak CJ in the Israeli case of *Migdol Village*,[78] Denham J

[72] *Per* O'Dalaigh CJ in *State (Quinn) v Ryan*, [1965] IR 70, at 122.

[73] *TD*, [2001] 4 IR 259, at 369.

[74] Ibid, at 372.

[75] Kelly J had relied heavily on the fact that, as this right was available only until each applicant reached the age of 18, the government's delay in providing the necessary facilities effectively denied forever the individual's prospect of seeing their constitutional rights vindicated.

[76] *TD*, [2001] 4 IR 259, at 362.

[77] PP Craig, 'Public Law, Sovereignty and Citizenship' in R Blackburn (ed.), *Rights of Citizenship* (Mansell, 1993), at 330. Although Craig was not specifically discussing the separation of powers, he was criticizing the type of majoritarian distrust of judicial action as 'unelected' and, thus, potentially 'anti-democratic', which informed the majority's interpretation of the separation of powers in *TD*. As this section has shown, the formal model was simply the vehicle for the articulation of these counter-majoritarian concerns.

[78] *United Mizrahi Bank v Migdol Village*, 49 (4) PD 221 (1995).

expressed her preference for a doctrine of 'substantive democracy'. According to this conception of democracy, the protection of human rights takes precedence over bare majoritarianism. Denham J envisaged the separation of powers as a 'functional' theory which, she felt, should be subject to those higher principles expressly adverted to in the Constitution. She saw the document as requiring 'not [an] absolute system of separation', but rather 'a fundamental principle . . . applied in a functional manner' in order to achieve a 'just and constitutional balance'.[79] On the facts of the case therefore, although she felt Kelly J's actions lay 'at the extremity' of the court's power, she regarded them as justified by the 'firm constitutional grounding' of the right under discussion.[80] As a result, Denham J's judgment represents a more appropriate attempt at publicly justifying her position on the separation of powers. By clearly outlining the political origins of her particular interpretation of the doctrine, she allowed for the possibility that the public could engage with the issues being debated. The majority, on the other hand, failed to put forward the determinative reasons for their decision, thereby denying the public the opportunity to understand, evaluate, and be convinced by their conclusions.

(2) Public Opinion and the Separation of Powers

(a) A Divergence of Institutional and Public Opinion?

From the point of view of value reinforcement, the *TD* majority's failure to adequately and publicly justify the nature of the individual state's separation of powers theory poses obvious problems. The theory cannot be effectively employed by a court without the adoption of some necessarily controversial political values. The use of the theory, therefore, must always involve the implicit (and perhaps unwitting) invocation of a particular political perspective. This, in itself, is not objectionable. A successful state, Chapter 1 suggested, will usually coalesce around a specific political or normative vision. The contemporary tendency to treat the tripartite model as an objective in itself conceals its central political principles from public view, however. This means that the valuable process of unifying the public by institutional example is inhibited. More seriously, it allows for the possibility that the separation of powers theory might serve as a vehicle for the surreptitious introduction of subjective political beliefs into the fabric of the constitutional order. There is a clear risk that the court (perhaps unintentionally) will covertly adopt a political theory with which the public does not agree. Such a rupture in the relationship between the institutional and public perceptions of the state's normative foundations might not be instantly identifiable. In the long term, however, this type of value dislocation is likely to prove problematic. If the public believes that the separation of powers theory reflects one particular normative understanding of the state,

[79] *TD*, [2001] 4 IR 259, at 306–307. [80] Ibid, at 315.

whilst the organs of the state consistently rely on a competing institutional vision, social disharmony would seem to be inevitable. Public expectations of institutional conduct would be regularly disappointed in such a scenario. For how long could unrepresentative institutions claim continuing public confidence? Will the public feel bound to offer allegiance to an institutional system with which they do not identify? Ultimately, a constitutional system stripped of popular support is likely to function as a disruptive rather than a unifying force, thereby severely undermining the normative authority of the state.

(b) Disappointed Expectations—The Concentration on Institutional Interests

A similar situation could arise in the possibly more plausible event that consistent discrepancies emerge between the rhetoric and the reality of an institutional theory's actual operation. Public justification, as a process, operates by way of example as well as expression. Once again, if the institutions of the state declare the doctrine to guarantee particular normative values, the public will expect to see those values featuring prominently in any institutional invocation of the theory. A consistent failure to so feature would confound public expectations and, again, undermine the institutions' claim to normative authority. Yet, that is what appears to regularly occur in the case of the separation of powers. Courts, especially in the USA, are inclined to affirm the doctrine's libertarian credentials in strident and sonorous terms, perpetuating the historical assertion that 'no political truth is ... of greater intrinsic value, or is stamped with the authority of more enlightened patrons of liberty' than the tripartite understanding of the separation of powers.[81] The same courts then apply it without any practical consideration of the consequences for the citizen's liberty of the action impugned.

Brown, in particular, has been highly critical of how '[t]he brief bow to Madison so often performed ... is more a ritualistic gesture than a meaningful framework for the inquiry at hand'.[82] The focus of the court's concern is generally the inter-institutional framework of the tripartite theory. The court confines itself to examining the impact of the action impugned on the institutional prerogatives of the relevant branches of government. Thus, in *Chadha*, the legislature's vetoing of the decision to allow Chadha to remain in the USA (which approximated to the abuse of bills of attainder, which was one of the doctrine's earliest concerns) was not discussed by the majority in terms of its adverse impact on Chadha's interests, nor with regard to the obvious partiality inherent in a legislative organ acting against named individuals. Rather, the majority mechanically considered whether the veto process conformed to the strict letter of the constitutional structures. Although the process was adjudged unlawful on this basis, the obvious implication of so narrow a ground of challenge was that the legislature could have vetoed the deportation judge's decision in an individual

[81] Madison, note 6 above, at 153. [82] Brown, note 15 above, at 1515.

case if it had properly followed the constitutional requirements of bicameralism and Presidential seal. As Powell J, in his dissenting judgment, remarked:

> [Congress's defence] does not address the concern that the Congress is exercising unchecked judicial power at the expense of individual liberties. It was precisely to prevent such arbitrary action that the Framers adopted the doctrine of separation of powers.[83]

The individual citizen is thus excluded from an analytical process publicly proclaimed to secure his liberty:

> The judicial opinions addressing the separation of powers ... tend to place primary emphasis not on the prevention of tyranny or protection of individual liberties, but on the advancement of the institutional interests of the branches themselves, as if that goal were itself a good.[84]

This tendency to treat separation of powers issues as an 'institutional turf war' is evident in the Irish authorities on this issue as well. The majority decision in *TD*, as we have seen, concentrated chiefly on the question whether the judiciary had interfered in its institutional counterparts' sphere of influence. The earliest Irish case law to expressly consider the separation of powers theory was similarly concerned primarily with ensuring that the legislature or executive did not trespass upon the judicial function,[85] a theme repeated with regularity up to today.[86] Academic commentary, too, has tended to implicitly accept the institutional focus of contemporary Irish separation of powers case law, discounting the individual citizen from its analytical calculus. Morgan's discussion of the most recent Irish cases concerns itself, for example, with the inter-institutional implications of the relevant decisions. The focus of the separation of powers, on this view of Irish law, is 'the borderline between the judicial and political organs'.[87] The individual appears nowhere in the analysis—a peculiar position for a theory ostensibly aiming at the protection of the state's citizens.

(c) Executive Dominance

Nor do such questions of public credibility arise only in the context of the court's consistent focus on institutional rather than individual interests. The claim that the doctrine represents a normatively acceptable structuring of the state's public activities is further undermined by the extent to which the tripartite theory increasingly fails to reflect the reality of institutional activity. The continued deployment of the doctrine is publicly justified on the basis of two inter-connected assertions—that the tripartite model safeguards the citizen

[83] *Chadha*, 462 US 919 (1983), at 963. [84] Brown, note 15 above, at 1513.
[85] See, for example, *Buckley v AG*, [1950] IR 67, *Deaton v AG*, [1963] IR 170, and *Maher v AG*, [1973] IR 140.
[86] See, for example, *Blehein v Minister for Health*, [2004] 3 IR 610 and *Brennan v Minister for Justice*, [1995] 1 IR 612. [87] Morgan, note 11 above, at 143.

against government tyranny, and that it actually encapsulates the way in which state power is institutionally arranged and exercised. The modern phenomenon of executive dominance, however, severely undermines such claims. The unifying feature of contemporary separation of powers theories, this chapter has noted, is that they necessarily involve some three-way division of power between legislative, executive, and judicial branches. All understandings of the theory agree that the existence of three co-equal independent branches in some way counteracts the possibility of unilateral rule.[88]

In Ireland, for example, how can these claims be reconciled with the reality that its Westminster-influenced system of cabinet government produces a 'nearly complete fusion of the executive and legislative powers'?[89] A system of cabinet government inevitably blurs the division of responsibility, influence, and power between parliament and the executive. The rise of the centralized political party structure, to which legislators owe their primary allegiance, has necessarily undermined the assertedly essential ability of the legislature to supervise and, where required, obstruct the activities of the executive branch. There is, once again, a very obvious divergence between the rhetoric used to justify the importance of the tripartite separation thesis and the actual reality of its institutional operation.

Nor is the artificiality inherent in this depiction of the legislature and executive as entirely independent actors a uniquely Irish phenomenon. The realities of modern politics dictate that the dominance of the legislature by the executive organ is a feature of many states. Kopecky has described how the new democracies of Eastern Europe, virtually all of which were designed to create a strong legislature and weak executive, have almost universally experienced a shift in favour of the executive's power, so that 'the balance of power between the executives and legislatures has increasingly been tipped in favour of the former'.[90] The reasons for such changes are not surprising. Kopecky concludes that 'the stabilization of political parties . . . [has] enabled political leaders to organize the relationship between the executive and legislative branches much better and to impose a dose of party discipline and cohesion'.[91] This description could be applied to almost all European democracies.

History offers similar examples of systems that have succumbed to the inevitable consequences of centralized party politics. Ireland's first constitution, the Constitution of the Irish Free State of 1922, made a conscious effort to establish a system in which the executive and legislature would act independently of each

[88] As previous sections have shown, this is generally achieved either by a balanced system of institutional checks and balances or, in the alternative, by complete separation of these bodies in the belief that the three-way division, by its very nature, will produce a balanced system of government.

[89] Sir Walter Bagehot, *Bagehot's The English Constitution* (P Smith ed., Cambridge University Press, 2001), 8–9. See also I Ward, 'Bagehot: Critic, Constitutionalist, Prophet?' [2005] PL 67.

[90] P Kopecky, 'Power to the executive! The changing executive–legislative relations in Eastern Europe' (2004) 10 *Journal of Legislative Studies* 142, at 146.

[91] Ibid, at 148.

other. The document's adoption of a proportional representation system and express provision for so-called 'extern' ministers who would not be members of the parliament (*Dáil*), nor of any of the parties therein, reflected the vision of those, like the Minister for Justice Kevin O'Higgins, who felt that the legislature would be composed solely of 'small groups of seven or eight', rather than large 'parties on definite lines of political cleavage'.[92] Unsurprisingly, the extern minister experiment was quickly abandoned once the logic of the Westminster party system began to assert itself.

Even in the US system, with its institutionally distinct and separately elected organs, the anti-constitutional impact of the political party has been observed with some degree of apprehension. Jackson J warned in *Youngstown* of the importance of having regard to contemporary political realities when interpreting separation of powers arguments:

> [The] rise of the party system has made a significant extraconstitutional supplement to real executive power. No appraisal of [the President's] necessities is realistic which overlooks that he heads a political system as well as a legal system. Party loyalties and interests, sometimes more binding than the law, extend his effective control into branches of government other than his own, and he often may win, as a political leader, what he cannot command under the Constitution.[93]

Despite the stronger institutional separation which exists in the USA, the reality is that 'in the broad run of cases, . . . party is likely to be the single best predictor of political agreement and disagreement'.[94] The tripartite theory appears to provide an incomplete account of even American government:

> Ignoring the reality of parties and fixating on the paper partitions between the branches, the law and theory of separation of powers is a perfect fit for the government the Framers designed. Unfortunately, they miss much of the government we actually have.[95]

It is clear, therefore, that the tripartite model's vision of independent and co-equal legislative and executive branches bears little resemblance to the modern practice of politics. In reality, any separation 'really come[s] down to two, not three institutions: the judiciary and the "political organs" '.[96] This calls into question the doctrine's ability to adequately explain the practices and conduct of contemporary institutions. More significantly, however, it also undermines one of the doctrine's central guarantees of citizen liberty. As Nedham commented in the seventeenth century, such effective 'placing [of] the legislative and executive powers in the same persons is a marvellous in-let of corruption and tyranny'.[97]

92 FSL Lyons, *Ireland Since the Famine* (2nd ed., Fontana Press, 1985), at 475.

93 *Youngstown*, 343 US 579 (1952), at 654.

94 D Levinson and H Pildes, 'Separation of Parties not Powers' (2006) 119 *Harvard Law Review* 2311, at 2324.

95 Ibid, at 2314.

96 Morgan, note 11 above, at 142.

97 M Nedham, *A True State of the Case of the Commonwealth* (1654), at 10. Cited in Munro, note 16 above, at 297.

In spite of this, however, contemporary institutions continue to perpetuate the myth of a protective legislative–executive division. This practice arguably threatens the very notion of individual liberty which the theory so publicly espouses. The doctrine's very prominent promise of systematic protection discourages any attempts to readjust the institutional balance to produce more liberty-optimal outcomes. Citizens are instead encouraged to trust in an empty formalism which essentially absolves all institutional actors of the obligation to consider the impact of their individual actions on the liberty or interests of the citizen. The design of the system, they suggest, constitutes a more than sufficient safeguard. That this institutional device evidently does not operate in the way in which it was intended, however, must necessarily undercut any such public assertions of normative worth.

(d) The Administrative State

The contemporary relevance of the tripartite model has been further damaged by the gradual emergence of the administrative state. The breadth and diversity of the modern system of bureaucratic government—most notably the expansion of the powers and responsibilities of government agencies, and the proliferation of organizations in the penumbra between classically public and private bodies—defies the simplistically categorical approach to official actors demanded by the common three-way conceptions of the separation of powers.

> Both the variety and the dispersion [of administrative agencies] are inconsistent with any notion that the powers of government are or can be neatly parceled out into three piles radically separated the one from the other and each under the domination of its particular 'branch'.[98]

Although it may once have encapsulated the essence of state governance, the notion that government can be reduced to a trinity of functions is today anachronistic in the extreme. These bodies do not conform to any single design and are therefore almost impossible to corral within the narrow confines of even a broad threefold classification. Rather, they display an institutional fluidity which has come to characterize the administrative state's organizational complexity, exercising at once powers which would formerly have been adjudged as executive, judicial, or legislative in nature. The rise of supranational organizations, and other bodies which defy the traditional eighteenth century understanding of the state, has served only to further accentuate the present-day inadequacies of the conventional separation of powers theory.

The courts, wedded to an outdated understanding of the state, have struggled to conceptualize these developments. Administrative agencies have been uncomfortably shoehorned into the tripartite structure, their legitimacy located

[98] P Strauss, 'The Place of Agencies in Government: Separation of Powers and the Fourth Branch' [1984] *Columbia Law Review* 573, at 581.

in the normative authority of the nominated supervising branch. That they, in fact, tend to exercise a range of powers drawn from across the putative legislative–executive–judicial divide is explained away by the convenient invention of intermediate categories of quasi-functional classification. The 'evident conceptual embarrassment of the qualifying quasi'[99] demonstrates quite clearly, however, that the three-pronged model is terminally unable to accurately reflect, explain, or legitimize the way in which the organs of the state today exercise their powers. As Jackson J, in a dissenting judgment, admitted:

> The mere retreat to the qualifying 'quasi' is implicit with confessions that all recognized classifications have broken down, and 'quasi' is a smooth cover which we draw over our confusion as we might use a counterpane to cover a disordered bed.[100]

Furthermore, it can be argued, the tripartite model again impacts adversely on the protection of the very values which the theory publicly claims to uphold. The model's incompatibility with the administrative state has generally led the courts to simply classify these entities as aspects of the executive power of the state. This process of taxonomy by deduction tends to occur, however, without any consideration of the effect of such a move on the level of liberty protection. This question will be examined in greater depth in the next chapter but, in short, the practical outcome of the vesting of these powers in the executive branch is that they are exercised on a discretionary and often unsupervised basis by unelected bureaucratic officials. Ministers are too overburdened to involve themselves in every—or indeed most—departmental decisions. The legislature, controlled as it is by the executive, tends to delegate broad and effectively unlimited powers to these officials. The courts, meanwhile, encouraged by the tripartite theory's myopic ignorance of administrative power, offer only the illusory protection of ineffective formal devices like the non-delegation doctrine.

> The court's approach seemed to be founded on a concept of its institutional competence under the model of division and separation of powers in which it was not the function of the court to get entangled in issues involving policy choice. ... This [inactive formalist] solution ... required administrative procedures only for those aspects of administrative decision-making which most closely resembled adjudication [and thus the judicial process]. While this left a range of decision-making processes free from judicial review, the courts preserved the form of the traditional model in suggesting that such processes are subject to legislative scrutiny.[101]

Judges felt that the separation of powers dictated that they not involve themselves in what the doctrine defined as executive or legislative functions. They therefore withdrew to oversee a narrowly drawn judicial area within which they could feel completely confident in their unquestioned hegemony. A wide range

[99] Ibid, at 639. [100] *FTC v Ruberoid Co.*, 343 US 470 (1952), at 488.

[101] M Loughlin, 'Procedural Fairness: A Study in the Crisis in Administrative Law Theory' (1978) 28 *University of Toronto Law Journal* 215, at 219–221.

of administrative actions were left effectively unchecked, restrained only by the platitudinous constraints of formalistic devices like ministerial responsibility and the non-delegation doctrine. For example, the Supreme Court's justification of a broad and essentially unfettered delegation of power to an executive official on the basis that 'the Constitution affords a strikingly wide latitude to the *Oireachtas* in adopting whatever form of legislation it considers appropriate'[102] entirely ignores the reality that, in an administrative state of executive dominance, the citizen is thereby placed at the mercy of an arbitrary exercise of discretionary power by unelected individuals. Fruitless limitations of form are offered as protection in place of real and proper scrutiny. Often, in more recent decades the separation of powers, originally 'adopted . . . to preclude the exercise of arbitrary power', has actually protected such situations from an appropriately intensive level of examination. Once again, there is a clear discrepancy between the rhetoric by which the doctrine is publicly justified, and the reality of its everyday operation.

D. Conclusion

The contemporary curial treatment of the separation of powers theory is institutionally deficient in several significant respects. The separation of powers is, put simply, an institutional vision in search of an ideal. This poses a number of practical problems. In the first place, the courts have failed to adequately define the nature and characteristics of the theory which they so regularly employ. This has generated considerable uncertainty over what the doctrine actually entails—an unacceptable situation for a theory apparently concerned with practical matters of power ordering and distribution. The theory, it would seem, is functionally ineffective.

In addition, however, the courts have relied on an underdeveloped version of the tripartite theory as a rhetorical device which provides an *ex post facto* explanation of a decision reached on other grounds. This ensures that the doctrine, as an ostensible constitutional theory, also fails to fulfil its socially significant role of reinforcing the shared normative values of the state. Institutional theories generally perform this function by publicly reasoning and justifying their actions, thereby providing demonstrable examples of the constitutional good in action. The separation of powers, by contrast, is typically used to conceal the court's political or normative principles from public view. This obviously limits the extent to which the theory can institutionally reinforce its central values.

Furthermore, its indeterminacy can result in the courts adopting and enforcing principles which fail to reflect either the public's particular normative views, or

[102] *Leontjava v DPP* [2004] 1 IR 591, at 636 *per* Keane CJ. The power in question in this case had been held in the High Court judgment of Finlay-Geoghegan J to be impermissibly broad.

their perception of what the doctrine actually entails. Thus, the Irish courts' particular interpretation of the separation of powers has embraced majoritarianism as a matter of high constitutional fact—a questionable normative development in a state traditionally committed to principles of intensive judicial review and substantive human rights. Crucially, this change of values occurred without any attempt to publicly rationalize or justify the change in its own terms.

Similarly, the Irish and American courts have, in practice, cut the doctrine adrift of its libertarian moorings. The courts have enforced an imprecise tripartite model as an end in itself rather than as an institutional attempt to serve a particular conception of the public good. This has not, however, prevented them from continuing to rhetorically rely on the citizen's liberty as the idea's normative anchor. There has been a notable and consistent failure to interpret and apply the separation of powers theory in a sufficiently public and transparent manner. This failure calls into question not only the doctrine's utility as an institutional theory, but also the extent of public support for the normative authority of the state. The practice of surreptitiously enforcing a particular political viewpoint while publicly declaring the state's support for an alternative position is not a viable long-term option. That this normative divergence might occur unwittingly does not detract from the potential threat it poses to the unity of a state's shared social vision, nor from its objectionability in a polity ostensibly committed to representative governance.

Finally, the tripartite model lacks real descriptive power. Incapable of accurately depicting the institutional reality of the contemporary state, the theory has proved unable to cope with either the executive dominance of the cabinet system or the emergence of powerful administrative agencies. That it continues to be used in spite of its descriptive inadequacy has had the unfortunate effect of perpetuating public reliance on hopelessly ineffective structural safeguards. The risk is that it has arguably undermined the libertarian values which it is publicly pledged to support.

There is, therefore, a notable discrepancy between the way in which the theory is publicly justified, and the way in which it actually operates. This cannot but undermine the theory's ability to perform its necessary normative-systemic role on an ongoing basis. As Chapter 1 argued, an institutional theory, if it is to function effectively, must reflect and reinforce the public's equation of the authority of the state with the pursuit, enforcement, and achievement of socially-accepted normative goods. These are objectives which the courts' treatment of the separation of powers has conspicuously failed to achieve, and which it, arguably, has actually managed to frustrate.

3

Institutional Legitimacy and the Administrative State

A. A New Understanding of the Administration?

(1) Exceptions, Counterprinciples, and the Process of Reform

Uncertain in its ideology and indeterminate in its details, the tripartite theory of the separation of powers remains a doctrine to which the organs of the state have surprisingly regular recourse. The inadequacies identified in Chapter 2 have not prevented it from being invoked and applied whenever issues of institutional power allocation arise. The ubiquity of the theory, it has already been argued, is attributable in part to the way in which it provides support for a range of alternative—occasionally even opposing—positions. However, it also proceeds partly from the residual attractiveness of some system of institutional separation. This work has not taken issue so far with the notion of a separation of powers, but rather with the particular tripartite model which presently predominates. As the previous chapter noted, this Montesquian model suffers from a number of critical flaws. Some of these are inherent in the theory itself. Others, however, relate to its dysfunctional relationship with contemporary governance. Even a doctrine as intrinsically malleable as the tripartite theory of the separation of powers has been unable, for example, to adequately account for the emergence of an administrative branch of government. The theory has instead attempted to preserve its explanatory power through the creation of convenient fictions and unconvincing exceptions. A dubious reliance on the notion of ministerial accountability is but one example of the way in which the doctrine has been stretched to accommodate contemporary developments. The model's continued descriptive capacity has been maintained only by the elaboration of a strained conception of tripartite separation. The presence of these analytical pressure points necessarily undermines the theory's claim to institutional appropriateness. However, arguably they also provide valuable guidance in the search for a more suitable scheme of governmental separation. The noted Critical Legal Studies scholar, Roberto Unger, argued that the existence of such counter-normative exceptions would not only undermine the ostensible authority of the dominant ideology (in whatever area of law is under examination), but also hesitantly intimate the outlines of an available alternative model.

When you add up the exclusions, the exceptions, and the repressions, you begin to wonder in just what sense traditional ... theory dominates at all. It seems like an empire whose claimed or perceived authority vastly outreaches its actual power.[1]

Unger thus argued in favour of a greater academic focus on these areas of 'deviationist doctrine', seeing in these exceptions and counterprinciples the potential for the articulation of more appropriate normative models. 'Once the crucial role of the counterprinciples has been recognized, the appeal to a larger vision of the possible and desirable models ... becomes inevitable.'[2]

Those situations in which the separation of powers is discovered to be descriptively inadequate are, on this analysis, more than merely atypical exceptions. On the contrary, they should be understood as challenges to the theory's underlying ideology, the very existence of which necessarily undermines any claims on its part to political or constitutional primacy. That problems occur at this superficial level of legal practice automatically calls into question the accuracy and appropriateness of the deeper normative judgments from which such everyday practices proceed.

Each time the next deepest level is exposed, the exposure produces a twofold destabilising effect. The more superficial level is shown to be but a flawed realisation of the deeper one, while the empirical and normative beliefs that constitute this deeper level are made controversial, if not implausible, in the very process of being exposed. Alongside these vertical tensions between levels of legal analysis, the reconsideration of law in untried contexts generates horizontal conflicts within each level. For each is revealed as the stage for a contest of ideals, a contest that becomes fiercer as we move down the sequence of levels.[3]

As a constitutional principle, the separation of powers already operates at one of these more subterranean levels of systemic abstraction. The difficulties which the doctrine encounters when seeking to describe and explain the structure and conduct of contemporary government should therefore be understood as the localized foci of a deeper normative debate. The internal weaknesses of the tripartite theory itself are not at issue here. Rather, the theory's relationship with the external reality of governmental power—and thus its position of constitutional pre-eminence—is in question. Those instances in which the doctrine is unable to account for the way in which contemporary governance functions evidently reveal the instability of its constitutional foundations. Crucially, however, they also serve to expose the presence in the system of competing normative visions. The tripartite model's persistent problem with administrative

[1] R Unger, 'The Critical Legal Studies Movement' (1983) 96 *Harvard Law Review* 561, at 617. The focus of Unger's analysis in this article was the law of contract.

[2] Ibid, at 618.

[3] Ibid, at 647.

power provides not only a ground of criticism but also a focus for possible reforms.

This is especially appropriate in light of the administration's own systemic significance. '[A]dministrative law is about the exercise of power in society; it cannot be divorced from broader political choices about the structure of government and the constitutional order.'[4] An intensive examination of the relationship between administrative process and the separation of powers can thus be regarded as 'part of a wider debate about the forms of political and legal accountability'.[5] Whereas Chapter 2 simply identified the many difficulties inherent in the tripartite model of separation, this chapter will seek to examine and explain precisely how the theory's difficulties with external reality occur. This is done in the hope that the insights thereby obtained might ultimately allow the articulation in later chapters of an alternative, more institutionally appropriate, scheme of separation. In this way, this book will attempt to 'transform the deviant into the dominant for the sake of a vision which becomes clearer in the course of the transformation itself'.[6]

B. Administrative Power

(1) The Need for Normative Justification

Liberal democratic theories have traditionally been suspicious of any exercise of the coercive powers of the state, fearing the subjugation of the individual citizen to the oppressive claims of collective interest. Hart maintained that 'the use of legal coercion by any society ... [is] something prima facie objectionable to be tolerated only for the sake of some countervailing good'.[7] Liberalism's instinctive opposition to the deployment of public powers required that there be a 'sound normative justification' for any action undertaken on behalf of the state.[8] 'The decisions of officials exercising public power should comply with certain principles of justification.'[9] Legitimacy must be earned, not assumed. Individual power-wielding decisions should be capable of being demonstrably legitimized by reference to accepted normative criteria. In liberal democratic systems, this legitimation has traditionally been achieved in one of two ways—through the

[4] AE Boyle, 'Sovereignty, Accountability and the Reform of Administrative Law' in G Richardson and H Genn ed., *Administrative Law and Government Action* (Clarendon, 1994), at 103.

[5] Ibid.

[6] Unger, note 1 above, at 618.

[7] HLA Hart, *Law, Liberty and Morality* (Oxford University Press, 1963), at 20.

[8] N Bamforth, 'The Public–Private Law Distinction: A Comparative and Philosophical Approach' in P Leyland and T Woods eds., *Administrative Law Facing the Future: Old Constraints and New Horizons* (Blackstone Press, 1997) at 138.

[9] G Richardson, 'The Legal Regulation of Process' in Richardson and Genn, note 4 above, at 124.

personal consent of the individual citizen; or by way of the impersonal application of suitably general principles.[10] These justificatory techniques aimed to protect the individual from arbitrary or majoritarian rule, thereby acknowledging the normative importance of securing each citizen's autonomy of thought and deed. In this way, liberal concerns about centralized government have historically been assuaged.

Liberal democratic theories have thus traditionally refused to tolerate the exercise of discretionary power by unelected officials. Contractarian conceptions of government located the state's legitimacy in the individual citizen's putative consent to the jurisdiction of an elected law-making organ. On such a view, the vesting of any form of creative rule-making capacity in bureaucratic officials was normatively illegitimate. Dicey, for example, abhorred the idea of discretionary power, disparaging it as an unjustifiable affront to the rule of law.[11] Kenneth Culp Davis similarly equated the pursuit of justice with the elimination of excessive administrative discretion.[12] Liberal democracy has hence been understood to demand that creative power be exercised only by elected—and thereby publicly accountable—officials. In this way, the citizen's consent to what would otherwise be regarded as arbitrary rule is secured. 'Accountability for the exercise of public power lies at the heart of democratic government ... [and] is fundamental to the concept of representative democracy.'[13] Unelected officials lack such direct democratic accountability. The liberal insistence on either generality or consent has been taken to dictate that they must be denied the possibility of ever exercising such powers. Discretionary decision making on their part is, from this traditional liberal perspective, arbitrary, unaccountable, and illegitimate.

(2) The Legitimacy of Discretionary Power

This antipathy towards discretionary power poses considerable problems for the administrative branch of government. Administrative officials habitually employ an extensive range of discretionary powers. Discretionary decision making is, in fact, a central, some might say defining, feature of the administrative process. It is clear, however, that it also contravenes the foundational principles of liberal democratic thought upon which so many of our constitutional and political structures are based.

[10] JL Mashaw, *Due Process in the Administrative State* (Yale University Press, 1985), at 224–225.

[11] Dicey 'associated discretion with arbitrary power, and hence found it to be incompatible with the rule of law as he understood it': P Leyland and T Woods, 'Public Law History and Theory: Some Notes Towards a New Foundationalism' in Leyland and Woods, note 8 above, at 390.

[12] K Culp Davis, *Discretionary Justice: A preliminary inquiry* (University of Illinois Press, 1971).

[13] N Radford, 'Mitigating the Democratic Deficit? Judicial Review and Ministerial Accountability' in Leyland and Woods, note 8 above, at 35.

The ultimate problem is to control and validate the exercise of essentially legislative powers by administrative agencies that do not enjoy the formal legitimation of one-person one-vote election.[14]

The traditional solution to this dearth of bureaucratic accountability has been to identify the offending administrative entity with one of the three 'legitimate' Montesquian organs of state. Administrative bodies obtain a form of parasitic legitimacy, finding normative justification in the authority of their parent institution. Any capacity for independent decision-making on their part is denied. They are instead accorded the status of institutional underworkers, adhering faithfully to the orders issued by the presumptively legitimate organs of the state. Officials are characterized as directed drones rather than autonomous actors in the policy-making or policy-implementing processes of government. Power is instead nominally confined to the parent organs of the executive, legislative, or judicial processes. This approach is prompted by an obvious elision of the separation of powers and liberal democratic thought. Stewart concludes that:

the traditional conception of administrative law does ... bespeak a common social value in legitimating, through controlling rules and procedures, the exercise of power over private interests by officials not otherwise formally accountable.[15]

This approach has been applied, most particularly, to those bodies exercising ostensibly creative powers. The process of creating new rules, policies, or administrative guidelines carries with it the ever-present threat of arbitrary governance. Creative power, by its very nature, is effectively unguided. Guaranteeing the general applicability of newly formed rules does little to mitigate the adverse effects of any rules which, in their basic content, are objectionable. In Ireland, therefore, this legislative power has traditionally been confined to the elected organ of the state. As a result, administrative agencies have consequently been identified with such bodies. They are, to adopt Stewart's seminal terminology, 'conceive[d] of ... as a mere transmission belt for implementing legislative directives in particular cases'.[16] Administrators carry out the commands received from other legitimate organs without personal input or decision-making power. The image of the transmission belt underlines the unreflecting machine-like nature of their role. The spectral vision of administrators exercising discretionary power is exorcized by promises of specific statutory guidance, or ministerial control. Popular accountability is preserved by the involvement of elected officials.[17]

[14] R Stewart, 'The Reformation of American Administrative Law' (1974–75) 88 *Harvard Law Review* 1667, at 1688.

[15] Ibid, at 1671.

[16] Ibid, at 1675.

[17] The USA has a different approach which accepts agency rule-making but requires it to observe particular procedural requirements.

(3) The 'Transmission Belt' Theory and the Courts

This 'transmission belt' theory of legislative power allows the judiciary a very limited role. Given the courts' equivalent lack of a direct electoral mandate, the involvement of judges in the supervision or direction of administrative agencies was normatively unnecessary. Furthermore, the separation-of-powers-inspired identification of any agencies exercising creative power with the elected institutions of the state discouraged an active judicial involvement in their operation.

It has already been noted in Chapter 2 how the formal understanding of the tripartite theory has tended (in decisions such as *TD*,[18] *Dupont Steel*,[19] and *Chadha*[20]) to encourage the courts to avoid the active scrutiny of elected organs. This has even been the case in the United Kingdom, where it has been argued that 'some notion of separation of powers, though scarcely articulate, has acted as a constitutional restraint'.[21] As Chapter 2 demonstrated, however, the theory of the separation of powers is, of itself, insufficiently specific to demand the adoption and observance of this particular conception of electoral pre-eminence. This attitude to the review of elected bodies follows, rather, from the way in which supporters of the formal theory are inclined to refract the Montesquian model through a majoritarian prism. In the English system, this deferential attitude to the creative competence of elected bodies has obviously been influenced by the orthodox doctrine of parliamentary supremacy. *Leontjava* and *TD* illustrate,[22] however, the extent of this idea's influence in the Irish courts as well. The formalists' insistence on all rule-making powers being vested in the legislature is the product, not of a tripartite institutional model, but of a majoritarian belief that creative power can only be validly exercised by elected officials. The separation of powers is a vehicle for the expression of these deeper demands. This means that it is not strictly accurate to speak of the influence of the separation of powers theory on the court's approach to the problem of administrative discretion. It must instead be understood as but one element of a more expansive model of majoritarian rule.

Identified with the other branches of the tripartite model, the administration thereby becomes a matter of presumptively non-judicial concern. The formal theory's focus on separation and restraint, rather than supervision and checks and balances, has encouraged the judiciary to withdraw to an 'inactive formalist' position, according to which they intensively engage only with those adjudicative bodies whose processes approximate to those of the courts themselves. These

[18] *TD v Minister for Education*, [2001] 4 IR 259.
[19] *Dupont Steel v Sirs*, [1980] 1 All ER 529; [1980] 1 WLR 142.
[20] *INS v Chadha*, 462 US 919 (1983).
[21] Boyle, note 4 above, at 81–82.
[22] *Leontjava v DPP*, [2004] 1 IR 591.

procedural resemblances to the judicial process justify the courts' involvement in areas automatically committed by the formalist conception of the state to the other branches of government. As Loughlin remarked, reviewing the response of courts in Canada and the UK to the rise of the administration:

> This solution, the one adopted [by the courts], required administrative procedures to conform to minimum requirements of judicial procedure only for those aspects of administrative decision-making which analytically most closely resembled adjudication. While this left a range of decision-making processes free from judicial review, the courts preserved the traditional model in suggesting that such processes are subject to legislative scrutiny.[23]

Irish authorities such as *Lynham v Butler (No. 2)*[24] and *State (Crowley) v Irish Land Commission* can be seen in the same light.[25] In these decisions, the court's conclusion depended on its preliminary finding as to whether, in the case in question, the body was exercising a judicial or an administrative function. If the power at issue was adjudged to be judicial, the body was obliged to act judicially. As a result, the applicant was then entitled to demand that officials observe the requirements of natural justice.

In respect of all other (non-judicial) administrative bodies, the transmission belt theory of the administration found normative justification in the supervisory involvement of the elected organs. Individuals seeking procedural protections beyond those set out in statute were met with the brusquely excusatory response that 'the discretion of [administrative officials on such matters] is quite unfettered'.[26] The courts were accordingly cast in the minor technical role of policing the boundaries of administrative powers. The nature and quality of decisions made was outside the designated area of curial concern. 'Judicial review was designed to keep administrators within their jurisdictions and harnessed to the values and purposes expressed in the macropolitical process of legislation and electoral accountability.'[27] Judges were charged simply with ensuring—through the use of devices such as the non-delegation doctrine, ministerial accountability and ultra vires review—that these bureaucratic bodies adhered to the instructions given to them by the elected (and thereby legitimately creative) institutions of the state. In this way, popular accountability, and consequently normative legitimacy, would be preserved.

[23] M Loughlin, 'Procedural Fairness: A Study of the Crisis in Administrative Law Theory' [1978] 28 *University of Toronto Law Journal* 215, at 221.

[24] [1933] IR 74.

[25] [1951] IR 250, expressly applied in *Foley v Irish Land Commission*, [1952] IR 118.

[26] *State (Costelloe) v Irish Land Commission*, [1959] IR 353, at 375, *per* Maguire CJ. The Supreme Court held that, regardless of the desirability or otherwise of the applicant's request to be furnished with inspectors' reports upon which the Commission might rely, the court could not review the officials' exercise of what were found to be administrative powers.

[27] JL Mashaw, *Greed, Chaos and Governance* (Yale University Press, 1997), at 112.

C. The *Imperium* Model of Government

(1) Electoral Legitimacy and the Sovereign Power

Administrative law, as Boyle has noted, forms but one element of a wider constitutional conversation about the nature and legitimacy of government rule. The development of a particular understanding of the administration necessarily rests on broader notions of legitimacy and accountability. The transmission belt theory must be conceived of as part of a more expansive image of constitutional governance. According to this, legitimacy lies in the connection of an individual decision-maker to a normatively superior authority. This logically requires the existence of a defined hierarchy of power. It is clear that this understanding of the administration implicitly connotes the presence of a central repository of creative power, to which all decisions must ultimately be attributable. This authoritarian model has obvious common law origins.

> [L]egal philosophy in Britain was [historically] dominated by the Hobbesian theory that at the foundation of every legal system there is a 'sovereign', who is the creator of all law and whose power is therefore above the law ... [F]or every law there had to be a law-maker ... But since there cannot be an infinite regress of law and law-makers, it seemed reasonable to postulate the existence in every legal system of an ultimate law-maker, or sovereign.[28]

Government, in such a view, is primarily a matter of command and control. Orders are centrally issued, officially applied, and individually obeyed. Furthermore, this model retains its explanatory power even if the anachronistic Hobbesian idea of an individual authority figure is discounted. The authoritarian structure survives the death of Leviathan.

> In HLA Hart's modern legal philosophy, the authority of the sovereign is replaced with that of secondary rules.... The decisively rejected image of domination by a personal sovereign gives way to an image of domination by impersonal rules—the rule of law.[29]

The transmission belt model of administrative organs as the meek handmaidens of a central sovereign can therefore be represented as a modern incarnation of an age-old understanding of government. This hierarchical conception of a top-down authority represents what Cotterell calls the *imperium* image of society—'an image of individual subjects of a superior political authority'.[30]

[28] J Goldsworthy, *The Sovereignty of Parliament: History and Philosophy* (Clarendon, 1999), at 236–237.

[29] R Cotterell, 'Judicial Review and Legal Theory' in Richardson & Genn, note 4 above, at 20–21.

[30] Ibid, at 20.

(2) Sovereign Authority and the Democratic State

Contemporary developments have, of course, required the details of this model to be amended. The advent of democracy (or at least the majoritarian understanding of it under examination here) dictated that creative power should reside in the elected organs of government. Generalized rules have replaced the arbitrary whims of an absolute leader. The conduct of government is conceived of as a rule-governed activity. The legitimacy of government actions depends upon the identity of the rule-maker rather than any external assessment of the quality of the conduct in question. The system, however, is still recognizably one of centralized authority.

> The hierarchy is now conceived in abstract, impersonal terms . . . But the fundamental conceptual structure of authoritarian (even fascist) legal systems would not be significantly different, in terms of Hart's central theoretical preoccupations, from those of democratically based ones. Law for Hart, no less than for Austin, is positive law; posited on the basis of a hierarchy of authority.[31]

The formal theory of the separation of powers is also infused with the ideology of the *imperium* model. Montesquieu's three branches of government are defined by their place in the process under which rules are enacted, interpreted, and applied. Authority, in a formal separation of powers system, is centrally located in the institutions of the state. Each institution exercises complete authority in its particular area of competence, conforming to the theoretical image of a hierarchical structure. The mechanics of the institutional separation are dictated by the organ's involvement in that rule-making process which the model regards as the central case of government activity. Government action is again epitomized by the top-down declaration of general rules.

(3) Sovereign Authority and the Limits of State Power

From the liberal point of view, the existence of such an omnipotent centralized power was permissible in part because of the restricted scope of state competence. Eighteenth century ideas of political authority and separation of powers regarded the state as an essentially negative instrument of limited social control. The liberty of the individual was secured by the extensive freedom which he enjoyed in arranging his relationships with other members of society. This was reflected, for example, in the way in which American administrative law was historically confined to the protection 'of a small class of private liberty and property interests against unauthorised governmental intrusions'.[32] This limited review was seen as sufficient to cover the likely extent of government activity. In this, the influence of Locke's limited conception of the state can clearly be discerned.

[31] Ibid, at 23–24. [32] Stewart, note 14 above, at 1716.

Man, in Locke's view, was 'born ... with a title to perfect freedom, and uncontrolled enjoyment of all the rights and privileges of the law of nature'. As a corollary of this entitlement, he also had an inherent power to act so as to 'preserve ... his life, liberty and estate, against the injuries and attempts of other men'.[33] In a pre-legal society, his ability to do this was obviously dependent upon the strength and force of his own personality and position. With his 'enjoyment of [this right] ... very uncertain, and constantly exposed to the invasion of others', the individual entered into a social contract with his fellow citizens to ensure 'the mutual preservation of their lives, liberties and estates'.[34] This implied that '[t]he great and chief end ... of men's uniting into commonwealths, and putting themselves under government, is the preservation of their property'.[35] Civil society was based on a desire to secure 'comfortable, safe, and peaceable living [by citizens] ..., in a secure enjoyment of their properties, and [with] a greater security against any that are not of it'.[36] It was accordingly also so limited:

> [T]he power of the society, or legislative constituted by them, can never be supposed to extend farther than the common good; but is obliged to secure every one's property.... And so whoever has the legislative or supreme power of any commonwealth, is bound to govern ... [in such a way as] to be directed to no other end but the peace, safety and public good of the people.[37]

The state acted as a restricted 'neutral guardian of the social order'.[38] Public and private affairs were clearly delineated, with the organs of the state excluded from issues of private power ordering.

The traditional understanding of the administrative process is a specific instantiation of this historical model of government. The image of the elected organs of the state as politically pre-eminent, like the formal separation of powers theory and transmission belt conception of the administration, is premised on an *imperium*-inspired understanding of government. This places the central institutions of the state at the apex of a rule-governed hierarchy, in which an individual exercise of power is legitimized by reference to its direct connection to the elected repositories of creative authority. Again, there are strong echoes here of Lockean political thought. Occupying a position at the apex of the state's creative capacity, the legislature was regarded by Locke as the supreme organ of state power. What this chapter will now seek to assess, however, is the

[33] J Locke, *Second Treatise of Government: Of Political or Civil Society*, at para. 87, in I Shapiro (ed), *Locke: Two Treatises of Government* and *a Letter Concerning Toleration* (Yale University Press, 2003), at 136.
[34] *Of the Ends of Political Society and Government*, at para. 123, ibid, at 154–155.
[35] Ibid, at para. 124, page 155.
[36] *Of the Beginning of Political Societies*, at para. 95, ibid, at 142.
[37] *Of the Ends of Political Society and Government*, at para. 131, ibid, at 156–157.
[38] Unger, note 1 above, at 193.

extent to which this authoritarian model accurately reflects the reality of governance in a modern administrative state.

D. *Imperium* and the Administrative State

(1) *Imperium* Under Pressure

As the previous section has shown, the traditional model's response to the gradual emergence of an administrative branch of government was to downplay the development's institutional and normative significance. Administrative agencies did not exercise power in a manner consistent with the traditional commitment to government-by-rules. More generally, they also tended to involve themselves in areas conventionally regarded as being beyond the borders of the state's constrained competence. The transmission belt theory sought to cloak these changes in the orthodox fabric of conventional dogma. The well-recognized reality, however, is that this adherence to the idea of *imperium* studiously overlooks the very changed nature of the contemporary state.[39]

(2) The Interventionist State

Dicey, espousing the prevailing Whig wisdom of his day, rejected that '[collectivist] school of opinion ... [which] favour[ed] the intervention of the State, even at some sacrifice of individual freedom, for the purpose of confirming benefit upon the mass of the people'.[40] *Laissez faire* individualism eschewed public involvement in private matters, which were seen as falling outside the legitimate limits of state concern. The rise of the welfare state in Europe, however, and the New Deal reforms of the 1930s in the USA, rendered such a starkly privatist view essentially obsolete. The modern state has embraced precisely this type of interventionist approach, according to which the government seeks to organize and structure society in a generally beneficial way. The state exercises an increasingly pervasive regulatory power, ordering society in whatever manner it sees fit. As Bamforth has commented, the state today provides the legal and social framework within which individual activity occurs. In this way, it seeks to direct and shape the conduct of its citizenry.[41]

As a result, public power can no longer be regarded as a neutral guarantee of social order. It is perceived rather as an instrument of social reform. Improving the position of individual citizens—which was formerly seen as a purely personal

[39] Commentators have long identified the inconsistency between the traditional model of a neutral state and the more activist understanding of twenteeth century government. See, for example, JM Landis, *The Administrative Process* (Yale University Press, 1938).

[40] AV Dicey, *Law and Public Opinion in England* (2nd edn, Macmillan, 1914).

[41] Bamforth, note 8 above, at 141.

matter of self-arrangement—has instead become the paradigmatic focus of government action. 'The administrative state of the twenteeth century thus engages in a large number of managerial functions.'[42] Administrative-governmental bodies have accordingly proliferated in the increasingly uncertain penumbra between public matters and private affairs. 'Private ordering has been swallowed up by government, while government has become in part a species of private ordering. ... [T]he government and private spheres are thus melded.'[43] Officials who, on a transmission belt interpretation, adhere blindly to superior orders have, in reality, been entrusted with sweeping discretionary powers. The administration has become, 'to a great extent, the central core of the governmental process'[44] at the same time that traditional institutional theory has attempted to confine and incorporate it into an outdated ideal of eighteenth century governance.

> The traditional model is an essentially negative instrument for checking government power; it does not touch 'the affirmative side' of government 'which has to do with the representations of individuals and interests' and the development of government policies on their behalf.[45]

This move towards a more expansive conception of government also reflects the limitations of the traditional view of liberty as freedom from interference. Pettitt has argued that individual freedom must also be understood to include freedom from domination.[46] Individuals are free only where they are master of their own decisions. Where an individual is potentially liable to the power of another, the fact that this power is not actually exercised in a way which interferes with his or her intentions does not make the individual truly free. Given the danger that unrestrained non-state actors might come to exercise domination over the individual, Richardson has therefore argued that the state may in fact have a role to play in preserving individual liberty in this more expansive sense. This suggests that state action may legitimately regulate individual conduct where it does so for the purpose of securing freedom from domination:

> Government does interfere, and it does so by imposing duties, or purporting to do so; but if it is adequately checked and constrained, it will not be able to do so arbitrarily.... What is crucial to nondomination is that power is not arbitrarily exercised. An effective system of laws is a necessary condition for the exclusion of arbitrary power.[47]

This suggests that an institutional theory based on such a negative conception of state action not only fails to reflect contemporary reality, but also ignores the

[42] Loughlin, note 23 above, at 240. [43] Stewart, note 14 above, at 1760.

[44] Loughlin, note 23 above, at 220.

[45] Stewart, note 14 above, at 1687, citing RF Fuchs, 'Concepts and Policies in Anglo-American Administrative Law Theory' (1938) 47 *Yale Law Journal* 538, at 540.

[46] P Pettitt, *Republicanism: A Theory of Freedom and Government* (Oxford University Press, 1997).

[47] HS Richardson, *Democratic Autonomy: Public reasoning about the ends of policy* (Oxford University Press, 2002), at 35–36.

potential contribution which state intervention may make to securing the liberty and freedom of today's citizens.

(3) The Decentralization of Public Power

The descriptive incoherence of the traditional model is not confined simply to the question of the appropriate scope of state activity. There is a similarly stark divergence between theory and reality when we consider the centralized nature of public authority. The continuing influence of the *imperium* image of public governance has already been outlined above. This top-down conception of a hierarchical rule-making structure also fails to reflect more recent developments in the administrative and governmental spheres. The 'blurring of the division between the public and private spheres' has resulted in an increasing recourse on the part of the state to self-regulation—'the delegation of public policy tasks to private actors in an institutionalized form'[48]—to accomplish particular policy ends. As the accepted area of state competence has expanded, so its direct involvement in many of these matters has actually declined. '[E]ven if . . . central . . . government does not actually provide or administer the services concerned, the state still devises and administers the overall framework within which the service provision takes place.'[49] The service providers, however, are generally allowed considerable latitude in determining the details of their operations. Delegating statutes tend to offer few specific instructions, providing instead a broad framework for administrative action. The widespread privatization of these governmental processes has led to a centrifugal decentralization of the sources of social authority. Although the mandate of many of these bodies is, of course, traceable to the legislative organ of the state, this cannot conceal the fact that, in practice, they operate independently of any central scrutiny or control. Account must also be taken of those bodies exercising a historic supervisory jurisdiction over important areas of human activity which do not depend for their power on any statutory *fiat*. Organizations like the Takeover Panel or the Jockey Club are allowed to regulate the actions of individuals within their area of expertise without the detailed statutory delegation which a strict adherence to the traditional model would demand. The *imperium* image of a central sovereign power issuing specific orders, it would appear, has profound difficulties in adequately accommodating the contemporary trend towards state privatization.

(4) The Place of Rules in the Administrative State

This growth in administrative-governmental bodies has also undermined the traditional model's insistence upon a rule-based system of governance. The

[48] C Graham, 'Self-Regulation' in Richardson & Genn, note 4 above, at 189–190.
[49] Bamforth, note 8 above, at 141.

state's transformation from a directive sovereign to the facilitator of social frameworks has reduced the practical importance of generalized governing rules. Power is no longer exercised in accordance only with centrally created rules. Statutory delegations of power, it has been noted, are permissively framed, allowing administrative officials considerable latitude when choosing a course of action. 'Increasingly, ... primary legislation has become a skeletal enabling framework conferring not just the functions of detailed implementation but the power to determine major policy questions.'[50] Discretionary decisions, rule bargaining, transient policy positions,[51] principles-based or 'light-touch' regulation, and executive-adopted tertiary rules[52] now feature alongside legislative provisions as commonly used instruments of political or legal change. The traditional model nevertheless holds fast to a conception of the system according to which political choices are normatively obliged to be made by elected officials.

(5) Accountability Issues

This again illustrates quite clearly the extent to which adherents of the traditional theory are obliged to deny, or at least overlook, the realities of contemporary governance. More problematically, however, the traditional theory's insistence on the normative superiority of the elected organs of state perpetuates a belief in essentially outdated notions of liberal legitimacy. Historically, liberal theory, it was noted in Chapter 2, has required that government action be legitimized by obtaining the individual citizen's personal consent to the exercise of power, or by ensuring that any principles are impersonally applied. The liberal insistence on the presence of personal consent traditionally manifested itself in a belief in the political pre-eminence of the elected institutions of the state. This type of electoral exaltation, however, has been conspicuously undermined by the willingness of these bodies to delegate and decentralize extensive political powers. Supporters of the traditional model have sought to sustain the notion of a central elected authority by developing mechanisms of electoral control, such as the non-delegation doctrine, or the principle of ministerial accountability. These constitutional devices profess to ensure that government power remains vested in the normatively appropriate institutions of the state. In reality, however, these doctrines are legal fictions, offering illusory protection against potentially illiberal abuses of public power.

[50] JD Hayhust and P Wallington, 'The Parliamentary Scrutiny of Delegated Legislation' [1988] PL 547, at 551, quoted with approval in R Baldwin, 'Governing with Rules: The Developing Agenda' in Richardson and Genn, note 4 above, at 165.

[51] The practice of administrative adherence to these non-statutory policy 'rules' has been considered (and accepted as constitutionally permissible) in cases such as *British Oxygen v Board of Trade*, [1971] AC 610; *Re Findlay*, [1985] AC 318; *Association of General Practitioners Ltd v Minister for Health*, [1995] 1 IR 382; and *McCann v Minister for Education*, [1997] 1 ILRM 1.

[52] See Baldwin, note 50 above.

(a) Parliamentary Accountability

Ministerial accountability, for example, is premised on the idea that an executive official's answerability to Parliament preserves some measure of legislative (and thus elected) control over the exercise of administrative powers. In reality, however, the doctrine is the product of an acknowledgement by the courts of the unavoidably delegated character of contemporary executive action. Courts, noting how 'the giving of powers to a ... subordinate body ... has been a feature of legislation for many years',[53] have accepted it 'would do a disservice to the efficiency of government administration if [they] were to overlook the practical necessity for delegation in much of the machinery of State'.[54] The courts sought to justify this process by reference to the doctrine of parliamentary accountability. As Greene MR explained in the seminal English decision on this issue:

> In the administration of government in this country the functions which are given to ministers are functions so multifarious that no minister could ever personally attend to them. ... The duties imposed upon ministers and the powers given to ministers are normally exercised under the authority of the ministers by responsible officials of the department. ... Constitutionally, the decision of such an official is, of course, the decision of the minister. The minister is responsible. It is he who must answer before Parliament for anything that his officials have done under his authority.... The whole system of departmental organization and administration is based on the view that ministers, being responsible to Parliament, will see that important duties are committed to experienced officials. If they do not do that, Parliament is the place where complaint must be made against them.[55]

In contemporary terms this doctrine suffers from two key flaws. In the first place, the enormous expansion in the administrative functions of the state makes it effectively impossible for a minister to properly supervise the actions of those for whom (s)he is ostensibly accountable. '[M]inisters can expect to become personally involved only in the most important decisions and, inevitably, most of the work will be delegated to officials.'[56] In fact, the spread of privatization has removed even this minimal level of ministerial involvement from many areas of governmental activity. Greene MR's belief that the minister will be involved at even the basic level of allocating particular tasks to individual officials seems quaintly antiquated in the era of the shrinking state. Privatization and the process of contracting out previously public tasks means that administrative decisions are regularly made without any reference to the relevant minister. It has even been argued that the increasing move towards ever more autonomous entities allows the minister 'while retaining overall political responsibility ... to

[53] *Cityview Press v An Comhairle Oiliuna*, [1980] IR 381, at 398.
[54] *AG v Cooper*, [1974] 2 NZLR 713, at 724.
[55] *Carltona v Commissioner of Works*, [1943] 2 All ER 560, at 563.
[56] Radford, note 13 above, at 39.

pass the buck of operational responsibility to the executive agencies',[57] thereby further undermining the administrative process's claims to accountability:

> The danger as far as agencies are concerned is that 'there will be a bureaucratic Bermuda Triangle' into which accountability disappears with neither minister nor chief executive responding to troublesome questions.[58]

With such a stark decline in the practice of ministerial involvement in, or responsibility for, administrative actions, it is clear that the protection offered by the principle of parliamentary accountability is hopelessly insufficient.

Secondly, even in those atypical situations of actual ministerial supervision, the dominance of the executive organ, as identified in Chapter 2, means that, in practical terms, the legislature is 'too weak to vindicate to the just satisfaction of the citizen its historic power to control the Executive in the name of the people'.[59] Party political control of the legislature ensures that an embattled minister will inevitably survive unless 'his or her own backbenchers conclude that the political damage caused by resignation is less than that arising from the minister remaining in post'.[60] This is a result of the fact that:

> [i]t is a characteristic of the British [and Irish] political system that when the future of a minister is in question, it will be regarded as first and foremost an aspect of the continuing party conflict rather than as an occasion for the House to act collectively to discipline the executive.[61]

Noting these deficiencies, Austin has dismissed the convention of ministerial responsibility as a case of the Emperor's New Clothes, an 'old constitutional sacred cow' with little relevance to contemporary affairs.[62]

Yet, in spite of its evident inadequacy, the doctrine continues to be relied upon as one of the formal constituents of the constitutional order. This has a number of potentially debilitating effects. The continued invocation of this concept openly encourages the public to trust in a constitutional doctrine which, on even the most cursory examination, is revealed as an empty formalism. In addition, its persistence as a fanciful and ineffective guarantee of liberal legitimacy might also serve to discourage attempts to develop a more relevant model of normatively appropriate governance. Furthermore, the doctrine can be taken to inhibit the involvement of other branches in any examination of executive or administrative processes at the same time as it conspicuously fails to properly fulfil this function. Accountability, on this model of government, is defined as

57 R Austin, 'Administrative Law's Reaction to the Changing Concepts of Public Service', in Leyland and Woods, note 8 above, at 14.

58 D Woodhouse, *In Pursuit of Good Administration: Ministers, Civil Servants and Judges* (Clarendon Press, 1997), at 11, quoting Bogdanor's memorandum to the Treasury and Civil Service Committee (TCSC), HC 390–II (1992–3).

59 S Sedley, 'Governments, Constitutions and Judges' in Richardson and Genn, note 4 above, at 42.

60 Radford, note 13 above, at 41.

61 Ibid, at 40.

62 Austin, note 57 above, at 7–8.

'predominantly a political issue',[63] from which the courts are thereby presumptively excluded. Adhering to this logic, the English courts have historically regarded the merits or otherwise of official actions as a question for the legislature alone, confining themselves to the 'determination of the limits of [the] power' at issue.[64] In this way, the rhetorical commitment to this constitutional dogma can be argued to have precluded the use of one of the more obvious means of redressing both the absence of effective accountability and the resulting democratic deficit.

(b) The Non-Delegation Doctrine

The Irish and American experiments with a non-delegation doctrine have been similarly fruitless. Like the concept of ministerial accountability, the non-delegation doctrine aspires to act as a bridge between the strict dictates of the traditional model (that power be exercised by the elected sovereign authority) and the contemporary reality that the delegation of power to administrative bodies is a 'necessary evil',[65] 'by common accord, indispensable for the functioning of the modern state'.[66] Thus, the courts require that any statutory delegation to an inferior body be sufficiently specific to exhaust the normatively crucial task of policy creation. The Irish courts have therefore demanded that the delegation in question be no 'more than a mere giving effect to principles and policies',[67] thereby supporting the claim that all creative power remains vested in the elected institutions of the state. In practice, however, the Irish courts have tended to apply an understanding of the test which is so broad as to effectively exempt all but the most obvious abuses from challenge.[68] In *Leontjava*,[69] the Supreme Court was satisfied that a legislative direction that *some* regulation was required was sufficient to satisfy the *Cityview Press* test. As Casey observed in respect of an equally indulgent earlier decision, '[i]f provisions of such vagueness can pass muster, it is not easy to imagine what would not'.[70] The suspicion must

63 Radford, note 13 above, at 36. 64 Ibid.

65 B Ganz, 'Delegated Legislation: A Necessary Evil or a Constitutional Outrage?' in Leyland and Woods, note 8 above, at 80.

66 *Maher v Minister for Agriculture*, [2001] 2 IR 139, at 245 *per* Fennelly J.

67 *Cityview Press*, [1980] IR 381, at 399.

68 The Irish courts have adopted a two-pronged approach to Article 15. The 'principles and policies' test—which can be regarded as an illustration of the classic non-delegation doctrine—represents the first line of Irish authority. The second concerns the amendment or repeal of primary legislation by way of delegated legislation. The courts have consistently held this to be unconstitutional: *Harvey v Minister for Social Welfare*, [1990] 2 IR 232. However, this rule derives chiefly from a textual interpretation of Article 15 rather than a vigorous application of the non-delegation doctrine. Thus the court's strict approach to this second limb does not really address the academic criticism of the principles and policies test as unjustifiably weak. See G Hogan and DG Morgan, *Administrative Law in Ireland* (3rd ed., Round Hall Sweet & Maxwell, 1998).

69 [2004] 1 IR 591, at 624.

70 JC Casey, *Constitutional Law in Ireland* (2nd ed., 1992), at 181, cited in DG Morgan, *The Separation of Powers in the Irish Constitution* (Round Hall Sweet & Maxwell, 1997), at 239.

be that the Irish non-delegation doctrine, like its under-utilized American counterpart,[71] is 'little more than high-sounding hocus-pocus, in which the Court mutters beguiling incantations while blowing smoke in the face of statutory reality'.[72] It seems no more than an 'empty exercise in judicial rhetoric'[73] invoked for reasons of ritual rather than real analytical aid. Once again, therefore, the traditional model's attempts to preserve its conception of normative legitimacy in the face of contemporary reforms have been shown to be ill founded and functionally ineffective.

(6) The Citizen–State Relationship Redefined

The problems previously identified can clearly be regarded as evidence of a profound dysfunction in the traditional image of a sovereign power. The *imperium* conception of rule-based and centralized power bears little resemblance to the actualities of an administrative state in which discretionary powers are exercised by unelected officials on a broadly dispersed basis. Normative justification for the use of public power rests on an outdated understanding of the institutional structures of the state, which has been shown to be functionally ineffective when faced with the realities of modern government. This, in itself, seems sufficient to condemn the traditional model as a historical anachronism.

The weakness of its accountability arrangements, however, have been exacerbated by the development of a changed conception of the public service. Recent decades have witnessed a significant transformation in the relationship between the citizen and the state. Some of the preceding sections discussed how state power historically required some sort of special justification. This recognized the fact that '[u]nlike the free market where there is freedom of contract between individuals equal in the eyes of the law, there is an inherent inequality between state institutions and the individual'.[74] Thatcherite-style reforms recast the citizen in a more contractual and consumerist light.

Woodhouse contrasts the traditional 'public service' model of administrative action with this 'New Right' or 'public management' model. The public service model is predicated on a 'commitment to the public interest',[75] which manifests itself in the importance historically attached to the values of 'rationality,

[71] The US Supreme Court has struck down legislation on the basis of the non-delegation doctrine on only two occasions: *Panama Ref Co. v Ryan*, 293 US 388 (1935); *Schechter Poultry Corp v United States*, 295 US 495 (1935). Furthermore, these authorities are inspired at least in part by the peculiar environment of the New Deal era in which the Supreme Court conducted a long-running political battle with President Roosevelt's Progressive reform programmes. They thus cannot be taken as generally representative of the American courts' point of view.

[72] C Farina, 'Statutory Interpretation and the Balance of Power in the Administrative State' (1989) 89 *Columbia Law Review* 452, at 480.

[73] Ibid, at 480.

[74] Austin, note 57 above, at 23.

[75] Faulkner, Crouch, Freeland, and King, Memorandum to the TCSC, HC 27–III (1993–4), cited in Woodhouse, note 58 above, at 27.

consistency and justifiability'.[76] Parliamentary accountability is a cornerstone of this conception of the administration, operating as a constant reminder of the public nature of official functions, and of their associated need for normative legitimitation. This understanding of the administration fosters a culture of public service which 'encourages adherence to constitutional principles and to principles which protect the individual', taking as its operational lodestar the 'liberal values [of] fairness, equity and reasonableness'.[77]

By contrast, the public management model prioritizes a very different set of principles:

> Most significant is the domination of efficiency which is supported by the language of consumerism and the values of the competitive market. The mechanisms of control and accountability also have an emphasis which accords more readily with management theory and with accountability to the market rather than to the public interest.[78]

Officials' self-perception of their role, and the obligations which it imposes, have accordingly been altered. This managerial vision of the administrative process is 'largely uncluttered by notions of public service, or concepts such as fairness, equity and reasonableness'.[79] Whereas civil servants were formerly encouraged to consider themselves as representatives of the state who were thereby bound by certain principles of public service, officials are now presented as decentralized service providers, freed from any additional notions of public duty.

Baldwin has remarked that, on any examination of the way in which delegated powers are employed, 'it proves difficult to make clear-cut claims to legitimacy on their behalf other than on the bases of expertise and efficiency'.[80] This 'search for efficient government' has been argued to 'undermine the [impartiality, integrity and objectivity which have traditionally been regarded as] the key characteristics of the civil service'.[81] Traditional ideas of normative justification—the existence of a legislative mandate, the presence of accountability controls, fairness of action[82]—have been supplanted by the language of the free market contract. This is animated by a desire to empower the citizen-consumer to interact directly with the provider of his services, rather than encouraging a reliance on the state to allocate resources as it sees fit. However, this free market ideology overlooks the absence of a genuine freedom of contract between citizen-consumer and service provider. The citizen-consumer is in reality at risk of being presented with a contractual *fait accompli* which provides a lower level of protection and redress than that offered under judicial review's traditional ideals of legality and fairness. Public power has often been

[76] RGS Brown & DR Steel, *Administrative Process in Britain* (2nd ed., Methuen, 1979) at 199.
[77] Woodhouse, note 58 above, at 34. [78] Ibid, at 46. [79] Ibid, at 51.
[80] Baldwin, note 50 above, at 170. [81] Woodhouse, note 58 above, at 7.
[82] Baldwin argues that these are the other headings under which state actions have traditionally claimed legitimacy. See R Baldwin and C McCrudden, *Regulation and Public Law* (Weidenfeld & Nicolson, 1987), Chapter 3.

decentralized to administrative agencies at the same time that these bodies have begun to define themselves (and their duties) in terms of restricted privatist notions of efficient service provision:

> [P]ublic service is no longer the service of the public as a collective, but rather the service of the individual consumer of specific and limited public services. This is reinforced by the weakening or even removal of the traditionally public, institutional and constitutional mechanisms for accountability and redress ... and their replacement by individualised, atomistic relationships between the citizen *qua* consumer and the providers of public service.[83]

This cannot but exacerbate the accountability and legitimacy deficit inherent in the traditional model of centralized governance. The validity of a normative legitimacy which rests on the idea of ministerial accountability has already been rejected. Furthermore, it is now clear that the various devolved bodies—which constitute the real loci of administrative power—do not evince a particular commitment to the traditional requirements of liberally legitimate government. There is, therefore, a clear 'danger that real political responsibility and accountability to the public through its representatives will fall into this gap between traditional doctrine and the practical realities of the modern structure of government'.[84]

E. The *Imperium* Model and the Courts

(1) The Judicial Response

Cumulatively, these charges of explanatory incoherence and normative failure demonstrate quite clearly the incongruity of the *imperium* theory in the era of the administrative state.[85] Thus, it is scarcely surprising that, in recent decades, the courts' support for this idea has become increasingly inconsistent. With the *imperium* model exposed as an inadequate and anachronistic vision, there has been a steady, if gradual, decline in judicial adherence to it. Stringent compliance with the archetypal image of a dominant central sovereign invested with ultimate political authority required the courts, in the context of judicial review of administrative actions, to confine themselves to the enforcement of the limits and obligations laid down by statute. The courts could not intervene to examine the standard and quality of decisions by bodies which, in accordance with the separation of powers, were allocated to the elected branches of government. Judges were entrusted with a limited and technical task. It is notable, however,

[83] Austin, note 57 above, at 23. [84] Ibid, at 5.

[85] Given its derivative attachment to the idea of a central creative institution, obviously this implicitly affects as well the institutional appropriateness of the formal theory of the separation of powers.

how the courts have moved beyond these restrictive limitations at the same time that the state has moved beyond the eighteenth century characterization of itself as a neutral rule-governed hierarchy of limited competence. As the justification for the use of this model has evolved from the veracity of its normative vision to the simple fact of historical tradition, so the courts have been less inclined to abide by its restraints. Mr Justice Sedley, writing in an extra-judicial capacity, has expressly tied the expansion in the courts' administrative competence to the changing nature of the modern state. Actions which would have been adjudged impermissible under the traditional theory have been undertaken, in his view, 'as a response to the growth of a corporate state in which the executive, far from exercising restraint, was itself heavily interested'.[86] Judicial reforms should be understood as a response to the novel innovations of this 'great wave of regulatory governmental institutions'.[87] Lord Irvine too regarded 'the want of Parliamentary control over the executive' to have been 'to an important degree, mitigated by the rigours of judicial review'.[88]

That is not to say, of course, that the image of the *imperium* has been entirely abandoned by the courts. On the contrary, it continues to influence extensive areas of constitutional jurisprudence. However, recent decades have witnessed the creation of an increasing number of exceptions to its most rigorous requirements. In keeping with Unger's thesis, these exceptions deserve particular analysis. Representing those issues in which the existing orthodoxy has come under the most significant strain, these points of controversy identify the areas in which it is practically or theoretically deficient. They also illustrate, however, the attempts which the system's institutional actors have made to deal with these developments, thereby potentially providing some outline indications of the possible shape of an alternative model for legitimate governance.

(2) The Public–Private Distinction

It may therefore be prudent to look in more detail at the ways in which the courts have begun to move away from the *imperium* model. The judiciary's rejection of the historical insistence on a bright-line demarcation of public and private spheres is one of the changes which has, for example, attracted considerable academic attention. The decision in *R. v Panel on Takeovers and Mergers, ex p Datafin* is rightly regarded as a seminal constitutional moment, in which the traditionally restricted scope of judicial review was profoundly redefined.[89] The courts had previously followed the formalistic approach of categorizing administrative entities in accordance with their specific legal origins. In

[86] Sedley, note 59 above, at 40. [87] Ibid, at 41.

[88] D Irvine, 'Judges and Decision-Makers: The Theory and Practice of *Wednesbury* Review' [1996] PL 59, cited in Radford, note 13 above, at 37.

[89] [1987] 1 QB 815; [1987] 1 All ER 564; [1987] 2 WLR 699.

accordance with the idea of the legislature as the source of public power, the decisions of bodies whose authority was based on an express statute delegation were subject to scrutiny on the basis of their adherence to the provisions of the relevant parent statute. The court in *Datafin* reoriented this analytical approach, focusing not on artificial classifications but on the consequences of the impugned action for the affected individual. At the time, the corporate state was asserting its authority in areas historically regarded as outside its area of competence whilst also devolving significant powers to quasi-private bodies. It was telling, therefore, that the court eschewed the opportunity to provide a definitive formulation of the extent of judicial review. It concentrated instead on the more individually oriented criteria of the potential consequences of the act. From an institutionally categorical point of view, Donaldson MR envisaged only minor limitations on the courts' supervisory powers:

> Possibly the only essential elements [for an institution to be susceptible to judicial review] are what can be described as a public element, which can take many different forms, and the exclusion from the jurisdiction of bodies whose sole source of power is a consensual submission to its jurisdiction.

Review, the Court of Appeal therefore concluded, could lie against any body which could be said to exercise a 'governmental' function—a flexibly expansive approach which greatly increased the courts' capacity to investigate the actions of an ever-evolving administrative branch.

(3) The Relaxation of the Standing Rules

In addition to this broadening of the courts' supervisory jurisdiction, judges have also demonstrated a willingness to entertain challenges which would formerly have fallen foul of the rules on standing. There has been a noticeable worldwide move towards a more liberal *locus standi* regime. The traditional requirement of a direct personal interest in the subject matter of the dispute has been waived in instances where, for example, no other challenger was likely to emerge.[90] This reflects a very different interpretation of the purposes of the review process, and of the place of the courts in the constitutional structure. The *imperium* model provides that, when considering a judicial review case, the courts are being asked to correct a wrong allegedly perpetrated by an official body against the applicant. More recent authorities, however, demonstrate a general concern to ensure the legality of government actions irrespective of the specific impact of the impugned measure on any one individual. As Keane CJ

[90] See, for example, *IRC v National Federation of Self-Employed and Small Businesses Ltd*, [1981] 2 AER 93; *R. v Secretary of State for Foreign Affairs, ex p World Development Movement Ltd*, [1995] 1 AER 611; *Thorson v AG for Canada*, (1974) 43 DLR (3d) 1 (SCC); *SPUC v Coogan*, [1989] IR 734.

commented in the course of his decision in *TD*, the traditional insistence on a sufficiently individuated legal interest:

> must on occasions yield to the overriding necessity that laws passed by the *Oireachtas* or acts and omissions of the executive should not go unchallenged, simply because it is difficult, if not impossible, for individual citizens or groups to establish that their individual rights are affected.[91]

The Canadian courts have echoed this opinion, allowing standing to be asserted in the public interest so as to deny the possibility of legislation or official acts being effectively exempted from challenge.[92] This focus on the legality of the official conduct in question transforms the nature of the judicial review hearing from a bilateral adjudication to something approximating to a 'surrogate political process'.[93] This characteristic is one of those enumerated by Chayes as an *indicium* of public law litigation: '[t]he subject matter of the lawsuit is not a dispute between private individuals about private rights, but a grievance about the operation of public policy'.[94]

The decision of Otton J in *ex p Greenpeace* provides further support for this amended understanding of the judicial review process.[95] In that case, standing was granted to the applicant pressure group, not on the basis of any individual interest in the dispute at issue, but rather as a result of the judge's estimation that they were the body best equipped to put forward the case in question:

> It seems to me that if I were to deny standing to Greenpeace, those it represents might not have an effective way of bringing the issues before the court ... It is unlikely that [other individual applicants] would be able to command the expertise which is at the disposal of Greenpeace. Consequently, a less well-informed challenge might be mounted which would stretch unnecessarily the Court's resources and which would not afford the Court the assistance it requires in order to do justice between the parties.[96]

Otton J's decision has attracted favourable comment from some Irish judges.[97] Australian courts have also, on occasions, adopted a similar approach.[98] This concentration on the applicant's capacity to advance its case seems, logically, to support the view that the objective of the court in a judicial review application is

[91] *TD*, [2001] 4 IR 259.

[92] See *Canadian Council of Churches v R & Ors*, (1992) 88 DLR 193; *Hy and Zelaposs Inc v AG of Ontario*, (1994) 107 DLR 634.

[93] Stewart, note 14 above, at 1670.

[94] A Chayes, 'The Role of the Judge in Public Law Litigation' (1976) 89 *Harvard Law Review* 1281, at 1302.

[95] *R. v Inspectorate of Pollution ex p Greenpeace Ltd (No. 2)*, [1994] 4 AER 329.

[96] Ibid, at 350.

[97] *Per* Denham and Keane JJ in *Lancefort Ltd v An Bord Pleanála (No. 2)*, [1999] 2 IR 270; *per* Kearns J in *Murphy v Wicklow County Council*, High Court, unreported, 19 March, 1999; *Irish Penal Reform Trust v Governor of Mountjoy Prison*, High Court, unreported, 2 September, 2005 (Gilligan J).

[98] See, for example, the judgment of Wilcox J in *Ogle v Strickland*, (1987) 71 ALR 41; *Right to Life Association (NSW) Inc v Secretary, Dept. of Human Services and Health*, (1995) 128 ALR 238.

to ensure the legality of the administrative process. In contrast to the traditional understanding, it is not to defend the rights of the individual in a particular public law context. In response to the state's adoption of increased administrative powers and, arguably, the decreased utility of the traditional mechanisms of normative accountability, it appears as if the courts now conceive of themselves as a general check on unlawful (or, perhaps even, normatively illegitimate) governmental action, rather than as defenders of the restricted range of individual rights protected under the eighteenth century model of limited public power.

(4) Increasing Standards of Review

The traditional image of a rule-based sovereign power also logically dictated that, in the review process, the courts could investigate only the extent of administrative adherence to the rules at issue. The court could not examine actions undertaken within the parameters set out in the relevant statutory provision. Neither, as a sub-sovereign organ, could it question the merits of the political choices behind each individual rule. The judiciary was obliged to confine itself to a process of ultra vires review, in which acceptability of administrative action was equated with the presence of a sufficiently specific statutory jurisdiction.

Once again, however, the limitations inherent in the traditional model have been ignored with progressively greater frequency. The actions of administrative bodies—and indeed the ostensibly authoritative elected organs—have been subjected to an increasingly intensive examination. From the theoretical perspective, this more rigorous approach has crucially expanded the review process beyond the simple supervision of the rule-based boundaries of administrative power. Obligations have been imposed upon administrative bodies which are nowhere set down in statute. The development of the *Wednesbury* jurisdiction,[99] for example, has allowed the courts to consider the rationality of the official conduct in question, evaluating it in accordance with a judicially created duty of reasonable behaviour. The restrained formulation of the test does, of course, show deference to the elected organs of the state. However, the fact remains that the *Wednesbury* decision asserts a residual power of rationality review which is entirely inconsistent with the traditional conception of a central and all-powerful authority figure. The more recent elaboration of a sub-*Wednesbury* species of 'anxious' or 'heightened' review emphasizes the willingness of the judiciary to engage in a process of strict scrutiny whenever it is adjudged to be appropriate.[100] It also underlines the extent to which the courts now appear to regard themselves as an autonomous check on normatively unacceptable official action.

[99] *Associated Provincial Picture Houses v Wednesbury Corporation*, [1948] 1 KB 223.

[100] *R. v Home Secretary, ex p Brind*, [1991] AC 696; *R. v Home Secretary, ex p Bugdaycay*, [1987] AC 514; *R. v Minister of Defence, ex p Smith*, [1996] QB 517.

Such an attitude would not be tolerated under a strict application of the sovereign *imperium* model.

This pattern of expanding judicial authority is replicated in decisions such as *Anisminic*,[101] *Lain*,[102] and *GCHQ*.[103] In *Anisminic*, 'the Lords opened up to judicial review effectively every error of law, far beyond the strict jurisdictional error' to which the courts had traditionally confined their focus.[104] *Lain* rejected the historical limitations of rule-based statutory review, subjecting the exercise of prerogative powers to the scrutiny of the courts. In *GCHQ*, meanwhile, Lord Diplock famously outlined a series of independent heads of judicial review—illegality, irrationality, and procedural impropriety—which, again, effectively require administrative bodies to meet standards of behaviour above those expressly specified by any sovereign-issued rule. The courts have even shown themselves to be prepared, in appropriate instances, to examine the actions of the elected institutions of the state. Even in advance of the enactment of the Human Rights Act 1998, the English courts had claimed, in cases such as *Derbyshire County Council*,[105] the capacity to enforce positive common law rights. The incorporation of the European Convention on Human Rights obviated any necessity to rely on this power. Its assertion in *Derbyshire CC* did demonstrate, however, a belief on the part of some judges in the courts' ability to intervene in defence of rights adjudged to exist independently of any centrally enacted legal text. The Irish doctrine of unenumerated rights could arguably be seen in a similar light.[106] That the rule of law has replaced ultra vires as the academically accepted basis for English judicial review demonstrates quite clearly the changes which have been wrought in the relationship between the judiciary, the administration, and the elected organs of the state. The recent obiter observations of a number of the Law Lords on the possibility of imposing judicial limitations on the power of parliament are telling:

> The classic account given by Dicey of the doctrine of the supremacy of Parliament, pure and absolute as it was, can now be seen to be out of place in the modern United Kingdom. Nevertheless, the supremacy of Parliament is still the general principle of our constitution. It is a construct of the common law. The judges created this principle. If that is so, it is not unthinkable that circumstances could arise where the courts may have to qualify a principle established on a different hypothesis of constitutionalism.[107]

These comments are little short of revolutionary. It is evident that the orthodoxy of *imperium* is under severe pressure in a much-changed modern era. A very

[101] *Anisminic v Foreign Compensation Commission*, [1969] 2 AC 147.
[102] *R. v Criminal Injuries Compensation Board, ex p Lain*, [1967] 2 QB 864.
[103] *Council of Civil Service Unions v Minister of State for the Civil Service*, [1985] AC 374.
[104] Sedley, note 59 above, at 39.
[105] *Derbyshire County Council v Times Newspapers Ltd*, [1993] AC 534.
[106] See *Ryan v AG* [1965] IR 294.
[107] *R. (Jackson) v AG*, [2006] 1 AC 262, at para. 102, *per* Lord Steyn.

plausible argument can now be constructed for a form of judicial review which rests on the protection of external values rather than on the dependent idea of enforcing rule-based expressions of the sovereign will. As Hailsham LC observed in *Evans*, the purpose of judicial review arguably now appears to be 'to ensure that the individual receives fair treatment'[108]—a position seemingly dictated by the underlying substantive values of the current constitutional order.

(5) Procedural Fairness

In keeping with this analysis, the trend towards the judicial imposition of non-statutory standards has been most evident, perhaps, in relation to the development of a duty of procedural fairness. In Ireland, this duty was conveniently derived from the text of the Constitution. Walsh J's doctrine of constitutional justice, 'understood to import more than the ... well-established principles' of the common law notion of natural justice,[109] allowed the courts to rest their development of enhanced standards of administrative conduct on a firmly positivist footing. A contextualized and flexible concept, constitutional justice has been held to involve 'a range of (as yet) imprecise procedural guarantees which are designed to avoid the unfair treatment' of individuals.[110] The insistence on ensuring procedural fairness was presented as a by-product of the existing constitutional order, rather than as a challenge to the influential (albeit less so in an Irish context) idea of centralized electoral authority.

Not all courts have been able to invoke this sort of usefully justificatory device. However, in those jurisdictions which lacked a constitutional document (like England and, at the time, Canada[111]) the courts proved themselves to be nonetheless prepared to insist on certain autonomous standards of procedural propriety. 'Acting entirely on their own initiative, the courts ... developed common law standards which, in the absence of statutory provisions to the contrary, they ... require of public officials.'[112] This occurred in spite of the fact that the dominant Diceyan 'expression of the rule of law ... makes no commitment to a principle of procedural due process'.[113] Procedural obligations had traditionally been confined to a narrow doctrine of natural justice, which applied only to judicial or quasi-judicial bodies.[114] The courts, however, gradually

[108] *Chief Constable of North Wales v Evans*, [1982] 1 WLR 1155, at 1161.
[109] *McDonald v Bord na gCon (No. 2)*, [1965] IR 217, at 242.
[110] Hogan and Morgan, note 68 above, at 501.
[111] See, for example, Loughlin's discussion of this: note 23 above, at 230–236.
[112] Radford, note 13 above, at 47.
[113] DJ Galligan, *Due Process and Fair Procedures* (Clarendon Press, 1996), at 184.
[114] See, for example, *B Johnson & Co. (Builders) v Minister for Health*, [1947] 2 All ER 395, at 398 in which Greene MR opined that the appropriate remedy for allegations of unfair administrative actions lay in the political arena. Legal obligations arose only in relation to 'that particular stage [of the administrative process] ... [where] there is superimposed on [the Minister's] administrative character, a character which is loosely described as "quasi-judicial" '.

expanded both the scope and nature of the procedural review process,[115] identifying an independent 'duty to act fairly' which has subsequently served as the vehicle for the imposition upon administrative bodies of significantly broader legal duties.[116] The flexible and contextualized nature of this general duty has allowed the courts to considerably expand the range of administrative agencies to which the principle is applied. As Galligan has commented, 'all areas of administration are now, in principle, subject to the requirements of procedural fairness', which is accepted as a 'dynamic principle from which other doctrines besides the hearing and bias rules (which traditionally exhausted the duties entailed by the principles of natural justice) can be derived'.[117] Administrative bodies have been required to give reasons for their decisions,[118] to abide by previously announced policies,[119] and to allow affected individuals some say in the initial policy-forming process.[120] In fact, the 'most rigorous court-set standards' of procedure can, in reality,[121] often approximate to some form of substantive merits-based review of a type entirely alien to the traditional theory. The court's emphasis on procedural fairness can probably be regarded as an attempt to conform to the constitutional orthodoxy, given the fact that 'procedural fairness fits, by its very nature, within the notion of a truly supervisory jurisdiction'.[122] However, as the obligations required under its rubric increase, so the 'simple distinction between substance and procedure begins to blur',[123] taking the courts far outside their traditionally restricted role. At the very least, it seems plausible to treat these developments as an effort on the part of the courts to ensure that the actions of the administrative process are informed, to some degree, by substantive normative values of fairness and justice. This would be in keeping with the belief that:

> [p]ower is arbitrary when it is not adequately controlled by a fair process of decision in which those subject to it are treated as free and equal and their fundamental rights and liberties are protected.[124]

On this analysis, the development of a doctrine of procedural fairness relates to far broader considerations of normative value than a simple concern to ensure that administrative bodies do not act in a way which accords with the intentions of the legislature or the executive.

[115] *Ridge v Baldwin*, [1964] AC 40. [116] *Re HK (an infant)*, [1967] 2 QB 617.

[117] Galligan, note 113 above, at 330.

[118] *Stefan v General Medical Council*, [1999] 1 WLR 1293; *State (Daly) v Minister for Agriculture*, [1987] IR 165, at 172; *International Fishing Ltd v Minister for the Marine*, [1989] IR 149.

[119] *R. v Liverpool Corporation, ex p Liverpool Taxi Fleet Operators' Association*, [1972] 2 QB 299.

[120] *R. v Secretary of State for Health, ex p US Tobacco International Inc*, [1992] 1 QB 353.

[121] M Fordham, 'Surveying the Grounds: Key Themes in Judicial Intervention', in Leyland and Woods, note 8 above, at 189. [122] Ibid, at 188.

[123] Ibid, at 189. [124] Richardson, note 47 above, at 250.

(6) Legitimate Expectations

This duty has even extended, in certain cases, to the enforcement of what the court classifies as legitimate expectations. These entitlements do not exist in any historically familiar legal form. The courts, it has been explained above, could traditionally act only to prevent the infringement of a recognized legal right. In private law, these tended to be contractual interests. In public law, they would be based on statute. The recognition of legitimate expectations thus marks a further move away from the rule-centred positivist conception of state authority. Founded on an external idea of fairness, the development of a doctrine of legitimate expectations is but one more example of the way in which the relationships between the citizen and the state, the administration and the courts, and the judicial and elected organs of government appear to have been redefined in non-traditional terms.

Richardson has admitted that 'it is ... har[d] to find a justification in orthodox constitutional theory for the imposition of common law procedural requirements'.[125] It appears more accurate, therefore, to conclude that there has emerged:

> a new relationship between the courts and those who derive their authority from the public law, one of partnership based on a common aim, namely the maintenance of the highest standards of public administration.[126]

That these standards are defined independently of the putative sovereign power on the basis of an external conception of fairness illustrates quite clearly the contemporary incoherence of the traditional *imperium* model.

F. Conclusion

It is important, of course, not to over-extend this argument. The traditional model of centralized authority must continue to feature prominently in any analysis of the contemporary constitutional order. The formal conception of a sovereign, rule-based power colours the approach of the instititutions of state to many important areas of modern government. The courts, on the one hand, may have demonstrated a willingness to ignore the strict requirements of the model in certain situations but their attitude in other areas bears strong testimony to the enduring influence of the *imperium* image.

The insistence on a *procedural* notion of administrative fairness demonstrates, for example, a reluctance to move too far beyond the confines of the traditional

[125] Ibid, at 109.
[126] *R. v Lancashire County Council, ex p Huddleston*, [1986] 2 All ER 941, at 945.

theory. Even if Fordham is correct that, in many cases, procedural review is closer to a substantive examination of the merit of the action impugned, the fact remains that the courts continue to couch their approach in the language of orthodox constitutional theory. Similarly, many judges continue to espouse a commitment to the ultra vires theory of limited judicial review whilst simultaneously attempting to enforce what appears to be an autonomous understanding of the rule of law.

Nor is the impact of the *imperium* orthodoxy confined to the constitutional niceties of judicial rhetoric. Attempts to assert what seem to be novel powers on the part of the courts are regularly hampered by the decisions of subsequent judicial panels to reintroduce elements of the traditional theory. The development of a general administrative duty to act fairly has been qualified by a continued insistence on 'interference with the right or interest of an individual, and the decision of a body exercising a public function' as precursors to judicial scrutiny.[127] These requirements—which recall the image of strictly defined public and private spheres—can generate potential rigidity in an area where the overall trend appears to be towards contextual flexibility. The decision in *Aga Khan*, for example,[128] is strongly reminiscent of the sterile categorical approach previously adopted by the courts. Opting to ignore the effective monopoly powers of the body in question (and, by its inaction, the clear tacit approval of the body's position by the government), the Court of Appeal simply repeated the orthodox position that the courts could not review the decisions of associations whose powers were founded on the consensual submission of individuals to its authority. Similarly, the continued formal classification of interests as rights or privileges to be found in decisions such as *Schmidt*[129] or *McInnes*[130] seems to resurrect in part the approach which cases like *Ridge* and *HK* had appeared to abolish. The courts, it is suggested, seem torn between, on the one hand, the enunciation and adoption of a radically different theory of governance and, on the other, confining ideas of procedural fairness within the orthodox understanding of public power. It is clear, however, that the historical model cannot logically be expanded to comfortably embrace reforms which are, in their essence, entirely alien to its conception of the state. The latter attitude appeals to a non-existent normative consensus, and is accordingly doomed. The search for a unified approach seems futile.

> The key to the problem . . . lies in the failure to recognise the pervasive influence in administrative law of the traditional model and, in particular, to recognise the change in

[127] Richardson, note 47 above, at 115.

[128] *R. v Disciplinary Committee of the Jockey Club ex p Aga Khan*, [1993] 1 WLR 909; [1993] 2 All ER 853. Cf. *R. v Disciplinary Committee of the Jockey Club, ex p Massingberd-Mundy*, [1993] 2 All ER 207.

[129] *Schmidt v Home Secretary for Home Affairs*, [1969] 2 Ch 149.

[130] *McInnes v Onslow-Fane*, [1978] 1 WLR 1520; [1978] 3 All ER 211.

the method of legal discourse and function of the courts required if the [alternative fairness-based] approach is to be adopted.[131]

The next chapter will therefore seek to explore more comprehensively the way in which this type of alternative approach could take shape. The 'contradiction between ideal and reality within the traditional [image]' makes it an unsustainable model for an administrative state.[132] The challenge, therefore, is to construct from the courts' initial efforts at escaping its outdated strictures a more appropriate theory of normative and institutional arrangement.

131 Loughlin, note 23 above, at 236.

132 Ibid, at 241.

4

The Search for Institutional Legitimacy

A. Issues of Institutional Design

(1) The Need for a New Model of Separation

At this point, a brief overview of the general arguments advanced thus far is apposite. Chapter 2 sought to critically assess the theory of the separation of powers. It concluded that the dominant tripartite understanding of the doctrine is indeterminate, underdeveloped, and functionally ineffective. Chapter 3 further suggested that the theory, in its current guise, is inapplicable to our existing system of governance. Based on an anachronistic eighteenth century understanding of society, the separation of powers theory is unable to adequately account for or explain the emergence of the administrative state. This chapter will attempt, therefore, to address what must logically be the next stage of this study—the development of a more appropriate theory of institutional separation.

(2) Assessing Institutional Success

Questions of institutional appropriateness, it is obvious, can only be considered adequately in the context of some conception of the place and purposes which institutional ideas serve in our governing structures. Chapter 1's examination of the social utility of constitutional thought is an instructive starting point for this analysis. That chapter, it will be recalled, rejected the common perception of the constitution as a fixed statement of static normative values. Instead, the constitution was instrumentally regarded as a socially centralizing force. The elaboration of an ostensibly authoritative normative text, it was suggested, had the doubly-unifying effect of declaring the existence of a shared social consensus which, by virtue of an assertion of authority in the present, demanded individual citizens' continued allegiance in the future. In this way the central state's authority was both proclaimed and perpetuated.

The establishment of a constitutional order, however, was only one element in this process of social construction. The simple articulation of a specific normative understanding is not sufficient, of itself, to command the continued acclaim of the public. The presence of public support for government is predicated on an enduring public belief in its values. A system of government must continue to be seen as a good if it is to retain the support of the majority of its citizens. The confidence of the citizen in his government's normative merits must be supported and secured on an ongoing and continuous basis. Institutions play an important part in underpinning such perceptions. As the representative agents of this central normative authority, they are obliged to adhere to its values in both word and deed, thereby providing for the individuals with whom they deal an example of the suggested social norms in action, and thus also a reason to expect, and believe in, their continued enforcement into the future. Government bodies must publicly fulfil their functions in an effective and—crucially—norm-appropriate manner. The means adopted (at least in public) are as important as the ends achieved. The actions and decisions of government institutions must be publicly justifiable if they are to exemplify and inculcate the constitution's normative vision successfully.

It is clear, therefore, that an institutional theory will fall to be assessed on the basis of both its instrumental efficiency and its normative appropriateness. Thus, the choice of a particular institutional model ought to be determined by the application of combined criteria of efficacy and value. This echoes Rawls's imprecation to the constitutional creators in his original position. Their task, in his view, was to 'choose the most effective, just constitution, the constitution that satisfies the principles of justice and is best calculated to lead to just *and* effective legislation'.[1] Institutional design is clearly an important part of this process. As outlined above, the bare delineation of a normative blueprint is insufficient, of itself, to counter the centrifugal forces of domestic political conflict. A constitution can only be successful when it is supported by an active institutional structure. Acting as the persuasive personification of the constitution's normative vision, these bodies should be designed in such a way that they sustain public confidence in their everyday operations. The particular model of institutional arrangement should therefore be one which not only is founded upon the constitution's normative values, but also is likely to demonstrably reflect these principles on a regular basis.

(3) The Failure of the Traditional Separation of Powers Theory

Can the separation of powers be considered as adequately fulfilling this function? Chapters 2 and 3 would seem to suggest not. From the point of view of normative value, the honourable aspirations of its creators are beyond reproach. The doctrine was intended as a foundational principle of good governance. It sought to ensure the establishment and development of a system which the public would be entitled to regard as just and fair. In practice, however, these

[1] J Rawls, *A Theory of Justice* (revised ed., Oxford University Press, 1999), at 173. Emphasis added.

aspirations have not been met. Chapter 2 addressed the doctrine's inability to successfully perform even the most basic task of an institutional theory—that of providing determinate criteria for the resolution of any questions of institutional competence which arise. In fact, this indeterminacy has even led to its occasional invocation in support of arguments and outcomes which are normatively alien to its original formulation. That the doctrine in its tripartite form is functionally incapable of ensuring the adoption of a norm-appropriate process (let alone result) indicates that it is deficient on the grounds of both efficacy and value.

Chapter 3 further queries the theory's utility, decrying its anachronistic inapplicability to contemporary governance. Issues of efficacy and value can only be assessed properly in the context of a specific social system. Rawls's own effort at social construction implicitly demonstrates this by removing the original position's constraints of ignorance at the point of constitutional creation. 'They are no longer limited to the information implicit in the circumstances of justice.' On the contrary, his would-be framers 'now know the relevant general facts about their society, that is, its natural circumstances and resources, its level of economic advance and political culture, and so on'.[2]

Ideals of justice are quite capable of being considered in the abstract. To put forward a model of justice is to make an obvious claim to universality on its behalf. A constitution, on the other hand, is inextricably tied to the political and social context in which it is developed. Constitutions, it should be remembered, aim to achieve a unifying effect in a particular society. They must therefore be carefully and contextually calibrated to increase their chances of success in that specific social environment. The institutional architect, after all, is charged with the creation of a normatively appropriate *and effective* system. Any scheme of institutional interaction must necessarily draw on and reflect the reality of the social and political structures within which it operates.

As Chapter 3 indicates, however, the separation of powers has been unable to cope with the emergence of an administrative state. The doctrine's authority has been disfigured by its numerous normative and descriptive inadequacies. In an era of decentralized decision-making bodies, the separation of powers theory's vision of a unitary, *imperium*-inspired legislative organ seems startlingly incongruous. Similarly, the extensive exercise of discretionary powers by administrative agencies makes the traditional model's commitment to a rule-based conception of government appear hopelessly outdated. A similar charge can be laid against the theory's continued reliance on notions of limited and tentative government, even as the organs of the state adopt an ever more interventionist role. In fact, the doctrine's continued insistence on the legislature's position as the sole legitimate source of creative power has only served to exacerbate the accountability deficit in modern governance, by attempting to perpetuate the public's belief in a system of parliamentary accountability which is patently

[2] J Rawls, ibid, at 172–173.

unsuitable to achieve this end. Contextually neither just nor effective, it is plain that the tripartite theory is an inappropriate institutional choice for the modern administrative state.

(4) Justice as Legitimacy

The challenge in this chapter, and for the remainder of this work, is therefore to design and develop an institutional model which is capable not only of addressing these administrative innovations, but of doing so in a normatively appropriate manner. The issue of appropriateness is, of course, contextual. An approach can only be adjudged appropriate in the light of a clear understanding of the purpose it aims to achieve. It is important, therefore, to draw a distinction between the way in which the abstract constitution, on the one hand, and the institutional structure on the other, support and sustain social unity.

Chapter 1 has already discussed the importance of publicity in some detail. As Machiavelli noted, political success depends not on the realities of government action, but on the public's perception of that activity, 'because the masses are always impressed by the superficial appearance of things'.[3]

> Political power depends primarily on what the people believe. The distinction between appearance and reality is irrelevant to the pursuit of politics: appearances—what the people believe—is the reality of politics.[4]

Thus, 'to govern well, rulers must be able to cultivate a reputation for being good'[5]—an analysis underscored by Allan and Rawls's previously observed insistence on the essentiality of institutional public reason.

Justice—or rather, the public's perception of justice—is, therefore, the foundation of governmental authority. The constitutional and institutional orders, however, contribute to this perception in quite different ways. A constitutional text tends to operate in the abstract, affirming the normative superiority of very broadly defined principles of justice. Freed from the complicated nuances of factual situations, the constitution can be regarded as part of a general social discourse with which individuals can relatively easily engage. Furthermore, the very vagueness of the constitution's principles will usually allow it to assert and establish its normative merit without difficulty. It is much simpler to construct a social consensus in support of ambiguous ideals of equality, fairness, and justice (for example) than it is to apply those values to complex or emotive cases. Who would claim to oppose justice in the abstract? Or fairness? The constitution, therefore, will generally derive its unifying force from broad notions of normative value.

[3] N Machiavelli, *The Prince* (2nd ed., R Adams, ed., Norton, 1992) Ch. XVIII, at 49.

[4] M Loughlin, 'Constitutional Law: The Third Order of the Political' in N Bamforth and P Leyland eds., *Public Law in a Multi-Layered Constitution* (Hart, 2003), at 27.

[5] Ibid, at 37.

There are significant problems, however, with an institutional reliance on such imprecise concepts. Broad ideas of justice or fairness do not always produce determinate outcomes in individual cases. These principles are of limited value for the institutional actor. Furthermore, this indeterminacy risks allowing the emergence of a divergence of individual views on the appropriate course of action in any context—thereby undermining the very social unity which the system is supposed to support.

In addition, the decentralized nature of contemporary decision-making makes it impracticable to ensure that a norm-appropriate outcome results from every individual exercise of public power. Any student of the law and economics movement will be painfully aware of the enormous informational costs associated with any effort to comprehensively examine, let alone respond to, the innumerable outputs of government bodies.[6] These analytical difficulties obviously become even more pronounced in the case of the individual citizen. If the government, with the resources of the state and its agencies at its disposal, cannot inform itself about the normative outputs of its decision-making bodies, the citizen cannot hope to come to any sort of concrete opinion on the merits or otherwise of these institutions' actions. In fact, this lack of information is also likely to affect the individual's understanding of individual decisions of the system. Most citizens will have neither the ability nor the inclination to fully inform themselves about the facts and circumstances of the many cases that administrative bodies must decide on a daily basis. Their perception of the system is ill informed, and thus highly unpredictable. This uncertainty of support has the capacity to seriously undermine the ostensibly unifying effects of the institutional order. To design and develop an institutional structure based only on notions of abstract justice would seem an imprudent and potentially ineffective choice.

The idea of institutional justice is of a very different order to its more abstract constitutional counterpart. Public justice—in the sense of being seen by the citizenry to be just—requires in the institutional context that the actions of government agencies be perceived to be taken in accordance with fair and just procedures. These procedural or (to use the term favoured by the more extensive American literature on this topic) process values are based not on esoteric notions of extant moral right, but rather on a more grounded estimation of the type of institutional techniques that will generally be regarded as just. Evidently, these techniques must conform to the normative tenets of the overarching constitutional vision. Their immediate concern, however, is not with the outcome of specific cases but with the regular public application of procedurally fair processes. This consistency of use ensures the repeated exposure of the public to these processes in a wide variety of situations. Individuals are accordingly better

[6] See, for example, the discussion of the issue of externalities in D Kennedy, 'Cost–Benefit Analysis of Entitlement Problems: A Critique' (1981) 33 *Stanford Law Review* 387.

equipped to arrive at an overall (and, if the principles of justice are well chosen, presumably positive) impression of the institutional system. In this way, the institutional order is able, through the typical process of normative exposition and advertisement, to perform its vitally unifying social function.

These distinct conceptions of constitutional and institutional justice do, of course, operate in tandem. The normative claims of institutional justice rest on the more abstract merits of the constitutional principles which the individual agencies are asked to interpret and apply. The consistently fair treatment of normative commands is without benefit if those commands are themselves misconceived:

> Only against the backdrop of a just basic structure, including a just political constitution and a just arrangement of economic and social institutions, can one say that the requisite just procedures exist.[7]

In this way, the system is one of cascading normative legitimacy. The claim to moral authority is based, not on the intrinsic merits of the individual decision, but on its adherence to the normative judgement of a higher power. The individual decision maker attributes his authority to the principles of institutional justice, the moral worth of which depends upon the normative vision which the constitution aims to instantiate. By allying decisions with the more general (and popular) attractions of abstract principles, the institution increases the possibility of public support, thereby reinforcing its own moral authority, as well as that of the system as a whole. More pragmatically, 'the practical advantage of pure procedural justice is that it is no longer necessary to keep track of the endless variety of circumstances and the changing relative positions of particular persons'.[8]

Institutional justice is distinguished by its relative lack of concern for more lofty discussions of abstract principle. Connected to the constitution's claims of normative value, it obviously plays an important part in legitimizing the actions of government in the eyes of the general public. This legitimacy, however, depends upon the procedures which it employs when faced with concrete and specific cases, rather than on the claims of individual administrators to moral or normative enlightenment. This has its disadvantages as well as its benefits. On the one hand, it avoids the apparently impossible task of convincing individual citizens that those amongst them who serve in an institutional capacity in some way exercise a higher moral power. On the other hand, it requires the institutional architects to develop notions of procedural justice capable of operating effectively in a host of very different situations. This is no easy task.

[7] Rawls, note 1 above, at 76.

[8] Ibid, at 76. Of course, as Rawls notes, it is impossible to construct a system of perfectly pure procedural justice. There is, therefore, a recurring necessity to monitor the general outputs of the system as a whole. However, this analysis does usefully illustrate the more restricted claims which institutional justice makes to moral value.

In the context of this book, however, it is useful to bear the moral limitations of this undertaking in mind. If it is to be successful, an institutional theory must be seen to be just. This justice is, however, a considerably constrained concept. An institutional theory makes no claims of abstract normative worth. It does not derive its force from external moral values. On the contrary, it seeks simply to establish a series of procedural or process values which, if properly applied, are likely to prove effective. This efficacy of course involves, in part, the public application (and propagation) of moral principles, but the system's overall assertion of moral authority is based, in large part, on the constitutional statement of abstract principles. Procedural justice is insufficient, of itself, to shore up the authority of an immoral system. It is but an instrument (albeit an important one) of a higher normative vision, upon the popularity of which the systems will succeed or fail. This book does not concern itself primarily with abstract philosophical notions of justice, morality, or right conduct. Rather, it proceeds on the assumption that the system's—any system's—constitutional basis has been established and accepted as just. The question, at that point, is how best to design a system to support that claim to justice in practice. The actions of the institutions must be procedurally just if they are to sustain the state's claim to moral authority, and legitimacy. The search, therefore, is for a theory of institutional justice which is capable of effectively and convincingly legitimizing the actions of our administrative state.

B. The Search for Legitimizing Process Values

It is a truism of liberal thought, already addressed, that the power-wielding actions of organs of government are presumptively illegitimate. Legitimacy is afforded only to those activities undertaken in accordance with accepted principles of good governance. As the previous section sought to show, this 'goodness' of government is generally based on a public perception that the system, as a whole, is just and effective. In normative terms, this claim to justice rests on the system's commitment to the procedurally just pursuit of that society's stated moral vision. It is obvious that procedural justice and administrative legitimacy are inextricably linked. The system's legitimizing value(s) must be demonstrably and defensibly just if it is to succeed on an ongoing basis. This section will seek to assess the relative justice of contemporary criteria of legitimacy.

(1) Democracy, Accountability, and Consent

The tendency, in recent times, has been to equate democratic accountability with normative legitimacy. The existence of an electoral mandate has been accepted, in decisions such as *TD*[9] and *Leontjava*,[10] as de facto evidence of an office-holder's or institution's legitimacy and, thus, decision-making authority. Some courts and commentators have acclaimed and exalted popular sovereignty as the superior norm in our law-making system, thereby following 'Bickel['s] conflat[ion] [of] very different strains of thought from Thayer to Wechsler into a single, national commitment to majority rule, or democratic faith'.[11] Such conduct draws on the traditional liberal belief that individual consent is one of the primary means of allowing 'the state [to] exercise power while avoiding the legitimation of [normatively unacceptable] personal domination'.[12] From an institutional design perspective, this preference for popular accountability and control has operated in two obvious ways.

In the first place, the apparent creative hegemony of 'pure' democratic organs has encouraged the courts to constrain the competence of unelected bodies. This perception of electoral primacy has even encouraged the courts (and other unelected organs) to defer to elected agencies in areas in which their own ability to act has already been clearly established, either by statute or tradition. Thus, as detailed at some length in Chapter 2, the Irish Supreme Court refused in *TD* to issue a mandatory expenditure order to the executive in a situation where an express constitutional right was at issue. This decision demonstrates the extent to which this exaltation of an electoral mandate has conditioned the courts to allow the *Oireachtas* a 'strikingly wide latitude' in the exercise of its powers.[13] Nor are the Irish courts alone in this attitude. As the statements of the *Chadha* majority showed,[14] the American Supreme Court has adopted a similarly permissive position, being apparently prepared to tolerate the actions of the legislature in singling out specific individuals for arbitrary treatment, largely on the basis of that body's electoral legitimacy.

That a democratic mandate may be taken by many courts to confer legitimacy and authority without the imposition of any additional requirements of justice was further confirmed by the decision of the Canadian Supreme Court in *AG v Inuit Tapirisat*.[15] This case concerned a challenge to an appeal decision of the Governor in Council in respect of the fixing of telecommunications rate structures. This appeal power was conferred on the body by statute. The seminal *Nicholson* judgment had previously held that there existed a duty of fairness in

[9] *TD v Minister for Education*, [2001] 4 IR 259. [10] *Leontjava v DPP*, [2004] 1 IR 591.

[11] R Brown, 'Accountability, Liberty and the Constitution' (1998) 98 *Columbia Law Review* 531, at 550.

[12] JL Mashaw, *Due Process in the Administrative State* (Yale University Press, 1985), at 224.

[13] *Leontjava*, [2004] 1 IR 591, at 636 *per* Keane CJ.

[14] *INS v Chadha*, 462 US 919 (1983).

[15] [1980] 2 SCR 735. This case continues to be affirmed by the Canadian courts. See, for example, *Wells v Newfoundwell*, [1999] 3 SCR 199. Cartier suggests that the decision in *Baker v Canada*, [1999] 2 SCR 817 might ultimately lead to a change in this line of authority. See G Cartier, 'Procedural Fairness in Legislative Functions: The End of Judicial Abstinence?' (2003) 53 *University of Toronto Law Journal* 217.

the context of administrative decisions.[16] The appeal decision in question occurred in the context of a regulatory statutory regime, and was delivered by what would have to be categorized as an administrative body. Crucially, however, the members of this body were all directly elected ministerial members. The duty to act fairly was therefore judged by the Supreme Court not to apply in this case, in part as a result of the 'very nature'[17] of the Governor in Council.[18] This is a clear affirmation of the democratic belief that 'legitimacy stems from the [fact] that the views of the citizen have already been taken into account through the electoral process'.[19] In this way, their activities are alleged to be just. By reason of that electoral link, it would appear, elected bodies are automatically accorded decision-making authority.

The second obvious consequence of the widespread attachment to this idea has been to encourage a reflexive reliance on ideas of electoral accountability in cases of questionable legitimacy. The discretionary powers of administrative agencies, it has previously been argued, are difficult to justify in a liberal democratic state. The academic, political, and curial reaction to this legitimacy crisis has been to introduce and develop notional electoral controls. The transmission belt theory of the administration is one obvious example of the judicial deployment of this technique. The concepts of parliamentary and ministerial accountability have also been advanced in a similar vein. The limitations of invoking ideas which, in a system characterized by the dominance of the executive organ, must be regarded as either 'dangerous myth or ... dangerous reality' have already been canvassed.[20] However, even the more sophisticated modern efforts at justifying the administration as an extended system of interest representation continue to rely on democratic participation as the primary criterion of institutional legitimacy. It has been suggested that in recent decades judicial developments have moved towards a model according to which:

> the function of administrative law is not the protection of private autonomy but the provision of a surrogate political process to ensure the fair representation of a wide range of interests in the process of administrative decision [*sic*].... Faced with the seemingly intractable problem of agency discretion, courts have changed the focus of judicial review so that its dominant purpose is ... the assurance of fair representation for all affected interests in the exercise of the legislative power delegated to agencies ... Agency decisions [so] made ... would have, in microcosm, legitimacy based on the same principle as legislation.[21]

16 *Nicholson v Haldimand–Norfolk Regional Board of Commissioners of Police*, [1979] SCR 311.

17 *Inuit Tapirisat*, [1980] 2 SCR 735, at 753.

18 Ibid.

19 Cartier, note 15 above, at 242.

20 L Sutherland, 'Responsible Government and Ministerial Responsibility: Every reform is its own problem' (1991) 24 *Canadian Journal of Political Science* 91, at 91.

21 R Stewart, 'The Reformation of American Administrative Law' (1974–5) 88 *Harvard Law Review* 1667, at 1670, 1712.

The influence of the idea of democracy-as-legitimacy here is obvious. It is therefore appropriate to examine and consider its claims as a theory of institutional justice in greater detail.

(2) The Majoritarian Idea of Legitimacy

The majoritarian claim to creative authority is founded, in large part, on the way in which democracy functions as a universalist calculus of political preferences. The mass aggregation of individually expressed desires both directs and justifies the taking of particular policy decisions on the basis of their superior social support. Numerical supremacy is the majoritarian democrat's criterion of legitimacy. Proposals are adopted or dismissed by reason of their public popularity. The fact that a majority of people in a specific society demonstrably favour a particular policy creates an expectation that the state should accede to their so-stated views. In an election (on this analysis), society speaks—and its edicts ought to be observed, and enforced.

At first glance, the majoritarian appeal to justice appears premised on the presence of popular support for the impugned programme of governance. Government action is attributable to, and thus legitimated by, the enumerated opinions of the majority of the state's citizenry. Lincoln's familiar and oft-invoked refrain that democracy is a system of government 'by the people, for the people' is confirmed by the direct involvement of the citizens in determining the political direction of their state. Political decisions are centrally taken but popularly inspired. The liberal objection to the adverse impact of state rules on individual freedom is avoided by the system's invocation of a contractarian conception of governance. The institutional reliance on elections as structured mechanisms of social choice confirms the citizen's status as societal stakeholders. Such ballots also thereby affirm the authority and legitimacy of the institutions of state that are so selected.

(a) The Concern for Electoral Accuracy

Majoritarian legitimacy, on this analysis, would seem to depend on the extent to which the democratic system accurately monitors and reflects the popular preferences of the state's citizenry. The capacity of the system to properly gauge public opinion is central to its appeal. It seems logical, therefore, to expect a democratic system to attach particular importance to ensuring and, where possible, improving the accuracy of its enumeration process. Democracy, as currently incarnated, however, does not appear to demonstrate this type of concern.

In the first place, the general election, as an occasional national consultation of the electorate, does not really allow for the expression of nuanced or individualized views. Voters are asked to adjudicate on the rival merits of broadly drawn (and often poorly explained) political programmes. The system does not allow the citizen to communicate his opinion on specific issues. Rather he must choose the package which most closely approximates to his general political preferences. A referendum process is one way of offering the individual an opportunity to adjudicate on a particular policy matter. Such appeals to popular judgement are only made, however, on a sporadic and intermittent basis. The continued deployment of these crude metrics of popular preference must call into question the seriousness of the system's commitment to the accurate assessment (and thus representation) of its citizens' wishes.

Ely suggests, however, that this institutional insistence on reducing complex political questions to a single moment of electoral communication is, in fact, an attempt to calculate the relative intensity of competing individual preferences. The voter cannot simply insist upon the satisfaction of all of his desires. On the contrary:

> more often than not we will be confronted with a choice amongst candidates who all hold some positions with which we disagree. How, then, do we choose? In large measure by placing greatest stress on those issues about which we care most, that is by taking into account our various intensities of preferences.[22]

In this way, 'our democratic system is one that is ... programmed, at least roughly, to register intensities of preference'.[23] The questionably blunt election process is, by this argument, in fact transformed into a positive institutional acknowledgement of the importance of enumerative accuracy which operates as a sophisticated tool of preference aggregation.

The majoritarian account of democracy as responsive government writ large continues, however, to lack sustained explanatory power. A closer examination of our democratic structures demonstrates clear discrepancies between the system's suggested adherence to a model of accurate preference aggregation, and the everyday reality of its actual operation. That a system, which ostensibly seeks to account for, and act upon, the views of the majority of its citizens, at the same time tolerates the non-expression of individual political preferences seems somewhat incongruous. If an elected institution's legitimacy does, indeed, rest on the extent to which its actions are directed by the registered desires of those over whom it exercises power, it would seem logical to establish a system of compulsory voting. If, come election time, every citizen was forced to select their favoured outcome, the result of the relevant ballot could truly be acclaimed as an authoritative statement of popular preferences. The legitimacy of actions undertaken in accordance with this result would thus also be assured.

Technological developments have similarly undermined the system's insistence on a one-vote-fits-all approach. Ely, it has been noted, sought to justify this as a means of ascertaining the relative intensity of particular preferences. The

[22] JH Ely, *On Constitutional Ground* (Princeton University Press, 1996), at 13.
[23] Ibid, at 14.

very rough calculation involved in this single electoral system evidently deprived individuals of the ability to accurately register their views on a range of important issues. This crude approximation of public demands may have been appropriate at a time when it was administratively impractical to allow individuals direct input into each policy debate. In this logistically limited scenario, requiring individuals to personally assess the importance to them of specific issues could plausibly be construed as a way of ensuring that the system remained proportionately attuned to public opinion on the most critical matters. Technological improvements, however, have removed the majority of these administrative constraints. Today individuals regularly participate, often at personal expense, in privately organized surveys of public opinion. Television shows have quite clearly demonstrated the capacity of modern communications technology—be it the internet, text message, or mobile phone—to calculate popular preferences on an ongoing and very regular basis. For the first time since the age of Athens and Rome, it is practically feasible to call for the construction of a system of government by perpetual plebiscite. That governments have failed to demonstrate much interest in this type of project belies the majoritarian definition of democracy as a simple exercise in opinion aggregation.

(b) Historical Scepticism

In truth, these examples are specific instantiations of a more general difficulty with this characterising democracy as the merely instrumental mechanism by which society's political preferences are measured. These cases demonstrate quite clearly that a description of democracy as a simple tool of social accountancy does not tally with our intuitive understanding of the system.

Past constitutionalists certainly did not seem to equate democracy with majoritarian governance. Madison, Alexander, and Jay, in their *Federalist Papers*, in fact 'eschew[ed] what many thought [(and seem, again, today to think)] democracy to be about—local autonomy, direct citizen participation, and the sovereignty of popular majorities'.[24] They saw in such majority control the 'dangerous vice' of factionalism.[25] Noting the tendency of all individuals to exercise power in accordance with the interests of either themselves or a group to which they happen to belong, Madison insisted that the creative power of the majority should be curtailed rather than acclaimed:

> When a majority is included in a faction, the form of popular government . . . enables it to sacrifice to its ruling passion or interest both the public good and the rights of other citizens. To secure the public good and private rights against the danger of such faction . . . is then the great object to which our inquiries are directed.[26]

[24] JL Mashaw, *Greed, Chaos and Governance* (Yale University Press, 1997), at 4–5.

[25] J Madison, *Federalist Paper No. 10* (1788) in *The Federalist Papers* (I Kramnick, ed., Penguin, 1987), at 122.

[26] Ibid, at 125.

Madison's constitutional project was dedicated to the restriction rather than the facilitation of majority rule. Pure democracy, as evidenced in the ancient 'petty republics of Greece and Italy', would inevitably result in a 'state of perpetual vibration between the extremes of tyranny and anarchy'.[27] Majoritarian influence, on this view, was an 'imperfectio[n] ... [to be] lessened and avoided',[28] rather than a foundational democratic principle to be observed.

(c) Normative Intuitionism

Of course, the opposition of historical figures, no matter how eminent, is not a reason, of itself, to reject a particular theory of government. The contemporary conception of democracy, however, seems equally to regard the doctrine as more than the instrumental means by which the aims of the collective are assessed. It is instead understood as a process which is in itself normatively significant.

A simple example will suffice to illustrate this point. Dworkin distinguished between the ideas of 'bare' and 'moral' harm. Bare harm, in his view, is that injury or inconvenience suffered by an individual adversely affected by the actions of the state. Moral harm, on the other hand, refers to the idea that the unjust or undeserved infliction of injury or inconvenience is, in fact, a matter of more serious and objectionable import. As he explains:

> We must distinguish ... between what we might call the bare harm a person suffers through punishment, whether that punishment is just or unjust—for example, the suffering or frustration or pain or dissatisfaction of desires that he suffers just because he loses his liberty or is beaten or killed—and the further injury that he might be said to suffer whenever his punishment is unjust, just in virtue of that injustice. I shall call the latter ... his 'moral' harm.[29]

Applying his analysis, Dworkin identified how a system designed for the sole pursuit of cost-efficient outcomes is unable to include this notion of moral harm in its utilitarian calculations.

In a similar way, a democratic model which concentrated solely on the ever-more accurate aggregation of individual preferences would not capture our understanding of the system's moral dimensions. A purely instrumental analysis of democracy would see only a minimal bare harm in any rejection of the individual's right to vote. The political choices of a solitary citizen are unlikely, after all, to alter the outcome of the majoritarian calculus. The bare harm thereby incurred is decidedly insignificant, carrying with it 'a loss of political power so minute that cold calculation should convince us that our personal franchise in practical, political terms is valueless'.[30] In reality, however, such

[27] A Hamilton, *Federalist Paper No. 9* (1788) in *The Federalist Papers*, note 25 above, at 118.
[28] Ibid, at 119.
[29] R Dworkin, *A Matter of Principle* (Harvard University Press, 1985), at 80.
[30] Mashaw, *Due Process*, note 12 above, at 163.

disenfranchisement would be understood to constitute an enormous injustice. To exclude a voter from the collective's act of conscious policy creation implicitly (and, to our minds, unacceptably) abjures the individual's status as citizen.

This illustrates, quite clearly, that our democratic system aspires to the protection and enforcement of values beyond those demanded by a simple pursuit of aggregative accuracy. As this section has shown, the 'involvement in the process of political decision making ... seems to be valued for its own sake'.[31] This protection of the individual's entitlement to participate in an election is evidently not mandated by a system of majority-oriented utilitarianism. More individualistic values are at work. Our system, as Mashaw notes, seems instead to be characterized by an intuitive commitment to some type of 'model of dignitary values'.[32] The individual citizen's status as the normative basis for all social action must be acknowledged and assured. A theory of institutional justice, if it is to operate successfully, must recognize and reflect such inbuilt intuitions. The asserted justice of the majoritarian paradigm must, therefore, rest upon its treatment of the demands and desires of the individual rather than those of the collective. The next section will therefore examine whether a majoritarian theory can be convincingly constructed from so individualistic an outlook.

C. Individualism in a Democratic State

(1) Democracy as Equality

The emphasis on the normative importance of the individual citizen reflects the liberal concern, already considered, to ensure that the interests of the collective do not displace those of the individual. The status of the citizen, it was noted in Chapter 3, has traditionally been secured by the use of one of two techniques. 'The first is consent; the second, the use of impersonal rules or principles.'[33] Democratic structures could arguably be justified on either of these grounds. It would not be difficult, for example, to construe the casting of a vote at election time as an act of individual consent to the authority and legitimacy of any institution established as a result. This analysis will be considered in due course. Advocates of democracy could, alternatively, rest its claim to normative justification on the system's evident impersonality.[34] Democracy in action is a grand exercise in non-discrimination. Every citizen of voting age is entitled to participate in the electoral process, regardless of religion, class, colour, and so on. Such absolute parity of treatment suggests a system-wide commitment to the concept of equality—a value which, by its impeccable impersonality, could quite plausibly support the system's claims to moral worth.

[31] Ibid, at 163. [32] Ibid, in Chapter 4. [33] Ibid, at 224.

[34] JL Mashaw classifies majoritarian voting as an impersonal means of resolving political conflicts, rather than one based on personal consent.

Democratic majoritarianism is, fundamentally, a strictly egalitarian theory. Consistent with the liberal insistence on the importance of the individual in society, majoritarianism offers each citizen an exactly equal opportunity to influence the actions and opinions of the government. The democratic system generally does not distinguish between citizens on the basis of wealth, intelligence, ability, moral capacity, or any other inherently individualized grounds.[35] All are equal in its eyes. Equality, for the majoritarian theorist, provides the necessary assurance of institutional fairness. Justice as equality is thus at the root of the majoritarian's assertion of normative legitimacy.

Is this trust in majoritarianism as the touchstone of normative legitimacy appropriate? Madison's and Hamilton's predictions of majority factionalism highlight an obvious potential criticism of the attempt to rely on majoritarianism as a legitimating value. The unfettered vesting of creative power in elected agencies has the clear potential to produce policies or decisions which adversely impact on the interests of specific groups or, in some cases, society as a whole. Is an equality of minimal involvement by each individual citizen in the framing of such policies sufficient to overcome this possible objectionability of outcome? Is this input equality enough to vindicate the majoritarian claim to justice? That Madison sees factional discord as the inevitable (rather than simply possible) consequence of any endorsement of this approach poses obvious problems for this contention. A constitution, it must be remembered, should be designed to be both just and effective—just in the principles it espouses, and effective in the way in which it is likely to produce just and effective outcomes. Placing sole reliance on the electoral system as a legitimizing value has the potential to result in tyrannical or anarchical rule. This necessarily calls into question the efficacy of a pursuit of justice based only on such grounds.

More profoundly, it illustrates the difficulties inherent in resting an assertion of justice on a narrow concept of equality of input. It is a truism that equality is an inherently empty principle. Devoid of any extant conception of moral right or wrong, it finds justice in a bare guarantee of equal treatment. It is just as capable of supporting deteriorating standards of state conduct towards individual citizens as it is of demanding an improvement in such activities.

> It is obvious ... that law and institutions may be equally executed and yet be unjust. Treating similar cases similarly is not a sufficient guarantee of substantive justice ... There is no contradiction in supposing that a slave or caste society, or one sanctioning the most arbitrary forms of discrimination, is evenly and consistently administered [so as to satisfy the requirements of the equality principle].[36]

This is especially so with a guarantee of equality of input. This aspiring principle of institutional justice does not offer the citizen any assurances that the organs of

[35] The obvious exception is jurisdictions where prisoners are denied the right to vote.
[36] Rawls, note 1 above, at 51.

the state will properly respect his rights or interests. Its justice speaks to Chance rather than to Reason. The individual is offered the institutional equivalent of an all-or-nothing gamble, a type of political Russian roulette in which the protection proffered is the structural guarantee that the citizen is (formally) no more likely to fail than anyone else.

In practice, of course, this emphasis on formal equality overlooks the systemic inequalities which Ely, Galbraith, and others have noted are likely to disrupt the individual's chances of success.[37] Can such a system truly be regarded as just? Or, in its failure to offer even minimal protection to the unlucky or the unpopular, does it fail to reflect the intuitive understanding of justice set out above? Such 'a purely formal conception of equality', it is clear, 'seems unacceptably narrow'.[38]

The indiscriminate nature of this particular conception of equality is also normatively unsatisfactory. The Aristotelian conception of justice famously required that like be treated as like, and that, accordingly, those who are different be treated differently. The utilitarian equality upon which the majoritarian principle is premised makes no such allowances for individual differences. Its equality is a matter of bare mathematics. The citizen is treated, not as an individual, but as a unit of preference to be aggregated in a grand electoral exercise in social calculation. In this way the individual is commodified. The unchecked creative primacy of elected institutions which majoritarianism seems to espouse ensures that the individual is only normatively and institutionally significant at specific intermittent moments of electoral addition. Upon the conclusion of these occasional ballots, the citizen becomes, once more, a passive object over which the state (as directed by the majority) is entitled to exercise full control. Such is the normatively unacceptable fate of the citizen in a majoritarian system animated by this starkly egalitarian understanding of democracy.

Democracy's asserted adherence to ideals of equality cannot provide adequate support for the majoritarian claim to moral legitimacy. As an apparently impersonal means of liberal legitimation, this egalitarianism goes too far. Offering impersonality without personhood, pure electoral equality actually subverts the individuality upon which it is ostensibly based. The system's insistence on such equality is justified as an acknowledgement of the normative importance of each individual being. Majoritarian democracy, it is claimed, is inspired and directed by a commitment to the autonomy and dignity of every citizen of the state. That democracy treats each person equally is said to affirm the individual's inherent normative value. This absolute equality in fact serves only to deny the individual's moral worth. The failure to recognize or react to individual differences dehumanizes rather than dignifies the citizen. Furthermore, the refusal to require

[37] See, for example, JH Ely, *Democracy and Distrust* (Harvard University Press, 1980); JK Galbraith, *The Culture of Contentment* (Penguin, 1993).

[38] TRS Allan, *Law, Liberty and Justice* (Clarendon Press, 1993), at 164.

the state to submit to any form of minimum substantive standards challenges the system's alleged belief in the value of each individual. That majoritarianism would, by itself, tolerate the unjust treatment of minorities or individuals must undermine its claimed commitment to individual dignity or autonomy.

Another ground of criticism is that the majoritarian interpretation of equality effectively treats it as a principle to be imposed by the centre, rather than as a general principle which derives from the moral autonomy of each individual citizen. It is treated as a formal tenet of institutional operation rather than a guiding principle of substantive moral value. Its dictates are determined by a centralized conception of public power—it is a principle which the system sees fit to observe in a particular political context, rather than one which is consistently respected as the normative foundation of legitimate rule. Taken together with the reasons considered above, these considerations undermine its claim to be regarded as a morally legitimate form of majoritarian governance.

(2) Democracy, Autonomy, and Consent

The alternative interpretation of majoritarian democracy as a system premised on the electoral provision of personal consent would appear to address a number of these concerns. Most obviously, this model relies on the conscious involvement of the individual voter as its central legitimizing value. This rehumanizes democracy's normative foundations. The individual citizen is a self-directed actor, contributing to his society's choice of suggested political options. The citizen helps to direct the institutional actions of the central political organs. He thereby becomes an active participant in the process of coordinating the collective, rather than the passive object of its operations. Even if an individual is unhappy with the results of the process, his voluntary submission to the rules and principles of the electoral procedure is sufficient to secure his personal consent, morally speaking. The consent provided by this personal involvement will suffice normatively, as long as it is treated in a just and fair fashion. After all, an individual cannot participate in a just and fair process, only to withdraw his consent when it produces an adverse outcome. Equality thus serves here as a supporting principle of institutional justice. Furthermore, the transient nature of any specific instance of majoritarian control guarantees the dissatisfied citizen a future opportunity to register his objections and attempt to amend the political direction of his state and society. The system recognizes and affirms the citizen's decision-making capacity on an ongoing basis, demonstrating a clear commitment to our intuitive ideals of individual dignity and autonomy.

This consent-based conception of majoritarian democracy echoes more closely our conventional understanding of normatively acceptable authority. However, on closer examination, the concept's application to contemporary governance is open to challenge. The system's assertion of legitimacy centres on the presence of individual consent to the actions of government. The casting of an individual vote is interpreted as providing implicit consent to the activities of state institutions over a number of years. This characterization is, however, tenuous in the extreme. The individual at the ballot box has not even anticipated, let alone approved of, the vast majority of future government actions. This is particularly true in the modern era of decentralized public power. Administrative agencies today exercise extensive discretionary powers, generally with little or no input from central government. It is no longer realistic (if it ever was) to describe our system of government in terms of the individual voter's consent to the creative authority of a single unitary and centralized institution. That approach strains the concept of consent to breaking point, as Cartier observes:

> [T]o argue that, by electing representatives, citizens consent in advance to abide by discretionary decisions made by administrative authorities under the authority of a statute legitimately enacted by the legislative assembly, assumes that the consent originally given is very broad.[39]

This is especially true in light of the usual lack of specificity in such statutes. The analysis of majoritarian democracy in terms of individual consent, like the equality rationale examined above, appears to depend on an emptily formal acknowledgement of the importance of the individual, rather than on any real commitment to ensuring the active participation of the citizen in the framing of public policy.

The actively interventionist character of the contemporary state offers further confirmation of the anachronistic nature of this notion of citizen consent. A reliance on the occasional presence of personal consent to legitimize the actions of central government would have been more justifiable in the eighteenth-century context of essentially negative and limited governance. In that environment, the potential risk of individually adverse government decisions was mitigated by the weakness of the central governing structures. The liberty, autonomy, and dignity of the individual was guaranteed, not by government, but by the lack of it. 'The old constitutional conception of government called to mind a policeman; government's role entailed minimal intrusion on private affairs and a *laissez faire* reliance on the invisible hand' of self-directed economic activity.[40] Individuals were charged with the basic protection of their own interests. The government's conscious inaction effectively affirmed the autonomy of individuals by entrusting them with almost complete responsibility for their own actions. State action was minimalist and sporadic. Its relative lack of impact could be regarded as justifying the insistence on only occasional individual consent.

[39] G Cartier, 'Willis and the Contemporary Administrative State: Administrative Discretion as Dialogue' (2005) 55 *University of Toronto Law Journal* 629, at 651.

[40] J Edley Jr, 'The Governance Crisis, Legal Theory and Political Ideology' (1991) 41 *Duke Law Journal* 561, at 581.

Today's managerial state, by contrast, functions in a much more interventionist manner, organizing and structuring the social framework within which individuals are entitled to operate. This is true even of jurisdictions which have enthusiastically incorporated private actors and free market principles into their process of governance. The state's continuing influence on the exercise of social power is illustrated by the way in which regulatory bodies have proliferated in such third-party systems. By simply establishing a regulatory framework, or even by allowing one to develop organically without hindrance, the state shapes the development of social policy. Furthermore, as the current economic crisis has starkly shown, the state retains a residual role as the problem-solver of ultimate resort. The result is that the contemporary state undoubtedly exercises influence over significant areas of social activity. This both restricts the decision-making freedom of the individual, and increases the possibility that adverse and intrusive measures will be enacted. The greater involvement of the state in the everyday activities of its citizens necessitates the incorporation of greater process values into the democratic system. The simple presence of a vague and poorly defined personal consent to government authority can no longer be regarded as a legitimate foundation for the actions of the multi-faceted contemporary state.

(3) The Enduring Importance of the Individual

This suggests that neither the equality- nor the consent-inspired conceptions of majoritarianism truly convince as methods of legitimate governance. Neither appears to attach sufficient significance to the adequate protection of the individual's position. Of course, these majoritarian models do allow the individual to engage with society's decision-making process, but they are primarily preoccupied with the examination and enforcement of the majority's desires. The constrained nature of this individual involvement does not tally with our intuitive understanding of institutional justice. Our system has traditionally and instinctively opposed the unjustified use of public power against a morally undeserving individual. Institutional guarantees such as the separation of powers were inspired in large part by the perception of such acts—for example in bills of attainder—as normatively unacceptable. Liberal theory could not countenance a sacrifice of individual interest for those of the collective, insisting instead that institutional respect for the citizen's dignity and autonomy is essential.[41] This individualistic outlook has permeated the fabric of our constitutional and

[41] For a recent affirmation of this principle in Irish law, see the decision of the Supreme Court in *CC v Ireland*, [2006] IESC 33, where Hardiman J struck down the strict liability offence of unlawful carnal knowledge. He objected to the utilitarian nature of the offence, decrying the way in which it 'permits the imposition of an admitted injustice on a discrete class of person on the sole justification of effectiveness ... To put it another way, it is not a balancing of the blameless [individual's] rights against those of the rest of society: it is a negation of those rights in the interest of a concept of the social good.'

institutional traditions. It underlies the democratic commitment to voluntary voting rather than obligatory aggregation. It supports the system's preference for a decision-making system designed with active participation rather than absolute accuracy in mind. It lies at the heart of our basic belief that the denial of the individual's right to vote is a matter of much greater injustice than the mere loss of that franchise's minimal influence would suggest is appropriate. Government, if it is to be legitimate and effective, must reflect these foundational values.

The contemporary trend towards majoritarianism, in reality, is nothing less than a move towards a modern absolutism. Legitimacy in a majoritarian system is based on the source of political power rather than the quality of its exercise. Just as the actions of the absolute monarchs of old were justified by the assertion of an inherent moral entitlement to direct and dictate public policy, so the contemporary majority claims superiority on the basis of what it is, rather than what it does. This is exactly the sort of logic which our institutional structures evolved to counter. Separation of powers, the guarantee of equal treatment, the insistence on institutional justice, and so on, were designed and defended as principles of good governance. As a defender of the New Deal once remarked, 'government, or any part of it, is not in itself something; it is for something'.[42] For the liberal thinkers of the past, that objective was the protection of the moral autonomy of the individual citizen from the dangers of self-animated factionalism. Majoritarianism undermines this value by presumptively doubting the normative acceptability of such individual-oriented restrictions. The People (or, more accurately, the majority) are instead invested with inherent political power, to be exercised as arbitrarily as they please. The voter is seduced by the tantalizing prospect that he might someday be in a position to have power exercised in *his* favour, rather than in that of his fellow citizens. A situation of unfettered, self-interested kingship is, after all, only objectionable to those excluded from court. Majoritarianism offers the individual the tempting possibility of an absolute furtherance of her own interests. *L'état, c'est vous.* Majoritarianism is less a theory of justice than an effective institutional strategy, the genius of which lies in the way in which it is able to broaden its appeal beyond those who will actually benefit from its adoption. Its popularity cannot, however, obscure its innate lack of regard for the excluded individual. In this, it contrasts sharply with our intuitive understanding of our institutional system. Thus it cannot convincingly serve as the constitution's organizing principle of institutional justice. On the contrary, there is a clear need to consider and construct a richer and more sophisticated conception of procedural justice. The system, if it is to be fair and effective, must insist on the protection of stronger process values, ideals which chime more closely with liberalism's central commitment to the dignity and autonomy of the individual. In this way, a more appropriate theory of institutional justice might be developed.

[42] RG Tugwell, *The Battle for Democracy* (1935), cited in Edley, note 40 above, at 581.

(4) Individualism, Citizenship, and the State

So far this chapter has argued in favour of a reorientation in our institutional outlook, away from the current concentration upon the claims of the majoritarian collective and towards a renewed emphasis on the interests of the individual. This individualism should not be interpreted, however, as an inherently anarchical force. An autonomy- or dignity-inspired theory of procedural justice will obviously regard the position of the individual citizen as the relevant departure point for its normative analysis. This concern for the citizen will inevitably inculcate a logical scepticism about any central organization of public power. This scepticism should not be confused, however, with an enduring or outright opposition to these activities. The demand for justification of state action does not arise from a desire to avoid the vesting of authority in central institutions, if possible. On the contrary, the interests of the individual are clearly served by such organized coordination of collective power. The construction of a power-wielding state has obvious potential benefits for the individual actor. The idea of public governance is premised on the advancement of the position of the individual citizen. This type of associative endeavour aims to secure increased advantages for the constituent members of the group. It is an idea of ancient standing that this type of activity satisfies the needs and demands inherent in mankind's characterization as a *politikon zoon*.[43] However, even aside from the intangible improvements this cooperative conduct might confer on individual citizens, it is beyond question that the machinery of the state provides each with the opportunity to achieve that which they, by themselves, could not.

The oft-cited example of the 'Tragedy of the Commons' is a useful illustration of this relational theory of the state. Rational self-interest dictates that, in all probability, the individual hunter will find his position greatly enhanced by the emergence of a system of public rules, enforced by way of centralized sanctions.[44] Some free riders might, of course, find themselves economically disadvantaged by such a development. However, this is a purely short-term analysis. If all are free riders then, ultimately, all will lose from the over-farming of the commons. The long-term advantages of this type of centralized system of coercive enforcement are even more assured if it is assumed that the hunters are

[43] Aristotle, *The Politics*, I ii. 9. Although this is often translated directly as a 'political animal', it must be remembered that Aristotle was referring to man's tendency to associate with those of his own kind. Political, in this context, is related to the *polis* or city-state unit of Ancient Greece, rather than the strategies for managing conflict which would more typically be found in, for example, the writings of Macchiavelli.

[44] Although he does not approach this issue from the point of view of a strictly economic analysis, Finnis agrees with the conclusion that the individual benefits from associative conduct. He regards communal life as the appropriate context for the pursuit of his self-evident human goods, listing 'sociability' as one of his seven forms of human good. See JM Finnis, *Natural Law and Natural Rights* (Oxford University Press, 1980).

concerned for the future of their families.[45] In this situation, centralized enforcement assures even the offspring of the free rider of a basic share in the commons, regardless of their capacity or strength. It is clear that, on the whole, each individual stands to significantly benefit from this type of system.

The advantages of a centralized system of rules are equally obvious from even a cursory examination of the Hobbesian individual in the pre-legal state. Free she may be, but this individual, dependent for her position on her own physical strength, is famously condemned to a life which is 'solitary, poor, nasty, brutish and short'.[46] The establishment of a system of public rules will inevitably restrict the theoretical autonomy of the individual citizen. The case of the Hobbesian citizen underlines, however, that abstract freedoms are effectively worthless without supportive legal structures. In practice, the citizen may retain an autonomy of action but this is not guaranteed for the future. Security is an essential prerequisite to the existence of assured personal freedom. Without it, liberty rests only on individual or group strength. Once again, the establishment of some form of governing, sanction-based structure will clearly improve the position of a significant majority of society.

Furthermore, it should be remembered that absolute freedom is a chimeric ideal. Aside from the issue of security, on a Hohfeldian analysis the existence of a guaranteed personal freedom depends on a complicated network of interlocking no-rights and freedoms, immunities and disabilities. Every individual freedom necessarily impacts on the liberty of action of some other citizen. A pornographer's freedom of expression will evidently impact on the freedom of the sensitive or moral citizen to inhabit a society devoid of this type of material. Individual freedom is necessarily dependent not only on the security or stability of a functioning rule-based system of sanctions, but also on the normative priorities enshrined in the rules of that system.

The existence of a centralized, public government does not necessarily represent a significant encroachment on the liberty of the individual. On the contrary, it enhances the citizen's situation by providing the stability and certainty necessary for any true autonomy of action—albeit only within the areas designated by the central authority. The individual citizen is better off in the legal, rather than the pre-legal state. There is, it is clear, a basic duality at the centre of the concept of government. The normative foundation of governance—a concern for the autonomy and dignity of the individual citizen—can be taken to justify both the facilitation and restriction of centrally organized rule.

[45] This could be argued to be a natural tendency in mankind, implicit in the emphasis attached by both Aristotle and Finnis to the communal aspects of life. The family, in most cultures, is the most accurate example of a functioning communal unit. However, even from the point of view of rational self-interest, this could also be justified as securing the position of farmers in their old age. In the absence of a centralized state system with some form of social welfare, they may be forced to rely on their offspring, so thus clearly have a personal interest in ensuring their children's long-term welfare.

[46] T Hobbes, *Leviathan*, Pt. 1, Chapter 13.

Liberal individualism is not a doctrine of disestablishmentarianism. The restriction of state power cannot rationally be justified for simple restriction's sake. An appropriate theory of institutional justice is necessarily more complex than one animated by an instinctive opposition to state authority. This type of theory must recognize and acknowledge that institutional action is socially essential, balancing the individual-inspired need for publicly exercised powers with a residual protection of the interests of each citizen. This affirmation of the individual as the normatively constituent unit of all social organization thereby demands the development of a much more subtle and sophisticated system of institutional justice.

(5) Universality and the Philosophy of Kant

This characterization the individual as the central criterion of normative value finds obvious parallels in the philosophy of Kant. The present chapter's earlier critique of majoritarianism focused on the essentially dehumanizing effect of its ideas of equality or consent. The key intuitive objection to its attitude towards the individual was its utilitarian treatment of the citizen as a passive unit of social accounting. At the moment of voting the individual was implicitly regarded as a means of calculating collective preferences, rather than as an active moral agent, deserving of respect and consideration in his own right. This contrasts with Kant's conception of the citizen as a 'noumenal being who is free'.[47] The right to vote was effectively treated under this model as an institutional instrument of aggregative accuracy rather than a normative recognition of the individual as a conscious and rational actor. This, to paraphrase Kant's most famous incantation, was to treat the individual as a means rather than an end, thereby undermining the majoritarian claim to justice, and, as a result, also to legitimacy. A bottom-up perspective, which takes seriously the normative challenge to defend the individual, is required instead.

The Kantian order to '[a]ct so that you use humanity . . . always . . . as an end, never merely as a means'[48] has, however, been criticized on the basis of its excessive individualism.[49] Society might be a relational structure for the advancement of individual interests but it does not provide a panacea for the absolute satisfaction of all individual wants. The inevitable contradiction of distinct individual desires ensures that the achievement of all individual ends remains an impossible project.

Mashaw persuasively disputes this reading of Kant. The instruction to treat the individual as an end is an imprecation to ensure a universality of principle,

[47] I Kant, *Political Writings* (2nd ed., H Reiss, ed., Cambridge University Press, 1991), at 18.

[48] I Kant, *Groundwork of the Metaphysics of Morals* (M Gregor, ed., Cambridge University Press, 1997), at 38.

[49] See, for example, R Scruton, *The Meaning Of Conservatism* (3rd ed., Palgrave, 2001).

rather than an effort to meet every demand that is made. This reflects the fact that this well known directive is but one element of Kant's overarching command—'act only according to that maxim by which you can at the same time will that it should become a universal law'.[50] Thus:

[t]he injunction to treat persons always as ends in themselves is derived from the universalization requirement of Kant's categorical imperative. [It] ... must be read as related to an objective or universal realm of ends or moral persons. So construed, the injunction relates not to the frustrating of any person's goals or purposes in life, but to frustrating that person's exercise and development of a good will. Each person thus is an end in himself *because* each person participates in, or strives for, objective moral goodness.[51]

In this way, Kant's theory of moral universality is 'rescued from the incessant and competitive claims of the self-realising ego'.[52] This insistence on universality echoes and explains the liberal preference for the impersonal application of institutional principles. Universality treats each citizen as an individual, but crucially does so in a manner which recognizes the person's normative worth. It rests not on an arbitrary egalitarianism, nor on an empty assurance of individual consent, but rather on a symbolic acceptance of the citizen's entitlement to individual respect. A system which attempts to adopt only truly universal rules thereby recognizes the individual as a morally important entity. It does not offer the dehumanizing prospect of absolutely equal inputs or outputs. It takes its responsibilities to each person seriously, refusing to tolerate the dismissive subjugation of the individual citizen to the interests of the collective. However, it also acknowledges the reality that an organized society cannot expect to satisfy all of the desires of its citizens. These facts are reflected in the system's normative insistence that '[t]he freedom of each individual has consequently to be regulated in a universally binding manner'.[53]

Universality, in effect, is a prudential principle of institutional operation, admitting the necessity for coordinated social action but restricting it to those situations in which the activities undertaken can be said to demonstrate an appropriate concern for the normative status of the individual. In so doing, the principle acknowledges the basic duality of our social structures in a way which reflects our intuitive understanding of justice. Universality affirms the moral autonomy of all persons at the same time that it justifies (and thus legitimizes) the possibility of individual-adverse outcomes. In its simultaneous approval of both action and restriction, it has obvious potential as an organizing principle of institutional justice.

[50] *Groundwork*, note 48 above, at 31.
[51] Mashaw, *Due Process*, note 12 above, at 193. Emphasis in text.
[52] Ibid.
[53] *Political Writings*, note 47 above, at 22.

(6) Universality, Rawls, and the Original Agreement

As Mashaw recognizes, a concern for such universality animates Rawls's idea of the original agreement:

> The original position might be viewed as an approach to the kingdom of ends; the veil of ignorance as a technique for protecting the universal or good will from the clash of contingent purposes that punctuate the phenomenal world. The choices of the disembodied rational wills posited by Rawls are universal by definition, and the pursuit of the principles of justice by a rational placeholder, who does not know where he will end up in the social scheme, necessarily treats all rational beings as ends in themselves.[54]

Rawls's seminal thought experiment can thus be construed as an imaginative updating of the Kantian requirement that 'our social and political relations should be governed and our public conflicts settled in a universal manner'.[55] A desire for universality is the key objective underpinning the use of Rawls's approach in this context. The invocation of the veil of ignorance is not intended to create the conditions in which a social contract could have been concluded in order to identify precisely what would have been agreed. It is instead a yardstick against which the general reasonableness of a model or proposal can be assessed. If a measure or value is one which might reasonably have been accepted by an individual citizen in the original position, then it is one which is likely to have the degree of universality required to serve as the foundational principle of a particular system. The claim being made is not that this is the model or approach which an individual placed behind the veil of ignorance *would* have chosen. Rather, it is only that the analysis is one which (s)he might reasonably have accepted.

The model of contextually ignorant actors also indicates, by its very neutrality, the normative importance of each person's moral autonomy. This is also relevant to its utility in this context. The citizen, unaware of his or her position in the society in question, is deployed as an evaluative tool as well as an instrument of theoretical creativity. This reliance on the putative consent of the imagined individual implicitly confirms the citizen as a rational and autonomous agent. The justice of the institutional order is examined from the perspective of an ideally universal person. The archetypal citizen serves as the directive inspiration for a notion of justice which thereby also affirms the individual's capacity for rational thought and moral action. This copper-fastens the citizen's status as the normative foundation of social action. Respect for the individual is 'the intuitive bedrock upon which ... bargains are based, and ... the test of the moral legitimacy and relative desirability' of these eventually agreed principles.[56] In this way, the theory of justice is freed of the distortion

[54] Mashaw, *Due Process,* note 12 above, at 194–195.
[55] *Political Writings*, note 47 above, at 20.
[56] Mashaw, *Due Process,* note 12 above, at 195.

caused by the chance concerns of personal circumstance, and is thereby rendered acceptably universal.

The model of the universal individual can both describe and explain the way in which we perceive particular conceptions of institutional justice.[57] This chapter's earlier examination of the majoritarian principle concluded that it failed to reflect our intuitive ideas of institutional justice. A consultation with this imaginary citizen confirms the veracity of this view, but also, crucially, identifies the reasons for this reflexive reaction. Would a person, acting under a veil of individual ignorance, consent to a system in which unfettered public power was vested in the representatives of a bare majority of voters? It is possible, of course, that a gambler would submit to this type of proposal. Would that constitute a rational choice, however? The rational autonomy of the individual citizen, it must be remembered, is the justification for the system's insistence on a universalist theory of institutional justice. It should obviously impact on the system's ultimate choice of institutional design, therefore. The abandonment of individual interests for an all-or-nothing gamble cannot reasonably be regarded as a prudent choice. Although it might appeal to individuals with particular reckless characteristics, it seems likely that the majority of citizens would not accept the risk that their desires or interests would never be considered as part of the governance process. It is not, therefore, a model which really falls within the range of social contracts to which all might reasonably agree. As a result, it lacks the level of universality required for it to act as the basis for a reasonable and rational social agreement. Majoritarianism is objectionable as an arbitrary, and accordingly irrational, way of structurally organizing a society of independent moral agents.

(7) Respecting Individual Autonomy

(a) Equality

How then should the system fulfil this normative obligation to recognize and respect the rational individuality of each citizen? That each must be dealt with as a distinct and autonomous entity would seem to suggest some institutional requirement of equality. Dworkin, for example, posits a notion of institutional integrity in which all individuals must be equal before the law. Decisions must adhere to principles which are expounded and enforced on a consistent, institution-wide basis. In this way, the individual is assured of equal treatment. This commitment to a concept of 'formal equality' does seem to demonstrate the requisite desire to secure the necessary universality of principle.

[57] It is important to underline, at this point, the limitations of this analysis. Rawls relied on his vision of the pre-constitutional original position to construct an overarching theory of social justice. Such an ambitious enterprise is far outside the ambit of this book. Rather, the original position of personal ignorance will be used in order to assess the attractions for the decontextuealized individual of a particular type of institutional order.

In reality, however, this notion of formal equality cannot adequately explain the actions of contemporary institutions. Disparities of treatment are not simply allowed but actually encouraged, provided that they proceed from an institutional recognition of rationally legitimate differences. A commitment to equality dictates only that 'we treat equals equally and unequals unequally'.[58] It does not require the establishment of a blind system of enduring egalitarianism. Dependent for its operation on the presence of an independent criterion of comparative value, it is a normative principle of ancillary importance, inspired by a deeper, more fundamental belief in protecting the autonomy of the individual. 'Formal equality reflects the principle that everyone should be accorded proper respect as a person of moral independence.'[59] It does not, therefore, exhaust the obligations imposed by ideas of institutional justice. The courts' interpretation of the constitutional equality guarantee, both in Ireland and abroad, tends to concentrate on ensuring that discriminatory state action has rational foundations rather than abstractly enforcing a dehumanizing egalitarianism.[60] 'Formal equality, in the sense of the equal application of the law, must, as a matter of logical consistency, be accompanied by [a] more substantive doctrine, forbidding hostile discrimination.'[61] The contemporary conception of institutional justice may be explained more accurately as a structural commitment to the rational treatment of the morally autonomous individual, than as an abstract belief in absolute equality.

(b) Institutional Rationality

There is a clear connection, therefore, between a systemic acceptance of the need for operational universality and a guarantee of rational institutional dealings. In keeping with the constrained focus of this book, on this idea of justice rationality does not attempt to assure the individual of perennially positive decision-making outcomes. It acts only as a process value, guaranteeing the citizen that any individually adverse (or indeed positive) exercise of public power will be justifiable objectively, and publicly so explained.[62] A rationality requirement confirms the entitlement of 'any citizen ... to an explanation of why her private harm is at least arguably outweighed by some coherent and plausible conception of the public good'.[63] This explanation thereby appeals to and affirms the individual's capacity for rational action. In so doing, it confirms the institutional order's reputation for justice. 'This reason giving is necessary, both to redeem

[58] *de Búrca v AG*, [1976] IR 38, at 68. [59] Allan, note 38 above, at 164.

[60] See, for example, *Brennan v AG*, [1983] ILRM 449; *Re Article 26 and the Employment Equality Bill 1996*, [1997] 2 IR 321; *An Blascoad Mór Teoranta v Commissioners of Public Works (No. 3)*, [2000] 1 IR 6. This, of course, is in part attributable to the fact that the text of Article 40.1 expressly permits discrimination on social, moral, and physical grounds.

[61] Allan, note 38 above, at 170.

[62] The need for public application of principles in a theory of institutional justice is explained in Chapter 1. [63] Mashaw, *Greed, Chaos & Governance*, note 24 above, at 68.

prior promises of rationality, and to provide guidance of the individual's future planning.'[64] The liberty and autonomy of the individual is supported by 'some notion of predictability or . . . rationality in government as a basic prerequisite to fair decision making'.[65] This tallies with the Hartean interpretation of law as a scheme of individual and social orientation, 'a stable framework of rules, which enables everyone to pursue his own aims in reasonable confidence about the likely conduct of others',[66] and the probable actions of government.

In the way in which it affirms the normative importance of the individual while facilitating the citizen's advantageous use of the available social structures, this process value has much to recommend it to our evaluative archetype.

(c) Non-Arbitrariness

Despite its obvious attractions, however, rationality is not sufficient of itself to secure the requisite level of institutional fairness. Pure rationality, after all, would tolerate the mistreatment of an individual citizen in situations where such conduct would be of long-term social benefit. Any procedural insistence on legislative rationality must therefore be connected, at all times, to the system's normative commitment to the protection of the individual. Institutional actions must be both rationally motivated and morally universal. It is arguably more correct, therefore, to characterize the contemporary system's requirement of rationality as the product of a more general belief in the normative essentiality of non-arbitrariness. This principle in effect unites the process values of equality and rationality. It allows for the possibility of individually divergent exercises of public power but demands that these differences of treatment be not only capable of rational justification but, in fact, based on a non-partial objective of universalist inspiration. This value speaks to the citizen's dual interest in state operations, by permitting public actions only when they cannot be construed as the targeted mistreatment of particular groups. State bodies are allowed the freedom to act in the way that they see fit, as long as they are able to justify their conduct rationally by reference to appropriately general principles. Non-arbitrariness effectively functions, on this analysis, as a form of modified rationality. It combines the positive benefits of a pledge of rationality—the recognition of the individual as rational agent, the establishment of expected norms of social and institutional action, the treatment of the individual as an active participant in the system rather than the passive object of its operations, and the acceptance of the possibility that collective acts will produce individually-adverse outcomes where that is required—with a universalist protection against the potentially dehumanizing effects of a purely logical system of governance.

[64] Mashaw, *Due Process*, note 12 above, at 176. [65] Brown, note 11 above, at 1534.
[66] Allan, note 38 above, at 24.

(8) Non-Arbitrariness as a Normative Value

There is considerable academic support for this suggestion of the systemic importance of the principle of non-arbitrariness. Bressman, for example, contends that the formative doctrines of American constitutional history 'understood the aim of the constitutional structure as the protection of individual liberty from arbitrary governmental intrusions'.[67] She argues that the 'risk of arbitrary ... decision-making' is a 'concern of paramount constitutional significance'.[68] Brown agrees, arguing that 'the separation of powers was adopted by the Convention of 1787 ... to preclude the exercise of arbitrary power'.[69] Allan, similarly, sees the rule of law in terms of 'its core ... conviction that law provides the means of protecting each citizen from the arbitrary will of others'.[70] Mashaw's remark that 'th[e] promise of non-arbitrariness helps make acceptable the inevitable sacrifice of private interests in pursuit of collective ends' encapsulates the essence of the principle's appeal for the idealized citizen, charged as that citizen is with assessing the suitability of an institutional theory for a system predicated on the attempted satisfaction of two, essentially opposing, individual desires.[71]

Non-arbitrariness offers a bridge between the citizen's interests in social action and individual protection. It is this duality of concern which underscores the principle's allure for our imagined institutional architect. Devoid of any knowledge of her own personal position, aware of her responsibility to construct an institutional model capable of according appropriate respect to the moral autonomy of each citizen,[72] this individual is torn between an appreciation of the benefits proffered by a system of social coordination and, on the other hand, a defensive desire to protect her interests from potentially adverse outcomes. Non-arbitrariness neatly avoids the worst excesses of these dual objectives. It accepts the possibility (in reality, a virtual certainty) that there will be some decisions which affect the individual negatively. However, it also provides an effective guarantee of institutional fairness, assuring the individual that any disagreeable decisions will be based on objective principles of universal application.

D. Conclusion

The rational assumption at the heart of this chapter's analysis is that, on balance, the situations of all shall be improved by the cohesive system of collective

[67] L Bressman, 'Beyond Accountability: Arbitrariness and Legitimacy in the Administrative State' (2003) 78 *NYU Law Review* 461, at 470. [68] Ibid, at 466.

[69] Brown, note 11 above, at 1534. [70] Allan, note 38 above, at 22.

[71] Mashaw, *Greed, Chaos & Governance*, note 24 above, at 52.

[72] Given that this seems to be the intuitive understanding of social justice upon which our system is based.

cooperation thereby created. As the Tragedy of the Commons demonstrates, organized society has its roots in a recognition that the occasional infliction of individual pain is offset by the advantages which the resulting social system makes available for all. The principle of non-arbitrariness proceeds from an equivalent insight—the willingness of the individual to accept the sporadic but inevitable injury of unfavourable public actions as the necessary price to be paid for an expected overall long-term gain. It thus matches the intuitive criteria outlined above. The fact that the theory rests on so logical an assumption confirms the model's foundational view of the individual citizen as a rationally autonomous agent. Its promise of protection against partial public conduct again reiterates the importance of the individual. Furthermore, its ancillary requirement of legislative rationality secures the citizen's capacity to consciously interact with the organs of the state, accepting their decisions and orienting his conduct accordingly, or questioning the state's reasons and thereby engaging in a dialogic effort to produce a more appropriate outcome. This commitment to rationality fosters the consistency and predictability necessary for individuals to autonomously position themselves so that they take advantage of the possible benefits of social coordination.

In short, therefore, the notion of non-arbitrariness organizes society in such a way that the individual is normatively acknowledged, structurally advantaged, and institutionally protected. It should thus serve as the principled foundation for the attempt to elaborate a theory of institutional justice for the administrative state.

5

A New Theory of Institutional Separation

A. Non-Arbitrariness and the Administrative State

(1) Introduction

It has so far been argued that the traditional tripartite approach to the separation of institutional power is both descriptively and normatively inadequate, and that it ought to be replaced by a new separation of powers system which shows due regard for both the realities of contemporary governance and the normative notions of non-arbitrariness. This chapter attempts to undertake this task. The previous chapter suggested that non-arbitrariness is a critically important principle upon which this proposed model of inter-institutional power distribution ought to be based. Developing a new model of institutional separation accordingly requires that consideration be given both to the way in which government is currently organized, and the extent to which prevailing practices are appropriately non-arbitrary. This should identify ways in which the system at present successfully prevents arbitrary action as well as areas where future reform may be required. As previous chapters have discussed, the emergence of an administrative state has posed perhaps the greatest difficulties for traditional accounts of centralized governance. Accordingly, it is to the current system's treatment of administrative discretion that this chapter will first look.

(2) Administrative Discretion and Non-Arbitrariness

(a) The Transmission Belt Theory

The leading doctrines of traditional constitutional thought, as Bressman noted, were largely animated by a concern to ensure the non-arbitrary character of all exercises of public power. The chief objection to the development of a more *dirigiste* state, as Chapter 3 commented, was its inherent reliance on administrative discretion. In its unpredictable lack of consistent principles or standards, this decision-making discretion carried with it an enduring risk of arbitrary rule. The liberal and Diceyan denunciations of discretion were both motivated by a belief in the law—in either its constitutionalist or rule-of-law form—as a bulwark against arbitrary governance. Discretion, as Davies demonstrated, was understood as both a practical and a symbolic threat to the position of the individual, allowing government agencies an unfettered creative freedom which could potentially be employed in an individual-adverse fashion.

The transmission belt theory of administrative bodies was conceived as a way of addressing the risk of partial or arbitrary rule. The court's insistence on a statutory basis for any delegation of administrative power was designed to link these bodies to the consent-based legitimacy of the elected organ, and also ensure that the powers ultimately exercised were dealt with by reference to clear statutory instructions. This, it was hoped, would avoid the dangers of uncertainty and partiality inevitably involved in discretionary decisions. The rationale for the non-delegation rule rested on the expectation that 'the requirement that agencies conform to specific legislative directives ... [would] cur[b the] official's exploitation of the governmental apparatus to give vent to private prejudice or passion'.[1] In addition, by placing its faith in the innate predictability of publicized statutory standards, the transmission belt model further affirmed the liberal conception of the citizen as an autonomous actor within an orienting legal framework:

> Private autonomy is secured in two ways by this [model]. First, it promotes formal justice by ensuring that the governmental sanctions faced by an individual are rule-governed, which facilitates private avoidance of sanctions and allows interaction with the government on terms most advantageous to the individual. Second ... the requirement [of statutory direction] ensures that sanctions have been validated by a governmental authority to which the individual has consented and therefore the restraints imposed ... may be viewed as self-imposed.[2]

The transmission belt theory is firmly located in the liberal philosophical tradition which treats the individual as the normative foundation of all public power—the very idea which, this chapter has argued, continues to inform our intuitive understanding of the state. As a result, its commitment to counteracting any risk of arbitrary governance is unsurprising. By focusing its efforts on an attempt to 'reduce opportunities for arbitrariness',[3] this model of administrative governance supports the assertion that 'the concern for arbitrariness can be seen as one of the primary evils at which [the] traditional checks and balances are aimed'.[4]

Although it continues to feature prominently in the Irish approach to the issue of administrative delegation,[5] the transmission belt theory has long been abandoned by American constitutionalists. '[A]dequate in theory [but] ... inadequate in practice',[6] it bore little resemblance to the reality of administrative

[1] R Stewart, 'The Reformation of American Administrative Law' (1974–75) 88 *Harvard Law Review* 1667, at 1673.

[2] Ibid, at 1673.

[3] L Bressman, 'Beyond Accountability: Arbitrariness and Legitimacy in the Administrative State' (2003) 78 *NYU Law Review* 461, at 470.

[4] Ibid, at 468.

[5] *Cityview Press v An Chomairle Oiliuna*, [1980] IR 381.

[6] Bressman, note 3 above, at 471.

operations. Transmission belt theorists had sought to deny the very existence in the system of any sort of creative discretion. The emerging administrative state, however, was chiefly characterized by its willingness to adopt such discretionary procedures. Advocates of the progressive approach did not apologize for discretion, but in fact celebrated it. In this situation, it would obviously be impractical and absurd for the courts to impose a constitutional requirement of statutory specificity.

> [M]odern administrative realities are so complex and governmental institutions so dependent on broad authorisations that it is highly unrealistic, if not also likely to be counterproductive, to seek to achieve a regime of narrow delegations.[7]

(b) Discretion as Expertise

A second rationale was thus suggested. This contended that the vesting of discretion in government agencies could be justified on the basis of the professional expertise of these bodies. Policy questions of particular technical complexity were argued to constitute 'precisely the sort of intricate, labour-intensive task for which delegation to an expert body [would be] especially appropriate'.[8] This specialization analysis accepted the place of administrative discretion within the state's governing structures, but did so in a way which sought to deny the possibility of (normatively objectionable) arbitrary outcomes.

> '[E]xpertise' could plausibly be advocated as a solution to the problem of discretion if the agency's goal could be realised through the knowledge that comes from specialized experience. For in that case, the discretion is more apparent than real.... [P]ersons subject to the administrator's control are no more liable to his arbitrary will than are patients remitted to the care of a skilled doctor.[9]

This emphasis on expertise posited the idea that there exists an objectively correct conclusion, to which the specialist administrator would reflexively come. US courts felt accordingly entitled to assert, with confidence, that these delegated powers could be 'expected to be exercised in the coldest neutrality'.[10] This addressed the enduring normative concern for non-arbitrariness by removing the risk of irrational or unpredictable decisions.

Echoes of this analysis appear intermittently in the Irish authorities on this issue. The conventional orthodoxy continues to regard the *Cityview Press* principle as the key criterion of constitutional legitimacy. The courts, however, have occasionally referred to the apparent expertise of subordinate agencies as an additional justification for an impugned delegation of discretionary power. Judges have repeatedly affirmed the appropriateness of delegating authority to

[7] TO Sargentich, 'The Uneasy Constitutional Status of Administrative Agencies (1987) 36 *American University Law Review* 419, at 429.

[8] *Mistretta v United States*, 488 US 361 (1989), at 376.

[9] Stewart, note 1 above, at 1678.

[10] *ICC v Chicago RI & P Railway*, 218 US 88 (1910), at 102, cited in ibid, at fn. 35.

government agencies when 'administrative, regulatory and technical matters' are in question.[11] This reflects an expertise-oriented belief that '[t]he evaluation of complex technical problems is better left to the implementing rules' applied by these bodies.[12] Thus, while the transmission belt theory continues to dominate Irish constitutional discourse on this issue, the asserted expertise of subordinate bodies provides a valuable ancillary support for the curial conviction that these delegations of discretion are, indeed, legitimate.

In the USA, however, the expertise approach ultimately foundered on the reality of administrative operations. An increasingly sceptical public began to 'doubt the very existence of an ascertainable "national welfare" as a meaningful guide to administrative decision[s]', thereby 'sapp[ing] faith in the existence of an objective basis for social choice'.[13]

> [Supporters of delegation] concentrated on the notion that agencies, as experts, would provide the best answers to social problems. No one paused to consider whether those technocrats also would provide the answers that the people wanted.[14]

Displaying a similar sense of world-weary scepticism, citizens no longer trusted in a simple assertion of expertise; they demanded instead to be demonstrably convinced of the benefits of specialized governance. In the absence of a general social consensus on what constituted good government, obviously this was almost impossible to achieve. Furthermore, the complex nature of governmental operations inhibited the ability of administrators to present the sort of record of achievement necessary to sustain public faith in the system's acceptability. Doubts were accordingly expressed over the level of expertise of these administrators, creating a climate of uncertainty which was only exacerbated by the institutional tendency towards non-transparent procedures. Specialization furthermore supported accusations of 'institutional capture' by those organized interests to which an agency was repeatedly exposed in its everyday actions.[15] The expertise which progressives had hailed as a panacea for public ills came thus to be regarded by many as an inegalitarian and inflexible force, wedded to inert and arrogantly misplaced convictions of objective expert 'fact'.[16] Like its transmission belt antecedent, the expertise approach to administrative discretion failed as a result of the reality that it 'described a government that, while perhaps legitimate, simply did not exist'.[17] Their mutual commitment to non-arbitrariness supplied the necessary normative foundations for these theories, but could not rescue them from their operational and descriptive inadequacies.

[11] *Laurentiu v the Minister for Justice*, [1999] 4 IR 26; *Dunne v Minister for the Environment*, [2004] IEHC 304.

[12] *Maher v Minister for Agriculture*, [2001] 2 IR 139, at 245, *per* Fennelly J.

[13] Stewart, note 1 above, at 1683.

[14] Bressman, note 3 above, at 479–480.

[15] Stewart, note 1 above, at 1684–1687.

[16] See JL Mashaw, *Due Process in the Administrative State*, (Yale University Press, 1985), Chapter 1, especially at 17–23.

[17] Bressman, note 3 above, at 464.

(c) Discretion as Interest Representation

Stewart's seminal article thus explained the American jurisprudence in terms of a move away from the transmission belt or expertise theories towards an approach which interpreted administrative discretion as a means of facilitating individual participation in the decision-making process:

> Today, the exercise of agency discretion is inevitably seen as the essentially legislative process of adjusting the competing claims of various private interests affected by agency policy.[18]

This 'interest representation' analysis represented one of the most significant and persuasive early academic attempts to set out a theory of administrative legitimacy which recognized the decentralized reality of contemporary authority. Previous theories could not cope with the fragmented character of the existing system of discretionary governance. Delegation, by establishing scattered repositories of creative power, necessarily obstructed any attempt to justify state decisions by reference to objective or unitary notions of centralized, top-down legitimacy. On the contrary, the 'interest representation' thesis embraced this idea of dispersed power, depicting it as a way of enhancing rather than inhibiting the acceptability of government. The theory equated personal involvement with normative legitimacy. Individual participation was presented as a means of institutional legitimation. The citizen's direct access to the decision-making process acknowledged and affirmed the vital value of individual autonomy, 'respon[ding] to [the] deep strains of individualism and political egalitarianism' in liberal democratic doctrine.[19] Institutional justice was supplied by the systemic 'assurance of fair representation for all affected interests in the exercise of the legislative power delegated to agencies'.[20] By '[s]uch a pluralist theory of legitimacy' could the dual demands of individual respect and collective action be satisfied.[21]

The attractions of this theory as a model of institutional justice were further enhanced by the way in which its belief in participation as a legitimizing value appeared to reflect the public's intuitive conception of procedural fairness. The development of this theory coincided with Thibault and Walker's famous series of sociological studies. These indicated a direct correlation between personal participation in an institutional process and the individual's associated opinion of the procedure's justice:[22]

[18] Stewart, note 1 above, at 1683.
[19] Mashaw, note 16 above, at 23.
[20] Stewart, note 1 above, at 1712.
[21] Ibid.
[22] J Thibault and L Walker, *Procedural Justice: A Psychological Analysis* (Hillsdale, 1975); L Walker, A Lind, and J Thibault, 'The Relation between Procedural and Distributive Justice' (1979) 65 *Virginia Law Review* 1401. See also G Klosko, *Democratic Procedures and Liberal Consensus* (Oxford University Press, 2000) at Chapter 8 for a discussion of the importance of procedural fairness to individual acceptance of particular outcomes.

> [A] litigation model that assigns a high degree of control over the process to the disputing parties . . . will be preferred and perceived as more fair. . . . [A]n adversary decision-making model enhances the perception of both procedural and distributive justice. . . . [They] are related by the element of actual participation in the decisionmaking experience.[23]

Their work 'tends to demonstrate that people seek to maximize their personal involvement in decisional processes and that they gauge the fairness of the process by the degree of that participation'.[24] Recognizing the normative necessity for individual respect, responding to the reality of a decentralized decision-making process, and intuitively reflecting the public's psychological understanding of administrative fairness, this interest representation thesis put forward a highly persuasive case for its adoption as the preferred model of just institutional process.

However, of itself participation does not provide any guarantees in respect of the eventual outcome of the decision-making process. To define the normative entitlement to institutional fairness in terms of pure participation secures only a right to raise individual arguments before the relevant government agency. This does, of course, generate an expectation that the administrative body in question will acknowledge and reflect these arguments in its ultimate conclusions. There is no enforceable requirement, however, to ensure that this is the case.

> [H]earing rights leave untouched the contemporary concern with . . . the unfairness and irrationality that seem to attend bureaucratic implementation of general rules.[25]

Unlike majoritarianism, the interest representation approach does acknowledge the normative importance of the individual citizen. Participation, in itself, is 'instrumental to the achievement of a moral purpose that is itself impossible to describe in instrumental terms, the purpose of treating a man not as a mere means but as an end in himself'.[26] A theory of institutional fairness must be both just and effective, however. An approach to institutional justice which is premised on the provision of pure participation rights lacks the instrumental efficacy necessary to support its claims convincingly. Participation, like majoritarianism, looks to accountability instead of non-arbitrariness as its chief criterion of legitimacy. A bare entitlement to participate in an institutional process cannot supply the assurances of impartiality or rationality which a complete doctrine of institutional fairness would provide. The concentration on interest

[23] Walker, Lind and Thibault, ibid, at 1416.

[24] Mashaw, note 16 above, at 162.

[25] Ibid, at 36.

[26] E Pincoffs, 'Due Process, Fraternity and a Kantian Injunction' in R Pennock and J Chapman (eds), *Due Process* (NYU Press, 1977), at 172, cited in Mashaw, note 16 above, at 191. This analysis can also be criticized on the grounds of its excessive individualism. To define participation in such stridently individualistic terms raises an obvious issue in respect of competing participatory entitlements. Pincoffs does not supply any criteria for distinguishing the claims of citizens to participation—this thus overlooks the universality which, it was argued, is an essential feature of any operable theory of social or institutional justice.

representation risks becoming 'so fixated on the concern for political accountability ... that [it] overlook[s] an important obstacle to agency legitimacy: the concern for administrative arbitrariness'[27] which 'is not only a ubiquitous feature of the administrative state but of the constitutional structure'.[28] The interest representation model effectively repeats the mistakes of majoritarianism by relying on an overly formal technique of egalitarian legitimacy. Allowing individual participation certainly appears to acknowledge the entitlement of each citizen to institutional respect. Without more, however, this ostensible commitment to individual autonomy is logically insufficient. To offer a guarantee of input without influence is effectively to deny the dignitary values upon which the entitlement is allegedly founded. Walker, Lind, and Thibault agree:

> We conclude that essential causal mechanisms [in the equation of fairness with participation] involve the participant's perception that he exercises some measure of control over the adversary process not only on the conduct of the proceedings *but also on its outcome.*[29]

Participation rights can obviously play an important part in the development of an appropriate process of institutional fairness. They do not exhaust the full range of procedural values which a normatively legitimate system ought to secure, however.

(d) Presidential Control

This objection applies with equal force to Mashaw's proposed solution to the difficulties involved in the delegation of discretionary powers to the diverse agencies of administrative governance. Relying on the President's position at the apex of the administrative system, Mashaw argues that 'vague delegations to administrative agencies' could be plausibly construed 'as a device for facilitating responsiveness to voter preferences expressed in presidential elections'.[30] Freed of the pork-barrel politics of locally organized legislative elections, Mashaw regards the presidential election as an opportunity for the citizen to put forward a more nationally oriented conception of good government.[31] 'Citizens', after all, 'vote for a president almost wholly on the perception of the difference that one ... candidate might make to general government policies.'[32] Furthermore, this identification of the presidency with the actions and operations of central government ensures the continued responsiveness of the incumbent office-holder to the demands of the public.

27 Bressman, note 3 above, at 462–463. 28 Ibid, at 502.

29 Walker, Lind and Thibault, note 22 above, at 1417. Emphasis added.

30 JL Mashaw, *Greed, Chaos, and Governance* (Yale University Press, 1997), at 152.

31 This view of the role of representation in government shares some similarities with traditional republican theories in the form discussed, for example, by Madison and James Harrington. See J Madison, A Hamilton, and J Jay, *The Federalist Papers* (I Kramnick, ed., Penguin, 1987); and J Harrington, *The Commonwealth of Oceana* (1656).

32 Mashaw, *Greed, Chaos, and Governance*, note 30 above, at 152.

Obviously, the preliminary problem with this theory of 'presidential control' is its inapplicability to the Westminster model of cabinet government. There is no equivalent direct election of an administrative or executive figurehead in the Irish or British systems of government.

It might be possible to construct an argument which approximates the doctrine of ministerial accountability to the idea of presidential control. Mashaw's model allows the individual voter distinct opportunities to separately express a local and national electoral preference. The fact that the Irish system conflates these choices into a single ballot could be characterized as a way of assessing the relative intensity of these discrete issues of local or national interest. Aware that they are being asked to elect an executive as well as a legislature, individual voters can act in accordance with the comparative strength of their concern for local representation or national administration.

Nonetheless, even if Mashaw's model of presidential control can be so revised for the Irish electoral environment, it remains normatively unacceptable. Mashaw's understanding of the administration simply replaces one form of accountability with another, on the basis of the latter's allegedly superior efficacy. It once again trusts to popular accountability as the touchstone of administrative legitimacy, thereby overlooking the normative importance of the non-arbitrary principle. In reality, it offers little more than a form of modified majoritarianism. As the previous section on participation showed, the process values of an institutionally fair system must extend beyond the provision of a bare individual entitlement to express an opinion.

(3) Non-Arbitrariness in the Courts

(a) A Concern for Non-Arbitrariness

Furthermore, the academic emphasis on popular accountability as a legitimating force is not reflected in the case law of the courts on agency actions. Chapter 3 described, in some detail, the increasing curial insistence on an administrative adherence to the dictates of procedural justice. It is widely accepted across the common law world that 'all areas of administration are now, in principle, subject to the requirements of procedural fairness'.[33] The aim of the *Nicholson–Baldwin–McDonald* line of authority is to secure an improvement in the quality of administrative decision making through the development of advanced procedural provisions. These judicial demands are inspired, therefore, by an enduring concern for non-arbitrariness rather than accountability. The doctrine of procedural fairness might provide the individual with increased opportunities to participate in the decision-making process but these are intended, not as an interactive acknowledgement of the citizen's autonomy, but as a means of

[33] DJ Galligan, *Due Process and Fair Procedures* (Clarendon Press, 1996), at 330.

enhancing the decision-making capacity of the administrative system. These process improvements do not provide a guarantee that the appropriate outcome will be reached in every individual case, of course.[34] They should generate the sort of system-wide enhancement that would support the state's assertion of institutional justice, however. Of course, this will often facilitate increased citizen participation in the decision-making process. To the extent that this provides individuals with greater opportunities for interacting with government, however, this is an ancillary benefit. Interest representation is not the dominant justification for these judicial decisions. Principles of good governance should instead be conceived and assessed in terms of their probable impact on the risk of arbitrary rule. Accountability is a subordinate concern.

Does this judicial process of proceduralization adequately protect the individual from arbitrary exercises of public power? The development in cases like *Re HK*[35] and *Schmidt*[36] of a general duty to act fairly, freed from the traditional fetters of the classificatory approach,[37] certainly seemed to indicate that this would, in time, be the case. Mullan welcomed the doctrine as an important institutional development:

> [F]airness, if developed properly by the courts, will lead to a highly desirable simplifying of the theoretical underpinnings of the law in this area. It will ... lead to a situation where the right question is at long last being asked: what procedural protections, if any, are necessary for this particular decision-making process.[38]

This confidence, however, proved to be misplaced. The potential of the doctrine of procedural fairness has in practice been hampered by a 'deeply fundamental and conceptually flawed reliance on separation of powers anachronisms'.[39]

(b) The Influence of the Separation of Powers

Historically the inactive formalism of the traditional approach had allowed the courts to involve themselves only in matters which were regarded as judicial (or, subsequently, quasi-judicial) in nature. Such 'procedural review proceeded from the assumption that the role of the courts could be limited to preserving the integrity of the judicial process'.[40] The risk of arbitrary action in areas formally defined as non-judicial was regarded as a matter occurring outside the presumed

[34] To provide such a guarantee of absolute veracity would obviously require the courts effectively to act as the decision-making body in every case. This would privilege the interests of the individual in personal protection at the expense of his interest in collective social action.

[35] [1967] 2 QB 617.

[36] *Schmidt v Secretary of State for Home Affairs*, [1969] 2 Ch 149.

[37] According to this approach (as discussed in earlier chapters) the obligations imposed on a body were determined by the court's classification of it as a judicial, or non-judicial matter.

[38] DJ Mullan, 'Fairness: The New Natural Justice' (1975) 25 *University of Toronto Law Journal* 281, at 315.

[39] J Edley Jr, 'The Governance Crisis, Legal Theory and Political Ideology' (1991) 41 *Duke Law Journal* 561, at 562.

[40] G Cartier, 'Procedural Fairness in Legislative Functions: The End of Judicial Abstinence?' (2003) 53 *University of Toronto Law Journal* 217, at 222.

parameters of legitimate judicial action. The interests of the individual in whole areas of government action were abandoned to the unacceptably bare accountability mechanisms of the electoral process.

The development of a general duty of fairness appeared to present the prospect of a more sophisticated and contextual approach to the issue of arbitrariness. The doctrine's utility has been constrained, however, by the effective reintroduction of formal institutional classifications. Motivated by the combined effects of the Diceyan distinction between law and politics, and, on the other hand, the institutional paradigms perpetuated by the tripartite separation of powers, the courts have proved unwilling to apply the doctrine to those matters of 'policy' which were traditionally reserved for legislative consideration.[41] Procedural fairness developed as a reaction to the restrictive futility of these institutional classifications. Separable in the abstract but indistinguishable in action, the tripartite notion of definable legislative, executive, and judicial functions could not be satisfactorily employed in practice. Yet the courts continue to resile from the active supervision of 'legislative' procedures. Decisions like *Inuit*, *TD*, and *Hammersmith LBC* demonstrate a continuing judicial reticence about involving themselves in those policy-making procedures from which they were historically excluded.[42] This is based chiefly on characterizing these questions as legislative concerns. This essentially reasserts the discredited rationale of the earlier case law, reiterating the idea that, by virtue of their innate characteristics, certain governmental functions can only be exercised by the relevant state institution. This approach perpetuates the failed institutional trichotomy—what Edley describes as the crude paradigms of judge as adjudicator, official as expert, and legislator as politician—upon which the separation of powers depends, thereby overlooking the lessons of earlier chapters that:

> [s]cholarship attempting to divine clear doctrinal guidance from these separation of powers nostrums will, like similarly reasoned judicial opinions, fail to persuade because the boundary problems of the trichotomy require that in interesting cases, we will be unable to disentangle the three paradigms.[43]

The courts, on this analysis, are restrictively conceived as capable of acting only when issues of adjudicatory fairness arise. This is reflected, for example, in the way in which the availability of judicial review was defined in *Datafin* in terms of the consequences for the citizen of the decision in question.[44] The review process was restricted to the correction of those institutional wrongs which have

[41] Obviously the Diceyan notion has been more influential in the UK and Canada, while the separation of powers has had more impact in the USA. The Irish case law has been affected by both ideas.

[42] *AG v Inuit Tapirisat*, [1980] 2 SCR 735; *TD v Minister for Education*, [2001] 4 IR 259; *R. v Secretary of State for the Environment, ex p Hammersmith and Fulham LBC*, [1991] 1 AC 521.

[43] Edley, note 39 above, at 574–575.

[44] *R. v Panel on Takeovers and Mergers, ex p Datafin*, [1987] 1 QB 815; [1987] 1 All ER 564; [1987] 2 WLR 699.

actually impacted on an individual. Judges will intervene where an individual alleges that he has been unfairly treated in the application or enforcement of a particular policy. They will not examine the procedure by which a policy was initially formulated, however, believing this to be outside their area of competence. Enquiries are not conducted into allegations of arbitrary action at the policy-making stage. This implicitly confines the scope of permissible court action to those administrative procedures capable of being approximated to the traditional judicial function:

> In other words, their involvement in the enlargement of the field of application of procedural fairness amounted to a recognition of the legitimacy of the administrative state, of the fact that, even though administrative decision makers take decisions based on policy, they exercise their powers in a sphere governed by legal principles and, notably, procedural fairness. . . . This evolution in the attitude of the courts . . . did not have its equivalent in the field of . . . decisions of a general nature and based on policy considerations. In regard to this kind of decision, the courts persisted in viewing their roles as preserving the integrity of the legislative process, which they did precisely by refraining from intervening, in procedure, as well as in substance.[45]

The courts' conception of procedural fairness thus appears limited to the enforcement of individualized justice in adjudicatory proceedings. On the basis of this case law, the obligation of government to act fairly in the exercise of public power does not extend to the way in which general principles are institutionally elaborated. Given the impact which such principles or policies can have on individual or social action, it is questionable whether the courts' absence from this area can be said to provide adequate protection for the critical value of non-arbitrariness.

(c) The Risk of Arbitrariness in Non-Judicial Areas

Is this limited procedural protection sufficient to satisfy the putative principle of institutional non-arbitrariness? This concept, it should be recalled, was argued to constitute a general legitimating value of good governance. Procedural fairness, in its present limited form, thus appears somewhat inadequate. The extension of the doctrine of fairness to administrative agencies was based, in part, on judicial recognition of the fact that these bodies now exercised extensive decision-making powers. It would have been remiss of the courts to abdicate their responsibilities in this area. The delegation of discretionary powers to subordinate bodies, however, has not been restricted to issues of an adjudicatory nature. These bodies typically wield a broad range of public powers, drawn from across the traditional trichotomy's range of institutional functions. Why then should judicial supervision occur in cases where policies are applied, but not where they are developed? The creative power of administrative bodies is currently justified by reference to the idea of ministerial accountability. However, as previous

[45] Cartier, note 40 above, at 237.

sections have shown, of itself accountability is insufficient to secure the interests of the individual citizen. This is especially the case in a situation where such electoral accountability is more hypothetical than real.

Furthermore, to constrain the development of process values by reference to the theory of the separation of powers betrays a lack of appreciation of the normative origins of the tripartite theory.

> Procedural requirements and separated powers are simply different limitations on the exercise of government power, sharing a common goal: to restrict arbitrary government action that is likely to harm the rights of individuals.[46]

A doctrine of procedural fairness taken seriously should attempt to ensure non-arbitrariness in the discretionary exercise of *all* administrative powers. The failure of the courts to enforce this doctrine is disappointing.

> When the court rejects a claim because it concerns a field of public responsibility, or department of government, which is inherently immune from legal control, it acts arbitrarily—failing to apply ordinary legal principles to the circumstances of the particular case.[47]

To confine the institutional assurance of non-arbitrariness to cases where policy is administratively applied does not reflect its asserted status as the central principle of procedural justice. This excludes the individual from the stage at which policy is actually established—which is also the point, therefore, at which appropriate procedural involvement would have the most impact.

> [O]ur self-respect is called into question not only when our rights are affected by procedures to which we are not admitted, but also when we are excluded from a process of social decision making that defines or elaborates the set of rights we all hold.[48]

In an era of decentralized administrative authority, a continued adherence to the simple tripartite conception of institutional operations is unacceptable and inappropriate. The functional paradigms upon which the separation of powers is predicated bear little resemblance to the realities of an administrative state in which a bewildering array of government agencies exercise a broad range of discretionary powers. In this organizational context, a three-sizes-fit-all approach—which was always problematic to apply—is simply unsustainable. Contemporary governance, if it is to be legitimate, must insist on the contextual enforcement of the principle of non-arbitrariness across the spectrum of administrative activity.

> If the justification for judicial review is the need for independent appraisal of administrative action, inspecting its impact on the persons most closely affected, the court's approach must be sensitive to all the circumstances.[49]

[46] R Brown, 'Separated Powers and Ordered Liberty' (1990) 139 *University of Pennsylvania Law Review* 1513, at 1556.

[47] TRS Allan, *Law, Liberty and Justice* (Clarendon Press, 1993), at 212.

[48] Mashaw, *Due Process*, note 16 above, at 178.

[49] Ibid, at 185.

To absolutely exclude the possibility of raising allegations of arbitrary action in certain contexts is impermissible:

> The application of a principle of justice or fairness in all the circumstances inevitably circumvents, and ultimately eliminates, narrower rules which unduly circumscribe the court's jurisdiction.[50]

The separation of powers, with its *a priori* insistence on legislative primacy (and, indeed, exclusivity) in particular affairs, thus represents a debilitating force in the prevailing institutional structure. The tripartite theory inculcates a judicial reluctance to scrutinize the administrative exercise of creative powers which is normatively unjustifiable.

> Administrative law doctrine therefore goes astray when it assumes (or pretends) that judicial deference is equivalent to political neutrality. . . . [B]road deference to the agency amounts to an alliance by the judiciary with the executive, which disservices the system of checks and balances; it abdicates any direct judicial responsibility for the quality of governmental actions.[51]

That the principle of non-arbitrariness is prima facie unenforceable in such significant areas of administrative activity fatally undermines the current system's claims of institutional justice. The next section will address this failing by attempting to imagine how this vital legitimizing value, freed of the functional limitations of the separation of powers, might be adequately enforced in the contemporary state.

B. A New Model of Non-Arbitrariness

(1) Legitimate Governance and Arbitrary Rule

The discussion has so far concluded that an intuitively appropriate theory of institutional justice should be founded on a principle of non-arbitrariness. The eighteenth-century conception of the state, for example, can be so understood. Consent and generality, as the traditional techniques of liberal legitimacy, derive their normative force from an underlying commitment to the defence of the individual against the arbitrary actions of the collective. Premised on the historical assumption that state power would only be exercised by means of public rules, this idealized procedure was perceived as a process of rule creation and rule application. The institutional insistence on the consistent application of general rules was obviously animated by a concern for non-arbitrariness. Generality removed the risk that rules could be unfairly targeted at particular groups. A guarantee of generality provided the universality necessary to properly protect the individual's autonomy.

[50] Ibid, at 196. [51] Edley, note 39 above, at 600.

Such universality was more difficult to secure at the legislative stage, however. At the moment of rule creation, the relevant body would obviously choose from a range of available options, most of which would adversely impact on particular groups. The danger of arbitrariness at this stage was addressed by the involvement of the individual in electing the relevant legislative institution. This direct input removed the threat that arbitrary provisions would be imposed imperialistically without reference to the desires or demands of individual citizens. Participation supplied the level of consent necessary to justify the possibility that the individual, or group, might be disproportionately affected by particular rules. Specific rules might impact on individuals but they would be rationally motivated by the proclaimed public interest rather than arbitrarily adopted by an unrepresentative elite. The possibility of legislative pain was accordingly accepted and shared on a rational and non-arbitrary basis. Consent and generality combined to ensure the non-arbitrariness of the historical conception of the institutional state.

(a) The Problem of Administrative Discretion

Legitimacy, from a liberal perspective, requires, therefore, that the state be structured so as to minimize the risk of arbitrary rule. The nature of the administrative state is such, however, that the traditional techniques of generality and consent no longer suffice. The central problem for contemporary institutional structures has been the proliferation of sub-governmental bodies with extensive discretionary powers. Statutory delegations to administrative entities have been expressed with such elasticity that it is impossible to claim with any conviction that the individual voter has consented to the exercise of these powers. Similarly, bureaucratic government has become so specialized and broadly dispersed that it is impossible to ensure generality across the system. The discretionary nature of most administrative powers has only served to exacerbate this issue. Inured against complaint by their assertion of expertise, these bodies tend to operate in an effectively rule-free environment, on a largely autonomous basis—thereby generating an obvious danger that individual administrators will adopt and enforce positions of unacceptable arbitrariness.

How then can these difficulties of discretion be addressed? As this chapter has seen, the earliest attempts to do so sought to deny the reality of administrative discretion. In a system of such extensively devolved decision-making powers, such an approach was inevitably doomed. Discretion is an inescapable element of the administrative state.

> Squeezing discretion out of a statutory-administrative system is indeed so difficult that one is tempted to posit a 'Law of Conservation of Administrative Discretion'. According to that law, the amount of discretion in an administrative system is always constant. Elimination of discretion at one choice point merely causes the discretion that had been exercised there to migrate elsewhere in the system.[52]

[52] Mashaw, *Greed, Chaos, and Governance*, note 30 above, at 154.

The acknowledgment of this institutional inevitability leaves the analyst with two choices: to accept the impossibility of elaborating a unified model of legitimacy for the administrative state; or to attempt to construct a theory of legitimacy which accepts, embraces, and, perhaps, even builds upon this administrative discretion.

(b) Procedural Justice as a Response to Discretion

The judicial development of a doctrine of procedural justice pursues the latter course. This approach acknowledges the existence of a rule-free void of administrative discretion, and attempts to fill it with procedural principles. Procedural justice is employed as an attempt to structure the exercise of administrative discretion in such a way that the risk of arbitrary decisions is thereby reduced.

The doctrine in its current incarnation is constrained, however, by the continued reluctance of the judiciary to involve themselves in presumptively 'legislative' issues of policy creation. The institutional paradigms at the heart of the tripartite separation of powers have conditioned the courts to restrict the doctrine's application to the administrative areas whose activities approximate to the adjudicatory individualism which typified traditional court action. The consequence of this is that non-arbitrariness is effectively enforced only in particular parts of the administrative system, exerting a limited level of influence which does not reflect its putative position as the foundational principle of institutional legitimacy. The solution, it would seem, is to extend the doctrine of procedural fairness to encompass all the administrative machinery of the state. The judicial imposition of process values across the administrative spectrum would address the danger of arbitrary action wherever it might arise. The abandonment of separation of powers notions of inherent institutional restraints would allow the courts to take seriously their task of securing the freedom of the individual from the risk of arbitrary rule.

This type of approach, if taken to its logical conclusion, would imply the existence of an unfettered curial power to enforce non-arbitrariness wherever judges see fit. The proceduralist project would expose all areas of administrative—indeed, governmental—action to the intensive scrutiny of the courts. Judicial insistence on enhanced procedural provisions, it is argued, would protect the citizenry from arbitrary (and thus illegitimate) government action. Separation of powers advocates, however, would oppose this development on the grounds that the courts are functionally ill equipped to exercise such an extensive and interventionist power. The separation of powers theory, in its most abstract form, is predicated on an assumption that governance requires the input of different types of institution. Chapter 2 has already outlined the limitations of the tripartite theory's particular conception of the functional capacities of existing institutions. The distinctions this specific model draws in the abstract cannot be so easily enforced in practice. However, there would appear to be some merit in the theory's more abstract insight into the organization of government. The courts, in their institutional operations, have frailties as well as force.

> [Judicial intervention] is praised for its neutrality, concern for consistency and attention to reasoned elaboration. However, this is accompanied by a set of companion vices: the method tends to be expensive, removed from political accountability, proceduralistic, stylistic, arcane, conservative and past-focused.[53]

Unrestrained proceduralism, by establishing an effective judicial hegemony over all decision-making processes, would be likely to result in institutional sclerosis. The theory of the separation of powers, with its model of discrete organizational structures, recognizes the operational importance of ensuring the existence of alternative methods of institutional action. The absolute dominance of a single institutional ideal (like the adjudicative fairness of the courts) would institutionalize in the system a series of debilitating weaknesses alongside the intended normative strengths—a problematic situation which the separation of powers seeks to preclude.

(2) Alternative Institutions and the Allocation of Power

A theory of separation can therefore be presented as a response to the structural necessity for a selection of institutional forms. The tripartite theory of the separation of powers seems to be based on relatively sound organizational instincts. The difficulty with any model of separated powers, however, is that it must also provide determinate criteria for the distribution of decision-making authority between the distinct institutional organs which it has established. A simple demand for structural separation in any form is normatively insufficient. Clear instructions for the assembly and operation of the system are necessary if the aspiring institutional architect is to have any hope of constructing a workable model of governance from the separate constituent elements supplied. A theory of separation must therefore provide normative justification for the particular power allocation it prescribes. It is not enough to propose a scheme of separation for separation's sake—the model must describe, explain, and, thereby, help to predict the vesting of particular powers in individual institutions.

(a) Functional Utility

As outlined in Chapter 3, the modern theory of the separation of powers tends to organize institutional competences by a process of functional classification. Administrative tasks are distributed in accordance with an initial identification of them as legislative, executive, or judicial in nature. Power is allocated on the basis of an analytical estimation that it 'belongs' to a particular body—that is, that it conforms to the institutional archetype according to which the body's

[53] Edley, note 39 above, at 570.

inherent competence has been defined. The theory of the separation of powers describes and depicts the organs of government in terms of the decision processes with which they are traditionally identified.

> [This] trichotomy of paradigmatic decisionmaking methods ... represent[s] different forms of reasoning which we might expect to be used by those who wield the state's power: adjudicatory fairness, science and politics. They are rooted in the crude images of the judge, the faceless technocratic expert and the politician.[54]

These institutional paradigms are taken to characterize the essence of each institution's function. The entitlement of an institution to exercise power is determined by reference to these set conceptions of the type of power typically vested in that institution.[55] The particular design of the overall system of power distribution is clearly premised on an overarching conviction that specific organs of government (or, more abstractly, the institutional paradigms which these organs represent) should be entrusted with particular powers and responsibilities. As currently constituted, the system depends, in its operations, on the existence of a determinate model of government in which function can be matched with institutional form.

The first problem with this approach is, obviously, that is has proved inoperable in practice. Chapter 2 detailed at some length the indeterminacy inherent in the tripartite understanding of institutional functions. In many cases, it is impossible to convincingly claim that a particular power can only be identified with a single organ of government. The procedural paradigms which define each function are practically imprecise, often failing to provide a clear answer to questions of institutional competence.

> Although the decisionmaking paradigms are arguably distinct in the abstract, in practice they are commingled and inseparable except where subjected to artificial and distorted conceptual violence. ... Where one paradigm ends and another begins is a matter of arbitrary perceptions or skilful advocacy.[56]

There is, however, a more foundational difficulty with this type of functional approach. Contemporary governance assumes that jurisdictional powers properly belong to those institutions with which they are formally identified. How do such ideas of institutional ownership arise? Chapter 2 has already identified the artificiality inherent in adhering to a formal understanding of government for the sake of form alone. Governance is a matter of administration, not art. The model of the 'separation of powers is not', after all 'an end in itself'.[57] A theory of government does not exist in the abstract—it is adopted on the basis of a belief that, in practice, it will prove effective. The process by which a power is allocated

[54] Ibid, at 568.

[55] For a discussion of the Irish and American case law in which this approach is evident, see Chapter 2.

[56] Edley, note 39 above, at 570–571.

[57] Brown, note 46 above, at 1516.

to a particular organ must be based on a belief that this body is especially suited to undertaking this task. Scrutiny of such allocations over time can, of course, allow careful observers to predict the pattern of future power distributions accurately. This is, however, a purely empirical approach. This type of analysis overlooks the casual origins of the institutional arrangement. It describes, but does not properly explain, why power is vested in an individual entity.

The formalistic approach to the separation of powers, which presently predominates, dictates, for example, that legislative tasks are those entrusted to the legislature. It does not seek to rationalize this occurrence, or to account for the way in which the idea or model of legislative tasks came to develop. Given the concern of any institutional theory to ensure operational efficacy, the model's initial determination of duties could only have been based on an assessment of institutional suitability. These bodies are, however, the individual incarnations of a generalized trinity of institutional paradigms. Such an assessment of suitability must be based on a conviction that the strengths of a particular institutional paradigm are especially appropriate for the exercise of the power at issue. The institutional or procedural characteristics of the legislature, for example, must have been regarded as rendering it the appropriate organ in which to vest those powers which would thereby come to be known as legislative tasks. The system thus depends on a model in which a body's functional qualities determine the institutional form. This, in turn, subsequently, determines and justifies its jurisdiction over particular functions.

If, however, the respective government body's functional or procedural characteristics decisively influenced the system's initial allocations of power, an obvious difficulty arises. Institutional or procedural characteristics are generally designed to perform a particular purpose. They do not spring fully formed from the brow of their constitutional creators. Rather, they are developed to address a particular need, or to advance an individual objective. A procedure is an inherently instrumental mechanism, established with a specific purpose, or purposes, in mind. Once again, questions of casual circularity arise. To return to the example of the legislature, this analysis does not advance our understanding of the system's foundations. If the system is to define legislative powers as those vesting in the legislature, a problem is thereby posed as to the conceptual origins of the initial notion of legislative competence. It was argued in the previous paragraph that the vesting of powers in the legislature could only have been justified by a belief that it was best suited to exercise those particular powers. This opinion must have proceeded from an assessment that the legislature's particular characteristics made it the most suitable body in which to vest 'legislative' functions. However, these institutional characteristics could only have been elaborated on the basis of an earlier conception of the legislature's competence. According to this explanation, institutional functions were defined by reference to a conception of institutional appropriateness which, itself, was determined on the basis of the qualities and characteristics which that institution established to allow it to fulfil its function. On this analysis, a particular procedural or decision-making paradigm is adopted to allow an institution to perform its function, the success of which is then argued to justify future allocations of functions. This logic is unacceptably circular. Procedural characteristics, it would seem, could not have served as the original foundation for the system's specific model of institutional design.

The contemporary approach to the separation and distribution of powers is thus confused by its focus on a reciprocal relationship between institutional capacity, function, and form. The prevailing judicial approach to the identification of functions seems to depend upon a capacity-oriented model of institutional forms. However, the ability of a government body to perform a particular function effectively should properly be understood as a response to, rather than a reason for, the allocation to it of such powers. Questions of procedural capacity and institutional competence are inextricably linked. Neither is, of itself, determinative of the issue at hand. Institutional paradigms do not exist for their own sake—they represent a particular approach, the suitability of which can only be assessed in the context of the exercise of an individual government power. Capacity and function can only properly be examined where they coincide. They must therefore be regarded as the product of some deeper conception of appropriate governance. The contemporary rationalizing of particular tasks as legislative, executive, or judicial on the basis of a belief that these institutions, designed to fulfil such functions, are thereby best equipped to undertake these tasks is an example of wholly inadequate *ex post facto* reasoning. It is but an empirical shorthand for the allocation of institutional responsibilities. Inspired by concerns of convenience rather than analysis, it offers guidance without enlightenment. The court's concentration on the elided issues of capacity, function, and form thus obscures the more foundational premises from which these organizational and institutional paradigms must have been developed.

(b) Decision-Making Processes as Normative 'Goods'?

An alternative explanation for allocating institutional competences in accordance with this decisional trichotomy might propose that each procedure, in itself, represents an objectively 'good' way of exercising public power. This rationale suggests that the procedures have certain normative advantages in themselves, which thereby legitimize their usage. This argument seeks to escape from the circularity of a function-oriented approach by offering an ontological rather than an instrumental justification for the techniques' institutional employment. The originating impulse for the tripartite theory is explained as an acknowledgement of the inherent merits of these threefold decision-making methods, rather than as a response to an impossibly *a priori* idea of institutional function. Adjudicatory fairness, science, and politics all have some intrinsic value, it could be argued, and deserve—if not require—institutional representation in any eventual organizational structure. Construction of an institutional model begins, on this analysis, with the decision-making paradigms, proceeding to allocate institutional tasks on the basis of the system's assessment of which approach is more appropriate. This therefore resembles the contemporary curial approach, differing from the dominant conception of the separation of powers only in the way in which it explains the origins of the tripartite model of institutional organization.

This analysis would obviously encounter the same difficulties of indeterminate functional identification as have afflicted the traditional approach. Again, however, there is a broader objection to the idea that the existing system of separation derives from an institutional trichotomy of 'good' decisional procedures. As Edley points out, the merits of a particular institutional paradigm depend entirely on the perspective from which they are assessed. To justify an individual allocation of administrative competence on the basis of the operational virtues of the institution in question is to overlook the fact that this qualitative calculation is entirely contextual. Any assertion of institutional suitability is necessarily affected by this 'notion of normative or attributive duality'.

> Each decision-making paradigm has associated with it a collection of positive and negative attributes, or normative associations—a kind of Jekyll-and-Hyde dualism that, in a given situation, may make it debatable as to which paradigm applies.[58]

The Janus-like merits of the judicial process, for example, have been outlined above. Such normative indeterminacy poses obvious practical problems:

> These dualities permit advocates or judges, in particular cases, to emphasise selectively one side or the other to support a particular claim . . . . The observer is often left confused and wondering what principle causes one side of the duality to prevail.[59]

More profoundly, however, this attributive duality undermines any suggestion that the processes can be normatively interpreted as inherently good. There is no objective criterion of decisional value which would support an assertion of intrinsic institutional utility. This is especially problematic in light of the fact that the very procedural quality which is argued to constitute a good is often simultaneously the source of opponents' objections to its use. Thus, for example, the 'politics paradigm promises participation, democracy, responsiveness and accountability' but 'carries with it the negative attributes of subjectivity, wilfulness, majority tyranny ... and even irrationality'.[60] In the absence of an authoritative yardstick of institutional utility, these decision-making processes cannot confidently be proclaimed as normative goods. Similarly, they thus cannot serve as the foundations for legitimate institutional action.

[58] Edley, note 39 above, at 570. [59] Ibid, at 570. [60] Ibid, at 570.

(c) A Duality of Interests?

Casting doubt on the possibility of any determinate estimation of institutional efficacy or value, this attributive duality raises considerable problems. As already detailed, the traditional approach seeks to address this duality by way of functional classification. The preliminary step of identifying the impugned function establishes a presumptive position on the advantages, or otherwise, of the institution in question. This indeterminate duality is refracted through the prism of asserted functional appropriateness. Thus, if it is decided that a power is legislative in nature, the court's preference for adjudicative proceduralism is interpreted as excessively inefficient, instead of suitably protective. However, it has been well established by this point that the initial stage in this analytical process is unacceptably imprecise. The identification of a specific function depends on a tripartite model of institutional paradigms which are, in practice, impossible to distinguish and employ. Any identification of the function depends on a necessarily circular analysis of institutional capacity and functional competence. Furthermore, an institutional process cannot be characterized as inherently good or bad on the basis of a particular functional perspective because that functional perspective cannot be authoritatively established.

This focus on function errs in attempting to avoid the effects of attributive duality, rather than to understand its origins. The traditional approach posits the existence of a trinity of procedural paradigms, thereby seeking to replace the indeterminate duality of values with a determinate, and thus operable, trichotomy of institutional images. The problem of these central case procedures appearing to be simultaneously good and bad is submerged by the introduction of an external frame of institutional reference. In the absence of an objective notion of institutional value, the asserted model becomes, in itself, a good. The utility of this approach has obviously been crippled by the fatal indeterminacy of the initial assessment of function. More seriously, however, a concentration on questions of functional identification has befuddled the courts, imposing a layer of conceptual confusion which directs attention away from the tripartite model's failure to engage with this normative duality. The model cannot claim legitimacy if it is unclear as to the merits or otherwise of its paradigmatic institutional processes.

There is a need, therefore, for a theory of institutional separation to examine and embrace this normative duality. Perceptions of institutional utility, it was argued, are entirely dependent on the point of view from which they are assessed. The key, therefore, is to contemplate the possible perspectives from which the value of particular institutional procedures might be considered.

That there is this conceptual duality suggests that the viewpoints at issue are twofold—a dichotomy of interests which might reasonably approximate to society's twin objectives. The individual citizen's relationship with the state, an earlier section argued, is characterized by his opposing interests in successful collective conduct. On the one hand, the entire purpose of the organized state is to allow individuals to achieve together that which they could not apart. However, the individual will also seek to ensure that this collective action does not impinge upon her own position. The advantages—from the citizen's point of view—of a specific institutional procedure thus depend on the individual interest being advanced at that particular time. This duality derives from the duopoly of individual interests at the heart of all societal action—the desire of the individual in the pre-legal position to obtain the benefits of associational activity while defending his own interests.

The attributive duality of the institutional paradigms can reasonably be so construed. If a procedure is intended to promote the individual's interest in effective collective action, any intervention on the part of the courts will be received with considerable scepticism. By contrast, the individual is likely to seek the protection of the courts' adjudicative proceduralism when her interests are under attack. Therefore, the objection to judicial involvement in 'legislative' affairs is not motivated by issues of functional capacity. Rather, it is a reaction to the excessive individualism which would result from a system-wide insistence on adherence to adjudicative procedures. In a similar way, the exclusion of the courts from whole areas of administrative action represents unacceptable prioritizing of the individual's interest in effective social action over that in personalized protection.

Of course, these interests tend to coincide in any administrative action. The government is forced at all times to attempt to balance the normative force of these opposing impulses. The systemic adoption of a single institutional process—such as the court's concept of procedural fairness—would thus be objectionable on the basis that it pursues only one of these foundational social objectives. Alternative institutional forms are required so that this duality of interests can be adequately catered for.

(3) Addressing the Duality of Individual Interests

The separation of powers attempted to achieve this by presumptively allocating particular functions to a series of institutional paradigms in which the relative importance of these two interests was appropriately and consistently calibrated. The utility of this approach has been crippled, however, by the fatal indeterminacy of its initial assessment of function.

The obvious solution would be to classify institutions by constituency instead of by function. This type of approach has been employed in the past, of course. The mixed theory of government—from which the contemporary concept of separation of powers in part evolved—rested on the idea of deriving socially appropriate actions from the intermingling of opposing interests:

Like ... distinct powers in mechanics the [different constituencies] jointly impel the machine of government in a direction different from what either acting by itself, would have done; but, at the same time in a direction partaking of each, and formed out of all; a direction which constitutes the true line of liberty and happiness of the community.[61]

The logic of the proposed approach is identical—only the identity of the constituent social elements differs.

This constituency-oriented technique directly addresses and resolves the central issue of attributive duality. If an institution is defined as attempting to further a particular interest, a clear view of its strengths and weakness can be authoritatively adopted. The normative basis for its actions is clarified, thereby allowing the appropriateness of its involvement in particular issues to be assessed adequately and consistently. This avoids the indeterminacy inherent in the functional approach, supplying the analytical precision necessary to assist efforts at striking an appropriate balance between the opposing impulses at the heart of the administrative state. The exaltation of one interest at the expense of the other can be prevented by involving institutions which represent each position in any process of exercising power. In this way, the traditional all-or-nothing arguments about matching functional capacity with institutional form can be avoided entirely.

(4) A Separation of Constituencies?

How might this type of institutional arrangement operate? The sole constituency in this appropriately liberal regime is, of course, the individual citizen in the pre-legal position. However, the conflicting nature of his or her central concerns for collective conduct and individual defence allows the system to treat each as a distinct constituent interest. These interests can be identified with existing institutional organs with relative ease. These matters are discussed in more detail in subsequent chapters but are sketched out briefly here.

(a) The Courts

The seriousness of the citizen's disquiet at any potential impingement on his personal affairs ensures that this interest should be committed to the courts. The rational individual, it should be remembered, does not object to the bare fact of an adverse exercise of power. The prospect of individual pain is one which all citizens in the original position would accept. The demand for robust defence of an individual's entitlements only arises in respect of those matters regarded as especially important—those rights or freedoms upon which the collective cannot blithely encroach. The judicial commitment to an adjudicative approach which concentrates on issues of individual fairness provides the sort of heightened guarantee of institutional non-arbitrariness which is commensurate with the protection of this type of interest.

[61] G Jones, *Selections from Blackstone's Commentaries on the Laws of England* (Macmillan Press, 1973), at 66.

(b) The Government

On the other hand, the electoral organs of government can easily be characterized as advancing the individual's interest in effective associational action. The citizen will not be advantaged by every exercise of such public power. The rational calculation of the pre-constitutional citizen is that this collective conduct, as a whole, will improve the position of all in society. The necessarily opposing nature of many individuals' interests ensures, however, that each action will generally produce an adverse impact on some citizen. Non-arbitrariness demands a much lower level of procedural protection in this context. Assuming that the individual's most important interests are secured by the courts, non-arbitrariness dictates that the citizen need only be assured that the political decisions of those organs charged with improving the position of the collective are rationally motivated as responding to a perceived public need or demand. The electoral institutions of the state are best placed to perform this task. The existence of an electoral mandate, which all individuals had an equal opportunity to influence, allows these bodies to be persuasively portrayed as acting in the public interest. Furthermore, the provisional nature of electoral hegemony obliges those elected to continue to monitor, and, indeed, to react to the demands of the citizenry. The key normative concern for non-arbitrariness is thus satisfied by the democratic origins of collective institutional authority. Elections allow for the expression and aggregation of individual preferences, supplying not only an important acknowledgement of the decision-making autonomy of the individual but also a rational foundation for all public action.[62]

It is important to note at this point that the model under examination here proposes, from the point of view of constituency representation, to treat all electoral organs as one. This is especially appropriate in the Irish or English scenario of an effectively fused legislature and executive. In contemporary politics, the cabinet government is generally regarded as controlling both the executive and legislative organs of the state. These cabinet members are almost always in a position effectively to dictate the measures enacted by the legislative chamber(s). In return, the electorate tends to assess individual members of the assembly largely on the basis of the adjudged achievements of the cabinet members with whom they are aligned.[63] The government (meaning here the

[62] Non-arbitrariness can also be argued to require that the actions of these institutions—specifically their motivations—be made to meet some threshold of demonstrable public regard. This argument tends to follow from the criticisms of public choice theory, which suggest a combined lack of confidence in the accuracy of the electoral system, and the extent to which those elected actually respond to the needs of all citizens. See Mashaw, *Greed, Chaos, and Governance*, note 30 above, Chapter 3.

[63] For an example of the practical effects of this tendency for individual legislators to be judged by reference to the achievements (or otherwise) of cabinet members, see N Whelan, 'FF backbencher's lot is not a happy one' *The Irish Times* (1 July 2006).

combined members of the legislative assembly—or at least the controlling majority of it—and cabinet) is responsible for dictating collective policy, and therefore for the creation and enactment of measures to achieve such selected ends. That is not to say, of course, that there should be no separation between what, up to now, have been termed the legislative and executive organs. On the contrary, such separation can be argued to provide a useful guarantee of legislative generality, thereby supporting the vital value of public reason, as outlined above. However, in the context of the discussion of institutional non-arbitrariness at hand (a value which, it must be remembered, is argued to constitute the system's foundational norm), these electoral organs are regarded as singly representing the citizen's interest in collective action.

On this model, the courts and the government serve as the twin pillars of decision-making authority, each representing a constituent social interest in an appropriately non-arbitrary way. This raises an obvious question in relation to the administrative organs of government. Any contemporary theory of governmental arrangement must address the issue of administrative power, prescribing some way in which these bureaucratic bodies can be incorporated into its institutional vision.

Practically speaking, the constituency-oriented understanding of institutional separation operates in a top-down manner. Although the normative authority of the two institutions is based on the extent to which they serve the dual interests of the individual, they effectively serve as the high repositories of legitimate power. Legitimacy, on this understanding of the state, derives from the normative mandates upon which these institutions act. This echoes the transmission belt theory of governance, under which authority was centrally vested in specific, normatively superior organs of the state. Like that theory, it would seem, therefore, that exercises of power in this structural scheme—if they are to be legitimate—ought to be linked back to either the government or the courts. As already noted, however, the discretionary nature of administrative powers confers an effective decision-making autonomy on such bodies, thereby imperilling the ability of this two-institution approach to describe, explain, or legitimize the everyday operations of government. In this way, the problems traditionally posed by the administration re-emerge.

(c) The Administration

The challenge, therefore, is to portray the administration as a structural support for the suggested system, instead of an obstacle to its operation. The previous paragraph highlighted a potential problem with the proposed model—the way in which, in keeping with traditional notions of government, it conceives of authority in a centralized, top-down fashion. As Chapter 3 concluded, this type of idea is increasingly anachronistic in an era of dispersed, discretionary powers. Discretion has undermined the notions of unitary governance upon which the system has traditionally depended, thereby calling into question its general legitimacy. However, the scope for individual involvement—and thus decisional readjustment—which such discretion provides should be treated, arguably, not as a problem for the system, but rather as an institutional opportunity. The existence of discretionary administrative organs of government might allow for a sort of institutional reorientation which would emphasize the bottom-up nature of all state authority. Power—from the liberal perspective—comes ultimately from the individual. Even the actions of the elected bodies acting on behalf of the collective are theoretically animated by a residual commitment to the advancement of each citizen. Administrative discretion acknowledges and affirms this vital normative value by proffering an avenue of institutional participation for citizens affected by a decision-making process. In this way, the individual's status is affirmed as the basic source of institutional sovereignty, and thus the enduring focus of its exercise.

This analysis embraces discretion as part of the system's family of structural values, rather than ignoring or concealing it like some sort of embarrassing institutional kinsman. In its celebration of discretion, this model echoes the theory of interest representation. Discretion here encompasses more than the provision of mere participation rights, however. It is instead interpreted as a type of institutional refinement to the decision-making process. Accuracy rather than involvement is the relevant concern in this case. Individuals are not afforded the opportunity to express their views simply as a way of affirming their autonomy. They are instead conceived as actors in the institutional process of producing appropriate state actions. This echoes Cartier's attempt to justify discretion as 'a dialogue between the decision maker and the individual affected by the decision'.[64] The idea here is that, at this discretionary stage, citizens with relevant complaints (a concept to be considered at a later point) can register their objections to a proposed course of action. Thereby better informed about the probable actual impact of general provisions on specific individuals or groups, the administrative official can amend a decision accordingly. The administration, with its discretionary procedures, is here depicted as a means of securing norm-appropriate outcomes at a micro level.

> When discretion is delegated, a margin of manoeuvre is conferred on the decision-maker, a margin that must be viewed as a space for deliberation, allowing individuals to participate in norm creation and value articulation.[65]

This administrative freedom offers an opportunity to affirm the autonomy of the individual as a rational moral agent, whilst ensuring an improvement in the decision-making process. Administrative discretion is accordingly conceived as a type of second-order decision process, providing a second-stage auxiliary mechanism to ensure that the state does indeed exercise power in a suitably non-arbitrary way.

[64] G Cartier, 'Willis and the Contemporary Administrative State: Administrative Discretion as Dialogue' (2005) 55 *University of Toronto Law Journal* 629, at 644.

[65] Ibid, at 645.

This notion of coordinated chambers of decision-making power seems peculiar when judged against the traditional concept of law as unitary command. The continuing court references in Ireland to the transmission belt theory, for example, are testament to the strong residual influence of this *imperium* image of power. As Chapter 3 explained, however, the idea of a single sovereign organ exercising authority is increasingly unsustainable. The model under examination here appears to chime more closely with the contemporary reality of overlapping public powers. The image here is one of inter-institutional dialogue, according to which power is exercised by means of a coordinated and communicative process. Understood to represent distinct but essential social interests, institutions are guaranteed an input into the decision-making process. Government bodies are no longer regarded as exclusively entitled to exercise particular powers. On the contrary, such unilateral action is prohibited, as befits bodies charged with the inevitably partial task of interest representation.

The prescribed institutional structure operates by inter-organ mingling instead of separation. Individual decisions are delivered at the end of a multi-institutional process, the central concern of which is to organize, structure, manage, and—crucially—ensure the input of all relevant institutional interests.

On this model, the government and the courts are presented as providing an orienting framework within which administrative decision-making will occur. These first-order organs function at the level of macro-social organization, adopting general measures which are expected to advance their constituent social interest. The government specifies the actions it feels are required (or requested) to enhance the position of the collective. The courts, for their part, insist on the process precautions necessary to secure individual protection. Issues of informational efficacy and non-arbitrariness combine to ensure, however, that these provisions are not particularized. Even the court, with its procedural emphasis on individualism, relies in its operations on general principles rather than shifting case-specific decisions.

These institutions thus allow administrative bodies a margin of decision-making discretion, within which there exists a range of possible and appropriate outcomes. Such scope for decisional freedom provides an opportunity for the administrative organ to consider the situation of those specifically subject to the exercise of the power in question. Individuals can put forward their claims directly at this final stage of decentralized decision-making. Thereby informed about the actual impact of a proposed action, the administrator can react accordingly, refining, if necessary, the crudely drawn general judgements of the other institutions.

In a system of scattered powers, this is a more manageable and effective institutional safeguard. Informational difficulties will inevitably affect any attempt to govern our interventionist state centrally. An elected government cannot hope to inform itself about the way in which the bewildering array of administrative powers might impact on particular citizens. Embracing discretion as a means of individualized impact-adjustment reduces this complexity, allowing those bodies in actual contact with affected individuals the autonomy to undertake this task. This provides an additional layer of normative protection, ensuring the existence of several stages at which the arbitrary treatment of individuals might be identified and redressed. This model not only recognizes the reality of administrative discretion, but seeks to embrace and employ it as a key institutional process.

Issues of efficacy aside, this model must also support the asserted normative merits of the suggested system. Non-arbitrariness, it was argued, is secured at the general level of courts and government by the particular procedures which they apply. Discretion, however, has traditionally been interpreted as presenting a risk of arbitrary rule. It is important, therefore, to re-emphasize the constraints this system imposes on administrative discretion. The twin organs of central government, it will be remembered, provide the orienting framework for administrative action. Any decisions taken within the parameters those organs set out cannot be challenged by an unhappy individual. The autonomy of the administration within its own area must be respected as a vital institutional process, but there must also be the facility to identify and correct cases where that body has strayed outside the range of permissible outcomes.

> Since dialogue [between the individual and the discretionary decision-maker] is shaped by ... [the dictates of other institutions], the requirement that the decision be an authentic reflection of that dialogue does not prevent the decision maker from making a determination that does not satisfy the demands of the individual. Rather it imposes on the decision maker a burden of justification in the light of the dialogue.[66]

In that way, normative appropriateness is secured by the ongoing supervisory involvement of both the government and the courts. The exercise of public power on this model is, after all, an evolving process of inter-institutional dialogue. No single body has unfettered or absolute power. Each represents a specific social interest, deserving of attention but not exaltation. Each is accordingly entitled to ensure that its central dictates are observed. Decisions are based on the cumulative wisdom of each organ, rather than any image of institutional primacy. Administrative conduct will be reviewable where it is argued to go outside the margin of permissible action, thereby preserving the necessarily coordinated and co-extensive nature of inter-institutional authority.

This analysis of the relationship between these institutions reiterates the extent to which this model allows for the representation of all key social interests. This section has already shown how the courts and government can be seen to act on behalf of the abstract individual's interest in personal protection and collective conduct, respectively. The representation of such abstract interests will inevitably result in a type of top-down institutional process. The citizen under

[66] Ibid, at 646–647.

the conditions of the original agreement—our analytical prototype—was instrumentally useful precisely because of the absence of distortive individual characteristics. Similarly, the institutions which represent this type of abstract interest must be removed, to some extent, from the situation of ordinary citizens if they are properly to assess the requirements of their conjectural constituency. The model under examination allows, however, for the development of an inclusive approach, which combines the top-down perspective of the notional citizen with a bottom-up acknowledgement of the actual individual.

This process has several advantages. In the first place, it obviously corresponds with the reality of a governmental system in which centralized institutions disseminate decision-making power. Secondly, the provision of a bottom-up mechanism of citizen involvement provides a tangible affirmation of the normative importance of individual autonomy. Most significantly, however, this double methodology neatly bridges the operational gap between theory and practice, ensuring that the system is motivated by suitably abstract and non-arbitrary objectives, but is also concerned to assess the actual impact of these actions. The individual, therefore, can be said to have a trichotomy of interests in the establishment of the state: the abstract pre-social interest in successful collective action; the abstract pre-social concern for individual protection; and, additionally, a partial desire for the concrete advancement of her particular real-life position. In this way, the ordinary citizen's more pressing aspirations are institutionally acknowledged alongside the more traditional contractarian foundations of social action. The system proposed strives to attempt to involve all interests, rational and universal, mercenary and specific, in the decision-making process, thereby striving to ensure more accurate and norm-appropriate institutional outcomes.

C. Conclusion

The analysis in this chapter seems to offer support for a constituency-oriented scheme of institutional separation. This model has several suggested attractions. Normatively, it acknowledges and reflects the autonomy of the individual citizen as the system's foundational value. It thus rejects majoritarianism, recasting the institutional understanding of democracy in an appropriately individualistic form. As part of this process of organizational reform, the model identifies the citizen's divergent interests in associative activity, thereby allowing for the establishment of a dispersed institutional structure which accurately echoes our intuitive conception of the citizen–state relationship. Collective action is encouraged rather than restricted by the system's emphasis on the interests of the individual. Furthermore, in its intuitive attractiveness, the theory attempts to avoid the conceptual confusion of the dominant functionalist paradigm, redefining the system so as to properly reflect the conflict of values with which all public—and thus institutional—activity must engage. This amended understanding of institutional competence thereby introduces some welcome conceptual and analytical precision into an area of the law that has been dogged by indeterminacy.

Intuitively attractive in the abstract, the theory, crucially, also seems concerned, in its practical applications, to conform to the defining features of contemporary governance. In its operations, it seems to reflect Chapter 3's discussion of the ways in which the administrative state is increasingly removed from the strict logic of the traditional *imperium* theory of government. The system, for example, not only accepts the reality of administrative discretion, but actively attempts to employ this to enhance its decision-making structures. This occurs as part of its general recognition of the reality of the interventionist state. The model also rejects the traditional idea of law as command, preferring to present the exercise of public power as the result of a multi-institutional process. Similarly, the suggested theory avoids the issue of executive dominance by treating all electoral organs as one for the purposes of power allocation. This ensures that authority is dispersed amongst properly independent entities, rather than entrusted to formally distinct institutions whose autonomy of action is more theoretical than real. In this pursuit of 'the Madisonian goal of avoiding tyranny through the preservation of separated powers',[67] as in its emphasis on institutional blending instead of separation, the constituency-oriented model seems to return to the type of checks-and-balances concern which animated the original tripartite theory of separation.[68]

Furthermore, arguably the idea under examination here would seem to support and explain a number of the more recent judicial developments which, it was noted in Chapter 3, cannot be justified by reference to any existing theory of the state. The system-wide concern for non-arbitrariness, for example, would require the involvement of the courts—newly charged with the defence of the individual from arbitrary attacks wherever they arise—in areas beyond their traditional role. The model would thus support, for example, the move away from the formal public–private distinction of former times. Similarly, the entitlement of the individual to ensure that power has not been exercised in an arbitrary way at any stage of the institutional process would require, in certain circumstances, the type of relaxation of the standing rules which, in part, has already occurred. An individual ought not to be denied a remedy against arbitrary rule simply because of the absence of any substantive legal entitlement. Securing non-arbitrariness in a scattered interventionist state requires the abandonment of all such artificially formal classifications, necessitating instead the adoption of a more fluid and contextually-oriented approach which is capable of

[67] Brown, note 46 above, at 1515.

[68] See E Magill, 'The Real Separation in Separation of Powers Law' (2000) 86 *Virginia Law Review* 1127; Brown, note 46 above.

applying across the governmental and administrative spectrum. This has occurred in part, of course, with the development of a doctrine of procedural fairness, which the courts have elaborated and enforced on a cumulative, case-by-case basis.

The parallels between existing institutional practice and this proposed model should not be overstated. As Chapter 3 admitted, the doctrine of procedural fairness, although revolutionary in its impulses, is constrained in its effects by the continuing influence of traditional notions of function, capacity, and form. The institutional trichotomy which this theory eschews continues to occupy a position of practical and analytical importance. The challenge, therefore, for the remainder of this book is to assess the extent to which this constituency-oriented structure either might, or already does, operate successfully in practice.

6

Institutional Legitimacy and Administrative Practice

A. Introduction

The previous chapter put forward a case for the administration as a normatively legitimate branch of government. It conceived of the administration as a key element of the new separation of powers—as an independent entity with the capacity to make a positive contribution to a renewed institutional effort to secure good governance. In comparison with the traditional separation of powers theory, this new model provides a radically altered template for contemporary administrative action. With its place no longer obscured by the traditional doctrine's twin preoccupation with command-based governance and a tripartite institutional arrangement, the administration emerges as an independent institution with a distinct and legitimate role.

This raises the practical question, however, of whether the administration is capable of adequately performing the task entrusted to it by this new separation of powers theory. Having identified the limitations of the prevailing tripartite institutional order, it was suggested that the administration could provide a means of remedying some of these defects. However, as consistently argued in the early chapters of this book, theoretical adequacy has limited value in matters of institutional organization. The traditional separation of powers theory was perfectly defensible—even positively attractive—in the abstract. It was in its actual practice that it proved notably deficient. Whether in the pure form established in a number of the early American states, or in the more modified form that has become a constitutional commonplace in many modern states, the tripartite theory's failings have been primarily operational rather than philosophical. Approval from the ivory tower is edifying but insufficient. Institutions must operate in the real world. This means that theories of institutional operation must be advanced with one eye on the possibilities for successful real-world elaboration. It is this issue which the present chapter will seek to address.

B. The Necessity for Multi-Institutional Analysis

The theory advanced thus far in this book was developed as a response to the perceived weaknesses of the current system of institutional arrangement. The model of institutional separation put forward emerged from an analysis of the limitations of the traditional orthodoxy. The legislature, the executive, and the judiciary in their current forms were argued to be incapable of adequately dealing with the realities of modern governance. Wedded in their institutional self-images to outdated notions of centralized, rule-based, and top-down control, their governing institutional norms served to conceal rather than to account for important aspects of state activity. In fact, the administration exercised real and significant influence within a system which in theory denied it the possibility of independent judgement or discretionary power.

Furthermore, it was argued that the individual institutional components of the tripartite model were unable to fulfil the functions which it conferred upon them. Multiple examples of these institutional failings were identified. In a Westminster system, for example, the legislature lacks the independence to consistently operate as a real check on the executive. The emergence of organized modern political parties increases the possibilities for factional or interest-group control of the political process in contradiction to the aims of the separation of powers system. The executive does not have the necessary direct control of its agents to convincingly claim a role for itself as the implementing organ of all government commands. The legislature similarly cannot claim a monopoly on the creative exercise of public power in a system in which administrative discretion is an institutional constant. Equally, the judiciary has found its central function of interpreting rules usurped, in part, by the exercise of discretionary judgement by administrators. Its ability to review the legality of government action is also inhibited by the exponential expansion in the scope and competences of modern government. This growth in government has raised serious questions about the resources, expertise, and sustainability of judicial scrutiny of such a diverse array of government actors. In turn, this has encouraged a judicial deference to electoral accountability or institutional expertise as a superior norm, which has further reduced the system's safeguards against factional control. And so on, and so forth. These issues were all considered at greater length in the earlier chapters of this book.

Following Unger's notion of counter-normative exceptions, these limitations and exceptions to the tripartite theory were used as a starting point for the articulation of an alternative institutional arrangement. It was suggested that at least some of these difficulties could be addressed by directly investing the administrative branch of government with specific responsibilities. This was, to some extent, an obvious conclusion. As many (although not all) of the traditional theory's difficulties are attributable to its inability to cope with everyday administrative action, the administration appears the natural choice of institution to address the issues so raised.

This process of reasoning from the weaknesses of particular institutions carries with it the danger of engaging in what Komesar has criticized as single institutional analysis. This, he explains, arises where an institutional choice is recommended, not on the basis of the relative merits of the relevant institutions, but by reference to the particular limitations of one of them alone:

> Frequently, any institutional choice inconsistent with the analyst's preferred law and public policy position is summarily dismissed after reciting a long parade of horribles. In a world of institutional alternatives that are both complex and imperfect, institutional choice by implication, simple intuition, or even long lists of imperfections is deeply inadequate.[1]

This reflects the fact that 'the choice [of institutions] is always a choice among highly imperfect alternatives'.[2]

It is not sufficient, therefore, to argue that matters ought to be entrusted to the administrative branch by referring to the 'parade of horribles' exhibited by the present legislative–executive–judicial axis of institutions. It is necessary to go further and to consider the capacity of the administration to fulfil these functions in its own right. It must be demonstrated that the administration is better equipped to perform these tasks when compared with the other institutions in which they could be vested. The analytical tendency to confer institutional functions by default rather than design must be avoided. A relative and multi-institutional assessment of the strengths and weaknesses of rival bodies should clarify whether or not the administration is, in practice, the best (or, on Komesar's more sceptical logic, the least imperfect) option available. In so doing, this assessment should also identify, not only those areas in which the advantages of administrative input are strong, but also those cases in which matters ought more properly to remain (or at least presumptively vest) in another institution. In addition, such a practical assessment of the relative merits of the administration is also likely to identify those internal aspects of the administration's organization which—although perhaps less imperfect than those of other institutions—could nonetheless be developed and improved further to perform these tasks more successfully.

(1) Defining the Subject Matter

Compiling such a comparative account of the institutional characteristics of the administration necessarily presupposes the existence of a reliable conception of

[1] N Komesar, *Imperfect Alternatives: Choosing Institutions in Law, Economics and Public Policy* (University of Chicago Press, 1996), at 5–6.

[2] Ibid, at 5.

what constitutes an administrative agency. The elaboration of any such central criteria of administrative identity does, however, pose significant problems.

One difficulty is the fact that contemporary governance is a diverse and very complex process. This is particularly the case since the collapse of the strict public–private boundaries which once distinguished governmental from non-governmental action. As governments have simultaneously both expanded and privatized their powers, a wide range of organizations have emerged which could quite plausibly be regarded as part of the process of government, broadly defined. The responsibility for pursuing governmental objectives, which was once the exclusive preserve of officials directly employed by the state, has been dispersed throughout 'an elaborate system of third-party government in which crucial elements of public authority are shared with a host of non-governmental or other-governmental actors, frequently in complex collaborative systems that sometimes defy comprehension'.[3] This means that administrative power is exercised by very different organizations in very different contexts, which makes the identification of any common qualities difficult. The result is that it is necessary to assess the characteristics of the administration at a very high level of abstraction.

Another problem is the distinct lack of consensus over the precise composition of the administration. This, in part, is attributable to the failure of traditional doctrine to accept and reflect the reality of administrative power. Conventional constitutional theory has sought to explain away the administration, rather than to define and develop it. This has created a significant divergence in the academic literature between those who regard administrative power as a necessary evil to be minimized and constrained, and those who see it as the most practical model for modern government. These differing views also influence each group's respective notion of what constitutes the administration. The former tends to define the administration by reference to traditional notions of direct, centralized government, whereas the latter may perceive the influence of administrative power in even the most devolved and decentralized informal networks. This illustrates the extent to which a definition of the administration is, inevitably, a contested choice which reflects a theorist's wider conception of government.

With that in mind, this chapter relies on an expansive notion of administration governance which covers the broad range of views held on this issue. It does not hold fast to the traditional image of the front-line administrator as either the executor of government commands or the adjudicator on individual claims. Rather, it accepts that the administration can potentially be required to perform a multitude of tasks of varying degrees of formality and requiring very different skills. What constitutes administrative conduct is not prescribed but remains instead an open-ended question. This flexible approach is based on the fact that these varying ideals of administrative action all have the potential to provide

[3] L Salamon, 'The New Governance and the Tools of Public Action' (2001) 28 *Fordham Urban Law Journal* 1611, at 1613.

some insight into the characteristics—or, probably more accurately, the potential characteristics—of the administrative branch. To define the administration in a particular fashion at the outset would pre-empt the purpose of the exercise at hand. It would be pointless to consider the potential institutional capacities of the administrative branch by reference to a partial understanding of it alone.

It should also be noted that the administration, broadly conceived, takes different forms in different jurisdictions. This renders the making of universal assessments of administrative capacity fraught with difficulties. It will also be recalled that this book is primarily concerned with the place and legitimacy of decentralized decision-making in a separation of powers system rather than with the mechanics of how this ought to be organized. The terminology employed in this chapter, as in the remainder of the book, is necessarily vague, therefore. The administration here means no more than that amalgam of institutions and organizations which exercise power at a certain autonomous remove from the central institutions of government. Where that line is drawn will vary from jurisdiction to jurisdiction.

In addition, the sheer diversity of administrative tasks means that there may be scope for a similar diversity of administrative forms. Traditionalist restrictions may be appropriate in one context, where another might require the less formal and more fluid approach of those theorists more comfortable with decentralized administrative power. 'There is no one-size-fits-all solution to the challenges facing the regulatory state.'[4] In terms of identifying the characteristics of the administration, there is no inherent necessity for an all-or-nothing choice between discretion and constraints. Both schools of thought might usefully contribute to the development of a suitable understanding of how, in practice, the administration could perform the role envisaged for it under the new separation of powers theory. They will both be considered, therefore, as part of this chapter's assessment of the potential strengths and weaknesses of the administrative process, *vis-à-vis* the other available institutional candidates.

C. The Characteristics of the Administration

(1) Bureaucratic Principles

The emergence of a government system in which administrative agencies wield considerable power prompted early attempts to develop a model of internal administrative organization which would reduce or address the legitimacy problems raised by this development. Weber's work on bureaucratic principles is perhaps the best known example of this early approach. Weber devised a system

[4] O Lobel, 'The Renew Deal: The Fall of Regulation and the Rise of Governance in Contemporary Legal Thought' (2004) 89 *Minnesota Law Review* 342, at 359.

of bureaucratic principles which aimed to address traditionalist concerns about discretionary administrative governance. Weberian theory 'portrayed bureaucracy as a rationalized, disciplined mechanism for implementing the wishes of its creators'.[5]

This model of administrative activity emphasized its objectivity. Administrative activity, it was suggested, is generally impartial and rule-bound. The exercise of power by an administrative official occurs within the confines of a hierarchical structure. In exercising such power, administrators are expected to act on the basis of expert technical opinion and 'scientific' management principles. These concepts of expert 'fact' and purportedly 'scientific' principles import a degree of objectivity into the administrative process, suggesting that the outcome produced is one which would inevitably have been arrived at regardless of which individual administrator(s) is involved. Administrative discretion on this analysis is more apparent than real.

Weber's work also presented the bureaucracy as a system organized along principles of impersonality and public service. Administrators are required to treat individuals in a manner befitting their status as citizens. In their actions they are obliged to separate the civic from the personal, adhering to 'the dominant norms [which] are concepts of straightforward duty without regard to personal considerations'.[6] The exercise of power is not a matter of personal prerogative. It is regulated by objective norms and standards, which the administrator internalizes and adheres to. As du Gay has summarized it:

> For Weber, the ethical attributes of the good bureaucrat [are] strict adherence to procedure, acceptance of sub- and super-ordination, *esprit de corps*, abnegation of personal moral enthusiasms [and] commitment to the purposes of the office.[7]

Administrators are also accountable in the sense that they are liable to have to answer for their actions to a superior with regard to the extent to which their conduct has complied both with the specific commands received and with more general administrative or bureaucratic norms of impartiality, integrity, and non-arbitrariness. '[T]he central feature of bureaucracy at work is hierarchical authority, underpinned by rationalisation and rule-governed behaviour.'[8] Accordingly, administrative action is dually accountable to a hierarchy of rules and to the demands of an impersonal order.

This model of formalist bureaucracy is generally regarded today as an anachronistic and inadequate account of administrative action. One of the most obvious grounds of criticism which can be applied to this model is that it is based on a system of governance which does not correspond to the realities of

[5] G Frug, 'The Ideology of Bureacracy in American Law' (1984) 97 *Harvard Law Review* 1277.

[6] P du Gay, 'Bureaucracy and liberty: state, authority and freedom' in du Gay, ed., *The Values of Bureacracy* (Oxford University Press, 2005) at 52.

[7] Ibid.

[8] P Thompson and M Alevsson, 'Bureaucracy at work: misunderstandings and mixed blessings' in P du Gay, ed., ibid, at 96.

the modern state. The Weberian bureaucracy is predicated on a model of direct government in which commands are issued by the central sovereign and conveyed down the administrative hierarchy for implementation by the front-line bureaucrat. This assumes, however, that government operates only through this sort of linear command-and-control system. At a time when most jurisdictions have moved to forms of decentralized, part-privatized, or third-party government, this model of direct governance does not account for a significant—perhaps even, the most significant—portion of contemporary government action.

In addition, the model provides only a limited advance on traditional theories, by embracing the existence but not the reality of administrative discretion. By assuming that discretion can be avoided though the development and use of a system of objective controls, the Weberian model encounters the same difficulties as formal separation of powers devices such as the non-delegation doctrine. It is unduly optimistic about the extent to which discretion at the lower levels of the bureaucracy can be supervised out of the system. This means that it 'suggests no way to prevent the subjectivity which is an inextricable attribute of bureaucracy from becoming the exercise of personal domination'.[9] From a normative perspective, this is problematic. The Weberian system places its trust entirely in the discretion-reducing effects of ostensibly objective standards. Once it is accepted that these constraints still leave considerable scope for administrative subjectivity, it becomes clear that a theory of bureaucracy is incapable, by itself, of providing a complete model of legitimate governance.

This does not mean, however, that principles of bureaucracy are irrelevant to the exercise at hand. Although, in the strict sense of the term as representing a system of direct government, the bureaucracy does not represent all aspects of contemporary administrative governance, it remains an important part of the state's structures. Similarly, Weber's bureaucratic principles of impersonality, accountability, and public service continue to inform elements of administrative conduct. Accountability to central institutions and, ultimately, to the public remains a central requirement for all administrators. Even where private actors are involved in the delivery of public services, their contractual obligations may be designed to provide a measure of public as well as purely commercial accountability. This indicates that the basic principles of Weberian bureaucracy may continue to have some resonance today. They might not provide a comprehensive legitimation of the modern administrative state but they do identify a number of important characteristics of administrative conduct which have the potential to make a significant contribution to just such an exercise. The principles of objectivity, impersonality, and accountability which Weber emphasized continue to influence administrative conduct. More importantly for present purposes, they also indicate potential characteristics of the administrative branch which may be taken into account as part of an overall inter-institutional

[9] Frug, note 5 above, at 1315.

assessment of its capacity to perform the role previously outlined for it in this book.

(2) Information Costs

A further characteristic of administrative agencies tends to be that they operate in closer proximity to those upon whom their decisions impact than centralized single institutions like the legislature or the executive. This proximity can have a number of different effects. One may be that information about the circumstances of those subject to a proposed course of action, and about the possible consequences of that decision for them and for the efficacy of the proposed action, may be easier or less costly for the administration to acquire than would be the case for other, more top-down institutions. Administrative institutions are frequently 'the proprietors of vast stores of information relevant to regulatory decisions'.[10] That is not to say that administrative agencies do not also encounter difficulties in obtaining relevant and accurate information about the localized geographical or subject areas for which they are responsible. However, the very fact that they do represent a less centralized form of governance means that they have greater possibilities for contact with relevant individuals or interest groups. The exercise of administrative power may involve engagement with particular interested parties, be it by virtue of an invitation for submissions on proposed actions, the holding of a consultation process with expert or experienced local interests, the receipt of appeals for special treatment for particular groups, or many other means. Direct government will often involve face-to-face contact between administrators and the public which presents an obvious opportunity for information retrieval. Devolved governance too may provide the administration with additional information through, for example, the submission of detailed tender documents or, at the other end of the process, the production of monitoring and outcome reports by third-party contractors. The simple fact that the administration is closer to the point at which the practical implementation of government occurs means that it is better placed than central institutions to obtain information about the realities of everyday governance.[11]

The information costs of the administration are also likely to be lowered by the fact that administrators tend to operate over a prolonged period of time in a particular field. This means, as discussed below, that they are liable to have, or to obtain, relevant experience and knowledge. Regulating such specialized fields generally requires a certain level of technical knowledge on the part of the decision-maker in question. An external or inexperienced decision-maker is likely to be required as a preliminary step to invest time and expense in educating

[10] E Kagan, 'Presidential Administration' (2001) 114 *Harvard Law Review* 2245 at 2262.

[11] See the more extensive discussion of this in JL Mashaw, *Greed. Chaos and Governance* (Yale University Press, 1997), at 142–145.

him- or herself to a particular standard of knowledge to be able to understand the issues at hand adequately. For an experienced administrator with specific technical expertise, any such preliminary instruction is generally unnecessary. This further contributes to the administration's potential institutional capacity to exercise power from a position of comparatively superior relevant knowledge.

(3) Expertise

Expertise is another characteristic which may legitimately be associated with at least some forms of administrative body. This expertise primarily takes one of two forms: specialist technical knowledge; or learned administrative ability. The first form of expertise tends to arise in the situation where an administrative body with responsibility for a particular technical matter recruits individuals on the basis of their relevant qualifications for the subject area in question. In addition, through prolonged experience in their position, administrators may acquire valuable and situation-specific skills. This provides a level of specialist knowledge which other more generalist institutions might lack.

The second form of specific expertise derives from the administration's proximity to the actual exercise of government power. This may support the development of specialist administrative expertise. Repeat efforts to secure the implementation of specified goals in a particular area may encourage the acquisition by administrators of an enhanced capacity for practical instrumental decision-making. Administrators may acquire not only additional information and knowledge but also a better understanding of the way in which particular measures or approaches might actually operate in practice. As Richardson has argued at some length, administrators may obtain a form of 'evaluative expertise' which is 'less easy to codify than empirical expertise' but which is valuable, nonetheless:

> What is involved is the kind of deeper understanding of a range of goods that comes from experience in seeking to promote or respect them in a range of concrete contexts. Civil servants come to know the goods they are charged with promoting and the ills they are charged with avoiding.... [T]hose with responsibility for promoting a range of goods or avoiding a range of ills have acquired not just information about how to do so or about the collateral effects of achieving or failing to achieve their goals but also an understanding of the detailed contours of the goods and ills in question. Each expert of this kind develops an expertise in distinguishing and classifying versions of the good or ill in which he or she specializes.... Through experience, each will also develop a sense for which aspects of good and ill are particularly relevant in which sorts of situation. In short, through their responsibility and specialisation, one skill these workers develop is a ready ability to pick out different ways that the general goals with which they are charged may be specified and sense of when one specification or another is apt in given circumstances.[12]

[12] HS Richardson, *Democratic Autonomy: Public reasoning about the ends of policy* (Oxford University Press, 2002), at 225.

(4) Operational Autonomy

The administration enjoys a practical, if limited, autonomy of action. It has repeatedly been stated that administrators enjoy a considerable degree of discretion in the performance of their designated functions. No matter how specific the instructions received from central government, the administrative entity in question will be required to make a certain number of autonomous decisions as part of its efforts to interpret and implement the relevant commands. Indeterminacy is inevitable in any system of communicated directions.

This discretionary freedom of action should not be confused with institutional independence. Traditional doctrine dictates that administrators are accountable to the relevant minister and subject to his or her direction as appropriate. It also distinguishes between the creation and the implementation of policy, reserving the former for the central political organs only. Thus, the administration is not independent, in the sense of being entitled to act in a way which contradicts the direct instructions of either the legislature or the executive.

Nonetheless, there is a practical autonomy which derives not only from the inevitability of administrative discretion but also from the fact that the central organs are required to issue such specific commands at all. For the model of power distribution under discussion here, this separation between instruction and application has considerable value. The administration's bureaucratic reliance on formal and hierarchical command and control systems means that, in directing an administrator to undertake a particular course of action, the central organ must do so in a suitably formal and specific manner. Although a minister may be able to issue direct or informal instructions to officials in immediate proximity, the devolved and hierarchical nature of the administration means that it is not practical for it to be exclusively organized or operated in this sort of face-to-face fashion. This limits the scope for the centre to exercise power through informal or concealed channels. If the intention is that a specific course of action be undertaken, or that measures be taken in respect of particular individuals or groups, the only way for the centre to be certain that this will occur is to formally indicate what is actually envisaged. If there is to be certainty for the centre, specific or targeted action cannot be concealed within general instructions. The requirement to issue formal instructions to the administration thus both restrains the instructing organ and creates scope for the administration to exercise autonomous judgement in its interpretation and implementation of the command.

(5) Flexibility

One of the most notable characteristics of the contemporary administration is its capacity for operational flexibility. In carrying out the tasks entrusted to it, the administrative branch frequently demonstrates a level of adaptability and flexibility which distinguishes it from other more centralized institutions.

In part, this reflects the diverse nature of administrative structures. Where power is dispersed amongst a wide range of separate agencies, this increases the possibility for the development by each body of different and diverse approaches to the operational issues at hand. With each administrative entity responsible for its own narrow area, it is relatively free to develop its own procedures and approaches. There is no necessity to develop a singular system which is capable of applying to all issues. This means that there is considerable scope for operational flexibility at the level of the individual administrative organ.

Flexibility is also inherent in the act of administration itself. As noted in the previous section, the performance of administrative functions necessarily involves a certain degree of decision-making autonomy. Instructions received must be interpreted and implemented. The limited nature of institutional resources often means that the relevant administrative entity must be selective in the way in which it exercises its powers. Even under traditional command-and-control structures, '[t]he dynamics of implementation demonstrate a process that is much more flexible than initially assumed'.[13] The opportunity for reflection and flexibility arises under even the more orthodox systems of direct bureaucratic government. These decisions can arise in relation to both macro-issues of policy and micro-issues of everyday practice.

If an official is charged with the organization of a specific bus route, for example, decisions may have to be made about the location of bus stops, the frequency of buses, the recruitment of drivers, the appropriate degree of expenditure on maintenance, and so on. Even after all of these initial decisions are taken, there will be an ongoing need to exercise judgement as new issues arise. These issues can be general or specific. If commuting patterns change, should the timetables be amended? Should fares be increased to cover more regular maintenance checks? More specifically, if one bus stop becomes subject to vandalism, should it be moved or should security be increased? When special events of local interest occur, should additional services be made available, or are the overtime costs involved too high? If one driver has a high absentee rate, is it appropriate to warn or to dismiss him or her? Countless discretionary decisions are taken on an everyday and on an ongoing policy basis. As each issue arises, the administrator is faced with a number of alternative options. This creates scope for flexibility and adaptability to local circumstances and interests.

The adaptability that derives from the nature of the act of implementation itself has been supplemented by the opportunities for flexibility and choice that have followed from the emergence of a contemporary state in which government has 'changed its role from one of doing to one of arranging'.[14] In more conventional terms, the government's role is no longer to 'row' but rather to 'steer' society.[15]

[13] Lobel, note 4 above, at 451. [14] Salamon, note 3 above, at 1622.

[15] F Mosher, 'The Changing Responsibilities and Tactics of the Federal Government' (1980) 40 *Public Administration Review* 541.

Coercive rule has been supplemented by a system of active governance in which the state's function has been expanded to include the facilitation and promotion of socially valuable standards of conduct. The state acts not only to coercively compel certain behaviour but also to educate, cajole, instruct, incentivize, and otherwise encourage the adoption of preferred forms of individual or institutional activity. This has enhanced the flexibility of administration action in two primary ways.

The first relates to the manner in which this expanded role for the state has encouraged the development of so-called 'soft law' techniques of governance. These are 'rules of conduct which in principle have no legally binding force but which nevertheless may have practical effects'.[16] These methods involve a simpler and more incremental approach to governance which focuses on persuasion and social learning rather than rule-based enforcement. From the point of view of the administration, 'soft law' measures provide additional potential options for decision-makers, thereby increasing the administration's capacity for flexible and adaptable action. For example, the administration might issue guidance or policy documents indicating the circumstances to which sanctions might be likely to apply. Education and information campaigns might be used to highlight the advantages of adhering to certain standards of behaviour. Administrative resources might be allocated to individuals or organizations who have adopted approved forms of conduct. These examples illustrate the extent to which the development of this 'soft law' system has significantly extended the scope for administrators to exercise their powers flexibly and selectively in accordance with the particularities of the specific situation.

Secondly, the collapse of the traditional public–private distinction and the emergence of a system of devolved third-party governance have also opened up a space in which decisions must be made in relation to the identity of those actors who are incorporated into the governance process. This reflects the fact that '[p]olicy instruments are not politically neutral, and the selection of one instrument or another for a policy intervention will generate political activity, and have political consequences'.[17] For example:

> When policy tools aim to change target groups' behaviour by inviting a market calculus, the action becomes individual, and people are encouraged to think like consumers. Such a stance is at odds with ... the disposition to take serious account of the good of others and not just oneself in public life.[18]

In addition to prioritizing certain approaches or principles, the administration's choice of instrument may also affect the relative input and influence of interested individuals and institutions. The selection of a specific instrument of

[16] F Snyder. 'The effectiveness of European Community law' (1993) 56 MLR 19, at 32.

[17] BG Peters, 'The Politics of Tool Choice' in L Salamon, ed., *Tools of Government: A Guide to the New Governance* (Oxford University Press, 2002).

[18] Smith and Ingram, 'Policy Tools and Democracy' in Salamon, ibid.

governance 'define[s] the actors that are centrally involved in particular types of programs and the formal roles they will play'.[19] This provides a fixed distribution of power, which, in turn, effectively establishes *a priori* power relations within the relevant field. The choice of instrument 'give[s] some actors, and therefore some perspectives, an advantage in determining how policies will be carried out', thereby privileging particular groups.[20] Different instruments create different bargaining relationships, which lead in turn to different coalitions or types of consensus.[21] Such decisions will not necessarily be taken by the administration itself, of course. The central organs might themselves make choices with regard to the appropriate tools to be deployed. However, in many cases it falls to the administrative entity to decide upon the instrument in question and thus, in turn, upon which actors ought to be comparatively embraced by, or excluded from, the implementation process.

These developments underline the considerable degree of discretion which is commonly enjoyed by the administrative branch. Administrative agencies are frequently entitled to themselves decide: what implementation entails; which of the available courses of action ought to be undertaken; and, where relevant, how much influence particular third parties ought to have on the governance process. At each stage, the contemporary administration has an extensive range of options available to it. This means that the administration retains an inherent level of operational flexibility. That it can perform the task of implementation in a wide variety of ways naturally equips it to adapt its actions to the specific factual situations with which it is faced.

(6) Administrative Characteristics

In conclusion therefore, this brief overview of the key characteristics of the administration indicates that it has many diverse forms; is flexible but rule-bound; tends to exhibit a certain basic level of expertise and experience; is sufficiently proximate to its subject to significantly reduce information costs; and is often regulated by norms of impersonality, impartiality, and accountability.

D. Applied Multi-Institutional Analysis

(1) Comparison with the Political Organs

In comparison with the administration, the political organs of government represent a more unified and obviously powerful force. The legislature in

[19] Salamon, 'The New Governance', note 3 above, at 1632. [20] Ibid, at 1627.
[21] PL Posner, 'Accountability Challenge of Third Party Government' in Salamon, *Tools of Government*, note 17 above.

particular enjoys relatively unconstrained power in the exercise of its creative rule-making function. Unlike the rule-bound and hierarchically subordinate administration, the legislature has the freedom to revoke or amend rules, or to frame new ones without reference to any other superior institution. Once it remains within the confines of the constitutional order, it may issue whatever instructions it desires. The executive does not enjoy unfettered freedom to the same extent. It may only operate on the basis of the instructions it receives from the legislature. However, those political figures who occupy positions at the head of the executive branch do retain relatively unrestrained decision-making power with regard to matters of practical implementation. They are not subject to the possibility of direct correction by a hierarchical superior in the same way that an administrative official or institution might be. Both of the political organs enjoy the primary entitlement to exercise decision-making authority within their own area of responsibility. This unchecked decisional primacy tends to confer a greater air of power and authority on the political organs than is often the case with administrative bodies which have traditionally and habitually been cast in a more institutionally subordinate role.

This powerful position obviously derives in part from the fact that the political organs are elected by the People. This provides these institutions with a level of popular accountability which, in a democratic system, is generally regarded as supplying valuable normative legitimacy. This supports the notion, discussed above, that these political organs retain institutional primacy in their relevant fields.

Furthermore, as smaller institutions with a limited range of constituent elements, the political organs of government, both legislative and executive, also tend to present a more unified and cohesive front. This follows in part from the fact that the same political party, or coalition of political parties, tends to control each institution. This is particularly the case in the Westminster system where the same party, or coalition of parties, usually controls both institutions at the same time. Party discipline ensures a level of consistency and cohesion in government policy.

The fact that these bodies are elected also ensures a regular periodic renewal of their membership. Such transience means that these bodies do not necessarily adhere to fixed institutional norms over time but can significantly alter their philosophy or approach if so desired. This allows these institutions to retain a level of consistency and coherence in their conduct while also incrementally responding to social developments over time.

A further important characteristic of the political organs is that they are top-down institutions which operate at a relatively distant remove from their subjects. This can generate informational and accountability issues. They tend to have some facility to acquire information through the initiation of formal inquiries into particular matters. These might be undertaken through the legislature's committee system, for example, or by the exercise by a minister of statutory powers to commission reports or appoint inspectors, where those are conferred upon him or her. In general, however, the political organs encounter a significant information deficit in respect of many matters upon which they make decisions. This reflects not only their inherent institutional limitations but also the necessarily panoramic nature of the tasks they tend to face. As central institutions, the political organs are expected to come to their conclusions on the basis of what is best for society as a whole. On many occasions, if undertaken in the most scrupulous manner possible, this task would require information to be obtained about the situations and circumstances of hundreds and thousands of individuals or organizations. Such information would be difficult both to obtain and to assess. It is difficult to see how the interests and demands of such a multitude of potentially affected parties could be weighed with any degree of accuracy or objectivity.

Even if this could be achieved, the question which would then arise is whether it would be possible to identify how this disparate array of groups might respond to the introduction of the proposed measure as any adjustments in their behaviour would obviously also be relevant to any assessment of both the individual impact and the overall social benefit of a particular proposition. It seems obvious that these are judgements of such baffling complexity that they cannot be objectively calculated by a small body of elected individuals. This means that the decisions of the elected organs are always, to a certain extent, made in an informational vacuum.

This is exacerbated by the fact that the political organs generally lack specialist knowledge or skills. Because potentially they must deal with all issues, they tend to lack the facility to deal expertly with any one of them. An incumbent minister may acquire such knowledge and experience over time but, in general, the transient nature of the political class, when taken together with the broad scope of their jurisdictions, mitigates against the development of specialist skills. This is particularly the case with respect to the legislature. When framing statutory rules, the reality is that it 'may have no expertise on the relevant issues and no sense for the best alternatives'.[22]

The centralized nature of these institutions may also limit their accountability. The elected organs are frequently described as popularly accountable. However, as Rubin has persuasively argued, elections do not, in fact, provide the level of accountability often claimed. Effective accountability, in his view, denotes 'the ability of one actor to demand an explanation or justification of another actor for its actions, and to reward or punish that second actor on the basis of its performance or its explanation'.[23] Voters cannot formally require the

[22] L Bressman, 'Procedures as Politics in Administrative Law' (2007) 107 *Columbia Law Review* 1749, at 1768.

[23] E Rubin, 'The Myth of Accountability and the Anti-Administrative Impulse' (2005) 103 *Michigan Law Review* 2073, at 2073.

political organs to provide an explanation for their actions. Such explanations might be furnished as a matter of political expediency but the political organs cannot be compelled to justify their actions in the same way that the administration is obliged to account for its conduct to other institutions and to affected individuals. Political actors might respond to preferences, especially at election time, but they cannot be required to acknowledge, let alone address, the concerns or demands of any specific individual or group. In fact, Rubin suggests that voters select candidates who share their own values and preferences precisely because the political organs will not be answerable to the People during the period between elections. This accountability gap is exacerbated by the geographic and social distance which may often exist between individual voters and the political institutions. As central institutions, these bodies are obviously located in a single place and are therefore necessarily distant from many individuals in the state. Individual representatives may come into contact with individuals in their own constituency but the individual voter or organization simply cannot formally hold the political institutions to account for their conduct. At best, they are periodically answerable for their actions but only then on the basis of their policy performance as a whole.

Comparing these characteristics with those of the administration, it is clear that the political institutions are more cohesive, more powerful, and more directly connected to the interests of the collective than the administration. At the same time, however, the electoral organs lack the experience and expertise in securing instrumental outcomes that administrators may have. The political organs have a direct relationship with the electorate but are not accountable to it in the same way as the administration, in the sense that they do not act under an enforceable obligation to explain or account for their individual decisions. This limits the extent to which they may be responsive to the interests or circumstances of particular groups or individuals, especially where those groups or individuals lack electoral influence. This reflects the susceptibility of the electoral process to produce outcomes that reflect either majoritarian or minoritarian bias. Political organs do not operate under the same requirements of impersonality, impartiality, or rational instrumentalism as administrative officials do. The result is that elected officials are likely to respond to the demands of the prominent and the electorally powerful. Administrators, in contrast, are obliged to respond to each individual as a citizen entitled to equal respect and regard.

The other significant distinction between the institutional characteristics of the political organs and the administration relates to the information costs which they may experience in the exercise of their functions. It seems clear that the process of obtaining information about the potential impact of a proposed measure is simpler and less costly for the administration than for the political organs. These lower costs reflect both the narrower scope of an administrative agency's area of responsibility, and the greater proximity of the administration to those upon whom their measures may impact. This means that the administration may be more suited to a task which requires power to be exercised in a way that responds to distinct individual circumstances.

(2) Comparison with the Courts

The judicial process is most typically characterized as a bilateral, adjudicative, and backward-looking system.[24] The courts, for their part, share some characteristics with the administration, most obviously in the rule-bound nature of judicial action, as well as in their attachment to notions of independence and impartiality. For the courts, these values are principles of fundamental and foundational importance.

This adherence to notions of independence and reasoned impartiality has the result that the courts apply rigorous procedural requirements to the actions coming before them. These have the effect of limiting both the range of claims and the type of information which the courts receive. These restrictions are designed to ensure that the matters brought before the courts are dealt with in a controlled, rational, and formally egalitarian manner. Evidence is adduced only after it passes the threshold standards of scrutiny, and in a manner which permits the court to weigh it with accuracy and care. These restrictions also mean, however, that the litigation process involves considerable expenditure for the parties to a dispute. The reality is that the courts' '[i]ndependence and even-handness come at significant cost'.[25] The judicial process offers a rigorously structured means for the reconciliation of competing bilateral claims but does so at considerable expense.

The strict nature of judicial procedures also reduces the amount of information available to the court in coming to its conclusions. In the first place, information is only presented to the court if it satisfies the necessary rules of evidence. Secondly, the information must meet the requirements of relevance. In a bilateral, adjudicative, and backward-looking forum, relevance is a significantly constrained notion. Information is only relevant if it pertains both to the strict issues being litigated and to the past or present circumstances of the two sides represented before the court. This ensures that the court will only act on information which has passed particular standards of reliability and relevance. However, it also means that the court does ultimately make its decision on the basis of partial information which might not provide a complete or accurate indication of the range of social interests potentially affected. Thirdly, the significant costs involved in litigating a claim before the courts mean that many issues are unlikely to be brought to the courts' attention. This is most obviously

[24] See, for example, the discussion of the limitations of court procedures for dealing with public interest issues in A Chayes, 'The Role of the Judge in Public Law Litigation' (1976) 89 *Harvard Law Review* 1281. See also L Fuller's classic work on 'The Forms and Limits of Adjudication' (1978) 92 *Harvard Law Review* 353.

[25] Komesar, note 1 above, at 123.

the case where the affected individuals lack the means to take a case to court, or where the affected interests are widely dispersed or impacted at a relatively low level. In the latter scenario, the cost of organizing or funding litigation, or even of obtaining sufficient information about the matter to make the decision to litigate, often outweigh the potential benefits of a successful action. This limits the range of situations upon which the courts are asked to adjudicate. The result is that the 'courts have the advantage of insulation from interest group politics, but [that] this comes at the cost of limited information and consequent bias in the development of rules'.[26]

The bilateral character of judicial procedures also means that the courts are ill equipped to examine or to address polycentric or policy questions which necessarily involve the weighing of multiple interests. The courts have neither the procedural capacity required to adequately investigate such issues, nor the range of remedies available to insist upon the most context-appropriate outcomes. This further restricts the types of dispute that are brought to the judiciary's attention. The courts, it has been argued, are normatively entitled to exercise their own judgement about the merits of a particular approach to reconciling competing public claims. As a body with an institutionally representative role, a court may assess whether a particular measure strikes an appropriate balance between social values. The particular institutional characteristics of the courts mean, however, that they are both empirically unlikely and practically incapable of being centrally involved in the determination of many forms of public dispute.

From the empirical point of view, it is instructive to consider the example of disputes over 'public goods' which involve polycentric or policy proposals in respect of matters in which a great many people or organizations have a low level of interest. As a matter of reality, these are unlikely to be brought before the courts:

> Public goods involve interests dispersed over most of the population. Although the social benefits can be vast, the per capita benefits are small—especially in comparison with the costs of production. In addition, excluding non-contributors from enjoying the good is impossible. The costs of litigation and enforcement are so high, the per capita stakes so small, and the free riding associated with the funding of the litigation so endemic that it is impossible to even imagine resolving public goods issues in the adjudicative process.[27]

Furthermore, as noted earlier, even if actions in respect of these issues were initiated before the courts, there would be a serious question mark over the capacity of an adjudicative framework to adequately engage with them. Traditionally courts have only been comfortable with weighing two sides. With public goods issues, such a bilateral balance will typically arise only after the political organs have already made an initial determination in respect of the relevant

[26] G Hadfield, 'Bias in the Evolution of Legal Rules' (1992) 80 *Georgetown Law Journal* 583, at 615.

[27] Komesar, note 1 above, at 129.

competing collective and individual interests, and expressed their support for a specific approach. It is only where the 'political process has already shouldered most of the decision-making responsibility and, by its presence, provided a concentrated interest' that the courts are likely to be invited to act.[28] This underscores the extent to which the court, in general, provides a reactive and backward-looking forum, more suited to a process of bilateral review than one of polycentric planning.

In comparison with the administration, the courts exhibit a greater institutional capacity for independence, impartiality, and procedural rigour. This means that their adjudications tend to be based on information which is more strictly relevant and reliable. This in turn means that they are less susceptible to the sort of targeted interest group efforts that can affect the administration. Parties, no matter how economically powerful, will be unable to intervene or make submissions to the court where their demands are not strictly relevant.

However, this also has the result that the courts consciously blind themselves to information which might have a more general social relevance. The courts' traditionally bilateral character reduces their capacity to have regard to other social interests in coming to their conclusions. These procedural restrictions also mean that the court is cast in a purely reactive role. Judicial involvement in social disputes is dependent on both the existence and the nature of a litigated action. In contrast, the administration enjoys a greater autonomy of action. It cannot, of course, undertake action in the absence of some form of central delegation or instruction. Implementing public policy or pursuing particular objectives is an ongoing role, however, which involves analysis, action, review, and possibly readjustment. This means that the administration can respond to particular developments on its own initiative instead of having to wait for a formal invitation to act.

Furthermore, the ongoing involvement of the administration in the governance process means that its officials are more likely than judges to have knowledge and experience of the practicalities of implementing public policy. Courts are more comfortable with correcting past errors than with solving future problems. Even where a court is asked to determine whether a proposed measure is appropriate, it usually will not learn whether this in fact proved to be the case upon implementation. This limits the possibility to develop learned expertise about the practice of governance. This suggests that, in comparison with the courts, the administration may have a greater potential institutional capacity for making practical judgements on issues of implementation.

(3) Comparison with the Market

In addition to these other central government institutions, the institutional merits of the administration must be compared with those of the market

[28] Ibid, at 133.

process. This is especially important given the extensive and sustained criticism which administrative governance has attracted in recent decades. The administrative bureaucracy has been criticized as an inefficient apparatus through which public power is exercised in an unaccountable and impenetrable manner.[29] Complaints have been made that the administrative branch has become rigid, ossified, and functionally ineffective:[30] 'an inert bureaucracy encased in an inert political system [which] grind[s] inflexibly ... toward (at best) irrelevance or (at worst) real harm'.[31] This apparent institutional sclerosis has been unfavourably compared with the responsive efficacy of market mechanisms. It is this unflattering contrast with the putative flexibility of the free marketeers which has provided much of the impetus for government reform of the administration in recent decades. Private actors have been invited to participate in previously governmental processes such as the delivery of state services, while market principles of efficiency and consumer service have been incorporated into the internal conduct and organization of the administration itself. The rise of the 'new public management' model may plausibly be understood as an attempt to make the administration more like the market[32]—in effect, to make an institutional choice in favour of market processes over traditional bureaucratic principles.

It might appear incongruous, therefore, to articulate a separation of powers theory which is predicated in part upon the positive input of administrative agencies at a time when governments in many jurisdictions have been moving responsibilities from the administration to the market. With apparently declining government confidence in conventional forms of administrative organization, it may seem incongruous to advance a theory which assumes that the administration should assume a significant and influential position as a pillar of institutional governance. This view, however, would risk falling into the trap of single institutional analysis against which Komesar has warned. Just as it is impermissible to argue for an institutional role for the administration on the basis of the limitations of the political or judicial branches, so it is equally impermissible to assert a general preference for market principles over bureaucratic values on the basis of the perceived inefficiencies of the administrative branch.

Nor is such a consistent preference for market principles necessarily well founded. In the first place, a number of empirical studies have suggested that the common portrayal of the administration as a defensive institution which is

[29] For an example of this kind of attack, see PK Howard, *The Death of Common Sense* (Grand Central, 1996).

[30] TO McGarity, 'Some Thoughts on "Deossifying" the Rulemaking Process' (1992) 42 *Duke Law Journal* 1385; RJ Pierce, Jr, 'Seven Ways to Deossify Agency Rulemaking' (1995) 47 *Administrative Law Review* 59.

[31] Kagan, note 10 above, at 2344–2345.

[32] D Woodhouse, *In Pursuit of Good Administration* (Clarendon Press, 1997).

hidebound by procedural and bureaucratic constraints may not be accurate.[33] Some commentators argue that the administration already operates in ways which emphasize the values of responsiveness and outcome-oriented efficacy more typically associated with the free market.[34]

Secondly, a preference for the market largely translates into a preference for instrumental or allocative efficiency as a superior institutional norm. The key attraction of the market process is its ability to generate efficient outcomes. Securing the efficient achievement of goals is, of course, a matter of considerable importance for an institutional theory. However, it was argued strongly in Chapters 3 and 4 that simple goal instrumentalism is not a sufficiently legitimate basis for state action. The autonomy of the individual citizen, it was contended, requires that the institutional system adhere to the principle of non-arbitrariness in order to operate in a normatively legitimate manner. Whether the market is as capable as the administration of integrating this necessary respect for non-arbitrariness into its efficiency-oriented processes is a much more open question than one framed solely in terms of the achievement of allocative goals. This is especially so given that the most obvious way of incorporating considerations of non-arbitrariness into market principles is by quantifying such considerations in monetary terms. This would allow the market's efficiency calculus to operate, but would do so by reducing the individual's interest in non-arbitrariness to a monetary value. As this interest derives from the individual's autonomy as a human person, effectively this approach would permit the individual's autonomy to be commodified. This would constitute a direct repudiation of the whole basis of the autonomy principle. The point of requiring non-arbitrariness in the exercise of public power is to ensure that the promotion of collective goals occurs in a way which takes due account of the interests of each individual in the particular actions envisaged. This might render the pursuit of such collective goals more inefficient or ineffective. However, regard for the individual is required because of each person's status as an autonomous entity. To reduce that status to a common reckonable figure to be factored into overall collective assessments of value dehumanizes the individual and would seem to contravene

[33] Bressman argues (note 22 above, at 1819–1820) that '[s]cholars have offered empirical studies that undermine the conventional wisdom that administrative procedures ossify the administrative process'. She cites, in particular, an unfinished study by Professor C Coglianese and AJ O'Connell, 'The Regulation Clock and Political Transitions: An Empirical Portrait of the Modern Administrative State' (UC Berkeley Pub. L Research Paper No. 999099, 2007), available at <http://papers.ssrn.com/s013/papers.cfm?abstract id=999099>. See also W Jordan, 'Ossification Revisited: Does Arbitrary and Capricious Review Significantly Interfere With Agency Ability to Achieve Regulatory Goals Through Informal Rulemaking?' (2000) 94 *Northwestern University Law Review* 393.

[34] Salamon has argued that 'the structure of modern government already embodies many of the features that ... reforms seek to implement. In point of fact, a technological revolution has taken place in the operation of the public sector over the past fifty years both in the United States and, increasingly, in other parts of the world; but it is a revolution that few people recognise'. See Salamon, 'The New Governance', note 3 above, at 1612.

the basic principles upon which, it was argued in Chapter 4, legitimate governance rests.

That is not to say that a system capable of accounting for non-arbitrariness and efficiency in an economic fashion would be impossible to devise. Whether or not that can be done is outside the scope of this book. The point being made here is that non-arbitrariness is not a value with which the market calculus is immediately comfortable. The market accordingly lacks the kind of demonstrably superior ability to deal with non-arbitrariness necessary to support any sort of general preference for market processes over administrative principles. To the extent, therefore, that critics of the administration or of bureaucratic principles assume an inherent superiority of market processes, their assumptions seem insufficiently thought-out to provide real assistance to the analytical exercises required in this chapter.

Thirdly, it must be remembered that there are a number of difficulties with applying any presumption of market supremacy, however well developed, to the actions of the state. As individuals faced with a monopolistic entity, there may be a limit to the extent to which the citizen stands to benefit from the use of pure free-market principles to regulate their interactions with the state. More fundamentally, any system premised on presumptive market efficiencies may encounter significant problems in situations where there is a skewed distribution of information or of transaction costs. Market ordering proceeds from prior allocations. The basic Coasean principle is that private ordering in a costless world will always produce an efficient outcome regardless of the previous allocations of power or assets. In reality, however, there are few situations, if any, in which transaction costs are zero, or even close to zero. This was a fact of which Coase himself was well aware. As Kennedy has observed, '[t]he historical irony of the Coase Theorem has been that it turned out to be the foundation of exactly the kind of elaborate law and economics theorising it purported to show was impractical'.[35] This means that, in practice, the capacity of the market to remedy anomalies in the initial distribution or to secure the most efficient outcome of the private ordering process is often quite limited. Where transaction costs are very high, for example, there will be a reduced likelihood of any change to the status quo, regardless of how inequitable, arbitrary, or inefficient this may be. 'Where impediments to successful negotiation are substantial, inefficiencies in the initial allocation may not be overcome through mutually advantageous exchange.'[36] Costs do not inhibit appropriate outcomes alone.

[35] D Kennedy, 'Cost–Benefit Analysis of Entitlement Problems: A Critique' (1981) 33 *Stanford Law Review* 387, at 397. See also Ellickson's observation that 'Coase's name is consistently attached to propositions that he has explicitly repudiated. Predictions identified as 'Coasean' are predictions that Coase would never make.' RC Ellickson, 'The Case for Coase and against "Coaseanism"' (1989) 99 *Yale Law Journal* 611, at 611.

[36] J Coleman and J Kraus, 'Rethinking the Theory of Legal Rights' (1986) 95 *Yale Law Journal* 1335, at 1335.

They can also serve to generate inappropriate transactions. Where the distribution of costs is skewed, skewed outcomes may occur. For example, where a proposed transaction confers significant benefits on a small group of individuals at the expense of a relatively smaller adverse impact on a widely dispersed group, so that the individuals involved have skewed incentives to support or to resist the transaction, it is more likely that the transaction will occur even if, by so doing, it produces an anomalous outcome.

The familiar law and economics example of a polluting factory can be used to illustrate this point briefly. The factory might be able to secure a situation in which it emits pollution to the detriment of the health of a wide range of citizens because of the fact that the financial benefits to it of so doing are so great that they justify its taking the risk of prosecution, or expending money on lobbying for government or regulatory approval. At the same time, the dispersed nature of the affected group, when combined with the fact that the impact on an individual's health is serious but not immediately obvious, make it unlikely that the group will be incentivized to acquire the necessary information, or meet the formidable transaction costs required, to organize opposition to the pollution. The skewed transaction and information costs in this example make pollution the likely outcome even though it might have serious long-term consequences for the health of a large group of individuals. It is obviously questionable whether this would be the appropriate outcome for any exercise of the state's power to regulate environmental issues.

What this indicates is that, while private ordering may have many benefits, it is not a panacea for all conflicts of interest, be they between different individuals, or between the individual and the collective, which can occur in an organized society. The costs of information and of transactions are rarely zero in the real world. In fact, they may be skewed in such a way as to destroy the market's ability to produce efficient outcomes. This undermines the extent to which it may plausibly be suggested that market calculus is an inherently superior instrument for achieving specific goals or objects, not least in matters of institutional choice. As Ellickson has remarked, '[t]ransaction costs ... are large'. Coase himself has said it. Field evidence shows it. Law-and-economics scholars should heed it.'[37] The question therefore is not whether the market is better than the administration per se. It is whether either the market or the administration is better equipped to perform a specific task, or series of tasks, in specific circumstances. This assessment is both contextualized and relative. This does not mean, of course, that the introduction of market principles into administrative procedures, or the delegation of particular tasks by the state to private actors, is necessarily misguided. The choice is not a binary one between opposing institutional forms. The allocation of institutional functions is a complex and contextual task which precludes the making of generalized judgements about the

[37] Ellickson, note 35 above, at 614.

merits of individual institutions. The point here is that this means that the qualities of the administrative branch cannot be dismissed as summarily as they have been by some pro-market critics. This is especially so when the discussion above of the relative adaptability of the administrative process indicates that criticisms of it as inherently inflexible may be based on caricature rather than reality. The market may be more suitable for some tasks but it does not enjoy an inherent institutional superiority over the administrative process.

Given the market's diffuse character, it is more difficult to make a global comparison of its institutional characteristics with those of the administration. Both may take many different forms. In general, however, it seems reasonable to suggest that the market's singular focus on efficiency maximization means that it may be more likely to carry out particular tasks in a cost-effective manner than the administration would. Relying on market processes should also encourage flexibility and responsiveness by incentivizing the monitoring and meeting of individual demands. However, the market's concern with considerations of profit also means that it may be less well equipped than the administration to take account of any public or civic dimensions to the exercise of power. In particular, there must be question marks over the extent to which an unfettered market would have regard to principles of fairness, justice, or non-arbitrariness. This is especially so given the fact that a focus on profit alone logically denotes that the objective of each actor is ultimately to reach a position in which it is able to maximize its profits. Having regard to the power imbalances inherent in the relationship between the government and the governed, this suggests that it would not be normatively appropriate to govern by market or efficiency-oriented principles alone.

(4) Comparative Conclusions

When compared with the political and judicial organs of government, the administration does appear to have specific institutional attributes which make it especially suited to perform particular tasks. It provides a comparatively cheaper and more effective means of obtaining localized information about the situation and circumstances of citizens and organizations. In practice, it allows the exercise of discretionary judgement by officials within the confines of a rule-bound and hierarchical structure. It is less cohesive or centrally powerful than the elected organs but is, at the same time, more impartial, more informed, more practically experienced, and more accountable. Its processes are less independent and rigorously structured than the courts, but it is also less costly, less rigid, and more capable of incorporating general public concerns and dispersed interests into its decision-making.

This combination of local information with evaluative experience, discretionary power with formal constraints, and impartiality with instrumentalist skills, appears to make the administration the appropriate institutional choice for the performance in practice of the role which has previously been proposed for it in the abstract in this book. That function, it will be recalled, was to serve as a second-order decision-maker, refining and recalibrating the determinations made by first-order institutions in matters of public governance. It was argued that effective constitutional governance requires the ongoing and normatively legitimate management of the recurring conflicts between individual and collective interests. In this regard, it was suggested that the administration could reconcile the abstract collectivist commands of the political organs and the abstract individual-oriented imprecations of the courts, with the practical implications of implementing such orders. This would have the particular benefit—from the point of view of both normative value and instrumental efficiency—of ensuring that the circumstances and interests of those subject to any proposed measures are adequately factored into the state's efforts to pursue the public good.

The discretion which necessarily inheres in the administrative process creates a space which permits the apparatus of the state to tailor the exercise of public power to individual circumstances in this way. Rules limit but do not exhaust administrative power:

> Rather than slavish adherence to rule-governed procedures the objectivity of bureaucracy is founded upon the use of judgement in complex, ambiguous and contested environments that constitute the everyday lived reality of the civil servant, health service professional or local government official.[38]

This reflects the reality of Mashaw's notion of enduring administrative discretion, which suggests that no system can ever provide guidance for every eventuality.[39] Once this is recognized as a potential virtue of the administrative process rather than as a threat to democratic governance, it becomes clear that the administrative process displays key institutional characteristics which permit it to play a valuable part in contemporary governance.

The administrative process also has distinct qualities when compared with the free market approach. Most notably, it would seem to have a greater inherent institutional capacity to take account of substantive normative values as part of its practical efforts to secure particular outcomes. It was argued in earlier chapters that efficacy cannot be the only yardstick of legitimate governance. It is not enough for government to simply generate social benefits—it must do so in a norm-appropriate manner. Market principles may make a useful contribution to this process but, of themselves, would not meet all of the requirements of good governance. In a devolved system of third-party government, it is instructive to note that the administration may employ market techniques where it is

[38] P Hoggett, 'A Service to the Public: The Containment of Ethical and Moral Conflicts by Public Bureacracies' in du Gay, ed., note 6 above, at 174–175.

[39] Mashaw, note 11 above, at 154.

considered appropriate. This indicates that it is not strictly necessary to consider the administration and the market as inevitably contradictory choices. In fact, the administration's ability to employ market instruments while operating within the substantive constraints of the constitutional order provides strong support for the assertions of instrumental adaptability previously advanced on its behalf.

Taken together, these factors would seem to suggest that the administration is best equipped to perform the function proposed for it in this book. The administration's combination of rule-based accountability with operational flexibility and expertise means that it 'stands apart with respect to the uniquely sweeping nature of its governing capability'[40] by providing a mechanism for both the 'impos[ition] [of] ... collective order that makes democracy possible' and 'the continuous readjustments to that order that are essential to democracy's fulfilment'.[41] The fact that it is both rule-bound and accountable to individuals means that it tends to have regard in its decision-making to civil society's dual impulses of collective and individual interest. The administration is centrally accountable but functionally dispersed, providing a system of '[c]oordinated decentralisation' which 'addresses the expectation of [citizens] that government policy will reflect their moral values and sense of fairness, but "efficiently, leav[e] the greatest possible amount of control in the hands of those closest to the problems" '.[42] This enables the administration to operate as a 'site for the continuous contestation of public purpose' which is such a prominent feature of constitutional governance.[43] The administration alone has the necessary capacities to act as a crucible of applied normative governance in which the interests of the constituent elements of the social order can be synthesized. As Hoggett concludes, the administration represents 'potentially the epitome of a substantive rather than an instrumental rationality; the one place perhaps where questions of technique ("what works") and questions of value stand a chance of being integrated'.[44]

E. External Implications for the Administration

This analytical overview of the relative characteristics of the relevant institutions does underline the extent to which the administration has particular advantages over the available alternative options. As discussed, its dispersed yet rule-bound character offers a useful combination of instrumental flexibility and normative

[40] CT Goodsell, 'The Bureau as a Unit of Governance' in du Gay, ed., note 6 above, at 22–23.
[41] Ibid, at 18–19.
[42] Lobel, note 4 above, at 443, citing P Osterman *et al.*, *Working in America: A Blueprint for the New Labor Market* (Osterman, 2001), at 152.
[43] Hoggett, note 38 above, at 168.
[44] Ibid, at 170.

accountability. Yet this dispersed and discretionary nature also limits the administration's utility as an instrument of legitimate governance in other ways. Although its positive attributes should be acknowledged, it is important that it is not presented as an institution of inherently superior value. The administration has many weaknesses as well as strengths.

For example, the breadth and diversity of administrative organizations in existence can make it difficult to subject all corners of the administration to appropriate levels of scrutiny. It is difficult, if not impossible, for external observers or for the public to understand and supervise all forms of administrative conduct. This reduces the transparency of administrative decision-making. Such a diffusion of discretionary authority across a wide range of officials and organizations also creates a significant risk of inconsistency in administrative action.

This susceptibility to inconsistency and impenetrability in turn leads to an increased danger of unnoticed, and thus unchecked, institutional capture or administrative groupthink. Where decisions are difficult for outsiders or superiors to supervise, and are understood only by those with a particular interest (be it professional or economic) in their outcomes, the possibility must exist that the decision-making process will become unduly influenced by these interested actors. This can occur in a number of ways—by the undue reliance of the administrator on the expertise or evidence provided by the well resourced and self-interested party; by encouraging the targeting of administrators with propagandist campaigns masquerading as informative specialist education; by the gradual learning effects of repeated exposure to the same arguments or ideas; by discouraging the presentation of perspectives from outside the core consensus of the relevant narrow peer network; as well as by making it more likely that simple corruption could succeed. These are important factors to consider, as they impose necessary limitations on the role and competences of administrative agencies. The unique qualities of these bodies may make them the least imperfect option for the task at hand—but the fact that such imperfections exist makes it necessary to devise an institutional arrangement which seeks to minimize their effects.

In particular, these issues of inconsistency, impenetrability, public non-awareness, and prolonged institutional capture do not affect top-down, centralized public institutions like the legislature or the courts to anything like the same degree. This suggests, in keeping with the thesis of earlier chapters, that the competences of these institutions may potentially be comingled in a way which allows the relative strengths of one to compensate for the weaknesses of others. Thus, just as the administration supplements the informational limitations of the political and judicial branches, so too can the courts and elected organs provide the sort of centralized, very public decision-making process which the administration may not. This means, for example, that the political organs constitute a much more suitable place for the conduct and resolution of collective debates about social and common goods. This is a necessary element of the constitutional system. Similarly, with their strict treatment of information and arguments, the courts are better equipped to provide an egalitarian framework for the resolution of those conflicts where the stakes and interests are sufficiently high to justify recourse to the greater rigours and costs of the judicial process. These are the roles envisaged for these institutions by the model of the separation of powers developed in this book—roles which are just as critical to the project of legitimate governance as the part potentially played by the administration. The relationship between these institutions is examined in more detail in the next chapter. At this point, however, it is sufficient to note that the concentration of this chapter on the institutional attributes of the administrative process should not obscure the fact that the system envisaged is one of collaborative interest representation in which each body plays an ongoing and co-equal part.

F. Internal Implications for the Administration

This chapter has concluded that, by comparison with the other available institutional options, the administration is best equipped to provide a mechanism of deliberative instrumentalism in which abstract choices about social value may be refracted through practical considerations of context. However, institutional choice is usually a matter of identifying the least imperfect option. If the administration has a legitimate role in governance, steps should be taken to enhance its ability to perform that role. Construing the administration's purpose in this manner carries with it a variety of implications for the future structure and organization of the administrative process.

(1) Appointment, Promotion, and Removal of Administrative Officials

As the earlier sections of this chapter make clear, the role prescribed for the administration by the new separation of powers theory is a difficult one. Refining the state's pursuit of specified objectives in a way which takes due account of local information, the need for effective action, and the interests of individual citizens is no easy task. For the administration to perform this function effectively, it must be operated by individuals with the expertise and experience to make such complex judgements. This logically requires the process by which individuals are selected to participate in the administrative process to be conducted with a view to appointment of persons or organizations with these necessary qualities of expertise and experience.

This requirement ought to permeate all aspects of the administrative process. It applies most obviously to the process by which administrative officials are recruited as employees of the state. It also applies, however, to the process by which third parties are identified to undertake tasks associated with the exercise of administrative power. One of the critical criteria for choosing the relevant actors should be that their expertise and experience makes them the most suitable individual or organization to perform that function in an effective and norm-appropriate fashion. Context-specific expertise should be present at all levels of administrative governance.

That has not always been the case. In terms of direct government, there has been a tendency in recent years for the administrative bureacracy to be deprofessionalized.[45] This has the consequence that administrative officials, especially at the lower levels of the state apparatus, have been portrayed as mere functionaries with little or no capacity for independent thought or judgement. Front-line officials are expected to reflexively adhere to the orders of superior institutions or officials. This conception of the role of the official does not accord with the new separation of powers theory, as put forward in this book. The theory requires the administration to play a positive and deliberative role which, in turn, demands logically that administrative positions be seen as professional posts which require a certain level of external competence and learned expertise. This means that the process for recruiting and appointing administrative officials should emphasize the necessity for these skills. The recruitment process must actively seek individuals with established expertise and, if possible, experience in the areas in respect of which they will be required to make decisions.

In addition, the model also attaches importance to the separation which exists between the administration and the central institutions of government. The value of this practical autonomy would be undermined if the administration's functions could be directly exercised by those centralized first-order institutions whose rules and commands it practically reinterprets and refines. The administration is instrumentally valuable for the proposed model because—in keeping with the original separation of powers device of avoiding tyranny by dispersing power—it provides the possibility for an autonomous second-stage application of proposed government actions. This requires the administration to bring its own judgement to bear on the orders issued by central government. If it passively adheres to these first-order decisions, a critically important element of the system's checks and balances is lost. This also has implications for the appointment process. It is essential that elected organs do not have direct and unchecked control of appointments to administrative posts. That is not to say that these bodies should not have an input into the process. However, a situation where officials are directly appointed by the *fiat* of elected organs risks undermining the independence of the administration. Where officials directly owe their position to the elected organ, they are less likely to be able to show the

[45] M Tushnet, 'Governance and American political development' in G de Búrca and J Scott (eds), *Law and Governance in the EU and US* (Hart, 2006).

necessary degree of independence in their deliberations and deeds. This may be because they are initially appointed on account of their subservient attitude to the elected organ, or because this type of direct appointment process supports the perception that the administration and its officials are inferior to the elected organs and accordingly obliged to give effect to their every demand.

This suggests that it is preferable for the appointment process to be organized by an independent body. Furthermore, the appointment process should be organized in a transparent and accountable way which attaches due emphasis to the necessity for relevant expertise and experience. In particular, there is a necessity to avoid the situation where support for a government party or elected organ is regarded as a criterion for appointment superior to external or established expertise. As stated, the vesting of the power to make appointments in an independent body should go a considerable way towards ensuring this is the case. This body should also give credit for the qualifications and experience of candidates in a way which accepts the basic premise that an administrative position, no matter how low-level, is a professional post in which a capacity for independent judgement is a necessary skill. Obviously, similar principles of independent judgement should also apply to the system in accordance with which third-party individuals or organizations are selected to assist in the process of governance.

Furthermore, it may also be beneficial to introduce a system whereby any proposal to appoint a particular candidate or select an individual organization is subject to an external review process designed to ensure that the proposed administrator is adequately qualified for the post in question. For high-level appointments, the review of an individual candidate could be conducted publicly. This would not necessarily be required for less high-profile positions. However, any review process of even such lower-level positions should also be transparent itself and open to public scrutiny where required. This would have the dual advantage of ensuring the appointment of suitably qualified candidates while also publicly reinforcing the view of the administration as a branch of government with a demonstrable capacity to contribute positively to good governance.

The concern for autonomy outlined above has similar implications for the tenure and promotion prospects of administrative officials, and for the process by which they may be removed from their posts. Again, it is necessary that they be able to exercise independent judgement about the instructions received from the political organs. This has the obvious consequence that the political organs should not be able to secure the removal of an administrative official or third-party organization for independently exercising its powers in a manner which does not accord with their preferences. Where this is even a possibility, this could produce a self-censoring effect on administrative independence. Similarly, where officials are required to regularly submit themselves to the political organs for reappointment or review, the necessary independence of this office may be compromised. An institution or official whose tenure is subject to very regular review may consider it more prudent to deliver decisions with which the political organs are content. The same phenomenon of self-interested self-censorship may also apply where the political organs have an unfettered or unsupervised entitlement to confer or withhold promotional advancement. This indicates that it may be desirable to ensure that administrative officials enjoy the protection of a reasonable tenure period and of a promotion and removal process which is supervised by a body that is independent of the direct control of the political institutions.

(2) Training

In a similar vein, the depiction of the administration as an institution characterized by the independent and dispassionate exercise of expert practical judgement has obvious implications for the internal training of directly-employed administrators. If the administration is to play the part assigned to it by the new separation of powers, it is necessary that officials understand their role and be adequately trained to perform it. They should not be discouraged from exercising independent judgement, nor encouraged to automatically respond to the demands of active or vocal interest groups.

The focus of many public service reforms in recent years has been on developing so-called New Management principles of administrative action. Under these principles the traditional concern of the administration with public service and impartiality is replaced by an approach which is focused on efficiency and consumer satisfaction. From the point of view of the proposed model of separation of powers, these reforms seem somewhat misconceived. Under this new model, administrators remain constrained by key institutional and hierarchical restrictions but are also required to act by reference, not only to considerations of efficiency, but also to substantive norms of non-arbitrariness and fairness. Efficiency is a relevant and important factor but it is not the dominant or sole concern for the administrative official. Training must encourage administrators to have regard to these substantive notions, and equip them with the skills to make independent judgements about what these values require in individual cases.

This again underlines the necessity to reverse any recent tendency to underplay the administration's capacity for independent professional judgement. Officials should obviously observe the constraints of the rule-bound hierarchy within which they operate. However, within those constraints, they should be encouraged and expected to make reasoned assessments about the 'best' way to pursue a particular objective. These assessments should integrate considerations of efficacy and of value in a way which is informed and logically defensible. The training of administrators should therefore equip them with the ability to undertake each stage of this process deliberatively. They should be able to investigate and inform themselves about relevant circumstances on the ground. They should be able to engage with interested parties and to rationally review their submissions. They should, crucially, be able to weigh all of these relevant considerations in coming to their conclusions, and to account for and defend any decisions reached. Training should be directed to the development of these skills.

From the perspective of third-party actors, it is unlikely that the state itself will be centrally involved in the provision of particular training or instruction. However, even here, the state does retain the capacity to act in an instructional role. It would seem appropriate for the actions of such third-party organizations to be subject to systems which encourage adherence to principles of good governance. This could be achieved in a number of ways. Where powers are devolved to third-party individuals or organizations, the state will usually be required to provide specific directions about particular aspects of the way in which the entity in question ought to perform its role. At present, many of these agreements are expressed primarily in terms of the delivery of particular outcomes. However, there is no necessary reason why the rules or contracts which govern the transfer of administrative powers could not also impose a series of substantive obligations on such bodies. Requirements to monitor and report on third-party activities should ensure a certain level of adherence to appropriate norms, as could a system in which third parties are encouraged to subject their practices to peer review. Central government may have a role in supervising the internal conduct of third-party actors, too. In particular, as will be argued later, the courts ought to be willing to review the procedures and activities of such bodies by reference to the normative principles of constitutional governance which have previously been discussed. The imposition of such substantive constraints, be they contractual or constitutional, could operate as a form of education by exposition and enforcement for these bodies, encouraging them to internalize the appropriate norms and thereby enhancing the administration's capacity to contribute to good governance.

(3) Self-Image of Officials

These recommendations for the training of administrative officials reflect a more general requirement for the development of an altered administrative self-image. As already noted, in the new separation of powers system it is necessary for the administration to act with due regard for principles of impartiality and non-arbitrariness, as well as notions of instrumental efficiency. This reflects the autonomous and positive role envisaged for the administration by the new model of institutional separation.

This role, however, requires a more radical rethinking of the administrative process than one which simply places greater emphasis on substantive norms. It is also necessary to develop a different conception of government itself, and of administrative power. The prevailing orthodoxy holds that the administration must implement the orders of the elected institutions. For administrators, this manifests itself in practice in the belief that they are subject to the direct control of the relevant minister or executive official. This is based, as previously discussed, on traditional *imperium*-inspired notions of government. This traditional view rests on the notion that central government may operate successfully by issuing rule-based commands which prescribe in sufficient detail what should be done in all eventualities. This approach assumes that top-down institutions are superior and that government by central decree produces immediate and effective outcomes. This is simply neither accurate nor realistic. Administrative discretion is not only inevitable but, as this book has argued, may also be normatively useful as a deliberative space for mediating between top-down commands and bottom-up circumstances, and between considerations of practical efficacy and substantive value.

If that is to be the case in practice, there is a need for the administration to adopt an amended understanding of how governmental power ought to operate. Governance must be seen as a collaborative inter-institutional process in which the administration is entitled and expected to play a distinct and valuable part. In particular, the issuing of commands by the elected organs must be understood as the starting point for the exercise of state power, rather than as an end in itself. This requires the administration to move away from a process of reflexive instrumentalism, where orders are blindly followed or ends unthinkingly pursued, towards one in which the administration independently examines how best to undertake the tasks entrusted to it.

In his work on deliberative democracy, Richardson argued that practical reasoning must necessarily involve 'reasoning about ends'—a process which acknowledges the possibility that, as the process progresses, it may become necessary to 'revis[e] the working conception of which ends matter'.[46] The unthinking pursuit of individual objectives is not an effective mode of governance: '[a]s Dewey most clearly recognised, an intelligent approach to practical problems, whether individual or public, requires above all a flexible willingness to remake one's aims in light of new information'.[47] This has obvious implications for an administration with superior local knowledge and practical experience. As Richardson suggests, administrative bodies are well equipped to 'reasonably take up the conclusions of democratic procedures as provisional premises of truth-oriented noninstrumental reasoning about what we ought to do'.[48]

That should not be taken to imply that the administration is at liberty to create entirely new objectives. Just as the political organs do not have a monopoly on determining state conduct under the new model of separation of

[46] Richardson, note 12 above, at 99. [47] Ibid, at 121. [48] Ibid, at 141.

powers, neither should the administration be entitled to make unfettered judgements about government action. The suggestion that the administration ought to be encouraged to think analytically about the orders it receives as part of its efforts to give effect to them reflects the fact that, with any form of proposed government action, there are likely to be a number of relevant ends which could be taken into account. These will include not only the general substantive norms, such as non-arbitrariness, which the administration must strive to secure. In many situations, there might be an overlap or even a contradiction between a variety of the ends identified as important by the elected organs. The pursuit of a particular specified purpose might conflict with a more general political desire: for example, to avoid excessive costs, or ensure economic stability, or avoid discrimination. Alternatively, where there is an overlap between identified objectives, it might be preferable to incorporate them into a single, amended end which will satisfy more of each than would be the case if only one were pursued. These are the sort of practical considerations that can arise in the course of the effort to give effect to political objectives.

If the administration is to fulfil the purpose newly prescribed for it, it is accordingly necessary for it to develop a self-image in which it is able to engage in just such forms of considered practical reasoning rather than simply pursuing individual political ends. This requires a rethinking of the administration's function and of its relationship with the political organs of the state. No longer should it be regarded as subject to the direct management and control of elected officials. Although still bound to act upon their direct instructions, the administration must exercise its own distinct judgement about the means by which such orders ought to be carried out in light of the additional information and expertise available to it. To put it another way, the administration must act autonomously but not unilaterally. It is not independent of the other organs in the sense of being able to act as it pleases, but it is entitled to bring its own judgement to bear on the task entrusted to it by them. Where the political organs are dissatisfied with its actions, they may issue amended instructions for the administrators to follow. What they may not do, however, is order the administrators to exercise their independent judgement in a specific way. To permit this would undercut the administration's proposed new purpose as a second-order application of first-order instructions on the basis of substantive principles of deliberative practical reason.

(4) Internal Administrative Procedures

Logically, the administration's own internal processes should also reflect the claims of institutional capacity advanced on its behalf. This means that internal procedures should seek to maximize the administration's purported institutional advantages and minimize its disadvantages.

In particular, given the continued assertion that the administration's proximity to the subjects over which it exercises authority enables it to make more informed and reasoned decisions, it seems sensible to suggest that the acquisition of information should be a key focus of internal procedures. This means that the administration should be organized in such a way as to encourage active engagement with interested parties. Through such engagement, officials acquire information about circumstances on the ground.

It may also be the case that administrative officials should be given investigative competence where appropriate, so that their ability to inform themselves about relevant considerations is not dependent upon the willingness of others to participate in the administrative process.

Similarly, the desire for an informed decision-making process also suggests that there may be a role for incorporating relevant expert views into the administration's deliberations. This may be achieved through the appointment of qualified officials. However, there may also be a benefit to involving external experts in the decision-making process. Subjecting the administrative process and outcomes to expert peer review, be it internal or external, could also be considered as another way of enhancing the quality of the conclusions reached.

Other important characteristics of the administrative process which have been emphasized in this chapter are its capacity for rational deliberative reflection and its accountability. Administrative officials are liable to account for their actions to their superiors, to the elected and judicial organs, and to substantive norms of impersonality and non-arbitrariness. There is a natural overlap between these characteristics, attaching emphasis as each does to the importance of reasoned decision-making. They logically suggest that the administration should organize its internal procedures in a way which both provides for the rational weighing of relevant considerations, and explains and justifies the eventual outcome. A duty to provide adequately detailed reasons would go a considerable way towards improving these qualities, not only enhancing accountability, but also by concentrating the attention of administrative officials on ensuring that their decisions are properly reasoned.

Furthermore, any such duty to provide reasons should also improve the responsiveness of the administration to local concerns by obliging officials to consider, and then rationally accept or reject the arguments of relevant affected interests. This strengthens the deliberative process and should accordingly improve the quality of administrative decision. In addition, however, the provision of adequate reasons may reassure participants that their interests are taken into account as part of the decision-making process. Unhappy as those whose arguments are rejected might be, such properly deliberative engagement at least involves these citizens in the governance process and—if properly explained—may remind them of how much government must involve the imperfect mediation between a multitude of conflicting interests. As considered in Chapter 1, this type of publicly reasoned proceduralism has an important role to play in ensuring the ongoing efficacy of a democratic system of government.

From the point of view of the administration's comparative institutional weaknesses, it is logical for it to structure its internal procedures in a way which reduces the dangers of poor institutional judgement. In particular, the heightened risk of bias associated with the administrative process raises serious questions over the extent to which it may be appropriate to regard it as a form of democratic representation. Stewart, it has been noted, suggested that the actions of administrative agencies in the USA could be so justified, so that they would provide an auxiliary avenue for the communication to the government of individual or group preferences. The administrative process, on this analysis, afforded the relevant interest group the opportunity to have direct input into the decision-making process, thereby ensuring the representation of their opinion in the process of governance.[49]

This chapter has already considered how the administration provides a valuable forum in which individuals or organizations who are potentially affected by a proposed exercise of power might make representations to the decision-maker about the appropriateness or otherwise of the envisaged course of action. There is a difference, however, between a process which permits the making of representations and one for which representation is an end in itself. It is important to remember that the reason why the making of representations was presented as an instrumentally valuable aspect of the process was because it was likely to enhance the administration's ability to make a more informed and reasoned decision. Allowing direct input from potentially affected parties provides additional localized information which might be difficult or costly for the state to obtain through its own agents. Similarly, where such parties have a significant interest in the eventual outcome of the process, there is a logical incentive for them to furnish appropriate technical evidence or reasoned argument to the administrative decision-maker in support of their position. Permitting the potentially affected to put their case directly to the decision maker reduces the information deficit between the government and the governed, promotes practical reasoning by providing a more precise focus on the possible real-world outcomes of any decision made, and enhances deliberative rationality by obliging the administration to consider and then rationally accept or reject arguments put forward by parties external to the governmental process. The key point is that this direct input is not intended to ensure that the state's actions accord more accurately with the wishes of the relevant interested parties. The role of the administration is not to advocate the views of these interested parties to central government. The administrative process does not provide a platform for the representation of

[49] R Stewart, 'The Reformation of American Administrative Law' (1974–5) 88 *Harvard Law Review* 1667.

their views. On the contrary, the interested parties are, in effect, co-opted into a deliberative process over which the administration retains control at all times.

It is the essence of democratic rule that government represents and responds to popular preferences. It is undemocratic, however, for government to reflexively privilege the preferences of either those specifically affected by an individual measure, or those who opt or are equipped to put their views to the relevant decision maker. The necessarily egalitarian regard for the interests of all that underpins the organized democratic state requires that decisions be taken because they are believed to serve the public interest best. The apparatus of the state is supposed to provide an independent means for rationally mediating between relevant interests. It is not an instrument of preference aggregation, nor of preference averaging. The administration contributes to this task, it has been argued, by providing a structure in which general judgements about social values, policies, or ends can be applied in a deliberative way which takes due account of practical considerations and individual circumstances. Any decisions taken must be accounted for to superior instititutions and substantive procedural norms.

To conceive of the administration as a form of auxiliary democracy, in which its role is to secure the representation of a narrow class of interests, is to put forward a case for administrative action which emphasizes a very different range of characteristics. This approach would attach particular importance to the administration's ability to engage directly with the relevant class while placing little or no emphasis on considerations of impartiality or rationality. That is not to say, of course, that the administration could not perform such a function. In the first place, however, such a role would seem to prioritize those characteristics which also give rise to the risks of institutional capture, bias, and groupthink outlined above. Secondly, it would seem that other institutions of government may be better equipped to perform the function of interest representation. In particular, the elected organs of government would seem better placed to play a representative role. The risk of bias clearly applies to them as well, but the centralized and public nature of their activities, coupled with their transient and shifting composition, make them less susceptible to long-term institutional capture than the more settled and sometimes impenetrable administrative process. Having regard to Komesar's insistence on multi-institutional analysis, as well as the notion that legitimate democratic governance requires more than mere interest representation, it seems reasonably clear that the administration is not best placed to carry out such a function.

This underlines the importance of properly calibrating the role of the administration under the new separation of powers. Its interaction with affected parties may improve the responsiveness of the governmental process, may promote civic engagement, or may ensure that the relevant parties are better represented in the decision-making process than might otherwise have been the case. Where appropriate, however, these are ancillary benefits. The primary purpose of the administration under the proposed model is to improve the quality of government decisions by providing a space for practical deliberative reflection upon the most effective and normatively appropriate means of implementing a particular measure. The focus of the administration is on securing the good rather than the agreed. Its priority should be to use its proximity to the subjects of government power to produce better decisions rather than consensus outcomes. The administration might refer to information and arguments provided by the relevant parties but the role envisaged for it here requires it to exercise independent and impartial judgement.

To understand the importance of this distinction, it is instructive to refer to recent experiences with the regulation of financial markets and products. It seems to have been the case in many jurisdictions that bodies with the responsibility for such regulation envisaged their role, at least in part, as being one of representing the interests of those organizations which operate under their remit. In Ireland, for example, the Financial Regulator favoured 'a model of regulation carved out of consensus' which was based on an 'open and collaborative approach between ourselves and our stakeholders in developing our strategy and our regulatory response to the best interests of consumers and investors, while maintaining sound and profitable financial businesses and markets'.[50] The Irish Financial Regulator, it seems, partly envisaged his role as one of advancing the interests of those over whom he exercised decision-making power by coming to consensus-based conclusions which responded to the preferences expressed by this narrow class in their engagement with the administrative process. As events have subsequently shown, the outcomes produced by this approach unduly favoured the interests of that class in a manner which was ultimately detrimental to the public interest and common good.

This example underscores the necessity for autonomous judgement in governance. It has been argued that the organized constitutional state is justified in part because of its capacity for considered and independent judgement. The state is normatively acceptable because it provides for the possibility of reviewing, reflecting upon, and appropriately reconciling the competing collective and individual interests engaged by government. That government must respond to the views and desires of the governed is a basic principle of democratic governance. Good governance requires more than mere responsiveness, however. There would be little logic, therefore, in a separation of powers system which conferred a primarily representative role on each individual institution. On the model proposed here, responding to preferences should be a greater concern for the elected organs; for the administration, the focus must be on securing context-sensitive decisions which appropriately marry considerations of efficacy,

[50] Comments of the Financial Regulator, Mr Patrick Neary, in a speech on 'The Evolution of Regulation in Ireland to Reflect the Future Convergence of Markets' at a Finance Dublin Conference, 27 March, 2007.

rationality, and non-arbitrariness. Accordingly, its internal procedures and self-image should reflect that fact. This suggests that, while procedures which increase the opportunities for input from relevant parties are to be welcome, it is also important that the procedures imposed provide space for independent judgement rather than the simple negotiation of an agreed consensus.

(5) Powers

Practical reasoning about the efficacy and value of proposed governmental action is a necessarily contextual process. Charged with devising the most efficacious way to implement political instructions while adhering to the relevant substantive norms, the administration is effectively asked to function as a context-sensitive, problem-solving unit. Different problems, however, require different solutions. In exercising its powers, the administration will often have to consider a significant range of factors and a considerable diversity of circumstances. It seems likely, therefore, that the appropriate action to take will vary considerably from case to case. This suggests that the administration must be equipped with an extensive and sophisticated range of powers if it is to be able to properly fulfil its functions.

Administrative discretion has a particular value for the new separation of powers system. Yet, this discretion is only as useful as the range of options open to the administration when actually exercising its powers. There is little benefit to a system in which an administrator is able to receive information about local conditions or arguments from potentially affected individuals if his or her options for responding to the issues raised are very limited. A one-size-fits-all approach to administrative power constrains the very administrative capacity to develop context-sensitive solutions upon which its proposed role in institutional governance rests. This indicates a need to examine the powers of the administration with a view to ensuring that it is equipped with the necessary tools for securing the most appropriate means of exercising state power.

In particular, there is a need to move away from the traditional *imperium*-based notion of government as a primarily coercive force. To a large extent, this has already occurred. The ability to punish individuals for their failure to observe government measures is undoubtedly a valuable power. However, it is also an essentially blunt instrument, which is only appropriate for particular situations. Typically, such punitive powers tend to be deployed in relation to the most serious infringements of government rules. This may lead, however, to an interregnum in which low-level disobedience is effectively tolerated by the state. This is particularly inappropriate given the more contemporary conception of the state as a positive instrument of social regulation with the responsibility for shaping the development of social norms. There has accordingly been a recognition that, while the capacity to punish may be useful in some situations, there is also a need in other contexts for the state to be able to guide, encourage, incentivize, or cajole. This has led to the development of the sort of 'soft law' powers discussed above. Adopting the separation of powers model proposed in this book would encourage the continued development of this process. In particular, it would call for the power of the administration to be kept under constant review so that it may be extended where necessary to ensure that officials have all the relevant options open to them when seeking to identify the most sophisticated and context-sensitive means of exercising public power.

(6) Reviews and Appeals

Acknowledging administrative decision-making as a distinct mode of practical reasoning which positively contributes to good governance suggests that it ought to be entitled to a certain level of respect as a legitimate form of judgement in its own right. This is particularly relevant to the way in which the institutional order deals with appeals from, or reviews of, administrative decisions.

The traditional separation of powers model regards administrative decisions as the mechanical application of political orders. Judgement is applied only to the extent that is required to give effect to the instructions received. This approach locates the exercise of independent judgement primarily in the political organs. This means, from the point of view of conducting a review or appeal of the exercise of power in question, that the primary decision-making responsibility rests with the political branch. Administrative conduct can be reviewed for its compliance with the orders issued by the political bodies. However, in terms of the policy choices made as part of the decision-making process, these determinations of social or political value are not matters for the administration. This has meant that the courts, when considering challenges to administrative decisions, have traditionally shown considerable deference to the actions of administrators. Decisions were reviewed to ensure that they were not ultra vires the orders given. There was a judicial reluctance, however, to engage in an intensive review of the merits of the administrator's decisions. This deference did not derive, however, from a judicial acceptance of the skill or judgement of administrators. It was, in reality, a deference to the political organs to whom the separation of powers attributes these determinations of social value. On the contrary, where legal or constitutional rights were engaged, the courts felt fully entitled to intervene and conduct intensive review. This again reflected a view of this matter as one which was primarily for the courts and in respect of which the administration was not entitled to exercise independent judgement.

Recognizing the positive role of administrators under the new separation of powers, and the practical reasoning abilities which it expects them to have, has two obvious implications for the conduct of appeals or reviews. In the first place, if administrative decisions represent the distinct application of independent judgement, a right of appeal in respect of them should be available. If administrators have a particular influence on the exercise of public power, those affected by that exercise should be able to have their decisions re-examined. Secondly, any such appeals or reviews should also reflect the distinct character of the judgement so exercised. In particular, appeals or reviews should recognize that administrative decision-making is not a purely mechanical process of giving effect to the earlier instructions of the judicial or political organs, but is rather a specific form of skilled practical reasoning.[51] This suggests not only that a review or appeal should show some degree of deference to the expertise involved in the exercise of such skills, but that it should be possible to review any such decision by reference to the relevant norms of practical reason. It shows insufficient regard for either the interests of affected individuals or the specific skills of administrators to review decisions on the basis of political or judicial norms alone. It should also be open to a relevant individual to challenge the judgement of an administrative official on the basis of his or her application of the modes of administrative reasoning where that is the real source of the individual's complaint.

G. Political Reforms of Administrative Practices

The specific details of the model of institutional separation set out in this book are informed by existing governmental practice. The development of this new separation of powers theory was, in part, designed to provide a more convincing account of the way in which the various organs of government currently interact. It is unsurprising, therefore, that the prevailing institutional practices already address some of the matters identified above. In both Ireland and the UK, for example, efforts have been made to introduce an element of independence and transparency into the public appointments process. The Irish Public Appointments Service and the British Office of the Commissioner for Public Appointments (OPAC) both provide a layer of independent scrutiny in relation to the appointment of officials to particular public posts. It is important not to overstate the extent to which this has occurred, however. From the point of view of independence, for example, the remit of OPAC is relatively limited, with ministers still involved in the appointment process for many civil service positions.[52] In Ireland, similarly, appointments to certain high-level public positions may be made directly by the government, with one recent *Taoiseach* (Prime

[51] This argument assumes, of course, that the sort of measures discussed above in relation to the recruitment and training of administrators have been implemented so that administrators are exercising such skilled judgement in fact as well as in theory.

[52] See, for example, the Civil Service Guide for Making and Managing Public Appointments (Cabinet Office, 2006) which reminds officials (at page 29) that the 'Minister is ultimately responsible for appointments' and 'may wish to take an active role' in the process. Good practice accordingly requires officials to '[m]ake every effort to ensure that Ministers suggest possible candidates at the outset'.

Minister) infamously explaining that he had selected particular candidates for such posts on the basis that they were friends of his.[53]

The issue of independence is one example of how current institutional practices provide some support for the principles of the new separation of powers theory, but in fact stop short of giving effect to its full logical consequences. In other areas, most notably the articulation of an institutional self-image which emphasizes efficient service delivery over substantive public-service norms, current practice may in fact conflict with the proposed theory. A comprehensive enumeration of how administrative practice as a whole fits, or fails to fit, with the new separation of powers theory is outside the scope of this book. Nonetheless, it is instructive to note that a number of recent or proposed government reforms appear to be informed by an understanding of the institutional order and, in particular, of the administration which corresponds closely with that upon which the new separation of powers theory is based.

(1) Macrory Report on *Regulatory Justice: Making Sanctions Effective*

As comparatively recent innovations in governance, regulatory bodies typify the sort of changed notions of administrative power which compelled a move away from traditional ideas of *imperium* and principal–agent control. Regulators are invested with significant discretionary powers and exercise considerable influence over the relevant sectors of society. In keeping with the modern conception of government as a positive regulatory force, they are usually charged with the responsibility for shaping and directing the social conduct of those individuals or institutions over whom they exercise power, in order to ensure that necessary restrictions are observed or specific outcomes attained.

As the relatively recent Macrory Report on *Regulatory Justice: Making Sanctions Effective* indicated, however,[54] their ability to perform this function in the most effective manner has been hampered, to a certain extent, by the fact that regulatory bodies tend to have a limited range of options for imposing sanctions open to them. Arguably, such a constrained power to sanction reflected traditional ideas of government as a central sovereign, exercising authority by the coercive enforcement of its decreed rules. For regulatory bodies, this meant that they were 'heavily reliant on one tool, namely criminal prosecution, as the main sanction should industry or individuals be unwilling or unable to ... comply with legal obligations'.[55] Macrory accordingly recommended a radical overhaul of the regulatory sanctioning regime in order that it be able to operate more effectively in the future. His recommendations have been accepted by the UK government and are expected to become law in the future. What is striking

[53] See, for example, F O'Toole, 'In the Long Shadow of the Boss' *The Irish Times* (5 April, 2008).

[54] *Regulatory Justice: Making Sanctions Effective* (Cabinet Office, 2006).

[55] Ibid, at E9.

about his Report, however, is the extent to which his understanding of the role of regulatory bodies, and the conclusions which he draws from that, quite closely approximate to the model of institutional order advanced in this book.

Macrory argues, for example, that regulators should not be regarded as primarily accountable to the elected organs of government alone, as would befit the traditional principal–agent relationship. 'Whilst accountability to Parliament and Ministers is important, it is equally important that regulators are clearly answerable to those that they regulate, and those on whose behalf they regulate.'[56] This posits a place for the regulators at the centre of conflicting social concerns, seeking to exercise power in a manner which reflects and is accountable to the interests of the elected organs, the public interest, and the affected individuals, which echoes that of the administration as a whole under the new separation of powers theory. Crucially, this accountability to individuals and to the public interest is as important as that to the elected organs. This underlines the administration's position as an independent branch of government, bound by an obligation to act within the limits placed upon it by others but entitled to exercise autonomous judgement about the most appropriate way to exercise power within those limits.

Like the view of the administration evinced in this book, the Report regards this administrative autonomy as useful because it allows the regulator the discretion to tailor the exercise of public power to reflect individual circumstances. Macrory recommends the introduction of a number of new and flexible forms of sanction so that regulators will be better equipped to adjust their actions to the particular requirements of an individual situation. These sanctions—which include profit orders, corporate rehabilitation orders, and publicity orders—will occupy the space between advice and criminal action, equipping the regulator with a 'suite of sanctions [to] ... be added to the regulators' enforcement toolbox'.[57] These, he argues, will 'allo[w] for a flexible and proportionate approach with a broad range of sanctioning options, where regulators can respond to the needs of individual cases and the nature of the underlying offence',[58] while 'ensuring the regulatory outcomes ... are not compromised'.[59] Such rule-bound flexibility in the pursuit of specified objectives is the very essence of the paradigmatic administrative process put forward in this book.

In addition, the Report also echoes the conclusions of this chapter in relation to the internal organization of the administration itself. It recommends, inter alia, that regulatory bodies should 'measure outcomes not just outputs', 'justify their choice of enforcement actions year on year', and 'enforce in a transparent manner'. These recommendations reflect the principles of transparency, publicity, and efficacy which have been consistently reiterated throughout this book. It has been argued that the administrative process should function as a

[56] Ibid at para. 5.30. [57] Ibid at 1.6. [58] Ibid, at 5. [59] Ibid, at E5.

deliberatively rational means of ensuring the 'best' outcomes available. Macrory's emphasis on the importance of measuring outputs reflects a similar concern to ensure the practical efficacy of the administrative process, while his insistence on the necessity for transparency and public justification chimes closely with the new separation of powers theory's attachment to public deliberation and civic engagement with the exercise of state power. The administration is valuable, in part, precisely because it provides the possibility of such rational public deliberation over individual circumstances, thereby providing accountability to relevant interests while also improving the quality of its decisions. If the administration is to fill this role effectively, it seems sensible to suggest that it ought to adhere to the same sort of principles as those set out in the Macrory Report. This underlines how the proposed model of institutional separation, with its revised view of administrative input into governance, may plausibly be seen less as a direct challenge to the status quo and more as a natural, if conceptually radical, evolution of contemporary attitudes towards the practice of government.

In terms of the issues addressed in the preceding section, it is also noteworthy that the Macrory Report recommends that regulatory decisions be heard by a 'separate tribunal for appealing administrative sanctions'. [60]

This, in his view, would provide flexibility in the appeal process and permit appeals to be dealt with by panels with 'both legal and specialist expertise'. As noted above, this sort of independent appellate system for regulatory or administrative bodies effectively acknowledges the legitimacy of administrative decision-making as a practice in its own right, with an entitlement to be assessed on appeal in its own terms. The creation of a distinct appellate body for administrative decisions might also have the effect of providing institutional definition for an administrative branch which, given its diverse and dispersed character, has often lacked an obvious centripetal point. From the point of view of the new separation of powers, this would be a useful step as it would emphasize the existence of the administration as a branch of government in its own right. It is instructive, therefore, that Macrory's recommendation in relation to a regulatory appellate body finds echoes in the introduction in the Tribunal, Courts and Enforcement Act 2007 of similar measures to remove administrative appeals to their own institutional forum.

(2) First-Tier and Upper Tribunal

The Tribunal, Courts and Enforcement Act 2007 established specific institutions for the hearing of appeals in respect of the decisions of administrative bodies. The new First-Tier and Upper Tribunals currently have jurisdiction over a specific number of administrative agencies but this may be extended by parliament at any time. The intention appears to be that, in time, these institutions

[60] Note 53 above, 54, para 3.59.

may have their powers extended to encompass most major areas of adjudicative administrative activity.

The First-Tier Tribunal is a generic body for the processing of appeals from particular agencies. Its decisions may be appealed to or reviewed by the Upper Tribunal, from which an appeal with permission may lie to the Court of Appeal.[61] The 2007 Act envisages this as a limited secondary appellate jurisdiction, providing in section 13(6) that the Lord Chancellor may limit the grounds upon which permission will be granted to situations where 'the proposed appeal would raise some important point of principle or practice' or where 'there is some other compelling reason for the relevant appellate court to hear the appeal'. Both Tribunals exercise full appellate powers over the decision under appeal, while the Upper Tribunal is also entitled to grant relief which would normally only be available under judicial review proceedings provided that, in so doing, it adheres to the judicial review principles which would be applied by the High Court in considering such a claim.

From the point of view of the theory under discussion here, the creation of these new Tribunals is significant for a number of reasons. In the first place, as discussed above, the very act of collecting administrative appeals into a single institutional structure lends credence to one of the theory's central propositions: namely, that, in contemporary systems of institutional arrangement, the administration has a distinct and independent role. It encourages observers to view the administration as a cohesive institutional entity, rather than as a collection of diffused and uncoordinated actors. In particular, it supports the argument that administrative decision-making is a distinct and cohesive form of institutional practice. By providing a system which—at least initially—allows the validity of administrative decisions to be examined outside the traditional fora of political and legal accountability, the 2007 Act implicitly accepts that these decisions can be made and reviewed on independent administrative grounds.

Secondly, the Act also appears to be based on a view of administrative decision-making which corresponds to that advanced in this book. Section 2(3) of the Act directs the Senior President of the Tribunals in carrying out his function, to have regard to a number of key principles. These are:

1) the need for tribunals to be accessible,
2) the need for proceedings before tribunals—
    a. to be fair, and
    b. to be handled quickly and efficiently,
3) the need for members of tribunals to be experts in the subject matter of, or the law to be applied in, cases in which they decide matters, and
4) the need to develop innovative methods of resolving disputes that are of a type that may be brought before tribunals.

[61] Section 13.

This statutory statement of principles reflects a very clear view of what Parliament regards as good administrative practice. It is telling that it emphasizes so many of the themes which have been identified thus far as the institutional characteristics which potentially equip the administration to make a positive contribution to legitimate democratic governance. The Senior President of the Tribunals is required to have regard at all times to the values of accessibility, fairness, speed, efficiency, and expertise. These are the sort of institutional norms which have consistently been reiterated as important in this book. The administrative tribunals are encouraged by section 2 (3) to act as innovative problem-solving units. This echoes the view previously advanced that the rule-bound flexibility of administrative bodies enables them to develop sophisticated and context-sensitive solutions to the issues raised before them. The administration is presented here as a fair, accessible, and expert institution with a particular capacity for the flexible, autonomous, and creative exercise of practical judgement. The extent to which this diverges from the traditional understanding of administrators as the unthinking implementers of government orders illustrates how much closer to an accurate depiction of contemporary governance is the characterizing of the administration under the new separation of powers system.

H. Conclusion

These latter examples are isolated instances of political developments which indicate at least some level of potential support for the conception of administrative action set out in this book. This chapter has concluded that the administration is functionally equipped, at least in principle, to perform the task which the new separation of powers model entrusts to it—that of providing an institutional space in which considerations of local context, normative value, and instrumental efficacy can be absorbed into the administration's decision-making process. The administration's particular characteristics, when set against those of the political organs and courts, make it a suitable candidate to fill this role. Equally, however, this chapter has indicated that these other institutions have particular qualities which must also be reflected in the overall governance process. Accordingly, a particular exercise of administrative power should not be seen as the final or binding determination of the polity's position. On the contrary, the relative strengths and weaknesses of these institutions mean that they each have a distinct and useful contribution to make to the process of exercising power in the interests of the common good—but a contribution which is of limited value. Good government requires ongoing input from each institution. The next chapter will therefore consider how such a system of overlapping institutional competences might operate.

7

The Relationship between the Administration and the Other Branches

A. Introduction

A separation of powers theory which rests its claims upon a system of inter-institutional balance must inevitably concern itself with matters of external as well as internal action. Striking the correct balance requires both separation and blending. An institution must organize itself internally so that it operates in the manner envisaged by the theory while also interacting externally with other institutions in a way which adheres to the system's intended overall structure. It is insufficient for the administration to carry out the functions conferred upon it by the new separation of powers system. Developing appropriate modes of interaction with other government bodies is equally important to the success of the system as a whole. Accordingly this chapter will examine the implications of the new separation of powers for the administration's relationship with the other key organs of government.

It is important to repeat at the outset a point made in the previous chapter. The vesting of particular powers in other institutions should not be considered as a response to the relevant weaknesses in the administrative process. That is not to say the process does not have such institutional frailties. The previous chapter's concern with the *potential* attributes of the administration may naturally have had the effect of portraying the administrative branch in an idealized fashion as a problem-solving entity of rare expertise and ability. To the extent that it might have developed, any such impression should be resisted. In the first place, the allegations of inefficiency and cost commonly levelled at the administration belie any such romanticized view. More profoundly, it should be remembered that the chapter concluded that, even in its most idealized form, the administrative process still contains certain institutional biases and limitations. The administration is not a Leviathan for our times. As Komesar notes, all institutions are imperfect. It is simply that some, in particular contexts, are less imperfect than others.

Of itself, this would be sufficient to justify a continued role in government for other distinct institutions. Dealing with the defects in one institution by involving another in the process of governance is a familiar technique for separation of powers systems. However, the distribution of power amongst different branches under the model proposed in this book is based on more than such practical concerns. The new separation of powers was elaborated as more than a merely prudential response to contemporary problems. It has instead been developed from, and designed to reflect, a number of underlying political assumptions. It is these principles, more than operational considerations of institutional practice, which shaped the particular pattern of power distribution advocated in this book.

B. Relevant Political Principles

(1) The Provisionality and Legitimacy of Institutional Perspectives

To recap briefly, the new separation of powers proceeds from an acceptance of the inevitability of political conflict in organized society. It rejects the possibility of a permanently fixed and common acceptance of what good governance involves. The range of interests which exist within an individual polity makes disagreement about any proposed act of governance inevitable. This has a number of implications for the system of government as a whole.

First of all, it implies that political perspectives must necessarily be provisional. Even where a proposal attracts considerable popular support, it is likely that opposition will emerge, whether at the time in question or at some stage in the future. This makes it impossible to identify a settled social consensus which will endure for all time. The system must accept that the ideal of universal social agreement is a chimera for which nonetheless the government must unsuccessfully strive. The contractarian foundations of the state compel the pursuit of universal value just as the individualist character of its most basic constituent authority dooms it to dissent and disagreement.

Accepting that the positions adopted by the state are only provisional in turn suggests that there is a basic legitimacy to the differing perspectives which may emerge. This does not assume, of course, that these contrary ideas will be objectively better than those of the government, or that they will ultimately persuade and prevail. The point is that, for the purpose of government, there is no such thing as the objectively correct view. There is only the current favoured conception of what is best for society as a whole, which is liable to refinement, amendment, or rejection over time. This indicates the necessity for a systemic tolerance of the articulation of alternative views. If a social consensus (to the extent that it exists) is provisional, it should always be open to the possibility of challenge.

This acceptance of the inevitability and potential legitimacy of alternative views, in turn, obliges the state as a matter of prudence as well as of principle to provide mechanisms for managing such social conflicts. The state's legitimacy and authority depend in part upon its ability to present itself as the representative embodiment of common social values at the same time as it tries to cope with the inevitable absence of true commonality. As Chapter 1 concluded, the state must internalize these conflicts in a way which engages the various opposing parties so that they are all drawn into a basic acceptance of the system's overall validity.

The model proposed by the new separation of powers is specifically intended to achieve that purpose. Its design is derived from an acceptance that different points of view are provisional and potentially legitimate. The separate and distinct roles which the model confers upon the relevant institutions reflect the assessment that they each represent a different constituent perspective. Because each of these constituent perspectives is likely to contribute to the ongoing social debate about common values and good governance, it is represented by a particular institution.

At the same time, these institutions are not expected to act as advocates for these particular views. The system does not envisage the courts as motivated only by the interests and concerns of individualism, just as it does not expect the political organs to be animated by a desire for collective action to the exclusion of all other interests. On the contrary, the model's calculation is that these bodies are all institutionally capable and empirically more likely to be influenced to a greater degree by a particular perspective. Each is still intended, however, to act in a way which it believes to accord with the requirements of good governance. The particular characteristics of each institution mean that it may be more or less equipped to engage with a specific point of view, but it is still intended to conduct itself in a way which supports the overall values of the constitutional order. However, the fact that the institutions are more or less susceptible to a particular form of argument means that the system as a whole has a greater capacity to ensure that inevitable conflicts of social value are addressed in one forum or another. Having separate institutions facilitates the incorporation of these varying views into the system's overall assessment of social value. This provides a measure of representative security for particular perspectives which should ensure that conflicts remain within the system and do not operate to destabilize it from the outside.

The separation of powers amongst these bodies accordingly reflects not confidence in their ability to act alone, but an acceptance of their inherent weaknesses and biases. Because each institution has particular biases, the new separation of powers seeks to correct these biases with those of other institutions. This acknowledges the legitimacy of the interests which they are likely to represent, but also the likelihood that vesting unfettered power in any single perspective is unlikely to produce good governance. In this, the system echoes the basic presumption of the Madisonian model of institutional separation—that, just as the problem of faction can be reduced by the dispersal of power amongst other factions, so inter-institutional bias may be used to avoid system-wide bias. The model is one under which the institutions are internally sovereign but externally accountable, being subject to an ongoing level of inter-institutional scrutiny which reflects both the legitimacy of their perspective and the system's lack of total trust in it.

(2) Coordinated Governance

This conception of governance has other notable implications for the theory's understanding of how the institutions ought to interact. Exercising power is portrayed by this theory as an ongoing and collaborative process to which all of the institutions may potentially contribute. The theory eschews formalist distinctions between creation, interpretation, implementation, and adjudication, presuming instead that each institution makes its own multi-faceted contribution to the system's overall efforts at governance. Because each represents a perspective which is both legitimate and provisional, it is neither logical nor justifiable for any one institution to have the final say in determining what the common good requires. The practical need for certainty in government means, of course, that there must be finality in the application of power to individual situations. In a broader sense, however, any institutional specification of social value must be susceptible to subsequent amendment by a different institution. If the inevitability of political conflict precludes the emergence of a social consensus, so too must it limit the possibility that any single institutional action can produce an appropriate accommodation of interests which is good for all time. This creates a level of in-built indeterminacy in government which supports the egalitarian nature of the institutional balance under the new separation of powers. The theory does not need to identify any one institution or set of institutions as dominant because it does not conceive of government as a linear process. An institutional decision is not the end of the process but is rather an opening position in an ongoing negotiation about governance. Exercising power is a collaborative and deliberative process in which each institution engages with the others' decisions on its own terms, subjecting them to its own internal scrutiny. Crucially, this also means that one institution's amendment of another's position is not decisive. The original institution will have the opportunity to respond to any such changes and to make any further amendments or refinements that it feels are appropriate. This introduces an element of flexibility into the inter-relationship between the branches which obviates the need for the sort of formal controls by which the traditional tripartite theory sought to regulate the respective institutional competences.

The basic political assumptions outlined above also underline the importance for the system as a whole of ensuring that the institutions together assist in the internalization and management of social conflict. This is a necessary element of any effective government system. As considered at greater length in Chapter 1, this aspect of the system is supported by the two-pronged approach of proclaiming the existence of a unified social system while at the same time engaging with any dissenting views. Centralized symbols and institutions, it was argued, were critical to the success of this strategy. The ostensible unity of these central symbols and institutions signals the existence of a cohesive society and state. The symbols contribute to the existence of a shared social identity. This vision of a unified society is supported by the actions of the very visible central institutions which invoke and exemplify the system's asserted values in their everyday conduct. Because of their visibility, these institutions also provide a means by which dissenting voices can be internalized into an ongoing process of value evolution and renewal. Although this theory attaches considerable importance to the administration's ability to operate in a devolved and context-sensitive way, it is important to bear in mind that the political views which value this dispersed flexibility also support the proposition that centralized government action is essential. For the polity to function effectively, decisions must be taken at central as well as local level.

C. The Inter-Institutional Relationship

(1) Institutional Blending

What are the implications of these considerations for the relationship between the relevant institutions? The first and most obvious is that the model is one of inter-institutional blending, as well as separation. Unlike those traditional formalist doctrines which emphasize internal sovereignty at the expense of external scrutiny, the new separation of powers theory not only accepts but requires the active supervision of each body by its institutional peers. It implies that the attitude of each institution to the other should be characterized by both deference and distrust—an acceptance that the other institution has a legitimate contribution to make to the process of governance, but also an awareness that its input is likely to emphasize considerations different to those which the other bodies value. The ongoing nature of the process also tends to support such a system of sceptical cooperation by assuring each institution that its own views will be incorporated into the evolution of public policy, but also that it will be liable to amendment by the other institutions where it contravenes their own idea of what constitutes good governance. With no body able to exercise absolute control, it is prudent for each to have regard to the other's views in coming to their own conclusions so as to avoid a situation in which their decisions are subject to a subsequent wholesale reversal.

(2) The Giving of Reasons

Institutional justification ought to be a prominent feature of any such system of mutual checking. As discussed above, the basic political logic of the model assumes that each institution must regard the views of the others as reflecting a legitimate if incomplete conception of the common good. This implies that the position of each institution ought to be treated with a certain level of initial respect. If this overlapping system of collaborative competences is to function effectively, the constituent institutions cannot simply continue to insist that power should be exercised only in accordance with their views. The result of that would be incoherence and, ultimately, gridlock in government. The system requires that, instead of simply substituting its view for those of the other bodies, an institution should engage with the decisions of those institutions with a view to improving the quality of the state's overall exercise of power. For that to occur, however, the institution must understand and take into account the actions of its counterparts. This indicates that there is a systemic necessity for institutions to justify their actions in order to facilitate cooperative governance. The giving of reasons to explain why a particular position was reached enables the other branches of government to consider the rationality of that determination, and to incorporate it into their own assessments of what the situation requires. Where one institution has the advantage of better or more relevant information, for example, it should explain and identify that advantage so that the other institutions can subsequently take account of it in making their own independent judgements. This suggests that a requirement to give reasons is a necessary element of the relationship between the institutions of government. Without justification or reasons, each institution will be left to insist on the veracity of its own position without having to engage in any sort of critical reflection on the rationality or plausibility of alternative views. In the absence of reasons, a system of separation is liable to descend into a Babelesque cacophony of institutional views expressed without any understanding of, or regard for, other opinions.

The model therefore places a considerable degree of faith in the proposition that a system of reasoned inter-institutional communication will produce better governance. There are similarities between this and deliberative theories of democracy. However, it is important to clarify that the model of institutional engagement considered here does not treat this deliberative process as a guarantee of agreed governance outcomes. Deliberation, on this analysis, does not need to produce an institutional consensus to be successful. This theory does not assume that the act of deliberation will necessarily have a transformative effect on the views or instincts of the individual institutions. In fact, given the extent to which the model assumes, not only that political conflict is inevitable, but also that institutions will retain a certain level of mutual distrust, the theory seems rather to regard it as highly unlikely that any such universal consensus will actually be established.

The model instead makes a much smaller claim for the utility of inter-institutional communication. It suggests that the provision of reasons by institutions will allow other institutions to understand the logic of an institution's position or the evidence upon which it is based, even if they continue to disagree with it. This may allow the other institutions to develop an alternative approach, for example, or to identify logical inconsistencies with that institution's position. It may encourage the other institutions to investigate other options entirely. Reasons do not need to persuade to assist in the development of more effective institutional strategies. In addition, the giving of reasons is important to ensure ongoing social cohesion, as summarized above. It provides a visible institutional means of presenting particular views. On balance, therefore, it is probably more correct to characterize this model as one of dialogic rather than deliberative engagement. The model sees dialogue as inherently valuable rather than as an instrument for the production of a fixed social consensus.

D. The Administration

These considerations have various consequences for the administration's external relationship with the other branches of government. The previous chapter detailed the range of institutional attributes which equip the administration to perform a valuable role in governance. This chapter makes clear, however, that the administration is not at large to act in whatever manner it deems appropriate. The administration has a particular capacity for problem-solving at a local and practical level. Problem-solving—no matter how successful or effective—is not sufficient to sustain a system of governance by itself. It is evident that the difficult task of balancing the necessity for social cohesion with an ability to engage with dissenting views requires a more complex system of institutional arrangement. Even if in practice the administration operated in the idealized way presented in the previous chapter, it could not effectively govern by itself. The new separation of powers theory insists that the administration has the potential to make a valuable contribution to government. It does not argue in favour of the delegation of all aspects of governance to an expert administrative elite, however. The administration has particular and specific qualities but is, at the same time, neither the Plato nor the Solomon of contemporary governance. On the contrary, it is required to justify its actions and decisions so that they may be subject to scrutiny by the other branches of government. Although its involvement may occur at a later stage of the process of exercising public power, it does not necessarily make the final determination of the appropriate balance to be struck. Rather, its decisions form part of an ongoing collaborative process in which it applies its own judgement to the instructions received from the political organs or the courts, only for its own conclusions to then become subject to scrutiny by those bodies. The exercise of decision-making power is both the coming to a conclusion in respect of the issue at hand, and the provision of a new starting point for further independent institutional analysis. This means that the administration is bound to explain why it interpreted and applied its instructions in the way that it did, so as to facilitate the continuation of the inter-institutional feedback loop which, for this separation of powers theory, is a critical element of good contemporary governance.

(1) Relationship with the Political Organs

This underlines the necessity for administrative independence from the political organs of government. The traditional doctrines of ministerial accountability and control are liable to inhibit the exercise by the administration of the sort of detached assessment expected of it under this model of institutional separation. If administrative bodies are intended to make a positive contribution to governance by subjecting the decisions of the political organs to more informed and practical scrutiny, they must be able to do this without the possibility of direct political interference in these assessments. The political organs may subsequently come to a different view but they cannot be allowed to dictate the outcome of the administrative process once initiated. This also means, however, that the administration itself must take responsibility for its own actions. If it is entitled to exercise independent discretionary judgement, it must do so—and be accountable for so doing. This implies the existence of an obligation to give full and proper reasons for its decisions. It cannot be sufficient for administrative agencies to indicate that they are simply applying instructions received from the political organs. The fact that they retain considerable discretion over the manner in which they comply with these instructions implicitly requires that they justify *why* they propose to implement them in a particular way.

Providing such reasons is not simply a matter of accounting to the affected individuals or groups for their actions. It is also logically required by the system's overarching assumption that each institution has a legitimate contribution to make to the ongoing process of government. The previous chapter argued that the value of the administration's input is, in part, attributable to the greater levels of information and expertise which it has, when compared to the political organs of government. These advantages justify the administration's entitlement to scrutinize the decisions of the political organs. However, if the administration is able to amend the legislature's view because of its greater proximity to affected interests, then it is incumbent on it to explain what particular information or expertise makes its decision the more appropriate choice. This is because the political organs also have specific institutional advantages over the administration and are accordingly themselves entitled to subject the amended decision to renewed analysis in light of the additional information provided. The requirement to give reasons is about more than mere accountability. It is also a means of enhancing the ability of other institutions to exercise their own judgement by providing them with the benefit of the relevant institution's particular perspective. From the administration's point of view, its purported advantages of information and expertise suggest that, in particular, it is obliged to provide reasonably detailed reasons for its actions. This also implies an additional requirement to ensure the ongoing monitoring of the outcomes of administrative acts. This reflects the fact that, as its decisions are based on its presumed facility for effective practical reasoning, it should ensure that measures adopted because of their putative efficacy do actually prove to be effective—and are amended where they do not.

The obligation to provide reasons which reflect an institution's particular abilities works both ways. It does not just impose particular obligations on the administration. It also suggests that the political organs should provide an adequate explanation of their own reasons for determining why a particular value or approach is appropriate. This, in turn, facilitates the exercise by the administration of its ostensibly superior practical reason by providing it with information about the objectives sought to be achieved, and of the political organ's justification for pursuing them in the manner proposed. The more information provided, the better able each institution will be to appreciate why its institutional counterpart decided to act in the way that it did. It means that the decision-making process is not a matter of starting afresh on each occasion, but of applying a particular institutional perspective to a balance already struck. This enables the institutions to approach each other's actions with the appropriate blend of scepticism and respect, accepting their entitlement to come to their own conclusion but enabling them also to subject the particular line of reasoning to their own independent judgement.

The requirement for the administration to justify its actions should also be seen as part of the process by which the state reaffirms its unity and cohesion. The central institutions, it has been argued, provide a very public framework for making determinations of social value. By so doing, these bodies implicitly proclaim the possibility of social cohesion while striving to secure it. There is a need, therefore, for the administration to visibly conform to this asserted social consensus in coming to its conclusions. This is especially so given the way in which it is often the administration itself which provides the citizen with a demonstrable example of these values in action. Regardless of how much the central institutions come to clear and visible conclusions about social value, it is frequently only when the individual citizen engages with the administration that the opportunity to provide a concrete illustration of good governance arises. 'It is at that moment that the social meaning of governance is created.'[1] This means that the administration must both conform to the stated public consensus put forward by the central institutions and also apply its power practically in a way which provides a real-world example of these principles in action. In some situations, this might require the administration to depart from the measures envisaged by the central political organs. Provided, however, that the administration draws upon the asserted social consensus in justifying any such departure, its actions are liable to strengthen rather than undermine the overall system's impression of conceptual unity by furnishing both rhetorical and real-world support for the principles in question. This again underlines the importance for the institutional order as a whole of ensuring that the administration provides full and proper reasons which accord with the system's overarching substantive values to explain and justify its actions in any individual situation.

(2) Relationship with the Courts

What of the administration's relationship with the courts? The recognition of the administration as a repository of discretionary power undermines the orthodox judicial approach of legitimizing administrative action by reference to the presumed vesting of instructional influence in an elected organ of government. It has already been suggested in earlier chapters that the limitations of this approach have encouraged the courts to effectively impose substantive restrictions on the actions of administrative bodies. The development of the doctrine of reasonableness,[2] for example, or of a general requirement to observe principles of procedural fairness, allows the courts to scrutinize administrative conduct on the basis of independent normative values.[3] The new separation of powers theory's open acceptance of the administration as a legitimate and influential branch of government would support the continuation of this move towards greater inter-institutional supervision. In particular, it would also imply that judicial review ought to be extended to encompass all aspects of administrative governance—including those third parties who are involved in the exercise of governmental power.

[1] CT Goodsell 'The Bureau as a Unit of Governance' in P du Gay, ed., *The Values of Bureacracy* (Oxford University Press, 2005), at 29.

[2] *Associated Provincial Picture Houses v Wednesbury Corporation*, [1948] 1 KB 223; *State (Keegan) v Stardust Compensation Tribunal*, [1986] IR 642.

[3] As previously discussed, it is telling that this has occurred in various constitutional contexts in various different ways but, by and large, all with the same result. See, for example, *Ridge v Baldwin*, [1964] AC 40; *McDonald v Bord na gCon*, [1965] IR 217; *Nicholson v Haldimand–Norfolk Regional Board of Commissioners of Police*, [1979] SCR 311; Article 33 of the South African Constitution.

This does not occur at present in many jurisdictions. In the USA, for example, the state action doctrine has restricted the range of actors who must observe and respect constitutional rights. The Irish courts, however, have notably developed a number of means of requiring nominally private actors to adhere to substantive norms of conduct. In *Meskell v CIE*, the Supreme Court confirmed that the obligation to respect constitutional rights applied to all individuals and organizations in the State, and that an action in tort was available under Irish law for breach of a constitutional right.[4] In *McCord v ESB*, meanwhile, the Supreme Court held that a semi-State company was required by law to act reasonably with regard to its contractual relations with private citizens.[5] The Electricity Supply Board had argued that its decision to disconnect the plaintiff was permitted by the contract of service agreed between them. Henchy J's comments demonstrate a welcome judicial awareness of the reality and of the dangers of delegated third-party governance, and, in particular, of the adverse implications which it may have for the constitutional order's protection of its central substantive principles:

> When the monopoly supplier of a vital public utility—which is what the Board is—forces on all its customers a common form of contract reserving to itself sweeping powers, including the power to vary the document unilaterally as it may think fit, such an instrument has less affinity with a freely negotiated interpersonal contract than with a set of by-laws or with any other form of autonomic legislation.

Henchy J accordingly held that the contract was subject to the same principles as would be applied to the actions of one of the central institutions of government. In particular, the ESB was required to act fairly and reasonably, and in accordance with the requirements of the Constitution.

These are examples of means by which the courts could supervise the exercise of government power by third-party agencies. Other methods could include the development of the concept of a 'public law contract' which would be subject to a more specifically substantively-oriented standard of scrutiny.[6]

Regardless of the way in which it is achieved, what the new separation of powers theory would logically require of the courts is a greater willingness to examine all aspects of administrative governance, including the delegation of functions to third-party actors, in order to ensure that all government actions undergo the requisite level of inter-institutional review. Institutions should obviously strive to demonstrate this fairness at first instance themselves, but this must be subject to the input of other institutions which might have a different conception of what fairness ought to entail. The courts, with their greater facility for the accurate weighing of individual interests, have a

[4] [1973] IR 121. [5] [1980] ILRM 153, at 161.

[6] See, for example, the discussion of the approach to this concept adopted by continental administrative law systems in J Auby, 'Comparative approaches to the rise of contract in the public sphere' [2007] PL 40.

particular ability to ensure that necessary standards of fairness are observed. This reinforces the fact that the courts must be entitled to subject all areas of administrative conduct to scrutiny on the basis of independent standards of procedural fairness.

In addition to requiring the existence of such broad supervisory powers itself, the vision of governance set out in this book also has implications for the content of any review jurisdiction. In particular, the theory's emphasis on the importance of normative notions of rationality and non-arbitrariness suggest that there ought to be the possibility to obtain an external opinion on the extent to which administrative action demonstrates due regard for these values. The courts are envisaged by this new model of institutional separation as a primarily individualist influence. This reflects the tendency of the judicial process to examine the appropriateness of a particular measure or proposition from the specific and singular perspective of the opposing party. This facilitates the representation of individualist ideas by providing them with an egalitarian framework in which their interests can be objectively assessed. This means that it is important that claims of non-arbitrariness can potentially be entertained by the courts regardless of the institutional context in which they are raised. From the point of view of the specific implications for the administration, this suggests that a general requirement of fairness and reasonableness is an important element in the process of ensuring that the interests of the individual are adequately protected. Subjecting government bodies, broadly defined, to independent scrutiny on the basis of these key substantive norms is an important part of the system's overall system of interlocking institutional checks as it secures a diversity of representative inputs into the governance process.

As described at greater length in earlier chapters, many jurisdictions have already developed general doctrines of procedural fairness which go some way towards providing the level of substantive scrutiny required by the theory. The experience of these systems also provides a useful illustration, however, of the fact that the relationship between the administration and the courts ought to be about more than ensuring the protection of the individual's interest. Insisting on appropriate standards of procedural fairness may also make a critical contribution to maintaining ongoing public support for the political system as a whole. The political science and sociological literature on this issue indicates that the perception that an institution adheres to principles of procedural fairness plays a vital part in ensuring public confidence in, and acceptance of, its decisions.[7] In fact, in terms of an individual's dealings with an institution, it has been argued

[7] See, for example, J Thibault and L Walker; *Procedural Justice: A Psychological Analysis* (Hillsdale, 1975); L Walker, A Lind and J Thibault, 'The Relation between Procedural and Distributive Justice' (1979) 65 *Virginia Law Review* 1401.

that the fairness of the procedures used may have more influence on the person's attitude towards it than the end result of the process:

[S]tudies strongly suggest that people's allegiance to authorities depends in large part on their perception of procedural fairness, and that allegiance can be retained in spite of how people fare in particular decisions, if they believe the decisions were made in a fair manner.[8]

Klosko notes that, given that governance will inevitably produce losers as well as winners, procedural fairness provides a valuable means of retaining the allegiance of the losers on an ongoing basis. As a crucial element of the overall institutional strategy to internalize social conflict, it is justifiable for standards of procedural fairness to be enforced across the institutional spectrum.

It is important to note also that procedural fairness, if it is to perform this function, requires more than the formal provision of impressive but empty procedural protections. An instructive example of the necessity for a substantive notion of procedural fairness is provided by the experiences of the Irish Refugee Appeals Tribunal. The Tribunal was charged with adjudicating on the appeals of unsuccessful applicants for asylum. The procedures which it operated, however, were regarded by many applicants as substantively unfair. Hearings were held in private and the Tribunal did not habitually publish its decisions. Without a process of visible and public reasoning, suspicions developed amongst applicants about the fairness, and thereby the legitimacy, of the institution.

The actions of the Tribunal prompted multiple legal challenges, including some which alleged, for example, that the Tribunal member who dealt with the largest number of cases had never been known to find in favour of an applicant for asylum.[9] Furthermore, concerns were expressed that the number of appeals allocated to him was influenced by his high rate of refusal. Although this matter was settled, it lent credence to the perception that the institution was not operating fairly.

A separate challenge to the Tribunal's refusal to provide appellants with previous decisions on issues relevant to their cases saw the Supreme Court find that the Tribunal had not demonstrated due regard for the constitutional principles of fair procedure. The Supreme Court held that it was 'blindingly obvious ... that fair procedures require some reasonable mechanisms for achieving consistency in both the interpretation and the application of the law', standards with which the Tribunal had failed to comply.[10]

Instructively, these controversies had a cumulatively detrimental effect on the reputation of the Tribunal amongst appellants, observers, and even some of its

[8] G Klosko, *Democratic Procedures and Liberal Consensus* (Oxford University Press, 2000).

[9] *Nyembo v Refugee Appeals Tribunal*, [2007] IESC 25. Later reports suggested that this member's refusal rate was actually 95 per cent. See, for example, 'Lawyer accused of bias against refugees quits Appeal Tribunal' *The Irish Independent* (4 March, 2008).

[10] *Antanasov v Refugee Appeals Tribunals*, [2006] IESC 53.

own members.[11] As an institution, it became 'plagued by allegations of bias, unfairness and non-transparency'.[12] It is somewhat unsurprising therefore that the Immigration, Residence and Protection Bill, 2008 proposes to replace the Refugee Appeals Tribunal with a new body, to be known as the Protection Review Tribunal. This appears to be intended, in part, to constitute an attempt to develop a new system with the necessary levels of legitimacy and public trust.

The Refugee Appeals Tribunal's experience demonstrates how a failure to follow principles of procedural fairness—or, more accurately, a failure to be seen to follow principles of procedural fairness—can inhibit the ability of an institution to carry out its administrative tasks. It also shows how such a failure can inhibit the efficacy of the administrative process itself. The Tribunal's lack of legitimacy amongst those subject to its jurisdiction contributed to the fact that its conduct was subject to numerous challenges before the courts. In 2006, for example, 909 judicial review actions connected with the asylum process were initiated in the Irish High Court. The next highest category of judicial review actions initiated consisted of cases seeking *certiorari*, of which there were only 289.[13] This latter category, of course, includes challenges to the conduct of a wide range of public and administrative bodies. This situation, where the actions of a single administrative agency gives rise to considerably more legal challenges than the rest of the administrative branch combined, demonstrates the difficulties that may follow from a perceived lack of procedural fairness. It not only impacts upon the individuals appearing before it but also undermines the operational efficiency which was one of the primary reasons for establishing a self-contained administrative process in the first place. This underlines the fact that *substantive* and *public* procedural fairness is essential, not only for the protection of the individuals in question, but also for the overall efficacy of the institution or institutions in question.

As the Refugee Appeals Tribunal example demonstrates, an important aspect of this notion of procedural fairness is the provision of adequate information about the decision-making process. This chapter has already discussed the importance of deliberation and dialogue to good inter-institutional governance. The requirement for an institution to rationally explain and justify its position partly reflected, it was claimed, the respect owed to each institution's position. While the organs of government are not obliged to agree with each other's views, they are expected to treat them as legitimate views which deserve a level of rational engagement. The requirement for the administration to provide

[11] It was reported that a number of members had sought to challenge the Tribunal Chairman's claim in the *Nyembo* case that the rates of refusal of the decision maker in question were not at variance with those of other members. See 'Members of refugee appeal body considered taking legal action' *The Irish Times* (4 March, 2008).

[12] T Ward, 'Independence, accountability and the Irish judiciary' (2008) 8 *Judicial Studies Institute Journal* 1, at 1.

[13] The Courts Service, *Annual Report 2006*, at 107.

information about its action does have the potential to contribute in other ways to the effective functioning of the new separation of powers system. Providing information facilitates external scrutiny. Such supervision, however, is not the exclusive preserve of the central organs of government. At the dispersed and decentralized level of the administrative decision-maker, those seeking information will usually be the interested or affected individuals. As noted above, engaging with such individuals in a rational and fair way can support the legitimacy of the administration. However, it may also provide a means for supplying the central institutions with additional information about the actions proposed or being undertaken by the administration. In the US context, Bressmann has argued that the judicial insistence on reasoned administrative decision-making can be understood not simply as an effort to protect fairness and non-arbitrariness but also as a way of enhancing the separation of powers by improving the legislature's ability to supervise the executive's actions. Providing information to individuals on the ground ensures the possibility of a 'fire-alarm oversight' which 'shifts to third parties the cost of gathering and processing information', thereby allowing the legislature 'to obtain more information than it would have otherwise, without incurring the costs of direct oversight'. That the administration is obliged to furnish information in a form which the individuals or public can understand improves the efficacy of this oversight:

> The reasoned decisionmaking requirement provides Congress (through its constituents) with access to information about agency action before such action is final. As a result of the reasoned decisionmaking requirement, an agency must reveal the factual and legal basis for its decision; it must demonstrate the alternatives considered and the reasons for selecting one over another; it must show that it has addressed the comments that run contrary to its policy choice. And it must do so in a common sense format, one that is accessible not only to judges but to members of Congress. This translation exercise ... serves a monitoring purpose. It requires agencies to filter information for ordinary consumption, minimizing informational asymmetries between administrator and legislator.[14]

Although Bressman's piece is specifically concerned with the American separation of powers system, its insights are relevant to the theory at issue here. It illustrates how the imposition of a requirement on the administration to account for its conduct rationally can have a systemic as well as an individualist value. Reasons inform not only affected individuals but also all relevant parties—including the other organs of government—about administrative action. The dispersed nature of the administration can make it difficult to monitor, which poses obvious problems for a theory of governance premised on the existence of a dynamic and dialogic inter-institutional relationship. The giving of reasons to

[14] L Bressman, 'Procedures as Politics in Administrative Law' (2007) 107 *Columbia Law Review* 1749, at 1780.

individuals creates a supplementary means of supervision which goes some way to addressing this issue. In addition to the advantages of fairness and public perception identified above, the imposition of an obligation on the administration to give reasons for its actions can also enhance the ability of the central organs of government to play their full part in the ongoing process of dialogic governance.

In terms of the implications for the courts, the new separation of powers theory dictates that it is necessary to regard the actions of the administration as the ostensibly legitimate products of an informed and expert decision-making procedure. Thus, although the theory posits that the courts must potentially be able to undertake a wide-ranging and substantive review of administrative conduct, it also suggests that it is appropriate for the judiciary to demonstrate a considerable degree of deference in exercising any such supervisory powers. As with the relationship between the administration and the political organs, so the courts must also engage with the administration's decisions on their own terms. They cannot simply replace its perspective with their own. The theory confers extensive powers of intervention on the courts but expects them to be used in a relatively non-intrusive fashion.

E. Regulating the Relationship

This raises the wider question of how these inter-institutional dealings ought to be regulated. This chapter has identified a need for mutual respect and dialogic engagement but these are broad notions which do not provide detailed guidance about how these relationships should actually operate. This is an area of particular potential difficulty given the way in which the model expects each institution to develop its own approach to the common pursuit of the public good. The theory assumes that each institution is imperfect but also accepts the legitimacy of their individual conceptions of good governance. This suggests that the system's overall approach is likely to be characterized by divergent institutional approaches to overlapping issues. With some level of institutional conflict seemingly inevitable, there would appear to be an obvious need for some form of firm regulation of the boundaries between each institution's area of action. Historically, the traditional doctrine's demarcation of specific spheres of institutional pre-eminence has provided this sort of guidance in situations where such inter-institutional disputes arise. The new separation of powers theory, however, rejects the utility of these strict formalist distinctions. It argues that the certainty or consistency provided by such formal classifications of functions is, in fact, illusory. The new theory instead favours a dynamic and flexible understanding of governance, in which the institutions make their respective contributions to an evolving, multi-stage, and multi-party process. The creation of policy, or the application of principles to facts, is not seen as the exclusive preserve of any one institution. Each represents a legitimate perspective and each is entitled to identify what it regards as the most appropriate way of exercising power. This begs the question whether this flexibility might more sceptically be seen as a crippling indeterminacy, however, which is liable ultimately to lead to an institutional free-for-all in which coordinated action is impossible because all are uncertain about specifically how such coordination should occur. Is it too naïve to trust a system of effective self-regulation?

One factor which may make a significant contribution to the success of a self-regulatory system is the role of individual citizens in determining when the opportunity for inter-institutional dealings will arise. The decision of each of the organs of government to undertake action in a particular area depends to varying degrees on the input of individuals. The courts, most obviously, require the initiation of a claim before they can have their input into the governance process. The exercise of administrative power too, depending on the process in question, may be shaped by the actions of individuals. A decision may be required, for example, by an application for a benefit or privilege, by the presentation of an individual with unanticipated needs, by the taking of an appeal against a previous decision, by a demand for explanation, or by an interested party's submission of new evidence or arguments in relation to a proposed or prevailing administrative practice. Even the political organs, which are formally entitled to legislate on their own initiative, tend to exercise power in response to the making of demands by interest groups or by the public. This illustrates the influence which civic action has on the focus and direction of the governance process.

This provides one potential solution to the problem of overlapping competences. Self-interest dictates that individuals or organizations are more likely to involve themselves in governance issues where their own interests are at stake. Furthermore, it would also seem logical to expect these claims to be initiated in the arena in which they are most likely to succeed. Such individual self-interest supports the possibility of a functioning self-regulatory system. The new separation of powers theory divides power between the identified organs of government because it assumes that they represent the relevant constituent social interests. These are the interests which must be reflected in the process of good governance. The whole point of this inter-institutional dialogue is that it is intended to ensure that state power is exercised after all relevant information and arguments have been taken into account. If a claim fails to convince in the receptive environment of its most favourable forum, it has, at most, a limited contribution to make to the state's pursuit of the public good.

This is also likely to prove an efficient system of allocating institutional tasks. The costs of going to court, for example, mitigate against the taking of a case by a citizen with little personal interest in the outcome. Actions are more likely to be taken by affected individuals, who are more likely to have access to all relevant information and to be able to furnish the institution with a practical and concrete example of the sort of individual circumstances which ought to be taken into account during the decision-making process. It is the nature of the adjudicative process which gives rise to this high level of costs, but it is also this factor which ensures that the courts are best equipped to provide an individual with a fair and rigorous assessment of what his or her interests required. This means that, in most cases, claims will only be taken where the stakes for the individual are sufficiently high that they justify recourse to the judicial process.

Where individual per capita costs are lower, arguments are more likely to be advanced in the political or administrative contexts. Where an individual's objection is based on wider considerations rather than personal circumstances, for example, this claim is more likely to be brought to the political arena where invocations of general or social good might receive a more favourable audience. Here the petitioning of individual representatives, or seeking media exposure for a position, may trigger a political response if the argument in question has sufficient popular resonance to attract an institutional response. In the alternative case, where the level of personal impact of a proposed measure is present but slight, a citizen may be more likely to bring his circumstances to the attention of the relevant administrator—either because of the lower costs of making submissions to such bodies, or because the nature of the scheme in question requires a level of face-to-face engagement which provides the citizen with an opportunity to explain his case.

These examples support the proposition that the problem of institutional overlap may be more significant in theory than it would prove in practice. By and large, the relationship between individual petition and institutional response is sufficiently close that rational self-interest will provide a level of self-regulation in the system. What this does not address, however, is the situation where a skewed distribution of impacts or incentives occurs. For a well-resourced citizen, for example, the costs of bringing a claim to court will not constitute as much of a disincentive as might be the case for other individuals. As a result, this could lead to a situation in which the courts are invited to intervene in situations where the individual's threatened interests are relatively undeserving of attention, let alone protection. Other skewed distributions could produce similarly unsatisfactory outcomes. There is accordingly a need for the institutions to retain a certain degree of residual discretion to refuse to entertain particular forms of claim. The new theory's distribution of power on the basis of comparative institutional qualities rather than formal categories suggests that it is these factors which should form the basis for the resolution of any disputes that arise over the appropriate institutional boundaries. In particular, it is necessary for each institution to have regard to its own relative limitations so that it can identify when a matter may be more appropriately dealt with by a different branch of government. This means, for example, that the courts should be reluctant to engage in the sort of balancing of multiple social interests for which the political organs are much better equipped. The political organs, for their part, should acknowledge the court's superior facility for considering whether the striking of a particular social balance showed due regard for constitutional values or individual interests. Both central bodies should recognize the administration's advantages of local information and expertise, just as it should defer to their greater accountability and deliberative visibility.

A doctrine of non-justiciability is one example of the sort of prudential institutional self-limitation envisaged by the theory. The concept of non-justiciability implicitly accepts that there are certain matters which an institution ought not to consider. The key difference between this theory, and ones which have operated in the past, however, is that it logically suggests that these assessments of non-suitability ought to be based on a flexible appraisal of the institution's own limitations, rather than on an *a priori* classification of forms or functions. It echoes, in particular, the 'lack of judicially discoverable and manageable standards' limb of the non-justiciability test outlined by the US Supreme Court in *Baker v Carr*.[15]

In fact, the Court's decision in *Carr* generally included the sort of pragmatic analysis of institutional separation which would be justified under the new separation of powers theory. The Court's references to 'an unusual need for unquestioning adherence to a political decision already made' or to 'the potentiality of embarrassment from multifarious pronouncements by various departments on one question' reflect a concern for the overall efficacy of government which is shared by the new separation of powers theory.[16] The model of separation presented in this book is not based on existing notions of pure institutional forms. It does not treat institutions as automatically entitled to unilaterally exercise particular powers. The theory instead supports a system of institutional separation on the basis of the belief that a system which provides for the distinction and subsequent pooling of inputs into the governance process is likely to produce better government, for all of the reasons of efficacy, publicity, norm adherence, constituency representation, and so on previously discussed. The relevant branches of government are entitled to exercise power because they each provide a distinct institutional structure which is liable, in its operations, to emphasize particular values and interests. Because these values and interests ought to inform the process of governance, so these institutions are expected to contribute to the system's overall efforts to produce acceptable and legitimate outcomes. As a purportedly multi-stage and multi-participant process, the refusal of an institution to act may undermine the efficacy of the overall system just as much as a unilateral insistence on a particular outcome or approach would. This suggests, therefore, that no areas of state activity should be automatically excluded from the competence of an institution. Because of the inherent legitimacy of the constituent interests they represent, each institution is in theory entitled to intervene and provide its input into any area of governance.

[15] 369 US 186 (1962). [16] Ibid, at 217.

Any institutional forbearance should be based not on a conviction that the subject matter in question is one which 'ought' to be decided by a particular body, but on an acknowledgement that the relevant institution is less well equipped to perform the required task adequately.

This concern for the institution's comparative ability to deal with the issue raised means that the focus of any doctrine of non-justiciability must be on the specific circumstances of the relevant question. When it cannot be said at the outset that certain matters are the exclusive preserve of a particular branch, context becomes all-important. To use a practical example, the relative inability of the court, with its bilateral adjudicative process, to assess polycentric issues means that it should not attempt to determine complex questions of public expenditure. Where, however, decisions have been taken which make expenditure issues more amenable to bilateral review, judicial input may be appropriate. If an administrative decision has reduced the complex public issues to a single position, the court may be more able to consider its merits in light of the rights of affected individuals. Where the legislature has specified the objectives which it is aiming to achieve with a particular course of action, or has identified values which it has pledged to protect, then the courts may be able to examine any suggestion that, in fact, its actions have departed from these positions.

To return to the example of the issue raised in *TD v Minister for Education*, it is arguable that the Constitution's acknowledgement of the existence of a right to education altered the nature of this claim from one for a particular form of public expenditure to one concerned with the state's level of adherence to an identified legal obligation.[17] The former question is one which the courts would be ill equipped to consider, whereas the latter is one more susceptible to adjudicative scrutiny. That is not to say, of course, that the claimant would necessarily have succeeded in his action. Institutional self-limitation should inform not only the initial decision to examine a claim, but also the extent of the organ's intervention. Although the specification of a particular social value might have made the claim suitable for judicial assessment, this does not alter the fact that the political and administrative processes are institutionally better equipped to take account of multiple interests in striking these initial balances of interest. As this chapter has emphasized, there is a need for each of the institutions to show deference when approaching a matter in respect of which its peers have particular expertise or experience. Applying this analysis to *TD*, therefore, the courts would have been entitled to consider whether the political organs had demonstrated due regard for the identified social value, but would have done so with deference to these institutions' initial assessment of the balance to be struck between the various social interests and values at stake. Deference would imply a low standard of scrutiny, perhaps by reference to requirements of bare rationality, consistency, or non-arbitrariness. The fact that the High Court was not

[17] [2001] 4 IR 259.

creating policy, but seeking to hold the political organs to their previously expressed view of what was appropriate, would also be relevant, as it would go a considerable way towards addressing the sort of institutional concerns which encourage judicial restraint on such issues. This underlines the significance of each case's particular factual context, and of examining in each case the extent to which what is required to address the issues raised would involve an institution in conduct for which it is ill equipped. What may have been appropriate in *TD* might not have been appropriate for another education-based claim for particular treatment.

This should not be taken, of course, to suggest that the adoption of the theory proposed here would necessarily have produced a different outcome in *TD*. It seems quite plausible to suggest that a court could have considered that the failure to implement the proposed policy was based on the political organs' obligation to have regard to multiple factors and interests, and that the way in which they had done so had sufficiently incorporated the claimant's right to education into their overall assessment of what the common good required. What the separation of powers theory in this book would not support, however, is an initial determination that the case itself is automatically outside the scope of judicial competence because of its connection with questions of public expenditure. Regulating the relationship between government branches in a fluid system of representative institutional separation cannot be reduced to such fixed categories or rules. It is a more complicated and sophisticated process which requires each institution to reflect critically on its own capacities, and on its ability to make a useful contribution to the resolution of the specific issue in question.

F. Conclusion

The bare outlines of the sort of inter-institutional relationship envisaged by this separation of powers theory ought by now to be apparent. The theory accepts, and indeed encourages, inter-institutional checking as a way of enhancing both the legitimacy and the quality of government decision-making. Where government action is taken on the basis of an informed and deliberative process amongst several institutions, it is less likely to favour a single perspective. When these institutions are structured and organized in a way that is liable to lead them to emphasize different social values and interests, the possibilities for arbitrary government action should be reduced further. In addition, involving different institutions with different capabilities in the taking of government decisions provides access to a more extensive range of information and abilities, which should produce better outcomes. Overlapping inter-institutional governance is accordingly a core part of the new separation of powers theory's efforts to ensure a legitimate governance system which is both effective and norm-appropriate.

Yet, as this chapter also illustrates, the relationship between the institutions under this model is difficult to identify with precision in the abstract. Because the model eschews the notion of hermetically sealed areas of institutional competence, it lacks the sort of structured formal or functional criteria which are typically used to assist in the regulation of inter-institutional activity. The scope and legitimacy of inter-institutional scrutiny, on this analysis, does depend to a large degree upon the particular circumstances in which the question arises. Because the model favours cooperative checking, it is unlikely to favour the sort of absolute formal restrictions which provide determinacy but which also discourage collaborative governance. It instead prefers a more contextual analysis of the extent to which an institution can usefully assist in the decision-making process at issue. This might appear to represent an unduly indeterminate standard to apply but, as the reference to *Baker v Carr* shows—and, indeed, as some of the English case law considered in the next chapter appears to suggest—it is possible to regulate inter-institutional relationships in practice by reference to such context-sensitive assessment of relative institutional capacity. It is thus to these factors, rather than to traditional notions of institutional competence, that the new theory of separation of powers looks for assistance.

8

From Exception to Orthodoxy? The Theory in Action

A. Introduction

One feature of the analysis and arguments advanced in this book has been their recurring concern with matters of institutional practice. In a book about institutional structures, this is hardly surprising. The purpose of a separation of powers theory is to provide a means of determining questions of inter-institutional conduct whenever they arise. Good governance is a matter of practice as well as of design. Accordingly, a model of institutional arrangement must consider not only what is normatively good but also what is operationally effective. Institutional analysis must be animated by considerations of what actually works—it must have regard to what is as much as what ought to be. This explains the focus of the preceding chapters on questions of institutional capability. There is no point in sketching out a separation of powers model which is unimpeachable in the abstract but likely to prove ineffective in practice. After all, it was this sort of divergence between theory and practice which prompted this book's initial criticism of the traditional theory. Scrutinizing the respective qualities of the various institutional actors is an important and necessary stage in assessing whether the model proposed here might actually represent an appropriate template for good contemporary governance.

From the perspective of the theory's overall efficacy, however, it is essential to go further than this consideration of bare institutional abilities. It has so far been suggested that the new separation of constituencies system is both theoretically defensible and practically possible. It is claimed that potentially the theory could serve as an organizing model of effective governance. It must be remembered, however, that our governing rules and institutions are operational phenomena of a firmly social nature. Constitutional structures do not exist in an asocial void. It is insufficient, therefore, to rest the claim for this theory on the conclusion that it could actually operate successfully in some real world. The argument must be taken further to show that it can, in fact, operate successfully in a specific social context.

This underlines again the importance attached throughout this book to social values and symbols. It has consistently been argued that such values or principles provide a unifying normative vision around which a particular social polity can cohere. As discussed at length in earlier chapters, this is not to say that these values cannot change over time. The persistent presence of varying internal views makes such changes inevitable. The key point is that, for reasons of social stability and effective governance, any such changes should take place within the confines of the prevailing institutional order. For there to be any real prospect of the separation of constituencies model replacing the traditional tripartite theory, it should therefore be capable of being incorporated into the current system. This technique of embracing new ideas on an incremental or evolving basis is encapsulated in Dworkin's theory of interpretative integrity:

> The notion of 'integrity' draws attention to the way in which the system attempts to seamlessly evolve to embrace any reflect any shifting social mores. Changes are publicly justified by reference to principles and values whose authority has been confirmed by consistent public repetition over time.... The state's institutions publicly invoke these tenets to justify any changes they adjudge to be necessary, thereby investing these 'new' social understandings with the authoritative reputation cultivated by the public use and repetition of the 'old'.[1]

The search for interpretative integrity is particular relevant to the model proposed here because of the way in which it has been developed out of those exceptional areas for which the traditional theory was unable to supply an adequate explanation. As a theory designed in part as a response to the realities of contemporary governance, it would be expected that there should be some degree of 'fit', either actual or potential, between the separation of constituencies model and existing institutional practice.

There might appear to be an element of circularity in evaluating a model in terms of existing case law upon which its conceptual origins in part depend. The book's earlier identification of particular areas of theoretical inconsistency was descriptive rather than doctrinal. The case law at issue was interpreted as evidence of a greater willingness on the part of the courts to subject the actions of administrative bodies to broader and more intensive scrutiny on non-statutory grounds. Very little attention was paid, however, to the jurisprudential justification offered for these developments. They were treated as externally observed phenomena in need of rationalization, rather than the internally explicable products of a particular judicial approach. These early chapters established the need for reform but did not offer a solution. Later chapters, for their part, focused primarily on abstract principles of normative value and institutional efficacy. There remains an open question, therefore, as to the extent to which the proposed model, with its commitment to non-arbitrariness and abstract institutional separation, can convincingly be accommodated by contemporary institutional practices.

[1] R Dworkin, *Taking Rights Seriously* (Duckworth, 1977); and *Law's Empire* (Fontana, 1986).

This chapter will focus in particular on the extent to which the constitutional and administrative case law of the courts can be said to provide support for any future adoption of this new separation of powers system. The reason for this concentration on the courts is that the judicial process provides a visible and particularly appropriate forum for the raising, assessment, and resolution of disputes about social values. Although these debates occur within each of the relevant organs of government, the judicial process has the advantage for the purposes of the exercise being undertaken here of providing a rigorous and public examination of the weight which that social system attaches to the values in question. Administrative assessments of value might be less visible or more narrowly focused, while the position of the political organs on debates about social values might be less considered or influenced by unacknowledged considerations. The twin commitments of the judicial process to precedent and to public reasoning means that this process provides the clearest insight into the way in which social values can shift over time. It was argued in the first chapters of this book that the limitations of the separation of powers system mean that inter-institutional issues are being resolved on the basis of other factors or considerations. It would be expected, therefore, that a new theory of institutional separation would fit with judicial developments in these areas if it was to provide even a vaguely credible model for the future regulation of any such disputes. Accordingly, this chapter will consider the extent to which the approach currently adopted by the courts to these issues might plausibly be presented as in keeping with the principles of institutional separation proposed in this book.

B. A Positive Conception of the Administrative Process

It has repeatedly been noted that one of the key differences between the new separation of powers model and the orthodox tripartite theory is their differing attitudes towards the administrative process. The approach put forward in this work is one which portrays the administration as a valuable aspect of contemporary governance. Specifically, it has been suggested that the administration's generally greater proximity to the subject matter of government decisions provides the opportunity for the making of a more informed decision about how power ought to be exercised. Administrators tend to be closer to those potentially affected by a government proposal. By virtue of their interest in the area, such potentially affected parties may have relevant personal knowledge and experience, as well as the incentive to ensure that it is incorporated into the decision-making process. In addition, the administrators themselves may possess specialist expertise or experience in the specific area in question. In contrast to the traditional model's concentration on linear command-and-control structure, the theory set out here conceives of governance, it will be recalled, as an ongoing multi-stage and multi-participant process. For this more flexible understanding of the decision-making process, such ready access to local information and expertise has obvious potential value. It was argued, therefore, that the administrative process provided a useful opportunity for government to engage with, and take account of, the position of interested parties with a view to producing more effective government actions.

Earlier chapters have already examined the way in which the administration was typically regarded by lawyers as a 'necessary evil'.[2] The exercise of power through the administrative process could not be avoided but the law sought to ensure that it was either minimized, or obscured. It is instructive, therefore, that a number of recent decisions appear to provide some support for the more positive conception of the administrative process put forward in this book. The decisions in *R. (Greenpeace Ltd) v Secretary of State for Trade and Industry*[3] and in *R. (Eisai Ltd) v National Institute for Health and Clinical Excellence,*[4] in particular, are notable for the way in which the English courts in both cases intervened to ensure that the administrative process operated in a way which maximized the potential for the ultimate taking of a better informed and reasoned decision.

In the *Greenpeace* case, the applicants sought to quash the Secretary of State's decision to recommend that nuclear power be included as part of the recommended future mix of electricity sources in the UK. The decision was taken after a consultation process which included, inter alia, the holding of conferences, seminars, and round-table meetings, as well as the issuing of a consultation document which attracted a number of responses from interested parties. The applicant's central objection was that this latter consultation document had appeared to be a preliminary 'issues paper', and had lacked the necessary information or level of detail to allow for 'the fullest public consultation' that had previously been promised by the government. In particular, the applicant relied upon the fact that information relied on by the government in coming to its conclusion had been released only after the consultation process had ended.

Sullivan J found that there had been a breach of the claimant's legitimate expectation that a full and proper public consultation process would be held. This legitimate expectation was derived, of course, from the government's initial promise that such consultation would occur. It was also relevant that the UK, as a signatory to the Aarhus Convention on Access to Information, Public Participation in Decision-making, and Access to Justice in Environmental Matters, has accepted the necessity for public consultation on important issues of environmental regulation. This decision, therefore, does not suggest that consultation is always a necessary part of the administrative process. What the decision does demonstrate, however, is a judicial willingness to ensure that

[2] G Ganz, 'Delegated Legislation: A Necessary Evil or a Constitutional Outrage?' in P Leyland and T Woods, eds., *Administrative Law Facing the Future: Old Constraints and New Horizons* (Blackstone Press, 1997), at 80.

[3] [2007] EWHC 311 (Admin).

[4] [2008] EWCA Civ 438.

consultation processes, where they occur, facilitate the sort of robust and informed participation which might produce better governance outcomes. Sullivan J criticized, for example:

> the contrast between the paucity of the information provided to consultees on the issue of economics in the 2006 Consultation Document and the wealth of highly-detailed information on the critical issue of cost–benefit analysis considered by the Defendant but not published until after (and in some cases well after) the consultation period had closed.[5]

The initial consultation document was, in the High Court's view, 'little more than an empty husk'. This was 'manifestly unfair' because it limited the ability of interested parties to make a fully informed and relevant contribution to the Government's consideration of the complicated issue. As Sullivan J explained:

> As *the* consultation paper on an issue of such importance and complexity it was manifestly inadequate. It contained no proposals as such, and even if it had, the information given to consultees was wholly insufficient to enable them to make 'an intelligent response'.[6]

This reference to the importance of organizing the consultation process so as to permit 'an intelligent response' is interesting because of the way in which it echoes the new model's image of the administrative process as a means of enhancing the deliberative rationality of government. Fairness, in this view, dictates that consultation, where it occurs, must operate in the manner which is most likely to produce better-reasoned outcomes.

This notion of the 'intelligent response' of interested parties also featured prominently in the Court of Appeal's decision in the *Eisai Ltd* case. The challenge here was to the failure of the defendant institute to provide the claimant company with an executable copy of the economic model upon which they based their assessment of the relative clinical benefits and cost effectiveness of particular courses of medical treatment. When considering whether to recommend the use of medical treatment for particular patients, the defendant institute typically engaged in a long and involved consultation process with interested parties. The Court of Appeal accepted that this process was 'exceptionally detailed and elaborate, involving extensive consultation and a high degree of disclosure at all relevant stages' and that the claimant company had been able to make informed comments on many aspects and at many points of the appraisal process. However, the Court nonetheless found that the failure to provide an executable copy of the relevant economic model was unfair because it prevented the participants from subjecting the institute's basic economic assumptions to rigorous scrutiny. The Court felt that '[i]n that respect, it limits their ability to make an intelligent response on something that is central to the

[5] *Greenpeace*, [2007] EWHC 311 (Admin) at para. 97. [6] Ibid, at para. 116.

appraisal process'.[7] This affected not only the company's ability to participate in the process, but also the strength of the process itself. Denying the company the ability to make an informed and intelligent response not only was unfair but also removed the 'possibility that work done by them on the fully executable version would bring to light hitherto unrecognized weaknesses in the model'.[8] Again, the court's concern for individual fairness manifested itself in a way which supports the principles of deliberative and rational governance.

While the significance of these decisions should not be overstated, they do typify the sort of valuable contribution to government which the administrative process can make. They illustrate how the interaction of government bodies (be they the political organs themselves or distinct administrative agencies) with interested and expert parties can encourage a more rigorous reasoning and decision-making process. More importantly, they suggest that the courts not only recognize the potential value of these procedures to the system of government as a whole, but also that they are willing, where appropriate, to compel the organization and operation of these procedures in a way which realizes that value. After all, it is important to note that some form of multi-participant consultation had already occurred in both *Eisai Ltd* and *Greenpeace*. This was particularly the case in *Eisai Ltd*, where the Court of Appeal accepted that the parties had already engaged in quite detailed and comprehensive consultations. That the courts refused to accept such procedures as sufficient demonstrates a readiness to look behind the formalities of a consultation procedure to ensure that a vigorous and fully informed process of engagement actually occurs. It implicitly accepts, not only the value of consultation, but also its appropriateness in a system of evolving multi-stage decision-making.

This robust conception of procedural fairness is in keeping with the new separation of powers theory's conception both of the normative utility of government's decision-making processes, and also of the way in which they ought to be organized. Much of the impetus for the particular design of the proposed model is based on its contention that the administrative process offers an opportunity to affirm the autonomy of the individual as a rational moral agent whilst simultaneously securing improvements in the governmental process. To the extent that the courts in both *Eisai Ltd* and *Greenpeace* invoked principles of procedural fairness to require the holding of a more extensive and fully informed consultation process, they reflect a judicial image of good governance which arguably has more in common with the new model's notions of collaborative decision-making than with traditional *imperium*-based conceptions of centralized and hierarchical rule.

[7] *Eisai Ltd*, [2008] EWCA Civ 438, at para. 66.

[8] Ibid, at para. 45.

C. Of Vires and Values: The Changing Basis of Judicial Review

(1) Competing Conceptions of Administrative Action

Another matter of some importance to the theory is the courts' attitude towards the administrative organs of government. It has been argued that it is the creation and proliferation of these agencies which poses particular problems for traditional accounts of institutional governance. Developing a model capable of acknowledging and regulating the influence of these bodies on the exercise of public power has been one of the primary concerns of this book. The new separation of powers theory has consistently been presented as a required response to the emergence of an administrative state. This is one area, therefore, in which a degree of overlap between the proposed model and existing practice might be expected to be found.

There is, of course, a degree of external correspondence between the current system's effective acceptance of administrative power as a political fact, and the proposed model's justification of it as an institutional means of securing norm-appropriate outcomes. From the point of view of the system's internal account of administrative action, however, there are clear discrepancies. A necessary evil for traditional theory, these bodies are characterized by this book as, on the contrary, an instrumentally valuable process. This logically shapes the way in which the judicial review of administrative acts is understood. Presumptively illegitimate on the analysis of one theory, administrative bodies are, in fact, depicted in a positive light by the other. On the first view, the courts are likely to regard these organs with suspicion, seeking to restrictively interpret their competences and abilities. On the second, more positive, model, judicial review is regarded as a means of ensuring that these bodies properly fulfil their institutionally legitimate function. An analysis of the courts' conception of the proper basis for judicial review should provide some valuable insight into the relative contemporary relevance of these rival theories.

As Chapter 3 noted, historically the law has been conceived in terms of its connection to an authoritative sovereign entity, from which all power emanates. This manifested itself in a reluctance on the part of courts and commentators to recognize the legitimacy of decentralized and discretionary exercises of administrative power. The increasing acceptance of administrative authority as a political and social reality, however,[9] has encouraged the elaboration of legal doctrines which seek to reconcile these developments with the dictates of traditional theory. Despite this, the continued attachment to the historical concept of a hierarchical sovereign power has prevented any acceptance of the basic

[9] See, for example, *Leontjava v DPP*, [2004] 1 IR 591; *Maher v Minister for Agriculture*, [2001] 2 IR 139.

validity of administrative acts. These bodies are denied any claim on their own behalf to substantive legitimacy. Their conduct cannot be authorized by reference to any independent values of institutional action. On the contrary, conventional wisdom insists on the parasitic justification of exercises of power on the basis of their connection to the ultimate sovereign agent. It is this attitude which underpins the traditionally dominant ultra vires theory of review.

(2) Ultra Vires and the Administration

The ultra vires approach tolerates the vesting of public power in subordinate bodies, but requires that any exercise of authority remain within the limits prescribed by the parent organ. The theory conforms to the courts' traditional insistence on the existence of a supreme and sovereign power, to which all authority must ultimately be attributable. Given the way in which the Diceyan doctrine of parliamentary supremacy has historically been treated as '[t]he bedrock of the British constitution',[10] it is unsurprising that the ultra vires theory, with its shared commitment to the concept of a supreme sovereign power, has traditionally dominated administrative and constitutional discourse in the United Kingdom. Courts, in their supervision of administrative bodies, have thus been tasked with ensuring the ongoing fidelity of these agencies to the intentions of parliament expressed in statute. Legitimacy is equated with declared parliamentary approval. External values ought not to intrude upon the review process. As Blackstone commented, 'if the parliament will positively enact a thing to be done which is unreasonable, I know of no power that can control it'.[11]

The supervisory jurisdiction of the courts was confined to mere questions of statutory competence within which considerations of external values could have no place. Without an error going to jurisdiction, no review could occur.[12] This was repeatedly emphasized by the courts. Lord Sumner, for example, conceived the courts as filling a very restricted function:

> [The court's] jurisdiction is to see that the inferior court has not exceeded its own, and for that very reason it is bound not to interfere in what has been done within that jurisdiction, for in so doing it would itself, in turn, transgress the limits within which its own jurisdiction of supervision, not of review, is confined.[13]

Brightman J's similar insistence in *Evans* that 'judicial review is concerned not with the decision but with the decision-making process' has been consistently regarded as an affirmation of the fact that the courts cannot question the outcome

[10] *R. (Jackson) v AG*, [2006] 1 AC 262; [2005] UKHL 56, at para. 9, *per* Lord Hope.

[11] Sir William Blackstone, *Commentaries on the Laws of England* (1765), cited in I Loveland, *Constitutional Law, Administrative Law and Human Rights* (Oxford University Press, 2006), at 32.

[12] See, for example, *R. (Martin) v Mahony*, [1910] 2 IR 695; *R. (de Vesci) v Queen's County JJ*, [1908] 2 IR 285; *R. v Governor of Brixton Prison, ex p Armah*, [1968] AC 192.

[13] *R. v Nat Bell Liquors Ltd*, [1922] 2 AC 128, at 156.

of the administrative process. Their concern is to ensure that the power at issue has been exercised in accordance with the instructions set out in statute. 'Judicial review is not an appeal from a decision but a review of the manner in which the decision was made.'[14] As the Australian courts explained in *Peko-Wallsend*,[15] their role is solely to patrol the parameters of the statutory power in question. Once the subordinate body remains within the 'four corners' of its competence,[16] the autonomous actions of the relevant authority cannot be impugned.

Despite the absence in Ireland of any equivalent conception of parliamentary sovereignty, judicial review of administrative action has often been interpreted in the light of the ultra vires theory.[17] Given the Constitution's express entrenchment of the sort of independent norms which should logically lead to more substantive notions of judicial review, this is somewhat surprising. Nevertheless, the doctrine of jurisdictional error, as set out in *R. (Martin) v Mahoney*,[18] 'seems to have almost hypnotized successive generations of judges'[19] who continued to insist on some form of 'jurisdictional frailty' as an essential prerequisite for review.[20]

(3) Ultra Vires under Strain

Over time, however, the judicial inclination to justify intervention by reference to specific legislative instructions became increasingly unsustainable. The English courts instead began to develop the idea of an implied parliamentary intent. Administrative actions could be reviewed on the basis of the extent to which they complied with independent ideas of legality which, the courts assumed, parliament would have expected them to observe. As the decision in *Anisminic* demonstrated, this approach effectively provided for the use of external criteria of judicial evaluation.[21] The Lords in that case employed the concept of a putative parliamentary intention to overturn the clear intention of the Commons, as set out in statute, to exclude the jurisdiction of the courts.

> [T]he reality [of *Anisminic*] is that the courts were reaching their decision by drawing upon a constitutional principle independent of Parliamentary intent.[22]

This decision indicated quite starkly that this doctrine of fictional intent actually operates in practice as an independent repository of supervisory values.

14 *Chief Constable of North Wales v Evans*, [1982] 1 WLR 1155, at 1173–1174.

15 *Minister for Aboriginal Affairs v Peko-Wallsend Ltd*, (1986) 162 CLR 24.

16 *Associated Provincial Picture Houses v Wednesbury Corporation*, [1948] 1 KB 223, at 228.

17 See, for example, *Cassidy v Minister for Industry and Commerce*, [1978] IR 297; *State (Kenny) v Minister for Social Welfare*, [1986] IR 693; *Doyle v An Taoiseach*, [1986] ILRM 693.

18 [1910] 2 IR 695.

19 G Hogan and DG Morgan, *Administrative Law in Ireland* (3rd ed., Round Hall Sweet & Maxwell, 1998), at 413.

20 *Lancefort v An Bord Pleánala (No. 2)*, [1999] 2 IR 270, at 310, *per* Keane J.

21 *Anisminic Ltd v Foreign Compensation Commission*, [1969] 2 AC 147.

22 PP Craig 'Ultra Vires and the Foundations of Judicial Review' (1998) 57 CLJ 63, reproduced in C Forsyth, ed., *Judicial Review and the Constitution* (Hart, 2000), at 52.

(a) Wednesbury *Review*

Developments in the English courts have continued this move away from the ultra vires theory's insistence on a specific legislative intent. The introduction of *Wednesbury* unreasonableness as a legitimate ground for review concentrated the attention of the court on the outcome of the exercise of administrative power, rather than on the way in which it was used. This required the courts to consider the merits of a decision by reference to residual values of rationality, rather than simply asking themselves whether the procedures adopted were within the scope of the body's delegated powers.

Rhetorically, of course, this jurisdiction was justified in orthodox ultra vires terms. A decision would only be struck down if it was 'so unreasonable as to go beyond anything that Parliament can have intended'.[23] The courts, wary of intruding in areas outside their competence, set the threshold of unreasonableness at a very high level. Thus Diplock LJ in *Mixnam* held that unreasonableness would only be found where there was:

> such manifest arbitrariness, injustice or partiality that a court would say 'Parliament would never have intended to give authority to make such rules; they are unreasonable and ultra vires'.[24]

This parliament-oriented formulation of the proper approach to judicial review was expressly affirmed as the 'correct test' in Ireland by Henchy J in *Cassidy*.[25] Decrying the failure of the Minister's price-control regime to distinguish between lounge and public bars, Henchy J concluded that 'Parliament could not have intended that licensees of lounge bars would be treated so oppressively and unfairly'.[26]

In its reluctance to involve itself in administrative matters generally, and in its invocation of the putative intention of Parliament that '[delegated] power ... should be exercised reasonably',[27] the *Wednesbury* doctrine evidently aimed to remain within the boundaries of the ultra vires theory. In reality, however, a jurisdiction which allowed for the review of the substance of an administrative decision was fundamentally incompatible with an adherence to the orthodox requirement that judicial scrutiny proceed from a specific and evident parliamentary intent. '[T]he more contrived the search for the legitimation of legislative intent, the more strained and implausible does the whole doctrine of ultra vires become.'[28] An implied intention on the part of Parliament to ensure reasonableness in all administrative acts effectively creates an independent ground of challenge.

It is notable that Lord Diplock's later decision in *GCHQ* described the standard of reasonableness without reference to the legislature's fictional will.

[23] *Hall & Co. v Shoreham-by-Sea UDC*, [1964] 1 All ER 1.

[24] *Mixnam Properties Ltd v Chertsey UDC*, [1964] 1 QB 214, at 237–238.

[25] *Cassidy*, [1978] IR 297. This case was cited with approval in *Kenny*, [1986] IR 693; *Doyle*, [1986] ILRM 693; *Purcell v AG*, [1995] 3 IR 287; [1996] 2 ILRM 153.

[26] *Cassidy*, ibid, at 311. [27] Ibid, at 310. [28] Craig, note 22 above, at 53.

Furthermore, in his view the ability of the court to intervene did not have to be justified on the basis of the inferred assumption that an unidentified legal error had occurred. Irrationality rather constituted an autonomous head of review in its own right, drawing on external ideas of rationality and morality to invalidate any decision which was 'so outrageous in its defiance of logic or of accepted moral standards that no sensible person who had applied his mind to the question to be decided could have arrived at it'.[29]

Traces of this type of judicial acceptance of the review process as autonomously inspired are also evident in the Irish decisions of this era. Lord Diplock's judgment in *GCHQ* was examined at some length by the Supreme Court in *State (Keegan) v Stardust Compensation Tribunal*.[30] Henchy J strongly rejected Lord Diplock's reliance on logic and morality, criticizing the former as an excessively narrow ground of review, and the latter as an indeterminate invocation of a 'vague, elusive and changing body of standards which in a pluralist society is sometimes difficult to ascertain and is sometimes inappropriate or irrelevant to the decision in question'.[31]

His own restatement of the appropriate standard of review was expressed, however, in similarly independent terms. Henchy J felt that:

> [t]he test of unreasonableness or irrationality in judicial review lies in considering whether the impugned decision plainly and unambiguously flies in the face of fundamental reason and common sense. If it does, then the decision-maker should be held to have acted ultra vires, for the necessarily implied *constitutional* limitation of jurisdiction in all decision-making which affects rights or duties requires, inter alia, that the decision-maker must not flagrantly reject or disregard fundamental reason or common sense in reaching his decision.[32]

[29] *Council of Civil Service Unions v Minister for the Civil Service*, [1985] AC 374.

[30] [1986] IR 642. [31] Ibid, at 658. This was approved by Griffin J in his judgment.

[32] Ibid, at 658. The Irish approach to reasonableness was confused by the later decisions of the Supreme Court in *P & F Sharpe Ltd v Dublin City and County Manager*, [1989] IR 701 and *O'Keeffe v An Bord Pleánala*, [1993] 1 IR 39. Although Finlay CJ approved Henchy J's formulation of the test in *Keegan*, he also went on to state that an applicant seeking to establish unreasonable conduct must show 'that the decision-making authority had before it no relevant material which would support its decision'. *O'Keeffe*, [1993] 1 IR 39, at 72. As Hogan and Morgan have argued, however, this stricter approach effectively elides two distinct conceptual issues, confusing reasonableness review with scrutiny based on actual legal or factual errors. See Hogan&Morgan, note 19 above, at 647–649. Although this disparity has not been resolved, it is notable that several subsequent cases have continued to use the *Keegan* formula. See, for example, *Matthews v Irish Coursing Club*, [1993] 1 IR 346; *EH v Information Commissioner*, [2001] 2 IR 463. Furthermore, in the High Court in *Gorman v Minister for the Environment*, [2001] 2 IR 414 Carney J relied, in his discussion of reasonableness, on both authorities. He omitted to refer, however, to the passage from *O'Keeffe* outlined above, citing it merely as an example of the conventional *Wednesbury* principle that a court cannot intervene on the basis that it would have reached a different conclusion on the facts of the case. O'Neill J similarly allowed for the possibility of review for 'an error of law' where 'there would have to be either no evidence at all to support the conclusion ... or alternatively that the decision must be one which on the basis of the facts, flies in the face of reason and common sense': *Gorman*, [2001] 2 IR 463, at 488.

This consideration of the courts' attitude to the review process is doubly interesting. In the first place, ideas of 'fundamental reason' and 'common sense', like Lord Diplock's discussion of logic and morality, clearly indicate a reliance by the courts on stand-alone substantive values outside the particular intention of Parliament. Secondly, Henchy J here describes the notion of ultra vires in notably non-statutory terms, deriving it, not from any doctrine of parliamentary supremacy, but from the tenets of the constitutional text. As this chapter's subsequent survey of the Irish concept of constitutional justice will show, to disconnect the ultra vires theory from a model predicated on the normative supremacy of Parliament's intent is to deprive it of both its logical basis, and any significant operational utility.

(b) Procedural Fairness

This tendency on the part of the courts to assess administrative activity by reference to non-statutory values is also evident in the development of the doctrine of natural justice which has latterly evolved into a more general duty of procedural fairness.[33] This case law was discussed to some extent in Chapter 3. The key point here, however, is that the decision of the court in *Ridge v Baldwin* to subject the decisions of non-judicial subordinate bodies to the requirements of natural justice has produced a situation in which the courts consistently impose procedural obligations on administrative actors which are not to be found in the relevant statutory scheme.[34] As Forsyth has accepted, it 'cannot be plausibly asserted that the implied intent of the legislature provides any significant guidance to the reach of the rules of natural justice'.[35]

This again reiterates the capacity of the courts to examine administrative actions on external grounds. Statutes, it would seem, have become more peripheral to the review process. Where the courts once could only act by reference to an express statutory term, they are now entitled to rely on autonomous values posing as an implied parliamentary intent. According to this constitutional vision, the courts are not bound simply to blindly apply the instructions of Parliament but in fact constitute, in reality, an independent check on government power. As Lord Diplock explained:

> The constitutional function performed by courts of justice as interpreters of the written law laid down in Acts of Parliament is often described as ascertaining 'the intention of Parliament' but what this metaphor, though convenient, omits to take into account is that the court, when acting in its interpretative role, as well as when it is engaged in reviewing the legality of administrative action, is doing so as mediator between the state in the exercise of its legislative power and the private citizen.[36]

[33] *Re HK (an infant)*, [1967] 1 All ER 226. [34] *Ridge v Baldwin*,[1964] AC 40.

[35] C Forsyth, 'Of Fig Leaves and Fairy Tales: The Ultra Vires Doctrine, the Sovereignty of Parliament and Judicial Review' (1996) 55 CLJ 122, reproduced in Forsyth, note 22 above, at 40.

[36] *Fothergill v Monarch Airlines Ltd*, [1981] AC 251, at 279.

That Lord Diplock went on to require the state to observe the principles of 'elementary justice' in its acts illustrates the extent to which the courts have evidently adopted a role beyond that of reflexively following express statutory instructions.

(c) Human Rights

The enactment of the Human Rights Act 1998 allowed for the creation of a review jurisdiction dedicated to the enforcement of independent values within the parameters of traditional theory. The ability of the courts to invoke substantive human rights in their scrutiny of government acts could be justified constitutionally by reference to the fact that these limitations were effectively self-imposed by Parliament. It has become common for the English courts to attribute their human rights competence to the provisions of this Act.

This overlooks, however, the pre-HRA development of a human rights regime which rested on the judicial assertion of inherent common law values. In *Derbyshire County Council*,[37] for example, Lord Keith insisted that the common law of England had long protected an independent value of free speech. He dismissed the attempts by the council in question to bring defamation proceedings as 'an undesirable fetter on freedom of speech'—a position which, he was at pains to indicate, he 'reached [based] ... upon the common law of England without finding any need to rely upon the European Convention'.[38]

Similar decisions were made in relation to the right of access to the courts, and the right to an appeal. The court's decision in the latter instance was particularly clear in its interpretation of judicial review as resting on independent substantive values.

> The [challenged measure] necessarily contemplates for some a life so destitute that, to my mind, no civilized nation can tolerate it. So basic are the human rights here at issue that it cannot be necessary to resort to the [principles of the Convention]. ... Nearly 200 years ago, Lord Ellenborough CJ ... said 'As to there being no obligation for maintaining poor foreigners ... the law of humanity which is anterior to all positive law, obliges us to afford them relief'.[39]

The recognition of a common law right of abode by a number of Law Lords in *R. (Bancoult) v Secretary of State for Foreign Affairs*[40]—in a case to which, of course, the Human Rights Act 1998 had no application—can be seen in a similar light.

Thus, even in advance of the Human Rights Act 1998, a number of English judges had already begun to explain their powers in autonomous terms. This supports the notion that English law contains a core body of enduring values,

[37] *Derbyshire County Council v Times Newspapers Ltd*, [1993] AC 534.

[38] Ibid, at 551.

[39] *R. v Secretary of State for Social Security, ex p Joint Council for the Welfare of Immigrants*, [1996] 4 All ER 385, at 400.

[40] [2008] 4 All ER 1055.

against which the acceptability of all government acts falls ultimately to be assessed. The Court of Appeal's discussion of the human rights competence of the English courts in *R. (Al Rawi) v Secretary of State for Foreign Affairs* seems to endorse this view.[41] The Court acknowledged the increasingly substantive nature of the courts' judicial review jurisdiction, referring to the fact that 'the rule of law requires not only that a public decision should be authorized by the words of the enabling statute, but also that it be reasonable and (generally in human rights cases) proportionate to a legitimate aim'.[42] Subjecting the actions of other bodies to review on the basis of their adherence to these 'substantive virtues' reflected the English courts' 'increasingly substantive' conception of the rule of law.[43] This was a development which, the Court felt, had occurred 'particularly since the HRA came into force'. It is notable that the Court of Appeal did not appear to envisage the enactment of the Human Rights Act as the exclusive source of these substantive values. Rather, the courts' asserted 'special responsibility in the area of human rights' was said to arise 'in part from the impetus of the HRA [and] in part from the common law's jealousy in seeing that intrusive State power is always strictly justified'.[44] On this analysis, the courts' jurisdiction to protect human rights does not depend solely upon the incorporation of the Convention. It also suggests that there may have been the possibility that some form of competence to require state conduct to be justified on substantive grounds might have been developed even in the HRA's absence. The basis for some type of human rights competence had long been established. As Laws has noted, '[t]he development of judicial review since the seminal cases of the 1960s . . . [had already] vouchsafed the submission of [government] to the rule of law'.[45]

(d) Non-Statutory Review

The increasingly astatutory character of contemporary curial review has also been reflected in other areas of the law. Judicial scrutiny, for example, is no longer confined to statutory powers. *GCHQ*, for example, subjected the exercise of the prerogative powers of government—for which there are obviously no direct statutory instructions—to the scrutiny of the courts.[46] *Datafin* similarly extended the scope of review to non-statutory bodies.[47] Prerogative legislation too falls to be scrutinized by the courts in order to ensure due observance of the rule of law.[48] Judicial review has clearly become a more general jurisdiction, requiring a broad range of governmental bodies to observe the substantive limitations imposed by the courts in the name of Parliament. With references to the

[41] [2006] EWCA Civ 1279. [42] Ibid, at para. 146. [43] Ibid, at para. 146.
[44] Ibid, at para. 147.
[45] J Laws, 'Judicial Review and the Meaning of Law' in Forsyth, *Judicial Review and the Constitution*, note 22 above, at 185. [46] *GCHQ*, [1985] AC 374.
[47] *R. v Panel on Take-overs and Mergers ex p Datafin*, [1987] 1 QB 815.
[48] *Bancoult*, [2008] 4 All ER 1055.

specific instructions of Parliament conspicuous by their regular absence from the review process, the continuing relevance of the traditional ultra vires model must be called into question.

(4) Academic Criticism

So it has been that the theory has come under sustained academic attack in the UK, being variously disparaged as 'indeterminate, unrealistic, beset by internal tension, and ... [unable] to explain all instances where the judiciary has applied public law principles'.[49] Whereas the courts' historical invocation of a directly didactic Parliament once provided jurisdictional content *and* legitimacy, the latter-day doctrine of implied legislative intent offers only bare legitimacy.

Supporters of the ultra vires theory have acknowledged its irrelevance to the actual deliberations of contemporary courts. As Elliott—who favours the retention of the notion of Parliamentary intention in some sort of constitutional role—has commented, '[a]ll modern writers recognize the necessity of moving beyond the unconvincing dogma of the orthodox ultra vires principle'.[50] Forsyth has instead attempted to portray the theory as a fictional but necessary 'fig-leaf',[51] continued adherence to which is required in order to 'preserve the decencies' of a 'constitutional order in which myth but not deceit plays so important a role and where form and function often differ'.[52] He has set out a modified form of the theory which, he feels, is capable of filling this legitimating role. His model argues that Parliament's failure to prevent the courts' expansion of the nature and scope of judicial review can be construed as constituting a tacit assent to that process. Elliot, similarly, argues that the courts' creation of autonomous rules of administrative review is based on a 'constitutional warrant, granted by Parliament'.[53] This amended interpretation of ultra vires 'sees general legislative intent merely as a key to unlocking the door to allow the courts to decide on the ambit of judicial review in accordance with the rule of law'.[54]

This imputation of an indirect relationship between legislative intent and judicial scrutiny is, however, only 'an elegant but doomed attempt to dress a fiction in the garb of reality'.[55] It cannot conceal the fact that the criteria of

[49] Craig, note 22 above, at 47.

[50] M Elliott, 'Legislative Intention *versus* Judicial Creativity? Administrative Law as a Co-operative Endeavour' in Forsyth, *Judicial Review and the Constitution*, note 22 above, at 368.

[51] This term first appeared in J Laws, 'Illegality: the problem of jurisdiction' in M Supperstone&J Goudie, eds., *Judicial Review* (Butterworths, 1992) but has since been used by many contributors to this debate, most notably Christopher Forsyth.

[52] Forsyth, 'Of Fig Leaves and Fairy Tales', note 35 above, at 42.

[53] M Elliott, 'The Ultra Vires Doctrine in a Constitutional Setting: Still the Central Principles of Judicial Review' (1998) 57 CLJ 63, reproduced in Forsyth, *Judicial Review and the Constitution*, note 22 above, at 96.

[54] PP Craig, 'Competing Models of Judicial Review' [1999] PL 428, reproduced in Forsyth, *Judicial Review and the Constitution*, note 22 above, at 376.

[55] Laws, note 45 above, at 76.

review employed by the courts have been autonomously elaborated by the judiciary without reference to the specific intentions of Parliament. The supervisory involvement of the courts is guided—as the theory set out in this book suggests it should be—by external and objective values. Ultra vires offers only an *ex post facto* (and unconvincing) justification of a review process conducted on entirely different grounds. '[L]egislative intent set at such a general level will not in any sense be determinative of what rights an individual should receive in court.'[56] As Craig, considering Forsyth's redefined model, remarked:

> The flexibility of the *ultra vires* principle can preserve the veneer that the courts are simply obeying the legislative mandate, but it is this very flexibility which ultimately robs the reasoning of any conviction. It is precisely because legislative intent can be used to legitimate almost all types of control that it loses its potency to legitimate any particular one.[57]

It is clear, therefore, that there is a considerable divergence between the rhetoric and the reality of ultra vires review. Constitutional orthodoxy continues, of course, to justify this jurisdiction as the judicial vindication of Parliament's intent. The case law shows, however, that in their use of their actual powers of review the courts effectively rely on external notions of legitimacy. This necessarily suggests, however, that these values are logically prior to the doctrine of parliamentary supremacy, upon which the ultra vires theory has traditionally been based. That the courts can assess the actions of administrative bodies in terms of their compliance with external norms implicitly constitutes those values as independent criteria of governmental legality.

There has therefore been an increasing academic tendency, beginning with Oliver's seminal attempt to connect judicial review with the objective of preventing abuses of public power,[58] to rest the competence of the courts on common law principles, or on the rule of law. In fact, on this issue common law models of review, under which the courts exercise independent supervisory powers, have now assumed a position of academic dominance in the UK.[59]

On this analysis, ultra vires theory is subordinated to superior values. Even the courts' continued reliance on traditional rhetoric presents no obstacle to an understanding of the British constitution as resting on some sort of residual norms. Woolf declared 'that there are ... limits on the supremacy of Parliament which it is the courts' inalienable responsibility to identify and uphold',[60] a contention echoed by Laws's professed opinion that 'a higher order law confers primacy on the doctrine of parliamentary supremacy ... and must of necessity

[56] PP Craig, 'Competing Models of Judicial Review', note 54 above, at 377.

[57] Craig 'Ultra Vires and the Foundations of Judicial Review', note 22 above, at 50.

[58] D Oliver, 'Is the Ultra Vires rule the basis of Judicial Review?' [1987] PL 543.

[59] T Poole, 'Back to the Future? Unearthing the Theory of Common Law Constitutionalism' (2003) 23 (3) OJLS 435, at 438.

[60] H Woolf, '*Droit Public*—English Style' [1995] PL 57, at 69.

limit it'.[61] Craig, Allan, Oliver, and Jowell are amongst the prominent constitutional commentators who have accepted the existence of such antecedent limitations on the power of Parliament. Contemporary academic discourse tends to agree that '[l]egislative authority is derived from, and must therefore be limited by, a collection of norms found in the rule of law'.[62]

It is important to note that the contributions of both Laws and Woolf to this issue (which were outlined above) were made in an extra-judicial capacity. Both were careful to ensure that their judicial pronouncements conformed to accepted constitutional orthodoxy. Their concerns were clear, however. As Woolf later put it, when considering government attempts to exclude the courts from the asylum appeals process:

> I am not over-dramatising the position if I indicate that, if this clause were to become law, it would be so inconsistent with the spirit of mutual respect between the different arms of government that it could be the catalyst for a campaign for a written constitution.[63]

If faced with the choice between preserving parliamentary sovereignty and, on the other hand, upholding fundamental normative values, the instincts of the judiciary evidently inclined towards the latter. It is in this context that the Lords' more recent input into this debate should be understood.

(5) Changes in the Courts: The Decision in *Jackson*

The decision in *R. (Jackson) v AG* concerned the enactment of the Hunting Act 2004,[64] which criminalized the hunting of wild animals with dogs, except in limited circumstances. The challenge to the Act was based not on its content, but on the way in which it had been passed by Parliament. The Act was introduced by way of a 1949 statute which allowed for the circumvention of the constitutional veto of the House of Lords, thereby permitting the Labour government to avoid the long-standing opposition of that chamber to the adoption of such anti-hunting measures.

The Parliament Act 1949, on which the government had relied, was itself an amendment of the Parliament Act 1911. This had been introduced by the government of the day in response to entrenched Conservative opposition in the Lords to many of the Liberal Party's reforming measures. Despite the electoral success of the Liberals, the Lords had refused to allow the enactment of a

[61] J Laws, 'Law and Democracy' [1995] PL 72, at 81.

[62] See further TRS Allan, 'The Rule of Law as the Foundation of Judicial Review' in Forsyth, *Judicial Review and the Constitution*, note 22 above; 'Legislative Supremacy and the Rule of Law: Democracy and Constitutionalism' (1985) 44 CLJ 111.

[63] Comments made by Woolf LCJ in a speech, delivered to mark the centenary of the Squire Law Library, University of Cambridge on 3 March, 2004.

[64] [2005] UKHL 56; [2006] 1 AC 262.

number of important Bills—most notably the 1893 Home Rule Bill, and the 1909 Finance Bill.

Section 2 of the 1911 Act provided that a Bill could be declared to have passed Parliament if it had been approved by the House of Commons in three successive sessions, and rejected by the Lords in each of those sessions, provided that at least two years had elapsed from the introduction of the Bill, and its adoption by the Commons for the third time. The Act also excluded money Bills and 'any provision to extend the maximum duration of Parliament beyond five years' from the scope of section 2.

The 1949 Act qualified the 1911 legislation by easing the original restrictions on the use of this process. It required only that a Bill be approved in two successive sessions of the Commons. Furthermore, the two-year time limit was reduced to one year.

It was argued in *Jackson*, however, that these 1949 reforms were unlawful. The case for the applicants effectively turned on their submission that the 1949 Act was a species of sub-primary legislation, which could not be used to amend the parent Act. The 1911 Act, however, had declared that 'any' public Bill passed by means of the procedure which it set out would 'become an Act of Parliament'. The Lords therefore concluded that the applicant's challenge should fail.

The central focus of this case, relating as it does to the details of a particular parliamentary procedure, is of limited general relevance. Of more interest, however, were the obiter responses of the Lords to the Attorney General's contention that, in principle, the 1949 Act could be used to introduce significant constitutional changes. Counsel for the applicants had argued that a decision to uphold the 1949 Act would logically allow the Commons, for example, to amend section 2 of the 1911 Act so as to extend its own lifetime indefinitely. Relying on the doctrine of parliamentary supremacy, the Attorney General concurred that this was the case.

Based on the 'strict legalism' of traditional ultra vires theory, this would appear to be correct.[65] Remarkably, however, the majority of the Lords seemed to suggest the existence of some inherent limitations on the legislative power of this ostensibly supreme organ. As Lord Bingham's acceptance of the Commons as an 'ultimately unconstrained power' showed, this position was by no means unanimous.[66] Furthermore, it should also be noted that, without fuller argument on this hypothetical point, the judges professed themselves only 'inclin[ed] very tentatively to the view that [the] instinct may be right ... that there may be a limit somewhere to the powers [of the Commons]'.[67] Allowing for these caveats, however, the fact remains that, as Lord Brown commented:

> in common ... I think, with the majority of your Lordships I am not prepared to give such a ruling as would sanction in advance the use of the 1911 Act for all purposes, for

[65] *Jackson*, [2006] 1 AC 262; [2005] UKHL 56, at para. 101. [66] Ibid, at para. 41.
[67] Ibid, at para. 178.

example, to abolish the House of Lords ... or to prolong the life of Parliament, two of the extreme ends to which theoretically this procedure could be put.[68]

Limited though it might be, this instinct towards restriction does not conform to the system's traditional conception of an absolutely unfettered Parliament.

The judgments of Lords Steyn and Hope went further, however, to expressly impugn the idea of parliamentary sovereignty. Lord Hope dismissed the concept of Parliament as an unconstrained organ:

[P]arliamentary sovereignty is no longer, if it ever was, absolute. It is not uncontrolled .... It is no longer right to say that its freedom to legislate admits of no qualification whatever. Step by step, gradually but surely, the English principle of the absolute sovereignty of Parliament which Dicey derived from Coke and Blackstone is being qualified.[69]

Lord Steyn, for his part, opined that:

[w]e do not in the United Kingdom have an uncontrolled constitution as the Attorney General implausibly asserts .... The classic account given by Dicey of the doctrine of the supremacy of Parliament, pure and absolute as it was, can now be seen to be out of place.[70]

Crucially, he then went on to suggest that—as the academics outlined above have argued—there may be some constitutional principles to which the sovereignty of Parliament is ultimately subject.

The judges created this principle [of Parliamentary supremacy]. If that is so, it is not unthinkable that circumstances could arise where the courts may have to qualify a principle established on a different hypothesis of constitutionalism. In exceptional circumstances ... the House of Lords ... may have to consider whether [a proposed change affects] a constitutional fundamental which even a sovereign Parliament acting at the behest of a complaisant House of Commons cannot abolish.[71]

It is obviously important not to overstate the significance of what remain only the obiter comments of individual judges. Nonetheless, the fact that several members of the United Kingdom's highest court offered at least intuitive support for the idea of independent constraints on parliamentary power indicates the extent to which rule of law conceptions of the constitutional order have supplanted those based on parliamentary supremacy and ultra vires review. The decision in *Jackson* suggests that the theory that there are inherent substantive limitations on the exercise of public power is gaining increasing acceptance as the courts' consideration of the English system's central values evolves.

[68] Ibid, at para. 194. [69] Ibid, at para. 104. [70] Ibid, at para. 102.

[71] Ibid, at para. 102–103. Lord Steyn used the examples of 'an attempt to abolish judicial review, or the ordinary role of the courts' to illustrate his point.

(6) Judicial Review as an Independent Jurisdiction

The implications of such a development for the model outlined in this work are clear. Traditional ultra vires theory, with its emphasis on a hierarchical and unfettered sovereign power, could not accept the way in which this work's suggested model equates the legitimacy of public actions with the extent to which they reflect particular substantive values. This necessarily implies that any exercise of power which contravenes these values will be unlawful. The identity of the institution in question is irrelevant. The body charged with ensuring the observance of this value (in this case, the court) is entitled to intervene as it sees fit, on the basis of its overarching obligation to enforce the system's foundational norms. That judicial review seems, increasingly, to be understood in the UK as an independent process of value-oriented review thus supports the claim of this book that the system can be (and, indeed, arguably is) founded upon its protection of certain fundamental principles. The marginalization of the ultra vires theory, and of the doctrine of parliamentary supremacy to which it adhered, removes one of the most obvious objections to the constitutional vision set out in this work.

This analysis is even more apposite in Ireland. As an earlier section of this chapter has commented, the continued Irish references to aspects of the ultra vires theory have been somewhat surprising. Arguably the existence of an entrenched constitutional commitment to secure denominated substantive values should have rendered the courts' jurisdictional reliance on a putative parliamentary intent obsolete.

This is particularly so given the elaboration by the courts of a doctrine of constitutional justice in administrative affairs. First set out by Walsh J in *McDonald v Bord na gCon (No 2)*,[72] it was explained by the courts in orthodox ultra vires terms. Echoing the UK courts' contention that parliament required that basic precepts of legality would be observed, the *Oireachtas* was assumed to intend that the principles of constitutional justice would be secured:

> [T]he presumption of constitutionality carries with it not only the presumption that the constitutional interpretation or construction is the one intended by the *Oireachtas* but also that the *Oireachtas* intended that proceedings, procedures, discretions and adjudications which are permitted, provided for, or prescribed by an Act of the *Oireachtas* are to be conducted in accordance with the principles of constitutional justice.[73]

That these values were, in reality, independent grounds of challenge was evidenced, however, by Walsh J's immediate proclamation that '[i]n such a case any departure from those principles would be restrained and corrected by the Courts'.

[72] [1965] IR 217.

[73] *East Donegal Co-op v AG*, [1970] IR 317, at 341.

This power of the courts to demand administrative compliance with extra-statutory conditions was set on a firmly constitutional footing in *Re Haughey* when the Supreme Court identified an independent Article 40.3 right to fair procedures:

> Article 40, s. 3, of the Constitution is a guarantee to the citizen of basic fairness of procedures. The Constitution guarantees such fairness, and it is the duty of the Court to underline that the words of Article 40, s. 3, are not political shibboleths but provide a positive protection for the citizen.[74]

The courts were constitutionally obliged:

> not [to] deny to the citizens the shield against injustice which th[e] guarantee [of fair procedures is] intended to provide.[75]

As has been the case in Britain, there has been a divergence between judicial invocations of ultra vires and the reality of the judicially permitted heads of review. In common with their English counterparts, for example, the Irish courts have allowed the use of *Wednesbury* unreasonableness as a ground of challenge. As the preceding sections have shown, such reasonableness review necessarily requires the courts to move beyond the constrained strictures of statute. 'No amount of judicial endorsement of Lord Brightman's dictum in *Evans* can disguise [the] essential legal reality' that 'when the court quashes a decision on grounds of unreasonableness, it is in effect saying that the merits of the decision are so plainly flawed ... that the courts will not stand over [it]'.[76]

In terms of procedural fairness, however, Irish judges have drifted much further from the ultra vires theory's traditional moorings. As the citations above make clear, the ability of the Irish courts to intervene is expressly justified by reference to external notions of justice and fairness.[77] In this context, the continued use of the language of ultra vires is very unconvincing. In Irish terms, it can only be explained realistically as some sort of instructional metaphor. Although incompatible with the justice-based competence of the courts, it does offer a colourful reminder of the importance of judicial deference in administrative matters. Employed for reasons of convenience rather than ideological clarity, its relevance to the Irish constitutional system is, at best, questionable. Certainly, it should not pose problems for any attempt to apply this book's theory to the Irish constitutional order.

[74] [1971] IR 217, at 264, *per* O'Dalaigh CJ.

[75] *Garvey v Ireland*, [1981] IR 75, at 100, *per* Henchy J.

[76] G Hogan, 'Judicial Review, the Doctrine of Reasonableness and the Immigration Process' (2001) 6 *Bar Review* 329.

[77] See also the earlier discussion of the decision in *Keegan*, [1986] IR 642.

D. The Search for Substantive Values

The preceding section has traced the gradual emergence in both Ireland and England of a judicial willingness to examine administrative acts on independent grounds. In this, it supports the argument, set out in Chapter 3, that a commitment to certain key autonomous values permeates the institutional order of the state. Justice, fairness, and the rule of law have all been invoked as objective criteria of governmental legitimacy. Thus far, however, this chapter has not considered the particular content of these principles. What does justice or fairness actually entail? The assumption by the courts of independent powers of review echoes the general republican thrust of this book. It does not automatically ensure that the substantive details of our existing system coincide with those described in Chapter 4, however. This section will therefore assess the extent to which recent developments in the case law of the courts can be said to sustain the suggested status of non-arbitrariness as the underlying value of our constitutional structures.

(1) The Doctrine of Legitimate Expectations

(a) The Duty to Act Fairly

One area of the law in which judicial references to fairness have consistently recurred is in cases concerning the comparatively emergent doctrine of legitimate expectations. In *GCHQ*,[78] Lord Fraser explicitly connected the entitlement of an individual to receive a benefit or privilege to which they had a legitimate expectation with the general obligation on government agencies to conduct themselves fairly when interacting with the state's citizens. Taylor J agreed in *Ruddock* that 'the doctrine of legitimate expectations in essence imposes a duty to act fairly',[79] a sentiment evidenced also in the judgments of Laws J in *Richmond LBC*,[80] O'Hanlon J in *Fakih*,[81] and Taylor J in *US Tobacco*.[82] That the courts' ability to enforce such benefits is founded upon its desire to ensure observance of this value was most strongly stated in *Hamble Fisheries*[83] and in *Coughlan*,[84] where the relative fairness of the acts impugned was regarded as the determinant touchstone of their ultimate legality.

United in their invocation of a general notion of fairness, the authorities do not, however, advance a single understanding of the specific content of this

[78] [1985] AC 374.
[79] *R. v Secretary of State for the Home Department, ex p Ruddock*, [1987] 1 WLR 1482.
[80] *R. v Secretary of State for Transport, ex p Richmond upon Thames London Borough Council*, [1994] 1 WLR 74.
[81] *Fakih v Minister for Justice*, [1994] 2 IR 406.
[82] *R. v Secretary of State for Health, ex p US Tobacco International Inc*, [1992] 1 QB 353.
[83] *R. v Minister of Agriculture, Fisheries and Food, ex p Hamble Fisheries*, [1995] 2 All ER 714.
[84] *R. v N&E Devon Health Authority, ex p Coughlan*, [2000] 2 WLR 622.

value. Craig has correctly identified the way in which this jurisdiction can be justified on various differing grounds:

> Th[e] [instrumental] rationale emphasizes the connection between procedural due process and the substantive justice of the final outcome. ... [T]he procedural rights perform an instrumental role in the sense of rendering it more likely that there will be an accurate decision on the substance of the case. ... Other [non-instrumental] justifications ... focus on formal justice and the rule of law ... [and] are also seen as protecting human dignity by ensuring that the individual is told why he is being treated unfavourably, and by enabling him to take part in the decision.[85]

There is the possibility, therefore, of some divergence between, on the one hand, those who equate this doctrine with an instrumental commitment to good administration, and on the other hand, those who deontologically envisage it as a jurisdiction founded upon a protection of important values.

Instinctively, these objectives incline in somewhat different directions. A focus on individual rights, for example, would require the actual infringement of some protected value as a prerequisite for judicial action. This is evident in the insistence of some Irish judges on some sort of detrimental reliance on the part of the particular claimant.[86] Alternatively, a desire to secure compliance with the principles of good administration could be satisfied by the simple provision of a procedural rather than a substantive remedy. This question has also previously led to a division of opinion between different courts.[87]

From the point of view of the theory at hand, however, non-arbitrariness can be taken to elide these instincts. In terms of its implications for the actions of administrative bodies, non-arbitrariness is obviously generally directed towards the quality of their decision-making procedures. An observance of the principles of good administration will generally preclude any challenge on this ground. However, the justification for its use is firmly rooted in its relationship with the individual's right to have his or her status as an autonomous agent acknowledged and affirmed. The principle's commitment to improved procedures is animated, not by a desire to ensure that all administrative decisions are always correct, but by a belief in the value of the individual autonomy. Its impact may often be procedural but there is no innate reason why it should be so contained.

This understanding of fairness would require a contextual assessment of the extent to which an administrative body took due account of the interests of relevant individuals in embarking upon its designated course of action. Significantly, the principle's emphasis on the importance of the citizen's autonomy ought not to inhibit its acceptance of the ability of the state to produce

[85] PP Craig, 'Legitimate Expectations: A Conceptual Analysis' (1992) 108 LQR 79, at 85–86.

[86] *Garda Representative Association v Ireland*, [1989] IR 193; *Cosgrove v Legal Aid Board*, [1991] 2 IR 43.

[87] See the discussion of *Hamble Fisheries*, [1995] 2 All ER 714; *R. v Secretary of State for the Home Department ex p Hargreaves*, [1997] 1 WLR 906; *Coughlan*, [2000] 2 WLR 622.

individually-adverse outcomes. It demands not that the desires of individuals are always secured but rather that their interests—considered in the context of the power in question—have been appropriately acknowledged. As the following paragraphs will argue, it can be submitted that this approach in fact underlies the development of the legitimate expectations doctrine.

(b) The Judicial Enforcement of Substantive Entitlements

As an 'evolving [jurisdiction] whose parameters have not yet been defined[,] ... whose scope has not yet been established'[88] and whose 'reach in practice is still being explored',[89] it is important to bear in mind that there are a number of outstanding issues in this area which continue to await a definitive resolution. Many of these questions arise as a result of the dysfunctional relationship between traditional ultra vires ideas and the emerging doctrine of legitimate expectations. The doctrine undermines the ultra vires theory in two main ways. In the first place, it casts doubt on the orthodox rule that a delegatee is unable to confer on itself the power to act outside its stated jurisdiction.[90] Secondly, the enforcement of an expectation on the basis of a body's making a previous representation has been argued to unduly fetter that body's discretionary powers. In *Amphitrite*, for example, the House of Lords was clear that it could not constrain a body's discretion by reference to its previous promise not to detain a neutral ship in port.[91]

As the previous section has shown, however, the influence of the ultra vires theory is gradually waning in the face of the courts' enforcement of external values. Legitimate expectations, with its fairness-oriented implementation of extra-statutory promises, can clearly be regarded as part of this process. Nonetheless, much of the confusion in the case law can be attributed to the residual influence of this theory.

One issue which has attracted a considerable level of academic and judicial attention is the question whether a legitimate expectation on the part of an individual claimant could give rise to a procedural or a substantive entitlement. In its initial formulation, the duty to act fairly, upon which judicial intervention was founded, was held to allow the enforcement of a 'benefit or advantage' to which an individual was due.[92] Several judges subsequently restricted the scope of such entitlements to procedural guarantees, however. In *Fakih*, for example, O'Hanlon J confined the applicants' claim to a right to have their cases determined in accordance with fair procedures.[93] Similarly, in *Tara Prospecting* Costello J equated the concept of legitimate expectations with the right to be heard.[94]

[88] *Hempenstall v Minister for the Environment*, [1994] 2 IR 20, at 31.
[89] *R. (Bhatt Murphy) v Independent Assessor*, [2008] EWCA Civ 755 at para. 27.
[90] *Re Green Building Co.*, [1977] IR 256; *Re Parke Davis & Co. TM Application*, [1976] FSR 195.
[91] *Redereiaktiebolaget Amphitrite v The King*, [1921] 3 KB 300.
[92] *GCHQ*, [1985] AC 374, at 408. [93] [1994] 2 IR 406.
[94] *Tara Prospecting Ltd v Minister for Energy*, [1993] ILRM 771.

Relying heavily on the Australian opinion of Brennan J in *Quin*,[95] Costello J argued that this right to a hearing, as an essentially procedural entitlement, could not be employed to compel an administrative body to act in contravention of its statutory duties or prerogative powers.

A similar principle was put forward in England in the judgments of Laws J in *Richmond LBC*,[96] and Hirst LJ in *Hargreaves*. Laws J advanced a procedural conception of the duty to act fairly, arguing that the observance of the principle of good administration would sufficiently address an asserted expectation. The enforcement of substantive benefits beyond the parameters of a body's particular powers was a constitutional 'heresy', which the courts could not allow.[97]

A number of other cases favoured a contrasting approach which appeared to eschew such ultra vires-inspired restrictions on this jurisdiction. In *Ruddock*, for example, Taylor J expressed the view that '[w]hile most of the cases are concerned ... with a right to be heard, I do not think that the doctrine is so confined'.[98] This idea of a more general jurisdiction to enforce administrative fairness was reiterated, and, indeed, expanded in the judgment of Sedley J in *Hamble Fisheries*. His extensive analysis of this nascent legal doctrine led him to conclude that the courts' capacity to act was founded upon their protection of the individual from unfair exercises of public power. Given the general nature of this commitment, Sedley J felt that it would unacceptable to restrict such protection to procedural affairs:

> It is difficult to see why it is any less unfair to frustrate a legitimate expectation that something will or will not be done by the decision-maker than it is to frustrate a legitimate expectation that the applicant will be listened to before the decision-maker decided to take a particular step.[99]

In the judge's view, 'principle, as well as precedent, points to these conclusions'.[100]

Doubted in *Hargreaves*,[101] Sedley J's judgment was subsequently approved by the Court of Appeal in *Coughlan*.[102] Here, again, the Court suggested a test in which the conduct of the authority in question would be examined in order to see if it was so unfair as to amount to an abuse of power. Like *Hamble Fisheries*, *Coughlan* treated the fairness of the impugned act, from the point of view of the individual, as the determining criterion of its validity. Crucially, however, the Court of Appeal interpreted fairness in an expansive fashion, maintaining that '[f]airness ... if it is to mean anything, must ... include fairness of outcome'.[103] The courts were obliged to move beyond the *Wednesbury* formulation to which the court in *Hargreaves* had insisted they adhere. Fairness, in the context of this

[95] *AG for New South Wales v Quin*, (1990) 170 CLR 1. [96] [1994] 1 WLR 74.
[97] *Hargreaves*, [1997] 1 WLR 906, at 921.
[98] *R v Secretary of State for the Home Department ex p Ruddock*, [1987] 2 All ER 518, at 531.
[99] [1995] 2 All ER 714, at 724. [100] Ibid, at 724. [101] [1997] 1 WLR 906.
[102] [2000] 2 WLR 622. [103] Ibid, at para 71.

case, required more than the raised rationality test that formula entailed—on the contrary, the actions of the body in this instance could 'only be justified if [required by] an overriding public interest'.[104]

Coughlan has since been cited with approval on a number of occasions, most notably by Lord Hoffman in *R. v East Sussex County Council, ex p Reprotech (Pebsham) Ltd*,[105] and by the Court of Appeal in *R. (Bhatt Murphy) v Independent Assessor*.[106] In the latter case, Laws LJ again made clear that he felt that, in an appropriate case, an action for legitimate expectations could support argument that the applicant had a legitimate expectation that a particular substantive benefit would be supplied. The Court emphasized that a 'much more rigorous standard' of scrutiny would apply to cases where claims to such substantive entitlements were made.[107] This reflected the importance that decision makers be permitted to exercise their powers to formulate and reformulate policy as they deemed appropriate. The courts retained, however, an enduring ability to intervene to prevent unfairness wherever it might occur. *Bhatt Murphy* and *Coughlan* appear to confirm that the courts' current view is that this judicial power to give effect to whatever fairness requires is not limited by traditional notions of ultra vires or political supremacy, but is rather the sort of distinct, substantive, and dynamic jurisdiction which is envisaged by the new separation of powers theory. As Bingham MR observed in *Unilever*, '[t]he categories of unfairness are not closed, and precedent should act as a guide not a cage'.[108] This indicates the extent to which the principles which underpin this area of the law seemed to have moved 'a long way distant from the archetype of public decision-making' associated with more traditional conceptions of English law.[109]

(c) *Collective* versus *Individual Interest—A Model of Institutional Balance?*

In this trend away from a rigidly categorical approach towards one based on the contextualized assessment of the fairness of the acts in question, the *Coughlan*/*Bhatt Murphy* conception of legitimate expectations supports the idea of a general, uninhibited judicial jurisdiction to secure external ideas of fairness. This was particularly noticeable in *Bhatt Murphy* where Laws LJ derived the doctrine of legitimate expectations from a more general principle of good administration, to which he appeared to attach quasi-constitutional status. His view was that:

> the underlying principle of good administration which requires public bodies to deal straightforwardly and consistently with the public, and by that token commends the doctrine of legitimate expectation, should be treated as a legal standard which, although

104 Ibid, at para 76.
105 [2002] UKHL 8 at para. 34.
106 [2008] EWCA Civ 755.
107 Ibid, at para. 35.
108 *R. v Inland Revenue, ex p Unilever*, [1996] STC 681, at 690.
109 *Bhatt Murphy*, [2008] EWCA Civ 755 at para. 41.

not found in terms in the European Convention on Human Rights, takes its place alongside such rights as fair trial, and no punishment without law.[110]

Significantly, however, the Court of Appeal in both cases was also clear in its acknowledgement of the need to balance the interests of the individual against the power-exercising primacy of the state. The case law, like this book's dual model of constituent interests, has consistently affirmed the importance of this latter aim. *Ruddock* noted that promises 'obviously' could not be upheld where to do so would conflict with statutory duties. McCracken J in *Abrahamson* agreed that legitimate expectations could only be secured where to do so would be 'lawful'.[111] In *Hamble Fisheries*, Sedley J insisted that the executive could be kept to its promises, but accepted that this could not restrict the liberty of government bodies to act within the scope of their discretion.[112]

Lord Woolf MR was at pains to point out in *Coughlan* that the recognition of legitimate expectations as a substantive guarantee did not unduly trammel the executive or legislative functions. In *Preston*, rather, he had adopted the position that a power abused is one unlawfully exercised, and set the threshold of invalidity accordingly.[113] The requirement that an act be so unfair that it constituted an abuse of power appeared intended to supply the appropriate level of judicial restraint. Intervention is justified as restraining illegality rather than restricting discretionary powers.

Thus the elevated nature of this threshold seems designed to guard against undue judicial interference on insignificant grounds. Lord Woolf MR further required the courts to accept an authority's suggested justification of its policy changes without equivocation. This constitutes a clear acceptance of the importance of allowing unfettered administrative action. Legitimate expectations should not be regarded as elevating the interests of the individual above those of the collective. Rather, it follows the approach of this book in resting institutional prerogatives upon a recognition of the basic duality in the exercise of public powers:

> The court's task in all these cases is not to impede executive activity but to reconcile its continuing need to initiate or respond to change with the legitimate interests or expectations of citizens or strangers who have relied, and have been justified in relying, on a current policy or an extant promise.[114]

The Court in *Coughlan* clearly sought to balance the courts' jurisdiction to defend the individual against the inherent capacity of the government to exercise power in the public interest. As Lord Woolf MR himself commented, its approach:

[110] Ibid, at para. 50.

[111] *Abrahamson v Law Society*, [1996] 4 IR 403.

[112] *Hamble Fisheries*, [1995] 2 All ER 714. The importance of securing the discretionary freedom of administrative bodies was also emphasized in, for example, *Wiley v Revenue Commissioners*, [1989] IR 350; *Gilheaney v Revenue Commissioners*, [1996] ELR 25.

[113] *Re Preston*, [1985] AC 835.

[114] *Coughlan*, [2000] 2 WLR 622, at para. 65.

recognises the primacy of the public authority both in administration and in policy development but it insists, where these functions come into tension, upon the adjudicative role of the court to ensure fairness to the individual.[115]

This acceptance of the necessity to balance the requirements of fairness with the decisional freedom of public bodies was also evident in *Bhatt Murphy*. Laws LJ emphasized the exceptional nature of the legitimate expectations jurisdiction, noting that the courts would not normally interfere with public bodies' ability to act in the way they deem most appropriate. The limited scope for intervention reflected the fact that:

> [p]ublic authorities typically, and central government *par excellence*, enjoy wide discretions which it is their duty to exercise in the public interest. They have to decide the content and the pace of change. Often they must balance different, indeed opposing, interests across a wide spectrum. Generally they must be masters of procedure as well as substance; and as such are generally entitled to keep their own counsel.[116]

This view not only accepts the value and necessity of government freedom but also implicitly acknowledges the courts' comparative inability to exercise such creative policy powers effectively. This echoes the analysis of institutional capacities set out in Chapter 6 and supports the argument that the development of the doctrine of legitimate expectations should not be regarded as an attempt by the courts to expand their decision-making authority into non-traditional areas. In *Coughlan* and *Bhatt Murphy* the Court of Appeal clearly, in both instances, acknowledged the primacy of the political or administrative bodies in coming to policy conclusions. What they also envisaged, however, was a role for the courts in checking to ensure that the procedures adopted, or the decisions taken, showed due regard for fairness, regardless of the form which these decisions took or of the context in which they were made. On this analysis, the doctrine of legitimate expectations seems to represent a variety of substantive judicial scrutiny which is not limited by formal notions of category or context. The courts may act to vindicate fairness as required, but must show due regard for the decisions and policy positions favoured by the other branches of government. This has obvious parallels with the forms of inter-institutional scrutiny favoured by the theory of separation set forward in this book.

(d) Balance, Justification and Non-Arbitrariness

The acknowledgement of the inherent validity of these dual interests logically requires that an attempt is made at mediating their claims in the individual context of each case. As this book argues in Chapters 4 and 5, non-arbitrariness supplies just such a means of meditation. As a principle, it recognizes the mutual veracity of opposing interests. It accordingly seeks to structure their interaction

[115] Ibid, at para. 70.

[116] *Bhatt Murphy*, [2008] EWCA Civ 755 at para. 41.

in a way which provides for the appropriate contextual reconciliation of competing impulses. This is achieved by concentrating on the reasons offered as justification for the exercise of an impugned power. Non-arbitrariness does not prevent the use of governmental power per se—it rather ties its legitimacy to the extent to which a particular decision can be shown to be the product of a contextually appropriate weighing of an individual's contrary interests.

In this, it matches closely the *Coughlan/Bhatt Murphy* approach to legitimate expectations. It is noticeable that the courts have consistently deferred to the decisional primacy of the challenged organ where they have been satisfied that there were objective grounds for the change in policy. National security,[117] the public interest,[118] previous decisions of the courts,[119] reasonable employment objectives,[120] and the existence of a compelling statutory obligation have all been accepted by the courts as valid reasons for resiling from an applicant's expectation.[121] Sedley J expressly tied the fairness of a proposed administrative change to the authority's reasons for undertaking it,[122] while Taylor J in *US Tobacco* accepted that the minister's freedom to depart from a previous representation was limited by the obligation that the decision be rationally based on objectively justifiable grounds.[123]

As the Court of Appeal in *Coughlan* declared, however, this emphasis on the acceptability of administrative reasons does not denote a basic rationality standard of review.

> It is when one examines the implications for a case like the present of the proposition that so long as the decision-making process has been lawful, the court's only ground of intervention is the intrinsic rationality of the decision, that the problem becomes apparent. Rationality, as it has developed in modern public law, has two faces: one is the barely known decision which simply defies comprehension; the other is a decision which can be seen to have proceeded by flawed logic (though this can often be equally well allocated to the intrusion of an irrelevant factor). The present decision may well pass a rationality test; the health authority knew of the promise and its seriousness; it was aware of its new policies and the reasons for them; it knew that one had to yield, and it made a choice which, whatever else can be said of it, may not easily be challenged as irrational ... But to limit the court's power of supervision to this is to exclude from consideration another aspect of the decision (fairness) which is equally the concern of the law.[124]

The simple search for the presence of some sort of rational and legitimate objective would not, therefore, properly protect the state's citizens.

[117] *GCHQ*, [1985] AC 374. [118] *Tara Prospecting*, [1993] ILRM 771.
[119] *Abrahamson*, [1996] 4 IR 403, based on the decision in *Bloomer v Law Society of Ireland*, [1995] 3 IR 14. [120] *Eogan v University College Dublin*, [1996] 2 ILRM 302.
[121] *Wiley*, [1989] IR 350. [122] *Hamble Fisheries*, [1995] 2 All ER 714.
[123] [1992] 1 QB 353. [124] *Coughlan*, [2000] 2 WLR 622, at para. 65.

> [A] bare rationality test would constitute the public authority judge in its own cause, for a decision to prioritise a policy change over legitimate expectations will almost always be rational from where the authority stands, even if objectively it is arbitrary or unfair.[125]

Woolf MR effectively imposed a standard of non-arbitrariness in this area, echoing Elliott's equation of the 'rule of law' with 'the exercise of public power in a manner which is fair and rational'.[126] Administrative decision-making, which the courts accepted as valid in its own right, can be challenged if it fails to take appropriate account of the interests of affected individuals. The status of these citizens as autonomous agents necessitates that the courts require more than a mere rationality of objectives, however. Reasons mean much more than a simple justifiability of objectives. They must be reasons which also justify the taking of a decision which will adversely impact upon the expectations of individuals. An action will be judged appropriate where it shows sufficient concern to protect affected individuals from arbitrary acts. The individual's fundamental entitlement to protection from arbitrary rule thereby provides the 'legal alchemy' necessary to render an expectation legitimate, and enforceable.[127]

Context here is all-important. Administrative bodies, the courts accept, are generally entitled to exercise their own policy choices. An individual who simply objects to such a decision will be unable to sustain a successful challenge outside the parameters of traditional *Wednesbury* review. Where, however, an individual has an expectation that the body in question will exercise its powers in a particular way, greater scrutiny of a change of policy will be required. In particular, the courts will have to assess whether, in deciding to undertake this change, the body gave due regard to the position of such expectant individuals. In this way, the doctrine of legitimate expectations 'operate[s] as an aspect of good administration, qualifying the intrinsic rationality of policy choices'[128] as an 'objective standard of public decision-making on which the courts insist'.[129]

In subsequent decisions of the courts the emphasis on detrimental reliance demonstrates the importance of the particular facts of a case quite clearly. Peter Gibson LJ observed in *Begbie* that '[i]t is very much the exception, rather than the rule, that detrimental reliance will not be present when the court finds unfairness in the defeating of a legitimate expectation'.[130] Schiemann LJ agreed in *Bibi*, but accepted the possibility that a successful claim could be mounted in the absence of such detriment.[131] This made it clear that detrimental reliance was only a

125 Ibid, at para. 66.

126 Elliott, 'Legislative Intention *versus* Judicial Creativity?', note 50 above, at 95.

127 *Hamble Fisheries*, [1995] 2 All ER 714, at 728.

128 *Coughlan*, [2000] 2 WLR 622, at para 71.

129 *Bhatt Murphy*, [2008] EWCA Civ 755, at para. 30.

130 *R. v Secretary of State for Education and Employment, ex p Begbie*, [2000] 1 WLR 1115, at 1124.

131 *R. (Bibi) v Newham London Borough Council*, [2001] EWCA Civ 607; [2002] 1 WLR 237, at paras. 29–30.

useful indicator of the possible presence of that arbitrary unfairness which will trigger the court's enforcement of a legitimate expectation. As Laws J noted in *Nadarajah*,[132] the questions in these cases centre on the balance struck between the position of the individual and the collective action of the administrative body. A simple departure from previous policy will not suffice to support a claim. Laws J, accepting that something more was needed to adjust the balance in favour of the individual, depicted detriment as a common but no means essential ingredient of a successful case. Rather than applying fixed criteria of illegality, the courts instead conduct a flexible and overall assessment of the fairness of the impugned act, interpreted in light of all the circumstances of the case.

The jurisdiction in question is focused on the contextual enforcement of administrative fairness. The impugned organ, in pursuing rational objectives, must ensure that its decisions do not impact on individuals arbitrarily. In many cases, as the authorities show, the provision of a hearing will suffice to satisfy such concerns. In certain situations, however, the entitlement of a citizen to protection from arbitrary rule may require the judicial enforcement of substantive benefits. As an overarching value, non-arbitrariness cannot be subjected to artificial ultra vires restrictions. Although it might conventionally require only the observance of particular procedural safeguards, it is clear, therefore, that the doctrine of legitimate expectations, as an expression of the system's concern for non-arbitrariness, can impose 'substantive limitations that in some settings lead to uniquely correct outcomes'.[133]

This analysis is supported by the judgments of Laws LJ in *Nadarajah*[134] and *Bhatt Murphy*.[135] Given his previous insistence on a purely procedural enforcement in *Richmond LBC*,[136] his endorsement of legitimate expectations as a generalized jurisdiction, capable of securing substantive benefits in an appropriate case, was significant. Furthermore, his exploration of the constitutional foundations of the doctrine effectively reiterates the normative importance of non-arbitrariness:

> Where a public authority has issued a promise or adopted a practice which represents how it proposes to act in a given area, the law will require the promise or practice to be honoured unless there is good reason not to do so. What is the principle behind this proposition? It is not far to seek. It is said to be grounded in fairness, and no doubt in general terms that is so. I would prefer to express it rather more broadly as a requirement of good administration, by which public bodies ought to deal straightforwardly and consistently with the public.... Accordingly a public body's promise or practice as to future conduct may only be denied ... in circumstances where to do so is the public

[132] *Nadarajah v Secretary of State for the Home Department*, [2005] EWCA Civ 1363.

[133] PP Craig, *Public Law and Democracy in the UK and the USA* (Clarendon Press, 1990), at 334, citing C Sunstein, 'Beyond the Republican Revival' (1988) 98 *Yale Law Journal* 1539, at 1550–1551. This passage was discussing the idea of deliberative rationality which, Chapter 4 showed, is closely related to the ideal of non-arbitrariness.

[134] [2005] EWCA Civ 1363.

[135] [2008] EWCA Civ 755.

[136] [1994] 1 WLR 74.

body's legal duty, or is otherwise, to use a now familiar vocabulary, *a proportionate response* (of which the court is the judge, or the last judge) *having regard to a legitimate aim pursued by the public body in the public interest.*[137]

Similar views were expressed by the learned judge in *Bhatt Murphy*. This echoes the analysis advanced in the preceding paragraphs. Like Lord Woolf MR before him (and as the theory in Chapter 4 suggested) Laws LJ regards the essential dilemma posed by the law of legitimate expectations as that of striking a 'balance between an individual's fair treatment in particular circumstances, and the vindication of other ends having a proper claim on the public interest'.[138] Similarly, he also sees the solution to this balance in a system of effective non-arbitrariness, in which the relative demands of the collective interest and the affected individual are rationally reconciled. His invocation of proportionality illustrates this quite clearly—as a later section will show, this value's contextual connection of a decision's relative aim with its impact offers considerable support for an analysis predicated on non-arbitrariness.

(e) A Dual Constituency Model in Action?

The institutional template set out in Chapter 4 seems perfectly capable of descriptively accommodating the development of a doctrine of legitimate expectations. Like the model described therein, the approach of the courts in *Coughlan* and *Nadarajah* is premised on an acceptance of the need to balance the collective conduct of government bodies with the state's defence of the individual's rights.

Furthermore, the suggested system's commitment to non-arbitrariness as an overarching institutional value seems to be reflected in the courts' contextualized approach to the enforcement of legitimate expectations. To accept non-arbitrariness as a general institutional norm is to require that the actions of state organs be capable of rational justification on the facts of each individual case. As the case law on legitimate expectations shows, however, the courts are increasingly insisting on this type of focused justification. Traditional *Wednesbury* review, appropriate to situations where no protected individual interest is at stake, is insufficiently vigorous when applied to cases of potential interest infringement. In this area the concentration of the courts on reconciling the reasons for administrative action with its adverse impact on affected individuals offers clear support for this book's suggested analysis of judicial intervention. Legitimacy is equated with more than mere rationality. Rather, administrative bodies must show that their policy objectives are not only valid, but also adequate to justify the practical implications of that action. The emphasis on individual context moves beyond objective rationality towards ideas of non-arbitrariness, imposing additional obligations on the basis of the particular

[137] *Nadarajah*, [2005] EWCA Civ 1363, at para. 68. Emphasis added. [138] Ibid, at para. 69.

situation of the individual citizen. Laws LJ expressly links the giving of reasons for action with the consequences of that conduct for the citizen, requiring the presence of a proportionate relationship between the two. Objective and outcome are intertwined, thereby emphasizing the status of non-arbitrariness as the underlying justification for judicial action.

In addition, the involvement of the courts can convincingly be construed as the deliberative supervision of administrative organs, charged with the mediation of collective and individual needs, by a body committed to the defence of abstract individual values. *Bhatt Murphy*, *Coughlan*, and *Hamble Fisheries*, like the Irish authorities, have been clear that public and administrative bodies are generally free to balance these interests as they see fit.[139] Operating at a micro-organizational level, the capacity to exercise autonomous discretionary powers has been consistently affirmed. It is only when their decisions fail to show appropriate respect for the individual's universal entitlement to non-arbitrary treatment that the courts will intervene. Like *Wednesbury* unreasonableness, it is a corrective jurisdiction, which—as the Chapter 4 model proposes—should be interpreted as but one element of the deliberatively participatory inter-institutional process of exercising state power.

(2) The Doctrine of Proportionality

This emphasis on contextual justification also appears in the case law of the courts on the proportionality doctrine. Here, again, recurs the image of the constitutional structure as animated by concerns of circumstantial non-arbitrariness and a duality of constituent social interest. Thus, it is submitted that an examination of these authorities offers further support for the suggested model which has been set out in this book.

In Irish terms, the proportionality doctrine was most authoritatively explained by Costello J in *Heaney*.[140] Relying on the Canadian case of *Chaulk v R.*,[141] he required that the *Oireachtas*'s asserted infringement of the Article 38.1 right to silence:

1) be rationally connected to the objective and not be arbitrary, unfair, or based on irrational considerations,
2) impair the right as little as possible, and
3) be such that their effects on rights are proportional to the objective.

This approach has since been widely approved, and applied by the Irish courts when considering alleged infringements of constitutional rights.[142] Furthermore,

[139] Sedley J for example, accepted that 'the balance [between expectation and policy] must in the first place be for the policy-maker to strike': *Hamble Fisheries*, [1995] 2 All ER 714, at 731.

[140] *Heaney v Ireland*, [1994] 3 IR 593, at 607. [141] [1990] 3 SCR 1303.

[142] See, for example, *Daly v The Revenue Commissioners*, [1995] 3 IR 1; *Iarnrod Eireann v Ireland*, [1996] 3 IR 321; *Re Article 26 and Part V of the Planning and Development Bill*, [2000] 2 IR 321; [2001] 1 ILRM 81.

the influence of the doctrine can also be discerned in a number of purely administrative law decisions, in which the courts have weighed the consequences of the measure in question against its impact on the individual applicant. Walsh J in *Fajujonu* allowed the Minister to deport a family only where he was:

> satisfied, for stated reasons, that the interests of the common good ... are so predominant and so overwhelming in the circumstances of the case that an action which can have the effect of breaking up this family is not so disproportionate to the aim sought to be achieved as to be unsustainable.[143]

From the point of view of English law, proportionality was first proposed as a ground for substantive review of discretionary powers by Lord Diplock in *GCHQ*. It has only been widely embraced as an independent ground of challenge since the enactment of the Human Rights Act 1998, however. The English courts now apply it in cases in which the violation of a protected Convention right is claimed. The House of Lords has therefore found, for example, that the indefinite detention of foreign terrorist suspects was unlawful as a disproportionate infringement of the right to liberty.[144] As Lord Bingham noted in that case, the standard formulation of the test in England is generally accepted as that set out by the Privy Council in *de Freitas*. In determining whether a limitation is arbitrary or excessive, the Privy Council stated that a court must ask itself:

> whether: (i) the legislative objective is sufficiently important to justify limiting a fundamental right; (ii) the measures designed to meet the legislative objective are rationally connected to it; and (iii) the means used to impair the right or freedom are no more than is necessary to accomplish the objective.[145]

The discussion by various English judges of the nature of this proportionality jurisdiction is instructive, providing considerable implicit support for this book's attempt to portray it as a species of contextual non-arbitrariness. The significance of a case's context was underlined by Lord Steyn in his leading discussion of this question in *Daly*.[146] Citing Laws J's observation in *Mahmood* that '[i]n law context is everything',[147] the judge explained the difference between *Wednesbury* and proportionality review. Sharing a common concern to ensure that the actions of public bodies are properly justified, he accepted that 'there is [obviously] an overlap between the traditional grounds of review and the approach of proportionality'.[148] Where these jurisdictions diverge, however, is,

143 *Fajujonu v Minister for Justice*, [1990] 1 ILRM 234, at 242.

144 *A v Secretary of State for the Home Department*, [2005] 2 WLR 87. This applied even though the Government had sought a derogation from Article 5 of the Convention.

145 *de Freitas v Permanent Secretary of Ministry of Agriculture, Fisheries, Lands and Housing*, [1999] 1 AC 69, at 80.

146 *R. v Secretary of State for the Home Department, ex p Daly*, [2001] UKHL 26; [2001] 3 All ER 433; [2001] 2 WLR 1622.

147 *R. (Mahmood) v Secretary of State for the Home Department*, [2001] 1 WLR 840, at 847.

148 *Daly*, [2001] UKHL 26, at para. 27.

in his view, in the relative weighting to be attributed by the court to the interests at issue in an individual case.

In a traditional *Wednesbury* case, the challenge rests on an assertion of irrationality in the actions of the authority in question. The applicant, therefore, is typically unable to point to any specific individual interest which has been infringed. He may disapprove of the body's policy, or may fear that it will adversely impact upon his personal preferences. Crucially, however, he cannot rest his claim on a potential violation of a constitutional or Convention right, nor on an expectation based on a previous policy or representation, nor—more generally—on a failure to have due regard to his particular circumstances. As this work has repeatedly emphasized, the fact that society has been constructed from two opposing interests dictates that individual misfortune is perfectly acceptable once it has not been arbitrarily secured. Classical *Wednesbury* review constitutes a very basic protection against arbitrary rule, applying to those situations in which no accusation is raised of a failure on the part of the collective to take account of an entrenched individual interest. This jurisdiction is still motivated by the system's overarching commitment to non-arbitrariness, of course. As Ryan J remarked, the essential 'rationality of decision making' still requires that 'the reason or reasons on which the decision is founded must be logically connected to the power or discretion being exercised'.[149] Without a countervailing affected entitlement, however, this abstract rationality constitutes the sole criterion for review. In such cases, the search for justification is therefore confined to a judicial examination of the legitimacy of the objective in question.

Proportionality, on the contrary, involves precisely those cases in which the applicant relies on her individual circumstances to claim that a government action is unjustified. Non-arbitrariness thereby requires a more sophisticated examination of the justification advanced in support of the impugned action. This necessarily requires the court to consider the way in which the dual social interests—the need for collective action, and the entitlement of the individual to protection from arbitrary governance—have been reconciled. As Lord Steyn commented in *Daly*, the 'doctrine of proportionality require[s] the reviewing court to assess the balance which the decision maker has struck, not merely whether it is within the range of rational or reasonable decisions'.[150] The issue is not one of bare rationality. Rather, proportionality 'require[s] attention to be directed to the relative weight accorded to [the] interests and considerations' at issue.[151]

149 *Fitzpatrick v Minister for Justice, Equality and Law Reform*, [2005] IEHC 9.
150 [2001] UKHL 26, at para. 27. 151 Ibid, at para. 27.

The court in these cases embarks on a flexible and contextualized assessment of whether a measure was justified in the circumstances of the case. 'The depth of judicial review and the deference due to administrative discretion vary with the subject matter.'[152] Where an individual is able to point to the infringement of some protected value, the courts will adopt an analytical approach in which, compared to the *Wednesbury* test, 'the intensity of review is somewhat greater'.[153] The doctrine of proportionality—like the earlier case law on the existence of a varying standard of review,[154] or decisions on the doctrine of legitimate expectations—effectively seeks to mediate between the competing claims of the collective will and individual interest. As Dyson LJ observed, '[i]t is important to emphasize that the striking of a fair balance lies at the heart of proportionality', a balance he defined as 'comparing the weight to be given to the wider interests of the community with the weight to be given to an individual's . . . rights'.[155] The 'critical question' for a court faced with a proportionality claim is typically whether there has been 'a fair balance between the rights of the individual and the interests of the community'.[156]

The English courts' discussions of these substantive grounds of review illustrate the growing influence, in practice, of a conception of judicial review as a form of independent assessment of the balance struck between the interests of the citizen and those of the state. The judiciary's increasing concentration on examining any asserted disparity between the impact of an administrative measure and its stated public objective demonstrates this quite clearly. Tellingly, however, the Court of Appeal has described even the more restrained types of rationality review in similarly interest-balancing terms:

> [W]here policy is the subject matter in hand, principle and practicality alike militate in favour of an approach in which the court's role is closer to review than appeal: where a degree of deference does no more than respect the balance to be struck between the claims of democratic power and the claims of individual rights.[157]

It is submitted, therefore, that the emergence in both Ireland and England of a proportionality doctrine indicates the intuitive veracity of this book's model of constituency-based institutional arrangement. The courts have portrayed ideas of proportionality, reasonableness, and legitimate expectations as an attempt to structurally reconcile the competing interests of the public, on one hand, and the individual on the other. The strength of applicants' challenges in all these areas

[152] Ibid, at para. 32, *per* Lord Cooke. [153] Ibid, at para. 27.

[154] See, for example, *Bugdaycay v Secretary of State for the Home Department*, [1987] AC 514; *R. v Minister of Defence, ex p Smith*, [1996] QB 517; *R. v Lord Saville, ex p A*, [2000] 1 WLR 1855.

[155] *R. (Samaroo) v Secretary of State for the Home Department*, [2001] EWCA Civ 1139, at paras. 26–28.

[156] *AS (Pakistan) v Secretary of State for the Home Department*, [2008] EWCA Civ 1118, at para. 24.

[157] *Huang v Secretary of State for the Home Department*, [2005] EWCA Civ 105; [2006] QB 1, at para. 53.

rests on the extent to which they can show an infringement of a protected interest. The intensity with which a measure is reviewed is directly related to the extent of its impact on individuals. The more important the interest in question, the more intensively will the court examine the suitability of the government's suggested justification for their act. This direct correlation underlines the balance which exists at the centre of all types of state action. On this analysis, judicial scrutiny fills its suggested role as one of the institutional order's key self-operating safeguards by reviewing the balance to ensure its non-arbitrariness.

Furthermore, the character of the proportionality jurisdiction also supports the inter-institutional model of participatory decision-making outlined in this book. Recognizing the justifiable entitlement of government and administrative agencies to impinge upon the interests of the individual, the proportionality doctrine casts the courts in the residual supervisory role of reviewing the balance struck by these bodies. The House of Lords in *Huang* emphasized the fact that, although proportionality principles require the courts to subject the actions of other institutions to 'a more exacting standard of review', 'it remains the case that the judge is not the primary decision-maker'. This echoes the deference to the decisional primacy of public bodies which has also been evident in the case law on legitimate expectations, and which was argued above to support the analysis put forward in earlier chapters. Courts, government, and agencies engage in a constitutional conversation in which all contribute to a non-arbitrary outcome which suitably respects the interests at stake.

This understanding of the doctrine has been echoed by Rivers's description of proportionality as 'a rational device for the optimisation of interests'.[158] His very detailed account of the way in which the European conception of proportionality operates fits neatly within the more general model set out in this book. 'A structured approach to balancing fundamental rights with other rights and interests in the best possible way', Rivers argues in favour of a proportionality test which variously involves:

> [a] very crude balancing exercise between the rights and public interests at the highest level of generality, ... [considering whether there is] a chain of justification from the decision back to the ... general public interest identified, ... [and] assess[ing] whether the degree of attainment of the legitimate aim balances the limitation of interests necessarily caused by the act in question.[159]

This tallies closely with the model of institutional interaction described in Chapter 5. At the first stage, Parliament and the courts collude in balancing the abstract interests of the collective against those of the individual. The focus of review then falls on the particular attempts of the state to implement this arrangement. Such specific measures must be connected to the objective in

[158] J Rivers, 'Proportionality and Variable Intensity of Review' (2006) 65 CLJ 174, at 207.
[159] Ibid, at 196–200.

question, and so justified in their effects. Significantly, however, the courts exercise restraint in their review of such administrative measures, accepting the discretionary nature of their acts. 'This discretion is important because it recognizes the contribution legislative and executive bodies make to the specification of the public interest.'[160] Government action appears here as a cooperative endeavour into which these diverse institutions, with their distinct competences and constituencies, all have an input.

This emphasis on the respective roles of each body perhaps explains the reluctance of some courts, most notably the Supreme Court in *Murphy v IRTC*,[161] to enforce the 'minimum infringement' limb of the proportionality test rigorously. In this case, Murphy was challenging a blanket ban on religious advertising on radio. Counsel for the applicant argued that the admittedly legitimate aim of avoiding religious tension could have been addressed by the creation of a panel to review (and, if necessary, exclude) proposed advertisements on such grounds. The Court accepted that this was the case but nonetheless upheld the *Oireachtas*'s designated arrangement, declaring that:

> once the Statute is broadly within the area of the competence of the *Oireachtas* and the *Oireachtas* has respected the principle of proportionality, it is not for this Court to interfere simply because it might have made a different decision.[162]

This arguably reflects the fact that:

> [t]he doctrine of proportionality needs structuring in such a way that, although applied by the judiciary, it is sensitive to the proper contribution of the other branches of government.[163]

Aiming to ensure the contextual justifiability of state acts, the judicial role under a proportionality approach 'risks treating the courts as the constitutional guarantors of the rationality of the entire state process' unless appropriate institutional restraint is shown.[164] Rivers has emphasized the importance for the proportionality doctrine of an overarching model of institutional separation in which the role of each body is acknowledged and defined. The courts are but a single (albeit vital) element in the participatory decision-making processes of the state.

The *IRTC* treatment of the 'minimum infringement' test arguably supports this point. Given the suggested position of the courts as the guardians, but not the supreme arbiters, of the proportionality of state acts, it may be more convincingly construed as a necessity-type threshold, in which some deference is shown to the instant decision-maker's entitlement to select what he regards as the most effective, and thus necessary, way of achieving the objective at issue.

Arguably, therefore, the courts are already playing the part outlined for them in Chapter 4—of ensuring that, in the context of the enduring social balance

160 Ibid, at 197.
161 [1999] 1 IR 12.
162 Ibid, at 27.
163 Rivers, note 158 above, at 176.
164 Ibid, at 181.

between citizen and state, the individual is not exposed to arbitrary exercises of power in which his or her *relevant* interests are not taken into account.[165]

(3) The Duty to Give Reasons

The suggested emergence of a justification-oriented conception of judicial review would necessarily focus the attention of the courts on the reasons put forward by a body to explain its actions. Arguably, therefore, it is no coincidence that the issue of the existence, or otherwise, of an obligation to offer reasons has featured prominently in the recent case law of both the English and Irish courts. Furthermore, the way in which the judges have depicted the provision of reasons as a prerequisite for the review process again reinforces the claim that judicial review effectively involves a non-arbitrariness-inspired search for contextual justification.

It should be noted that the courts continue to insist on the absence of a general duty to give reasons. Sedley J was clear in *Institute of Dental Surgery* that the administrative inconvenience which would be caused by the development of a universal obligation demanded that some limitations be placed on its scope.[166] Nonetheless, as Lord Clyde observed in *Stefan*:

> The trend of the law has been towards an increased recognition of the duty upon decision-makers of many kinds to give reasons. This trend is consistent with current developments towards an increased openness in matters of government and administration. But the trend is proceeding on a case-by-case basis ... and has not lost sight of the established position of the common law that there is no general duty, universally imposed on all decision-makers ... [but] [t]here is certainly a strong argument for the view that what were once seen as exceptions to a rule may now be becoming examples of the norm, and the cases where reasons are not required may be taking on the appearance of exceptions.[167]

It is clear, therefore, that 'the trend of the law has been towards an increasing recognition of a duty upon decision-makers of many kinds to give reasons'.[168]

This inclination has been attributed in England to a desire on the part of the courts to strengthen and improve the decision-making process, and also to increase the protection available to affected individuals. This latter objective, which echoes the analysis of the court's jurisdiction set out in the previous section, has been at the heart of decisions to extend the duty to give reasons to cases where there are, for example, unexplained errors,[169] a departure from

[165] Obviously, the issue of which interests are relevant is an important one. Space precludes an extensive discussion of this question here. As Chapter 4 indicated, however, non-arbitrariness is the key criterion of such relevance. In cases where no entrenched right is in question, an individual would have to demonstrate a failure on the part of the administrative body to have due regard to his or her situation to demand any more than general rationality review.

[166] *R. v Higher Education Funding Council, ex p Institute of Dental Surgery* [1994] 1 All ER 651.

[167] *Stefan v General Medical Council*, [1999] 1 WLR 1293, at 1300.

[168] *Mecca Bingo v Glasgow Licensing Board*, [2005] LLR 454, at para. 14, *per* Lord Clarke.

[169] *R. v Civil Service Appeal Board ex p Cunningham*, [1991] 4 All ER 310.

previous policy,[170] or a result giving rise to an inference that incorrect reasons have been applied.[171]

It has also been a recurring element of the Irish case law on this issue. The courts here have repeatedly discussed the duty to give reasons as the product of the required availability of review. Barron J in the Irish decision of *Daly* described the court's competence in precisely these terms:

> The court must ensure that the material upon which the Minister acted is capable of supporting his decision. Since the Minister has failed to disclose the material upon which he acted or the reasons for his action there is no matter from which the court can determine whether or not such material was capable of supporting his decision.[172]

Blayney J in *International Fishing Ltd* agreed that 'in refusing to give his reasons for his decision the Minister places a serious obstacle in the way of the exercise of that right [to obtain review]'.[173]

Costello P's decision in *McCormack* has generally been construed as a more restrictive analysis of the question of the existence, or otherwise, of an obligation to offer reasons for an administrative decision.[174] Stressing that '[i]t is not the law of this country that procedural fairness requires that in every case an administrative decision-making authority must give reasons for its decisions',[175] the President of the High Court held that the failure of the relevant body to account for its decision not to discipline an officer against whom the applicant had lodged a complaint was not unlawful or unfair. In his judgment, he repeatedly sought to underline the contextual nature of such claims. Previous precedents were therefore, in his view, of little assistance.

Costello P described the court's intervention in this area in firmly individualistic terms. In general, he concluded, cases concerning:

> [this] issue can largely be determined by considering whether some detriment is suffered by the applicant by the failure of the [body] to give reasons for the opinion which it reached because if no detriment is suffered then no unfairness can be said to exist.

This insistence on the existence of individual detriment could, on the one hand, be argued to evince a lack of concern for the rationality or non-arbitrariness of government actions. This would, of course, incline against an acceptance of the analysis set out in this piece.

It must, however, be remembered that non-arbitrariness is proposed as an underlying institutional principle in this piece precisely because of its ability to mediate between the opposing interests of the individual and the collective, thereby ensuring an institutional (and, by extension, constituent) balance.

170 *Fisher v National Greyhound Racing Club Ltd*, Court of Appeal, unreported, 31 July, 1985.
171 *R. v Secretary of State for Trade and Industry ex p Lonrho plc*, [1989] 1 WLR 525.
172 *State (Daly) v Minister for Agriculture*, [1987] IR 165, at 172.
173 *International Fishing Ltd v Minister for the Marine*, [1989] IR 149, at 155.
174 *McCormack v Garda Síochána Complaints Board*, [1997] 2 IR 489.
175 Ibid, at 500.

Costello P's conclusion was in large part inspired by his belief that 'a person aggrieved by a decision has no right to obtain reasons for it merely for the purpose of seeing whether or not the decision-maker had erred'.[176] By opposing the sort of fishing expeditions which would constitute the courts as a default avenue of effective appeal, his judgment can thus be regarded as an acceptance on his part that such balance is essential. As the discussion of proportionality above emphasized, the model set out in this book requires some restraint on the part of the courts when participating in its inter-institutional decision-making process. The system's insistence on contextual justifiability certainly attaches considerable importance to the giving of reasons in many cases. Costello P himself acknowledged as much, noting that in this instance the absence of reasons did not preclude the applicant from seeking a remedy via judicial review. It does not require the detailed rationalization of even the most ordinary administrative actions, however.

Furthermore, it should be borne in mind that non-arbitrariness, as a value, is really only determinate in the specific context of an individual case. Thus, the failure to provide reasons for a decision which seems objectively justifiable (which Costello P clearly felt was the situation in *McCormack*) does not indicate the presence of unacceptable arbitrariness. It is only when the facts of a particular situation suggest the existence of some species of administrative unfairness that the courts will intervene to review the act in question. In the context of that contextual assessment of the justifiability of the impugned act, the giving of reasons will almost invariably be required. *McCormack*'s emphasis on the necessity of individual detriment accords with this analysis. It should be noted that, as with the doctrine of legitimate expectations, detriment should be treated as a probable, but not obligatory, indicator of the need for judicial review. With this in mind, *McCormack*, it is submitted, should be treated as a fact-based affirmation of the individualistic nature of the court's jurisdiction in this area. Concerned that administrative procedures take due account of individual citizens, the courts must nonetheless ensure that they do not second-guess even apparently acceptable decisions. Charged with the defence of individual interests, some suggestion of arbitrariness should be required before the judges intervene.

This analysis is further supported by those Irish cases in which a duty to give reasons has been denied. The courts have tended to explain such denials in terms of the interests of the affected individual, generally justifying their decisions by reference to the absence of any possibility of review. This reiterates the concern for individual non-arbitrariness rather than absolute administrative accuracy. O'Flaherty J, noting the general immunity of decisions of the DPP from challenge, refused, for example, to require the Director to explain why a particular prosecution had not been brought:

[176] Ibid, at 502.

[A]s the duty to give reasons stems from the need to facilitate full judicial review, the limited intervention available in the context of the DPP's decisions obviates the necessity to disclose reasons.[177]

However, as Keane CJ subsequently noted in *Eviston*,[178] this did not forever exempt the DPP from an obligation to offer reasons for his acts. Examining the earlier case law, he remarked that:

[t]he decisions ... go no further than saying that the Court will not interfere with the decision of the respondent ... where: (a) no prima facie case of *mala fides* has been made out against the respondent; (b) there is no evidence from which it could be inferred that he has abdicated his functions or been improperly motivated and (c) the facts of the case do not exclude the reasonable possibility of a proper and valid decision of the respondent ... [179]

The Supreme Court therefore seemed implicitly to accept the possibility that a duty to give reasons could arise where there was some evidence of administrative impropriety on the part of the DPP. That an office so historically removed from scrutiny can hypothetically be obliged to explain its actions, albeit only in 'very limited circumstances',[180] illustrates the extent to which the courts seem increasingly to regard the provision of reasons as an essential element of their review powers.

This underscores the way in which reasons have become inextricably linked with the mechanics of the review calculus. Reasons are an essential prerequisite to any assessment of a measure's contextual justifiability. Without some statement of reasons, the courts are unable to ensure that the body in question has taken appropriate account of the individual's position. As the dissenting judges in *AO* observed, to allow a decision-maker to offer only a generalized reason as justification for its acts renders its decisions 'virtually immune from review'.[181] In their opinion, more recently echoed by Laffoy J in *Gritto*,[182] some contextually attuned reasons must be offered if the interests of the individual are to be adequately protected in a proper review process. In the absence of reasons, the courts are analytically impotent.

(4) Regulating the Inter-Institutional Relationship

As discussed, this overview of a number of developing areas of the law appears to demonstrate a trend towards the assertion by the courts of a free-standing jurisdiction to review government actions by reference to core substantive values. This implicitly confers a distinct and independent role upon the courts as a

177 *H v DPP*, [1994] 2 IR 589, at 603.
178 *Eviston v Director of Public Prosecutions*, [2002] 3 IR 260.
179 Ibid, at 294.
180 *Dunphy (A Minor) v DPP*, [2005] IESC 75.
181 *AO v Minister for Justice, Equality and Law Reform*, [2003] 1 IR 1, at 203.
182 *Gritto v Minister for Justice, Equality and Law Reform*, [2005] IEHC 75.

non-subordinate institution with primary responsibility for this process. However, the case law also appears to envisage this responsibility as one aspect of an overlapping system of inter-institutional governance. The strict model of separation of powers regulated such inter-institutional conduct by reference to of a clear (or, more accurately, ostensibly clear) and rigid demarcation of exclusive areas of competence. The case law on proportionality and legitimate expectations, on the other hand, seems to regard the making of government decisions as a matter of striking a balance between competing interests, in respect of which all institutions are entitled to have some input. The recognition of an obligation on public bodies in many situations to provide adequate reasons to justify their acts can also be seen as part of this collaborative process. However, as observed in the previous chapter, any move to a system of flexible inter-institutional scrutiny will inevitably raise issues with regard to the regulation of the relationship between the relevant branches. How can government be effectively organized if different institutions can exercise power over the same area? A strictly formal system has the advantage (at least in theory) of providing determinate criteria to resolve any such issue. The move to a more fluid or multi-participant form of institutional arrangement is likely to require the development of a similarly flexible system of regulating the inter-institutional relationship.

The decision of Court of Appeal in *R. (Al Rawi) v Secretary of State for Foreign Affairs* seems to support this analysis.[183] Having acknowledged the development of a more substantive conception of the rule of law by the courts, the Court of Appeal went on to note that one consequence of this had been that '[a] recurrent theme of our public law in recent years has been the search for a principled means of disentangling the functions of these different arms of government'. Recognizing a role for the courts in ensuring due observance of substantive values—described here as one connected with their 'special responsibility in the field of human rights'—necessarily implies that they retain an inherent entitlement to make this distinct contribution to the process of exercising public power. In turn, this logically requires the elaboration of some system for regulating how this sort of second-order scrutiny by one body of the decision-making process of another should be regulated.

The Court of Appeal in *Al Rawi*, in its efforts to identify appropriate criteria for this purpose, referred to considerations of both constitutional principle and institutional competence. 'Strategic fields of policy', like foreign affairs, were the 'special responsibility' of the elected government because of the electoral legitimacy and institutional characteristics of such bodies. Nonetheless, the Court seemed to envisage a role for the courts even in such areas. It was for the judiciary, the Court felt, to 'to see that the government strictly complies with all formal requirements, and rationally considers the matters it has to confront' even in these areas of decision primacy. The elected organs enjoyed 'an especially

[183] [2006] EWCA Civ 1279.

broad margin of discretion' in particular areas of activity, such as foreign affairs. This appeared to mean, in practice, that the courts would rarely subject decisions in these areas to intensive scrutiny.

It is notable that the Court did not refer to this discretion as absolute or unlimited. For pragmatic and constitutional reasons, these decisions were primarily entrusted to the elected organs. The Court of Appeal did not seem to deduce from that, however, that these were areas of exclusively political competence. Rather, as suggested, this decision seems to envisage scope for a limited degree of judicial scrutiny of the sort which might be consistent with the idea of respectful inter-institutional scepticism suggested in Chapter 7.

Arguably this preference for a flexible and pragmatic approach to this issue may also be detected in other recent decisions in this area. Like *Al Rawi*, many of these decisions have occurred in the context of individual challenges to decisions taken in the area of diplomatic or foreign affairs. Under the traditional understanding of the separation of powers, these are functions classically and exclusively reserved to the elected organs of government. In each of these cases, however, the courts do not seem to have disclaimed forever an entitlement to subject such foreign policy decisions to scrutiny. On the contrary, the courts' responsibility to uphold the rule of law has been expressed in sufficiently independent terms to suggest that in the appropriate circumstances a court could intervene and overturn a political organ's decision in this area. Yet, it is also instructive that the courts' conception of their own role, and of the decision primacy of the other branches, seems to indicate that it would require a truly exceptional set of circumstances for the court to feel justified in considering such a course of action. That the judges have attributed this self-restraint in part to their own institutional limitations is instructive because it supports the proposition, put forward in the previous chapter, that a new, more flexible system of separation of powers would replace the theory's traditional focus on demarcated areas of activity with an approach which accepts in principle the permissibility of institutional intervention in all areas, but which also constrains the actual extent of any such intervention by reference to the respective capabilities of the institution at issue.

There are shades of this sort of approach in *R. (Abbasi) v Secretary of State for Foreign Affairs*,[184] and in some of the speeches of the individual Law Lords in *Bancoult*.[185] In *Abbasi*, the claimant, who was detained in the Guantánamo Bay prison facility, sought to compel the Foreign Secretary to make representations on his behalf to the US government. It was argued in response, inter alia, that the executive conduct of foreign governments was not a matter which was justiciable by the courts. The Court of Appeal accepted that this was a matter which the courts would not generally consider but refused to treat this as an absolute principle. The Court cited with approval Lord Nicholls's comments in

[184] [2002] EWCA Civ 1598. [185] [2008] 4 All ER 1055.

Kuwait Airways Corporation v Iraqi Airways Co (Nos 4 and 5)[186] to the effect that, although the courts would often be unable to review actions where there were no manageable judicial standards,[187] they were not prohibited in principle from so doing where such standards were available. Given the similarities between English and American law, and, in particular, their traditional shared commitment to the importance of habeas corpus, the English courts were entitled to conclude that the denial of this remedy to the claimant left him subject to arbitrary detention in a 'legal black hole'.

It was also argued that the conduct of the Foreign Secretary was itself non-justiciable. The Court of Appeal accepted the primacy of the political organs in making decisions on matters of foreign affairs. However, it appeared to suggest that this meant, not that the courts were excluded from examining this area at all, but rather that they were obliged to show considerable deference and restraint in so doing. The question of whether to make representations or not was left 'entirely to the discretion of the Secretary of State' who was 'free to give full weight to foreign policy considerations'.[188] The Court emphasized, however, that this 'does not mean the whole process is immune from judicial scrutiny'. In fact, the Court went on to specify that, in an 'extreme' hypothetical situation, such as the scenario in which the Foreign Office refused to even consider acting on behalf of an individual whose rights were being infringed, the courts could intervene and issue a mandatory order obliging consideration to be given to the individual's case. In short:

> The expectations [which an individual can legitimately have] are limited and the discretion is a very wide one but there is no reason why its decision or inaction should not be reviewable if it can be shown that the same were irrational or contrary to legitimate expectation; but the court cannot enter the forbidden areas, including decisions affecting foreign policy.[189]

This latter reference to 'forbidden areas', following on from an earlier observation that foreign policy considerations 'are not justiciable' indicates that there are, of course, limits to the courts' ability to intervene. It is not clear precisely what the Court of Appeal meant by this, however. Although the notion of 'forbidden areas' would seem to suggest a particular subject matter or zone of activity from which the courts are entirely excluded, this would seem to be at odds with the Court's willingness to accept the possibility in principle, however remote, of the courts issuing mandatory orders directing the taking of particular steps with respect to foreign policy. It is certainly arguable that the Court may have intended to indicate that the courts are not entitled to substitute their judgment for that of the political organs in respect of matters on which they are

[186] [2002] 2 WLR 1353, at 1362.

[187] The case there concerned the courts' ability to consider the content of a foreign law when considering whether to recognize it or not.

[188] *Abbasi*, [2002] EWCA Civ 1598 at para. 99.

[189] Ibid, at para. 106.

ill equipped to adjudicate. The limitations of the judicial process, as considered in previous chapters, mean that it is particularly unsuited to the consideration of complex matters which require a wide range of factors and a large amount of information to be taken into account. Foreign affairs are a prime example of this sort of issue. It may be the case, therefore, that the reference to foreign affairs indicated a view that the courts should proceed from an acceptance of the political organs' foreign policy views as prima facie accurate—but not that the courts should be debarred from examining issues relating to foreign affairs where they are able and obliged to do so.

Some support for this interpretation of *Abbasi* can be found in *Bancoult.* There, the majority again adverted to the decisional primacy of political organs in matters of foreign and economic affairs. Lord Hoffman accepted that '[p]olicy as to the expenditure of public resources and the security and diplomatic interests of the Crown are peculiarly within the competence of the executive'.[190] However, he went on to rely on this statement in support of his assessment that the decision impugned in this instance could not be said to be unreasonable. He did not hold that reviewing a decision in these areas on reasonableness grounds was impermissible in itself. The fact that these issues are primarily entrusted to the political organs affected the level of scrutiny applied, rather than the fact of its application in the first place.

Furthermore, the primacy of the political organs was connected by some of the Law Lords not only with constitutional principles but also with the particular capabilities of each institution. Lord Carswell, for example, felt that '[d]ecisions about how far to accommodate [diplomatic] concerns and wishes are very much a matter for ministers, who have access to a range of information not available to the courts'.[191] Lord Rodger too referred to the courts' comparative inability to weigh multiple factors accurately when he observed that

> the government had to take account of the interests of the islanders, it was nevertheless entitled to give appropriate weight to the wider, economic, foreign affairs and defence interests of the United Kingdom when it decided whether to enact the orders in council. In the absence of any relevant legal criteria, judges are not well placed to second guess the balance struck by ministers on such a matter.[192]

Several of the judges also referred to the fact that the political organs are constitutionally entitled to make such decisions because of their elected character. The separation of powers theory set out in this book has disputed the notion that popular accountability necessarily confers superior decisional authority on the elected institutions of government. It has suggested, however, that the fact that the political organs are elected makes them the most appropriate places in which to conduct debates and assessments on complex questions of collective

[190] [2008] 4 All ER 1055, at 1080. [191] Ibid, at 1103. [192] Ibid, at 1097.

interest. This is the reason why the theory entrusts primary responsibility for such collective questions to the political organs of government.

The English courts' case law on non-justiciability is still at an early stage of its development. It does seem reasonable to suggest that the courts have moved to a situation in which they are reluctant to acknowledge any areas of government activity as inherently off limits. Equally, the courts do seem commendably conscious of their own institutional weaknesses, especially with regard to areas involving complex assessments of multiple interests and information of varying levels of reliability. These positions logically suggest the need to develop a flexible and pragmatic theory of inter-institutional relationships which accepts both the legitimacy and the limitations of each institution's perspective. The approach adopted in *Abbasi* and *Bancoult* can be interpreted in a way which accords with this form of approach. In both cases, the courts acknowledged their entitlement to scrutinize matters for which the political organs were primarily responsible. However, they also emphasized the need for the courts to accept the assessments of the political organs on matters for which they are particularly suited. This tallies quite closely with the brief discussion of non-justiciability set out in the previous chapter. It thus illustrates again the extent to which the new separation of powers theory is capable of accounting for, and fitting with, the courts' approach to these less traditional jurisdictions that have recently been developed.

E. Conclusion

Like the approach of the courts to legitimate expectations and proportionality, the case law on the duty to give reasons is argued to proffer persuasive support for the organizational model prescribed in this book. As this chapter has repeatedly emphasized, the adoption by the courts of a contextual and reason-oriented balancing approach, in exercising their powers of judicial review, matches characterization of our institutional order in Chapters 4 and 5 as a mixed system in which an overarching commitment to non-arbitrariness is employed as a way of reconciling the constituent interests of the individual and the collective. Traditionally confined to ensuring that the actions of individual bodies were intra vires their statutory orders, the courts are now increasingly subjecting individual exercises of public power to a form of scrutiny in which the objective sought to be achieved is weighed against its likely impact on the interests of individuals. As befits a system assertedly resting on non-arbitrariness, rational justification is always required. Just what passes for justification, however, falls to be determined in accordance with the contextual relevance of the interests in question. Judicial deference to the creative primacy of the collective organs will increase as the interests of the individual disappear from the process of review in a particular case.

Judicial review thus represents, in microcosm, that balancing exercise upon which, it is argued, our political and constitutional structures depend. There are, of course, many additional areas of the law which a fuller examination of the implications of this book would have to explore. The topics considered above, however, provide some indication of the extent to which emerging judicial doctrines—those which arguably stray furthest from traditional notions of *imperium* or ultra vires—can be accommodated neatly within the theory proposed in this book. In general—as the case law considered above shows—the task of contextually reconciling these opposing impulses falls to subordinate administrative bodies. Operating within the parameters set out by both collectivistic statutes and individualistic legal principles, these agencies tailor the use of public powers to the facts of particular cases, in the exercise of their discretion. Where their decisions contravene collective principles, they are liable to correction through statutory reform or ministerial *diktat*. Similarly, where a decision fails to demonstrate due regard for the interests of an individual, it is for the courts to intervene. As the survey of emerging trends in judicial review shows, however, such intervention is guided by an awareness of the importance of accommodating both constituent interests. The courts do not insist on the triumph of the individual over the collective, but confine themselves to ensuring that the actions impugned have taken due account of the constituency they represent. Recognizing the respect owed to the government in its pursuit of collective values, the courts require only an equivalent respect on its part.

Individual exercises of public power are thus presented as the product of a multi-stage process in which opposing values are abstractly stated, contextually reconciled, and, finally, secondarily scrutinized. In the way in which this analysis reflects the reality of the administrative state more accurately, and in the way in which it connects the direction and content of institutional actions with the foundational values of modern society, it is thus submitted that the theory outlined in Chapter 5 represents a more appropriate model of contemporary institutional arrangement than the pluralist or tripartite notions to which much of our constitutional discourse remains attached.

9

Conclusions: A Republican Theory of Institutional Separation?

A. The Myth of the Separation of Powers

For a discipline so firmly grounded in the everyday conduct of human affairs, the law is surprisingly susceptible to the beguiling mythologization of traditional orthodoxies. A professional attachment to precedent ensures that theories are received and reapplied with such frequency that they ultimately acquire totemic status as ideological pillars of the established order. So it has been with the separation of powers. Over two centuries of usage have secured it a position of prominence in the liberal pantheon of constitutional principles. Furthermore, its popularity certainly should not be dismissed as a matter of accidental acclaim. The tripartite theory combines conceptual simplicity with an impeccable academic pedigree. Invested with the weighty authority of Montesquieu, Madison, and Locke, the doctrine is nonetheless easy enough for the student to understand. That it has become a constitutional staple of recurring significance is attributable, at least in part, to these favourable qualities.

The theory is not without its flaws, however. Despite its paradigmatic status, the doctrine has failed to justify or explain the emergence of an interventionist administrative state, in which public power is exercised on a decentralized and largely discretionary basis. The effect of this is that the dominant institutional theory of the day is conspicuously unable to account for a significant *tranche* of government activity. For a theory which purports to organize the overall structure of government, this is plainly an unsatisfactory situation.

B. The Problems of the Separation of Powers

This book began as an attempt to address this descriptive inadequacy. As Chapter 2 demonstrated, however, the doctrine's difficulties are more than merely contextual. Closer analysis indicated that, in fact, the theory is internally incoherent. This manifests itself in a number of ways. For example, where an allocation of powers is in dispute, the doctrine can be argued to instinctively favour both institutional separation and blending. Aspirationally, the theory is similarly unfocused. Does it protect liberty or efficiency? Is it confined to the defence of the individual, or should the separation strive to promote the public interest? Further, from an operational perspective, the case law indicates that the trinity of functions upon which the doctrine is predicated in the abstract, is actually impossible to identify in practice. Uncertain in its objectives and imprecise in its application, the separation of powers doctrine seems hopelessly indeterminate.

This poses clear problems for any attempt to invoke the theory as a directive principle of institutional separation. Of itself, the doctrine is devoid of determinate details. The theory can only provide guidance on issues of power allocation if it is allied to some broader political conception of the state. This explains the doctrine's frequent appearances on opposing sides of the same argument. The theory's central vagueness means that it effectively functions as a rhetorical cover for discrete political judgements made on independent grounds. In this way, the doctrine serves only to obfuscate and distort political and constitutional discourse.

Taking these criticisms into account, why then is the theory so enduringly popular? In part, this is undoubtedly due to a combination of its simplicity and malleability. It is also likely that its invocation reflects, to some degree, a certain nostalgia for the glory days of eighteenth-century constitutionalism. Reliance on the tripartite model seems, in part, a romanticized reification of Enlightenment ideals, connecting our systems of government and our courts to the celebrated insights of that era's intellectual heavyweights.

In this context, Brown's critical overview of US case law is particularly instructive.[1] She demonstrates quite clearly that the American courts, like their Irish counterparts, have tended to employ the doctrine mechanically without any consideration of the libertarian values which originally inspired its elaboration. Detached from the fundamental principles which underpinned its adoption, for some judges the model has itself become 'a high constitutional value'.[2] This focus on the interests of state institutions creates the possibility, however, that in fact the doctrine might be used, in certain situations, to frustrate the liberal individualist values which originally animated it.

An institutional theory does not develop in a vacuum. It is intended to operate in a particular social and political environment. Its design is context- and society-specific. Where the political or constitutional context changes, so, therefore, should the specifics of the theory. To hold fast to the details of an outdated model risks allowing it to become a perversion of its original ideals. So it has proved with the separation of powers.

[1] R Brown, 'Separated Powers and Ordered Liberty' (1990) 139 *University of Pennsylvania Law Review* 1513.

[2] *TD v Minister for Education*, [2001] 4 IR 259, at 362 *per* Hardiman J.

C. The Theory and the Administrative State

What are the implications of this analysis for the institutional architecture of the administrative state? That the preferred model of institutional arrangement effectively ignores the presence in the system of extensive bureaucratic powers is unacceptable. From the point of view of the average individual, administrative agencies wield enormous influence.

> [W]hile the press reports endlessly on the machinations of national ... politicians, citizens mostly encounter administrators.... These are the 'devoted public servants' who lead us through the labyrinthian requirements of modern law, or the 'pointy-headed bureaucrats' who make our lives miserable.[3]

Administrative law constitutes the practical everyday expression of constitutional principle. It is probably no exaggeration to claim that the bureaucrats, administrators, and third-party agencies who are variously involved in the governance process have greater influence on the way in which law is interpreted, applied, and experienced by citizens than either the political organs or the courts. It is logical, therefore, that the actions of these bodies must be incorporated into any developed model of institutional interaction. As Chapters 2 and 3 demonstrated, this is an objective which the traditional tripartite conception of the separation of powers seems simply incapable of achieving.

The experience of the separation of powers also underlines the importance of an institutional theory's background conception of the state. The doctrine only becomes determinate (and thus employable) when interpreted from the perspective of a particular political theory. This obviously introduces an element of value-animated arbitrariness into what is an ostensibly apolitical model. More significantly, however, it leads to a situation in which the continuing utility of the separation of powers doctrine depends upon the extent to which its background theory remains apposite. Locke, it will be remembered, envisaged government in very restricted terms:

> And so whoever has the legislative or supreme power of any commonwealth is bound to govern by established standing laws, promulgated and known to the people; [and] by indifferent and upright judges, who are to decide controversies by those laws.[4]

Such a limited, statute-oriented conception of the state is anachronistic in an age of dispersed and discretionary governance. It is unsurprising, therefore, that the tripartite theory—extrapolated as it was from this idea of state action—has proved similarly unable to adapt to contemporary times.

[3] JL Mashaw, *Greed, Chaos & Governance* (Yale University Press, 1997), at 106–107.

[4] John Locke, *Two Treatises of Government* and *a Letter Concerning Toleration* (I Shapiro, ed., Yale University Press, 2003), at 156.

D. A New Theory for an Administrative State

From the point of view of this book, there were two lessons to be learned from this. The first is that an institutional model is necessarily subordinate to a broader theory of the state. Any attempt to establish or develop a new institutional theory must therefore also consider the background values upon which it will be based. Furthermore, as Chapter 1 suggested, these foundational norms must have relevance and resonance for the particular social and political system within which they are intended to operate.

The second proposition to emerge from the early analysis of the limitations of the separation of powers is that it is imperative that an institutional theory reflect the reality of contemporary governance. A model must be both practically and normatively coherent if it is to operate effectively.

The challenge for this book thus became one of developing a theory of institutional separation for the twenty-first-century state. In comparison with Locke's seventeenth-century and Montesquieu's eighteenth-century ideas, much has changed. The character, function, organization, and powers of the state have all been radically altered. As Chapter 3 indicated, the state is now *dirigiste*, discretionary, and broadly dispersed. A host of different organizations and actors participate in the business of government, broadly conceived. These are the operational characteristics which any aspiring model of institutional arrangement must take into account.

Normatively, however, much has remained the same. The contractarian understanding of the state which informed the theories of the seventeenth and eighteenth centuries retains a certain contemporary value. The political and constitutional controversies which tend to arise still involve, at their simplest, attempts to balance the interests of the collective against those of the individual. The state still strives to serve the good of all through the coordination of each. Even at a time of increasing majoritarianism, the constitutional case law of the courts exhibits an ongoing concern for the interests of the individual.

> It was ... to prevent such arbitrary action that the Framers adopted the doctrine of separation of powers.[5]

Chapter 4 has argued—and Chapter 3 has shown—that this desire is still relevant today. Non-arbitrariness was thus proposed as the foundational value upon which this work should be premised. As an institutional principle, it accepts the possibility of individual-adverse outcomes in the exercise of public powers but requires that they be capable of a rational justification which takes due account all of the circumstances of the individual's situation.

As the model's commitment to non-arbitrariness shows, there is much in the model proposed in this book which is consistent with previous theories of state

[5] *INS v Chadha*, 462 US 919 (1983), at 963.

and institutional action. In fact, in many ways, the model suggested here represents no more than a repackaging of the separation of powers theory for contemporary times. Montesquieu's tripartite theory was very much a product of its day. In that era, power tended to be understood as being primarily exercised in one way. The eighteenth century theorist was accustomed to, and thus predicated his analysis upon, a single process of power application—the exercise, by a limited central sovereign, of its authority by way of generalized rules. The Montesquian model of governmental functions makes sense in the context of such a singular and straightforward model. The identification of the necessarily distinct stages of creation, interpretation, and implementation is a relatively simple affair where purely statutory processes are involved.

Whatever its merits in the past, this idealized model of rule-based governance is grossly unsuitable for the administrative state. Government today acts in a bewildering variety of very different ways. Public power is conferred not only on the state bureaucracy but also on a range of independent specialist and regulatory agencies which exist outside direct political control. The state also entrusts particular tasks to quasi-private bodies, even as it assumes to itself the ability to act in ever-broader areas of social conduct. Created with a particular purpose in mind, these ad hoc bodies defy simple analysis, or clear-cut categorization. In many jurisdictions, third-party bodies are heavily involved in the organization and delivery of particular government projects. The basic tripartite theory is evidently unable to explain these developments. Power is diffused across a range of institutions, appearing in vastly varying forms in each. It is impossible for the analyst to reduce this broadly dispersed system to a three-way institutional model. The assorted administrative bodies of today's state are just too diverse to be convincingly corralled within Montesquieu's original trinity of functions.

There is a need, therefore, for a different sort of separation. In this regard, this book has argued in favour of a constituency model, in which the institutions of the state are identified with specific social interests. From the perspective of traditional theory, this constitutes a significant shift in analytical emphasis. In an age of egalitarian democracy, it is generally expected that public bodies ought to be animated by objective notions of public interest instead of sectional concern. As an area of the law, institutional separation has accordingly concentrated in recent centuries on questions of power, competence, and function. As the previous paragraph has noted, however, the likelihood is that the current system of public governance is so complicated that it cannot be considered solely in such terms. Power is no longer exercised by statute alone. Without this single central case of institutional action, it is difficult, if not impossible, to defend a function-oriented approach to issues of power exercise or allocation. Any system which is based upon a particular idea of institutional power, function, or competence will fail to account for a significant area of governmental activity. In the face of such unmanageable complexity, the theorist can only turn to more general ideas. Hence the move in this thesis from operational details to abstract aims.

Although the institutions in question are intended to continue to pursue whatever course of action they perceive to be in the public interest, the model assumes that they will emphasize different perspectives in so doing. Chapter 6 discussed how these institutions, in their current forms, are likely to reflect particular values. The courts are equipped to conduct the sort of rigorous assessment of a balancing of interests which is likely to reduce the possibilities for arbitrary interference with individuals' interests. The political organs demonstrate a degree of centralization, visibility, and responsiveness to public preferences which makes them more likely to emphasize the interests of the collective. The administration, meanwhile, being closer to the actual exercise of power, should have access to local information, experience, and expertise which enable it to prepare better informed assessments of how best to give effect to the measures proposed by other institutions. The model suggests, therefore, that the actions of an institution in a particular situation can be explained by reference to the values it consistently represents across all contexts. There is no need to consider which one of its multitude of tasks is actually at issue. In its comparative simplicity, this model attempts to address the indeterminacy and uncertainty associated with the existing system of separation of powers, while providing sufficient detail to allow the elaboration of some sort of determinate scheme of inter-institutional checking.

E. Republicanism and Mixed Government

There are echoes of classical republican theory in the way in which the model proposed in this book allocates power between different institutions. The details of this power distribution are based on an assessment that the participation of these bodies in the decision-making process will ensure the adequate representation of all relevant interests in government. The institutions are each identified with one of what are claimed to be the key constituent perspectives within an organized polity. The central premise of this approach is that dispersing influence and authority amongst different views will produce outcomes which better reflect the interests of all than would be the case if decisions were taken by a single institution alone.

This has been a theme of classic republican theory throughout the ages. Aristotle, for example, was amongst the first to develop a republican design which sought to achieve the universal by pooling the particular.[6] The perfect polity, in his view, was one in which all individuals could achieve their own

[6] Aristotle, *The Politics*.

ends. Of course, the vastly varying nature of these individual ends precluded the adoption of any single prescription for civic action.[7]

> The formal dilemma of the ... republic [was] that it was an attempt to realize *[sic]* a universality of values within a particular ... political structure.[8]

The satisfaction of all depended upon the recognition of the differences of each, and on each person's entitlement to a different end. Aristotle accordingly devised a model of mixed government in which the different categories of citizen would all be represented. He distinguished these categories—the one, the few, and the many—on the basis of the qualities of the citizen in each. The active interdependence of these constituent elements, if properly balanced, would adopt a suitably universal approach which would produce a perfect republic.

This mixed constituency approach was one to which republican theorists would return again and again. Machiavelli cited Rome as an example of republican perfection which, critically, had emerged as the cumulative result of a series of imperfect, particularist acts. Previous theorists had looked for their models of perfect republics to systems of government, such as those in Sparta or Venice, which had been established on the basis of the single act of a divinely ordained ruler. Machiavelli indicated to medieval minds that the perfect republic could be created, not only by the acts of an inspirational leader, but also by the more attainable means of properly organizing the ordinary conduct of political affairs. This encouraged scholars to treat political stability as a science to be studied rather than as the benevolent and fortuitous result of an example of God's grace in action. Once again, republican theorists began to argue in favour of a system of mixed constituencies in government. The Venetian system was especially influential in this repopularization of mixed models of government. A city whose centuries-old stability had led to its characterization as *la Serenissima*, its division of duties between Doge, Senate, and Consiglio Maggiore was interpreted by many as the medieval incarnation of Aristotle's harmonious interaction of one, the few, and the many.

> The image of Venice was ... the vehicle through which [republican writers] conveyed once more the categories of Aristotelian politics. Yet Venice became a myth, a paradigm exercising compulsive force on the imagination; and ... the force of the symbol surely lay in its perfection: in the vision it conveyed of a polity in which all particulars were harmonized and whose stability was consequently immortal.[9]

This led to the development of a 'Venetian' constitution in Florence, and to an ongoing political discourse in which disagreements were primarily focused, not

[7] He did make an exception to this in the case of the philosopher-king, whose intelligence would be as far above men, as man's was above beasts. Until such a man emerged, however, the republic would have to be ruled by those laws created by the participation of the different groups, with their different qualities, in government.

[8] JGA Pocock, *The Machiavellian Moment: Florentine Political Thought and the Atlantic Republican Tradition* (2nd ed., Princeton University Press, 2003), at 84.

[9] Ibid, at 102.

on the appropriateness of a system of mixed institutional governance in itself, but rather on the correct balance of classes within such a system.[10]

In his 1642 statement, *His Majesty's Answer to the Nineteen Propositions of Both Houses of Parliament,* Charles I's implicit acceptance of an image of England as a state in which the King, the Lords, and the Commons shared power encouraged a similar focus on mixed-constituency government amongst English republicans. For many in revolutionary England, the state was now conceived of as a republic of constituent classes rather than as a unitary reflection of monarchic authority. For some, however, the notion of residual constituent classes was a means of preserving the authority of an entrenched elite: the 'one' and the 'few' to whom, in the name of the 'many', power was to be exercised. This raised an issue which was to dog more modern conceptions of republican theory—how to develop a mixed system of constituent classes in an egalitarian or democratic polity which, by definition, regarded the notion of elite classes with suspicion. Harrington's *Oceana* dealt with this issue by arguing that power should be entrusted to an aristocracy based on natural talent rather than inherited privilege.[11] His work was particular influential on the development of republican theories in the new American colonies, where essentially agrarian understanding of political virtue was attractive to those who regarded England as the epitome of the corrupt and over-commercial state. The experience of the early American states, however, called into question the whole notion of the naturally differentiated class, in whom authority should vest. The absence of an existing nobility in the colonial states ought to have made the identification of these talented few an even simpler matter. The predicted elite failed to appear, however. This impugned the entire republican project. Since Aristotle, the republican system had centred on the existence in society of inherently distinguishable classes. Civic virtue itself was manifested in the act of recognizing and respecting the entitlements of a different class, thereby demonstrating confidence in the project of constructing the universal from a balance of particular classes. Republicans had always believed that a balance of particular elements would secure appropriately universal values. The American experiments, however, cast doubt on the existence of these particular elements, and therefore of the ability to strike a balance between them.

As Craig has argued, however, to view the Madisonian constitution as motivated by a fatalistic concession to the inevitably corrosive effects of self-interested action may be misguided.[12] Certainly, the apparent absence of a natural elite posed serious problems for a republican advocate. For centuries republicanism had been inextricably associated with the Aristotelian belief in a mixed

[10] See the treatment of the debates between Guicciardini, Machiavelli, and Giannotti in Pocock, ibid, and in JP McCormack, 'People and Elites in Republican Constitutions, Traditional and Modern' in M Loughlin and N Walker, eds., *The Paradox of Constitutionalism* (Oxford University Press, 2007) at 107.

[11] J Harrington, *The Commonwealth of Oceana* (1656).

[12] PP Craig, *Public Law and Democracy in the United Kingdom and the United States of America* (Clarendon Press, 1990).

government of qualitatively different classes. Relying on this fact, Wood famously went so far as to label the American acceptance of the citizen as a non-virtuous actor as 'the end of classical politics'.[13] Arguably, however, Madison's constitution actually constituted an attempt to apply republican teachings to this new scenario. Rousseau had insisted that corruption was an inherently human phenomenon. The desire of the individual to advance his interest would inevitably give rise to the growth of factionalism in a particular polity, as citizens identified, not with the common good, but with those in power who best reflected their particular interests. Madison openly admitted as much in Book 10 of the *Federalist Papers*. However, he also contended in that book that such factional politics could be contained by the development of a dispersed system of institutional authority. His model of the separation of powers was inspired, on this analysis, not by the objective of maximizing the number of discrete inputs into any exercise of power, but by his desire to construct a republican balance out of the self-interested actions of individual groups. This does not escape the difficulty, however, that 'the constitutions of modern republics almost invariably treat the people as a homogeneous unit: the people are a unitary and socio-economically anonymous collection of individual citizens, formally equal under the law'.[14] Without constituent social classes, how then can an interdependent polity be erected? Classic republicanism, after all, involved more than mere institutional separation. It required that separation be organized on the basis of a vision of government in which the constituent classes were all adequately represented.

This book's model can be portrayed as an attempt to adapt the theory of mixed constitutionalism to modern times. It advances an understanding of the state as a construct of constituent interests. This allows it to draw on the central tenets of republican thought, arguing that a universality of values can be achieved by the proper pooling of particular interests. Instead of examining contemporary social classes or divisions, the model seeks to avoid this issue by separating constituent interests from the particular contexts in which they occur. Abstracting these interests supplies the detail of the institutional separation. This identification of distinct interests does go some way towards avoiding the indeterminacy which has plagued classic republicanism since the age of the American colonies. Furthermore, the fact that they mirror the constituent foundations of the state allows the theory to put forward a reasonable claim that the separation it proposes will produce balanced outcomes which advance the objective interests of the state. In this way, it may be possible to argue that the model proposed falls within the republican tradition.

[13] GS Wood, *The Creation of the American Republic* (University of North Carolina Press, 1969), at 562.

[14] McCormick, note 10 above, at 107.

F. The Commitment to the Common Good

Other aspects of the theory can be identified with republican theory. The use of institutional separation as a means of preventing tyranny, for example, is a technique which has often been advocated by republicans. Another characteristic which the model shares with classic republicanism is a central commitment to non-arbitrariness which, as Pettitt's work has shown, reflects the republican conception of liberty as freedom from domination.[15]

In addition, the model, like republicanism, rests its legitimacy on the claim that it assists in the identification and pursuit of the common good. It implicitly assumes, therefore, that the common good exists as a distinct and tangible value. This is important as it underlines the extent to which this book does not advance a pluralist conception of institutional power. The theory's concern with the institutional representation of diverse interests in government bears a superficial resemblance to forms of politically pluralist thought. Such an interpretation of the theory would see in its particular institutional arrangement an attempt to foster interest competition through factional separation. To present the model as a primarily pluralist framework, however, is to overlook both its commitment to rational non-arbitrariness, and its insistence on the presence in society of distinct and identifiable constituent interests.

Pluralism is predicated on a refusal to accept the existence of an objective public interest. It finds its values rather in the broadly participatory articulation by discrete interest groups of their subjective desires. Pluralism privatizes the notion of public interest, identifying the interests of society with whichever values eventually prevail in its competitive institutional process. Its focus is primarily on ensuring that there is an extensive array of inputs into this process. External conceptions of the common good do not intrude. The rationality or morality of the system's institutional outputs are not of its concern. Instead, it is neutral between different claims about the good. The system's implicit assumption that the subjective preferences of individuals and groups are morally equal necessarily refutes the idea that there exists an objectively identifiable public or social interest. The theory described in Chapter 5, by contrast, proceeded from an initial commitment to the assertedly universal value of non-arbitrariness. In its dependence on an externally justified notion of objective good, it cannot therefore be convincingly classified as a pluralist theory.

This conclusion is further supported by the way in which the theory seeks to organize its allocation of institutional power in accordance with its understanding of society's constituent elements. Pluralism, on the other hand, does

[15] P Pettitt, *Republicanism: A Theory of Freedom and Government* (Oxford University Press, 1997).

not envisage society in such terms. Groups, in pluralist theory, are formed from a convenient confluence of individual desires. They may also be so defined thereby. The nature and membership of such groups can alter and evolve as the demands of individual citizens change. For the pluralist, there is no fixed conception of society, no balance of constituent interest. There is only the partial accommodation of shifting popular personal (and thus group) preferences. The model of the separation of powers in this book, by contrast, is organized by reference to what are argued to represent the key constituent elements of society. The input of these various institutional perspectives is required because of the belief that these institutions represent abstract constituent interests of which any effort to act in the public interest must take due account.

G. The Character of the State and its Constituencies

This element of the theory indicates that in some ways, also, it is similar to contractarian theories of the state. By assuming both that there are abstract constituent interests and that action in the public interest requires them to be reconciled, the model indicates that it is the purpose of the organized state to coordinate the striking of an adequate balance between these constituent interests. The particular interests identified further support this view. In proposing an institutional alignment premised on a dichotomy of individual and collective interests, the model aligns itself with the contractarian tradition. It sees the state as a collaborative construct, the utility of which is that it allows for a more effective and universalist advancement of individual and collective interests than would be possible in a disorganized pre-social state. This accords with Klosko's recent work on this issue, which concluded that citizens are subject to political obligations to the state because it provides them with the benefit of public goods which they could not provide themselves.[16] The state has a particular value and utility to individuals which legitimizes its existence and authority, and which an institutional theory should reflect. The model of separation of powers proposed in this book attempts to achieve this by arranging institutional power in a way that is intended to ensure that government decisions are taken by reference to both collective and individual interests.

It is also instructive to note that this approach draws upon the increasing contemporary tendency to consider legal and constitutional issues in such dualist terms. Sedley's model of bi-polar sovereignty is, perhaps, the most demonstrably developed example of this thinking in a British context,[17] although elements of it can also be discerned in decisions in cases like *Coughlan*[18] and *Bhatt Murphy*,[19] as discussed in Chapter 8.

[16] G Klosko, *Political Obligations* (Oxford University Press, 2005).
[17] S Sedley, 'Human Rights—a Twenty-First Century Agenda' [1995] PL 386.
[18] *R. v N&E Devon Health Authority, ex p Coughlan*, [2000] 2 WLR 622.
[19] *R. (Bhatt Murphy) v Independent Assessor*, [2008] EWCA Civ 755.

In distributing power amongst relevant institutions, however, the model in this book rejects this dualist conception of the state to argue that the administration too should be regarded as representative of a key constituent value—namely, the interest of contextualized individuals who find themselves actually subject to a proposed exercise of power. This approach has the added advantage of ensuring that the model accurately reflects the greater flexibility of the administrative branch. Despite the guiding presence of rules, policies, and bureaucratic strictures, there remains a significant discretionary element to much administrative decision-making. Traditional doctrine, however, has been inclined to ignore, excuse, or conceal the discretionary nature of administrative activity, reflecting the top-down, imperialistic understanding of the state upon which it is based. In reality, of course, the courts have accepted this as an inevitable feature of modern governance. The model proposed accordingly embraces the administrative branch, employing it as a positive means of enhancing the system's institutional protections. In contrast to the efforts of traditional doctrine to explain away the many 'incongruous' aspects of the modern state, the model grounds itself in the everyday realities of contemporary governance. It might be the case, of course, that the model is overly optimistic, seeing in its rationalization of the state a series of cross-institutional safeguards capable of ensuring the non-arbitrariness, and thus legitimacy, of government acts. At least, however, it describes a system of government which actually exists. In this, it represents a considerable advance on the theory of the separation of powers.

In its details, therefore, the model is motivated by a contractarian conception of administrative government. The traditional doctrine of the separation of powers assumed, to a certain extent, the dominance of each institution within its own specific sphere. This was a result of the fact that power was conventionally allocated on a formal or functional analysis of institutional competence. Each organ was entrusted with its tasks on the basis of its superior suitability, rather than because it represented a particular interest or value. Technical ability was the touchstone of power distribution.

This had two consequences. In the first place, if a body's competence derives from the fact that it is best equipped to undertake that task, it cannot sensibly be suggested that its use of the power should subsequently be questioned by organs which are, by definition, less well equipped to do so. This necessarily encourages unsupervised institutional conduct.

Secondly, this system of capacity-oriented allocation denied the presence in society of discrete competing constituencies. The distribution of institutional power was an objective question of technical expertise, rather than a subjective exercise in interest representation. There was no suggestion that a different allocation would produce aspirationally different outcomes. Any changes which would flow from an alternative arrangement would arise as the result of the system's use of less skilful organs, rather than from any change of emphasis on their parts. Each body was thus clearly assumed to serve the same, single, overarching public interest. It was only in their abilities, not in their aims, that differences could occur.

In contrast, the model considered in this book eschews the understanding of public interest as a monolithic notion. In its contractarian impulses, it accepts the possibility that there may (and usually will) be divergent views of any social actions. Institutions, on this amended model, are predicted to represent these disparate specific social interests. The model seeks unity from division, aiming to secure objectively beneficial outcomes for all from a rational amalgamation of the aims of each. In this, it constitutes an effective updating of the age-old republican idea, that the creation of an institutional balance on the basis of the relevant social interests will ensure the achievement of appropriately universal goods.

The system's acknowledgement of the existence of distinct constituencies of interest necessarily implies that each cannot, of itself, be absolute. No one constituency can have a monopoly on the notion of public interest. If the public good is served by the coordination of these interests, each must be guaranteed representation. Each, however, must also be denied automatic or unqualified success. Thus, the institutions which purport to represent each interest cannot be regarded as absolutely dominant within any individual area, as under the separation of powers theory. On this analysis, power is vested in a particular organ so that the interest which it represents can be assured of input into the participatory process of exercising public power. The competence of the body is based on the values which its particular abilities make it more likely to emphasize. In a positive sense, the constituency system produces cooperative institutional coordination. Negatively, it acts to inhibit unchecked unilateral action. In this, it chimes closely with the objectives of the separation of powers theory as they have traditionally been understood. Tied to an outdated institutional trinity, that doctrine, as Brown has noted, has ceased to have such effects. Inspired by similarly republican notions of objective good and public interest, but based, crucially, on the actual nature of today's institutional activity, it is submitted that the adoption of this amended model could potentially encourage a constitutional return to the values of the original theory.

H. Discretionary Power and Dialogic Institutional Interaction

In pursuit of such hopes, this thesis places its faith in the efficacy of rational inter-institutional discourse. It necessarily assumes that these distinct institutional bodies, with their particular approaches, will be able to organize their actions in a coordinated and participatory process. Taking institutional identities and professional jealousies into account, this may seem unduly optimistic. However, the multi-faceted character of today's institutional system—which undermined, in part, the contemporary utility of the theory of separation of powers—might actually rescue the constituency model from the effects of such inter-institutional rivalries.

In this administrative era of delegated, decentralized, and discretionary powers, government is an ever-evolving process. Policies are regularly updated or reversed. Decisions are adjusted to take account of new circumstances. New interpretations are applied to existing conventions. With discretionary power comes transient governance. In a system of purely statutory rules, government is fixed and inflexible. In a multi-constituent model, this would allow for the possibility of a victorious actor emerging from the inter-institutional process. This would discourage compromise, undermining the system's central reliance upon rational discourse as an institutional value. The discretionary character of the administrative state operates, however, to reduce the likelihood of the institutional process producing such fixed and unyielding outcomes. Administrative governance is, effectively, an adjustable issue of ever-ongoing concern. Without permanent rules there can be no permanent victors. Institutional actors may thus participate with confidence in what is a collaborative process of exercising power.

Of course, in reality, the system might not operate in such a civic-minded fashion. It may be more likely that the constituent organs will conduct their discourse through unilaterally amending the expressed earlier positions of other organs. The rules and principles set out by government and by the courts are likely to be adjusted in response to the way in which they are dealt with by administrative bodies. By such a system of reaction and retort should the quality of government actions improve overall. This may not be as maturely reflective a process as the pristine academic model might suggest, but—in its effectively cooperative outcomes—it is arguably apt, nonetheless. In these ever-decreasing circles of responsive interaction lies the possibility that a more appropriate and beneficial system of institutional governance could emerge.

Selected Bibliography

Ackerman, B, 'The New Separation of Powers' (2000) 113 *Harvard Law Review* 633.
Allan, TRS, *Law, Liberty and Justice* (Clarendon Press, 1993).
—— *Constitutional Justice* (Oxford University Press, 2001).
—— 'Dworkin and Dicey: The Rule of Law as Integrity' (1988) 8 OJLS 266.
Bagehot, Sir W, *The English Constitution* (Smith, P, ed., Cambridge University Press 2001).
Baldwin, R, *Rules and Government* (Oxford University Press, 1995).
Barber, N, The Academic Mythologians' (2001a) 21 OJLS 369.
—— 'Prelude to the Separation of Powers' (2001b) 60 CLJ 59.
Barendt, E, *An Introduction to Constitutional Law* (Oxford University Press, 1998).
—— 'Separation of Powers and Constitutional Government' (1995) PL 599.
Bator, P, 'Constitution as Architecture: Legislative and Administrative Courts under Article III' (1990) 65 *Indiana Law Journal* 233.
Bogdanor, V ed., *The British Constitution in the Twentieth Century* (Oxford University Press, 2003).
Bressman, L, 'Beyond Accountability: Arbitrariness and Legitimacy in the Administrative State' (2003) 78 *NYU Law Review* 461.
—— 'Procedures as Politics in Administrative Law' (2007) 107 *Columbia Law Review* 1749.
Brown R, 'Separated Powers and Ordered Liberty' (1990) 139 *University of Pennsylvania Law Review* 1513.
—— 'Accountability, Liberty and the Constitution' (1998) 98 *Columbia Law Review* 531.
Cartier, G, 'Procedural Fairness in Legislative Functions: The End of Judicial Abstinence?' (2003) 53 *University of Toronto Law Journal* 217.
—— 'Willis and the Contemporary Administrative State: Administrative Discretion as Dialogue' (2005) 55 *University of Toronto Law Journal* 629.
Chamberlain M, 'Democracy and Deference in Resource Allocation Cases' (2003) 8 *Judicial Review* 12.
Charles I, *His Majesty's Answer to the Nineteen Propositions of Both Houses of Parliament* (1642).
Chayes, A, 'The Role of the Judge in Public Law Litigation' (1976) 89 *Harvard Law Review* 1281.
Coase, R, 'The Problem of Social Cost'(1960) 3 *Journal of Law & Economics* 1.
Coleman, J and Kraus, J, 'Rethinking the Theory of Legal Rights' (1986) 95 *Yale Law Journal* 1335.
Craig, PP, *Public Law and Democracy in the United Kingdom and the United States of America* (Clarendon Press, 1990).
—— 'Legitimate Expectations: A Conceptual Analysis' (1992) 108 LQR 79.
—— 'Democracy and Rule-Making Within the EC: An Empirical and Normative Assessment' (1997) 3 *European Law Journal* 105.
—— 'Ultra Vires and the Foundations of Judicial Review' (1998) 57 CLJ 63.

—— 'Competing Models of Judicial Review' [1999] PL 428.
—— 'Public law, political theory and legal theory' (2000) PL 211.
Curtin, D, *Postnational Democracy: The European Union in Search of a Political Philosophy* (Kluwer, 1997).
Daintith, T and Page, A, *The Executive in the Constitution* (Oxford University Press, 1999).
Day O'Connor, S, 'Altered States: Federalism and Devolution at the Turn of the "Real" Millennium' (2001) 60 CLJ 493.
Dehousse, R, 'European Institutional Architecture after Amsterdam: Parliamentary system or regulatory structure?' (1998) 35 CML Rev 595.
DeSmith, S, 'The Separation of Powers in New Dress' (1966) 12 *McGill Law Journal* 491.
Dicey, AV, *Law and Public Opinion in England* (2nd ed., Macmillan, 1914).
du Gay, P ed., *The Values of Bureacracy* (Oxford University Press, 2005).
Dworkin, R., *Taking Rights Seriously* (Duckworth, 1977).
—— *A Matter of Principle* (Harvard University Press, 1985).
Edley Jr, J, 'The Governance Crisis, Legal Theory and Political Ideology' (1991) 41 *Duke Law Journal* 561.
Ellickson, RC, 'The Case for Coase and against "Coaseanism"' (1989) 99 *Yale Law Journal* 611.
Elliott, M, 'The Ultra Vires Doctrine in a Constitutional Setting: Still the Central Principles of Judicial Review' (1998) 57 CLJ 63.
—— 'Sovereignty and the New Constitutional Settlement: Legislative Freedom, Political Reality and Convention' (2002) 22 LS 340.
Ely, J H, *Democracy and Distrust* (Harvard University Press, 1980).
—— *On Constitutional Ground* (Princeton University Press, 1996).
Fanning, R, 'Reflections on the legislative process following *Leontjava*' (2004) XXXIX *Irish Jurist* 286.
Farina, C, 'Statutory Interpretation and the Balance of Power in the Administrative State' (1989) 89 *Columbia Law Review* 452
Fisher, E and Schmidt, P, 'Seeing the Blind Spots in Administrative Law: Theory, Practice and Rule-Making Settlements in the United States' (2001) 30 *Common Law World Review* 272.
Forsyth, C, ed., *Judicial Review and the Constitution* (Hart, 2000).
—— 'Of Fig Leaves and Fairy Tales: The Ultra Vires Doctrine, the Sovereignty of Parliament and Judicial Review' (1996) 55 CLJ 122.
Fried, C, 'Is Liberty Possible?' in *Liberty, Equality and the Law* (University of Utah Press, 1987).
Frug, G, 'The Ideology of Bureacracy in American Law' (1984) 97 *Harvard Law Review* 1277.
Fuller, L., 'The Forms and Limits of Adjudication' (1978) 92 *Harvard Law Review* 353.
Galligan, DJ, *Due Process and Fair Procedures* (Clarendon Press, 1996).
Goldsworthy, J, *The Sovereignty of Parliament: History and Philosophy* (Clarendon, 1999).
Greco, G, 'Standards or Safeguards: A Survey of the Delegation Doctrine in the United States' 8 *Administrative Law Journal of the American University* 567.
Griffith, JAG, 'The Political Constitution' (1979) 42 MLR 1.

—— 'The Brave New World of Sir John Laws' (2000) 63 MLR 159.

Hadfield, G, 'Bias in the Evolution of Legal Rules' (1992) 80 *Georgetown Law Journal* 583.

Hale, R L, 'Bargaining, Duress and Economic Liberty' (1943) 43 *Columbia Law Review* 603.

Harrington, J, *The Commonwealth of Oceana* (1656).

Hart, HLA, *The Concept of Law* (Clarendon, 1961).

—— *Law, Liberty and Morality* (Oxford University Press, 1963).

Lord Hoffman, 'The COMBAR Lecture 2001: Separation of Powers' (2002) 7 *Judicial Review* 137.

Hogan, G, 'Judicial Review, the Doctrine of Reasonableness and the Immigration Process' (2001) 6 *Bar Review* 329.

Hogan G and Whyte G, *Kelly: The Irish Constitution* (4th ed., Butterworths, 2003).

Hogan G and Morgan DG, *Administrative Law in Ireland* (3rd ed., Round Hall Sweet & Maxwell, 1998).

Irvine, D, 'Judges and Decision-Makers: The Theory and Practice of Wednesbury Review' (1996) PL 59.

Jennings, I, *The Law and the Constitution* (5th ed., University of London Press, 1959).

Joerges, C and Neyer, J, 'From Intergovernmental Bargaining to Deliberative Political Processes: The Constitutionalisation of Comitology' (1997) 3 *European Law Journal* 273.

Jones, G, Selections from Blackstone's Commentaries on the Laws of England (Macmillan Press, 1973).

Jowell, J, 'Beyond the rule of law: towards constitutional judicial review' (2000) PL 671.

Kagan, E, 'Presidential Administration' (2001) 114 *Harvard Law Review* 2245

Kant, I, *Groundwork of the Metaphysics of Morals* (Gregor, M, ed., Cambridge University Press, 1997).

—— *Political Writings* (2nd ed., Reiss, H, ed., Cambridge University Press, 1991).

Kennedy, D, 'Cost–Benefit Analysis of Entitlement Problems: A Critique' (1981) 33 *Stanford Law Review* 387.

Klosko, G, *Democratic Procedures and Liberal Consensus* (Oxford University Press, 2000).

—— *Political Obligations* (Oxford University Press, 2005).

Komesar, N, *Imperfect Alternatives: Choosing Institutions in Law, Economics and Public Policy* (University of Chicago Press, 1994).

Kopecky, P, 'Power to the executive! The changing executive–legislative relations in Eastern Europe' (2004)10 *Journal of Legislative Studies* 142.

Kronman, A T, 'Contract Law and Distributive Justice' (1980) 89 *Yale Law Journal* 472.

Laws, J, 'Law and Democracy' [1995] PL 72.

Lenaerts, K, 'Constitutionalism and the Many Faces of Federalism' (1990) 38 AJCL 205.

—— 'Some Reflections on the Separation of Powers in the European Community' (1991) 28 CML Rev 11.

Lord Lester of Herne Hill, 'Developing constitutional principles of public law' (2001) PL 684.

Leyland, T and Woods, T eds., Administrative Law Facing the Future: Old Constraints and New Horizons (Blackstone Press, 1997).

Lindseth, P, '"Weak" constitutionalism? Reflections on comitology and transnational governance in the European Union' (2001) 21 OJLS 145.

—— 'The Paradox of Parliamentary Supremacy: Delegation, Democracy, and Dictatorship in Germany and France, 1920s–1950s' (2004) 113 *Yale Law Journal* 1341.

Lobel, O, 'The Renew Deal: The Fall of Regulation and the Rise of Governance in Contemporary Legal Thought' (2004) 89 *Minnesota Law Review* 342.

Locke, J, *Two Treatises of Government* and *a Letter Concerning Toleration* (Shapiro, I, ed., Yale University Press, 2003).

Loughlin, M, 'Procedural Fairness: A Study in the Crisis in Administrative Law Theory' (1978) 28 *University of Toronto Law Journal* 215.

—— 'Constitutional Law: The Third Order of the Political' in Bamforth, N and Leyland, T eds., *Public Law in a Multi-Layered Constitution* (Hart, 2003) 27

—— and Walker, N, eds., *The Paradox of Constitutionalism: Constituent Power and Constitutional Form* (Oxford University Press, 2007).

Loveland, I, *Constitutional Law, Administrative Law, and Human Rights* (4th ed., Oxford University Press, 2006).

Macchiavelli, N, *The Prince* (2nd ed., Adams, R, ed., Norton, 1992)

Madison, J, *The Federalist* (2nd ed., University of Chicago, 1990)

Madison, J, Hamilton, A, and Jay, J: *The Federalist Papers* (Kramnick, I, ed., Penguin, 1987).

Madwick, P and Woodhouse, D, *The Law and Politics of the Constitution* (Harvester Wheatsheaf, 1995).

Magill, E, 'The Real Separation in Separation of Powers Law' (2000) 86 *Virginia Law Review* 1127.

Malleson, K, 'Modernising the Constitution: Completing the Unfinished Business' (2004) 24 LS 119

Marshall, G, *Constitutional Theory* (Clarendon, 1971).

Mashaw, JL, *Due Process in the Administrative State* (Yale University Press, 1985).

—— *Greed, Chaos and Governance* (Yale University Press, 1997).

Masterman, R, 'A Supreme Court for the United Kingdom: One Step Forward, Two Steps Back' (2004) PL 48.

Merry, H J, Five-Branch Government: *The Full Measure of Constitutional Checks and Balances* (University of Illinois Press, 1980).

Morgan, DG, *The Separation of Powers in the Irish Constitution* (Round Hall Sweet & Maxwell, 1997).

—— 'Judicial-o-centric separation of powers on the wane?' (2004) XXXIX *Irish Jurist* 142.

Mosher, F, 'The Changing Responsibilities and Tactics of the Federal Government' (1980) 40 *Public Administration Review* 541.

Mullan, D J, 'Fairness: The New Natural Justice' (1975) 25 *University of Toronto Law Journal* 281.

Munro, C, *Studies in Constitutional Law* (2nd ed, Butterworths, 1999).

Oliver, D, 'Is the Ultra Vires rule the basis of Judicial Review?' [1987] PL 543.

Pocock, JGA, *The Machiavellian Moment: Florentine Political Thought and the Atlantic Republican Tradition* (2nd ed., Princeton University Press, 2003).

Poole, T, 'Back to the Future? Unearthing the Theory of Common Law Constitutionalism' (2003) 23 (3) OJLS 435.

Pym, J, *On Grievances in the Reign of Charles I* (1640).
Rawls, J, *A Theory of Justice* (revised ed., Oxford University Press, 1999).
—— *Justice as Fairness: A Restatement* (Belknap, 2001).
Richards, DAJ, *Foundations of American Constitutionalism* (Oxford University Press, 1989).
Richardson, G, and Genn, H (ed.), *Administrative Law and Government Action* (Clarendon, 1994).
Richardson, HS, *Democratic Autonomy: Public reasoning about the ends of policy* (Oxford University Press, 2002).
Rivers, J, 'Proportionality and Variable Intensity of Review' (2006) 65 CLJ 174
Rubin, E, 'The Myth of Accountability and the Anti-Administrative Impulse' (2005) 103 *Michigan Law Review* 2073.
Salamon, L, (ed), *Tools of Government: A Guide to the New Governance* (Oxford University Press, 2002).
—— 'The New Governance and the Tools of Public Action' (2001) 28 *Fordham Urban Law Journal* 1611.
Sargentich, TO, 'The Uneasy Constitutional Status of Administrative Agencies (1987) 36 *American University Law Review* 419.
Schmitt, C, *The Concept of the Political* (1932), (G Schwab (tr.), University of Chicago Press, 1996).
Sedley, S, 'Human Rights—a Twenty-First Century Agenda' [1995] PL 386.
Shapiro, MH, 'The Technology of Perfection: Performance Enhancement and the Control of Attributes' (1991) 65S *Southern California Law Review* 11.
Stevens, R, *The Independence of the Judiciary* (Clarendon, 1993).
—— 'A Loss of Innocence: Judicial Independence and the Separation of Powers' (1999) 19 OJLS 365.
Stewart, R, 'The Reformation of American Administrative Law' (1974–5) 88 *Harvard Law Review* 1667.
—— 'Administrative Law in the 21st Century' (2003) 78 *NYU Law Review* 437.
Lord Steyn, 'The Case for a Supreme Court' (2002) 118 LQR 382.
Strauss, R, 'The Place of Agencies in Government: Separation of Powers and the Fourth Branch' (1984) *Columbia Law Review* 573.
Thibault, L and Walker, J, *Procedural Justice: A Psychological Analysis* (Hillsdale, 1975).
Tribe, L, *American Constitutional Law: Volume 1* (3rd ed., Foundation Press, 2000).
Unger, R, 'The Critical Legal Studies Movement' (1983) 96 *Harvard Law Review* 561.
Verkuil, PR, *Outsourcing Sovereignty* (Cambridge University Press, 2007).
Vermuele, A, 'Our Schmittian Administrative Law' (2009) 122 *Harvard Law Review* 1095.
Vile, MJC, *Constitutionalism and the Separation of Powers* (Clarendon, 1967).
Wade, W & Forsyth, C, *Administrative Law* (9th ed., Oxford University Press, 2004).
Walker, L, Lind, A, and Thibault, J, 'The Relation between Procedural and Distributive Justice' (1979) 65 *Virginia Law Review* 1401.
Weiler, J, *The Constitution of Europe: 'Do the New Clothes Have an Emperor?' and Other Essays in European Integration* (Cambridge University Press, 1999).
Weinrib, E, 'Legal Formalism: On the Immanent Rationality of Law' (1988) 97 *Yale Law Journal* 949.

Whittington, KE, 'Legislative Sanctions and the Strategic Environment Of Judicial Review' (2003) 1 *International Journal of Constitutional Law* 446.

Wolff, J, *An Introduction to Political Philosophy* (Oxford University Press, 2006).

Woodhouse, D, *In Pursuit of Good Administration: Ministers, Civil Servants and Judges* (Clarendon Press, 1997).

—— 'The Constitutional and Political Implications of a United Kingdom Supreme Court' (2004) 24 LS 134.

Woolf, H, '*Droit Public*—English Style' [1995] PL 57.

—— 'Judicial review—the tensions between the executive and the judiciary' (1998) 114 LQR 579.

Index

The manufacturer's authorised representative in the EU for product safety is Oxford University Press España S.A. of el Parque Empresarial San Fernando de Henares, Avenida de Castilla, 2 – 28830 Madrid (www.oup.es/en or product.safety@oup.com). OUP España S.A. also acts as importer into Spain of products made by the manufacturer.

www.ingramcontent.com/pod-product-compliance
Lightning Source LLC
LaVergne TN
LVHW011915200926
848484LV00002B/627

9780199568673